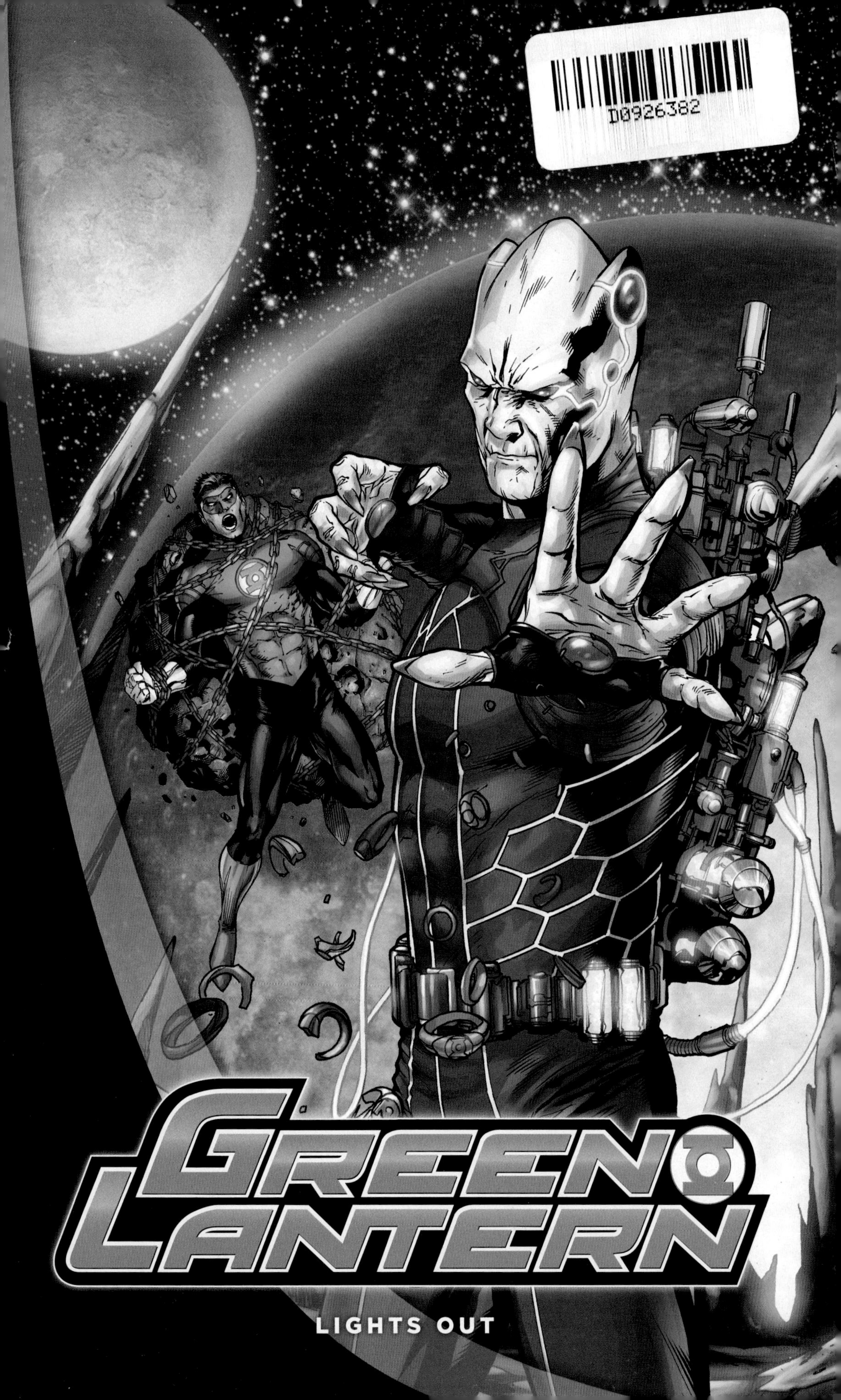
GREEN LANTERN
LIGHTS OUT

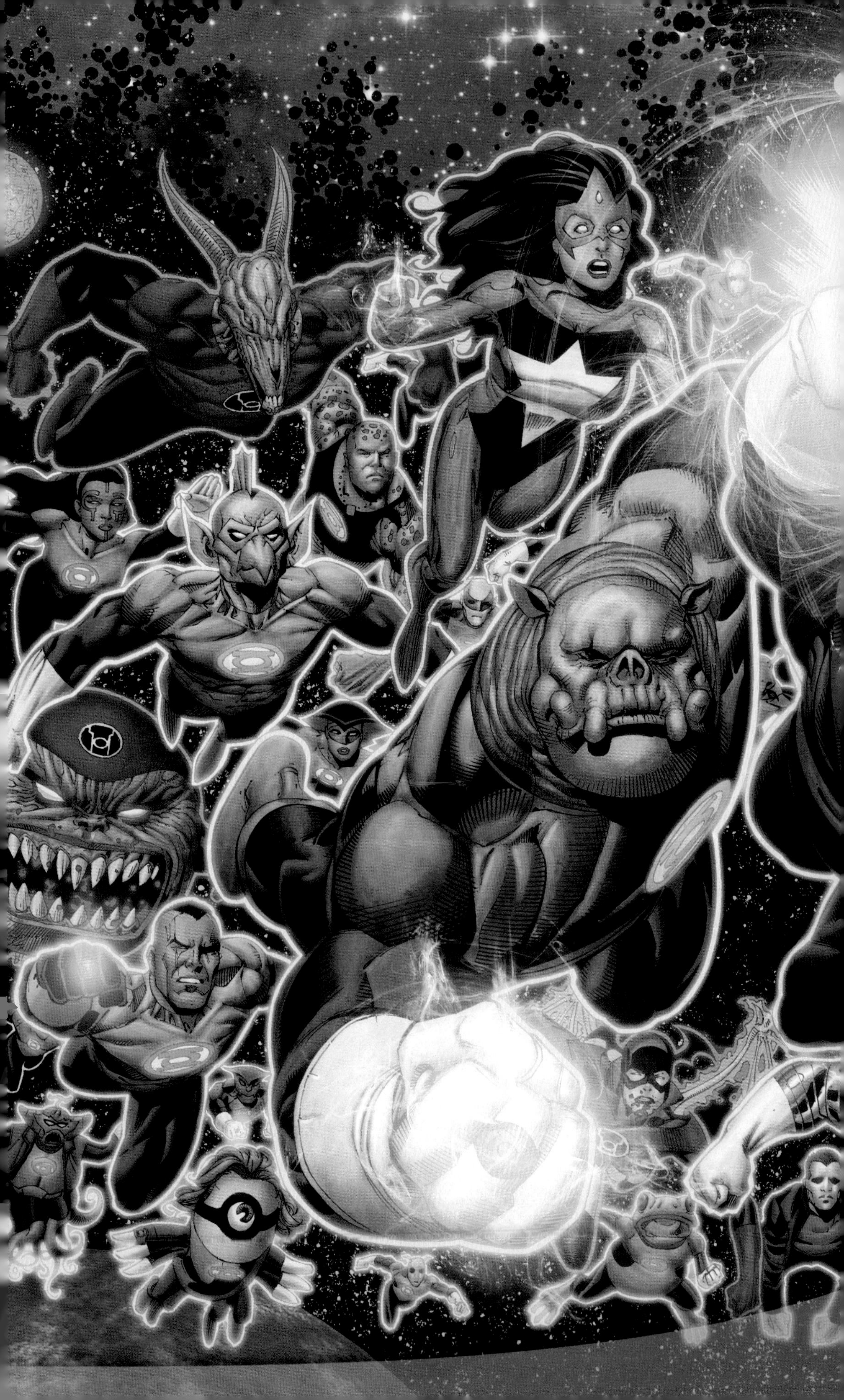

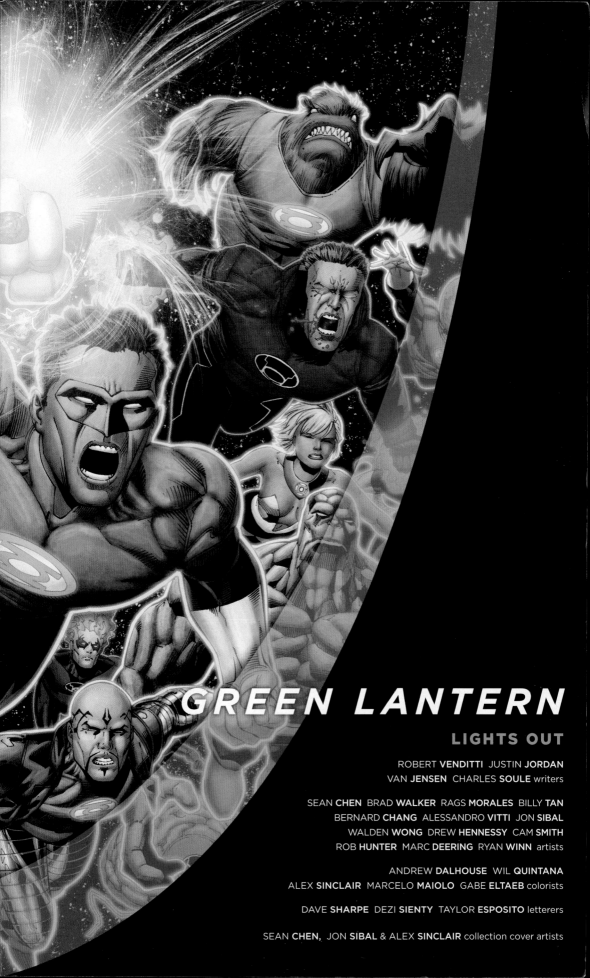

GREEN LANTERN

LIGHTS OUT

ROBERT **VENDITTI** JUSTIN **JORDAN**
VAN **JENSEN** CHARLES **SOULE** writers

SEAN **CHEN** BRAD **WALKER** RAGS **MORALES** BILLY **TAN**
BERNARD **CHANG** ALESSANDRO **VITTI** JON **SIBAL**
WALDEN **WONG** DREW **HENNESSY** CAM **SMITH**
ROB **HUNTER** MARC **DEERING** RYAN **WINN** artists

ANDREW **DALHOUSE** WIL **QUINTANA**
ALEX **SINCLAIR** MARCELO **MAIOLO** GABE **ELTAEB** colorists

DAVE **SHARPE** DEZI **SIENTY** TAYLOR **ESPOSITO** letterers

SEAN **CHEN,** JON **SIBAL** & ALEX **SINCLAIR** collection cover artists

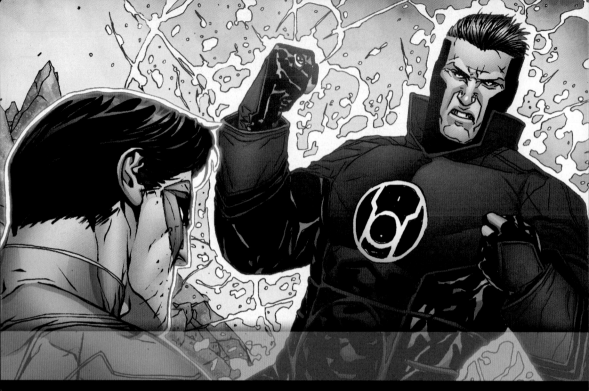

MATT IDELSON CHRIS CONROY Editors – Original Series ROBIN WILDMAN Editor
ROBBIN BROSTERMAN Design Director – Books ROBBIE BIEDERMAN Publication Design

BOB HARRAS Senior VP – Editor-in-Chief, DC Comics

DIANE NELSON President DAN DIDIO and JIM LEE Co-Publishers GEOFF JOHNS Chief Creative Officer
AMIT DESAI Senior VP – Marketing and Franchise Management
AMY GENKINS Senior VP – Business and Legal Affairs NAIRI GARDINER Senior VP – Finance
JEFF BOISON VP – Publishing Planning MARK CHIARELLO VP – Art Direction and Design
JOHN CUNNINGHAM VP – Marketing TERRI CUNNINGHAM VP – Editorial Administration
LARRY GANEM VP – Talent Relations and Services ALISON GILL Senior VP – Manufacturing and Operations
HANK KANALZ Senior VP – Vertigo and Integrated Publishing JAY KOGAN VP – Business and Legal Affairs, Publishing
JACK MAHAN VP – Business Affairs, Talent NICK NAPOLITANO VP – Manufacturing Administration SUE POHJA VP – Book Sales
FRED RUIZ VP – Manufacturing Operations COURTNEY SIMMONS Senior VP – Publicity BOB WAYNE Senior VP – Sales

GREEN LANTERN: LIGHTS OUT

DC Comics, 1700 Broadway, New York, NY 10019
A Warner Bros. Entertainment Company.
Printed by RR Donnelley, Owensville, MO, USA. 11/21/14. First Printing.
ISBN: 978-1-4012-4943-4

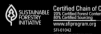

SUSTAINABLE FORESTRY INITIATIVE
Certified Chain of Custody
20% Certified Forest Content,
80% Certified Sourcing
www.sfiprogram.org
SFI-01042
APPLIES TO TEXT STOCK ONLY

Library of Congress Cataloging-in-Publication Data

Venditti, Robert, author.
Green Lantern. Lights Out / Robert Venditti , Justin Jordan; [illustrated by] Billy Tan.
pages cm.
ISBN 978-1-4012-4943-4
1. Graphic novels. I. Venditti, Robert, illustrator. II. Tan, Billy, illustrator. III. Title. IV. Title: Lights Out.
PN6728.G74J68 2014
741.5'973—dc23

2014008616

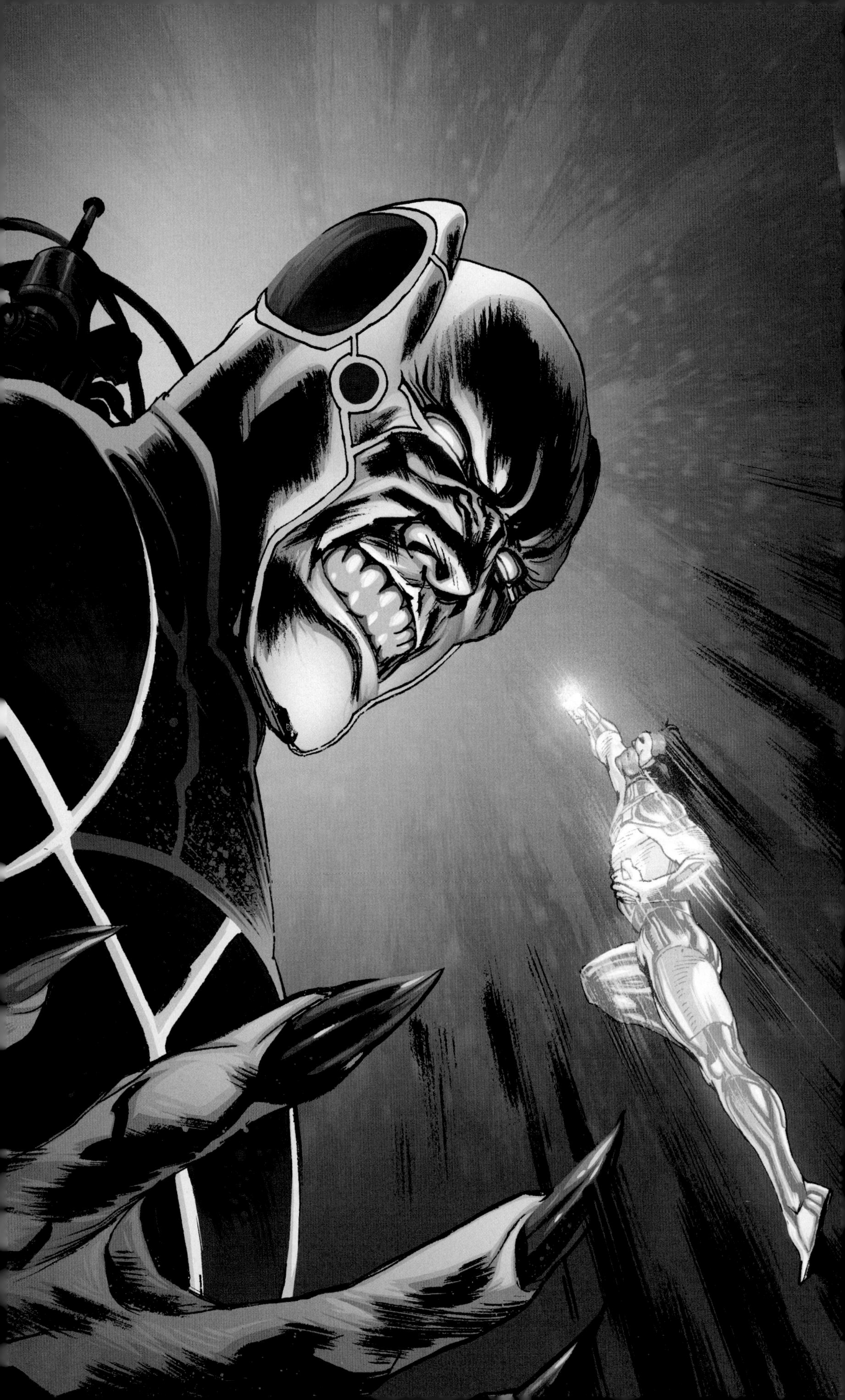

KEEP HOPE ALIVE

JUSTIN JORDAN writer BRAD WALKER penciller DREW HENNESSY inker WIL QUINTANA colorist RAFAEL ALBUQUERQUE with DAVE McCAIG cover artists

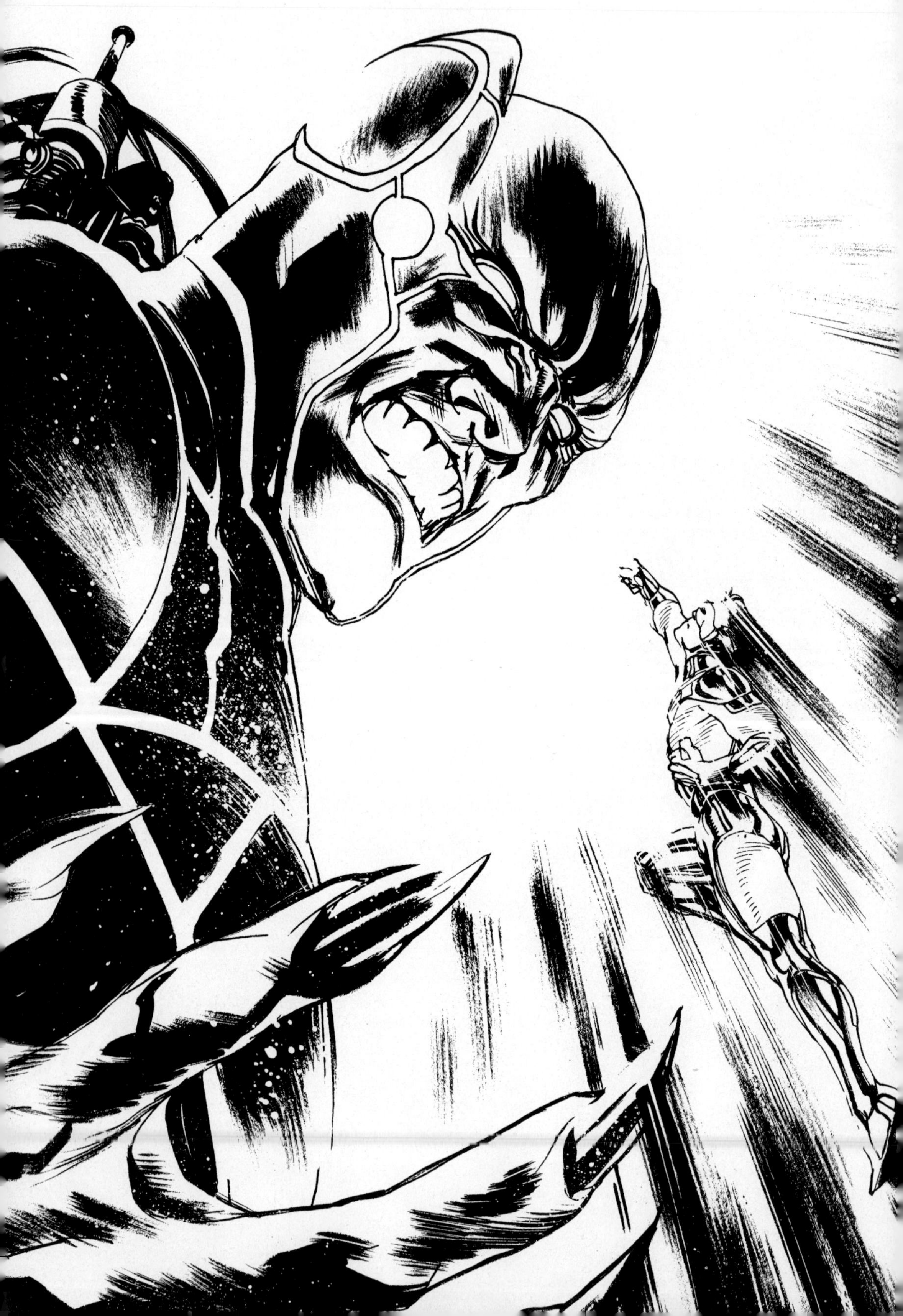

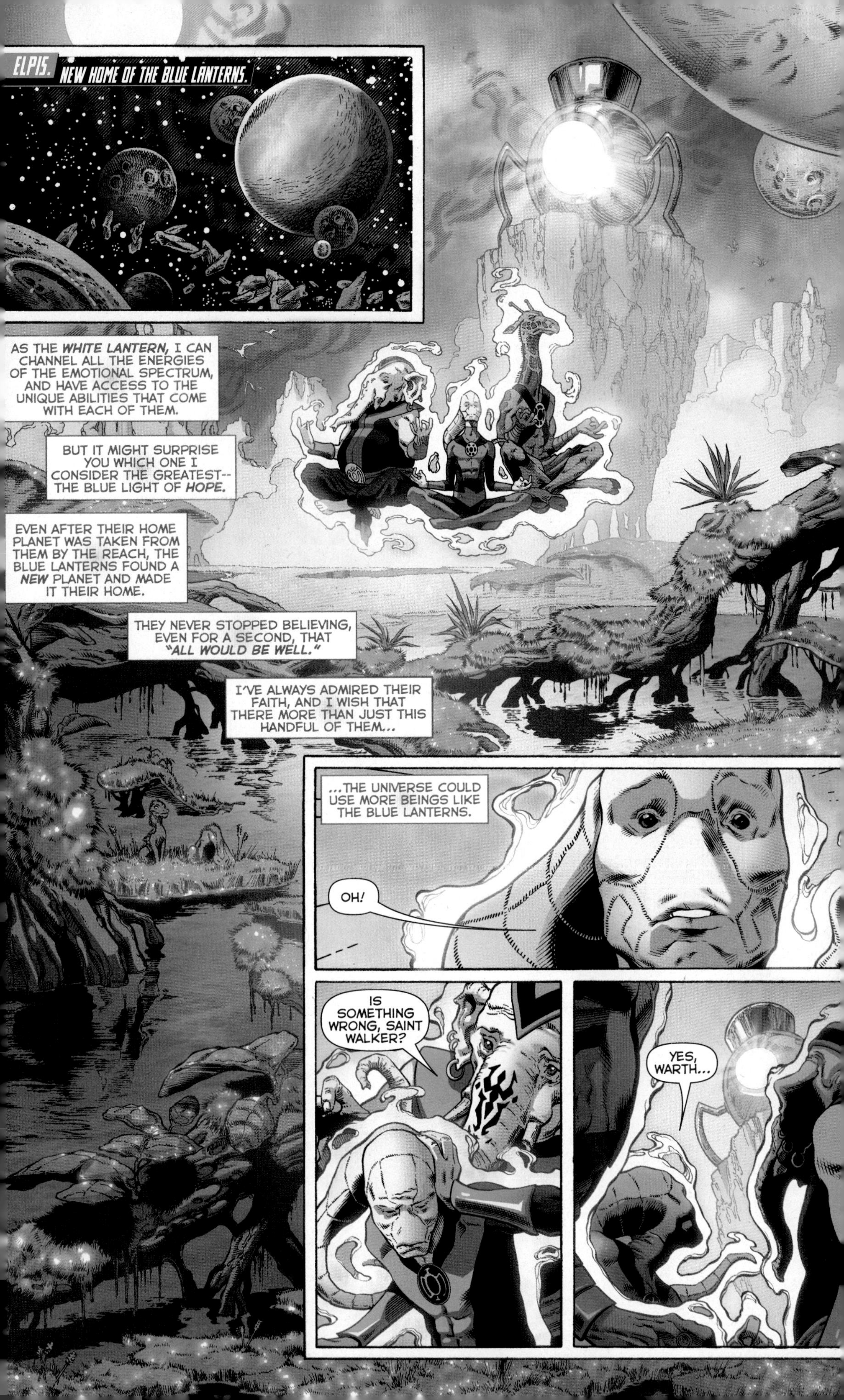
ELPIS. NEW HOME OF THE BLUE LANTERNS.
AS THE WHITE LANTERN, I CAN CHANNEL ALL THE ENERGIES OF THE EMOTIONAL SPECTRUM, AND HAVE ACCESS TO THE UNIQUE ABILITIES THAT COME WITH EACH OF THEM.
BUT IT MIGHT SURPRISE YOU WHICH ONE I CONSIDER THE GREATEST-- THE BLUE LIGHT OF HOPE.
EVEN AFTER THEIR HOME PLANET WAS TAKEN FROM THEM BY THE REACH, THE BLUE LANTERNS FOUND A NEW PLANET AND MADE IT THEIR HOME.
THEY NEVER STOPPED BELIEVING, EVEN FOR A SECOND, THAT "ALL WOULD BE WELL."
I'VE ALWAYS ADMIRED THEIR FAITH, AND I WISH THAT THERE MORE THAN JUST THIS HANDFUL OF THEM...
...THE UNIVERSE COULD USE MORE BEINGS LIKE THE BLUE LANTERNS.
OH!
IS SOMETHING WRONG, SAINT WALKER?
YES, WARTH...

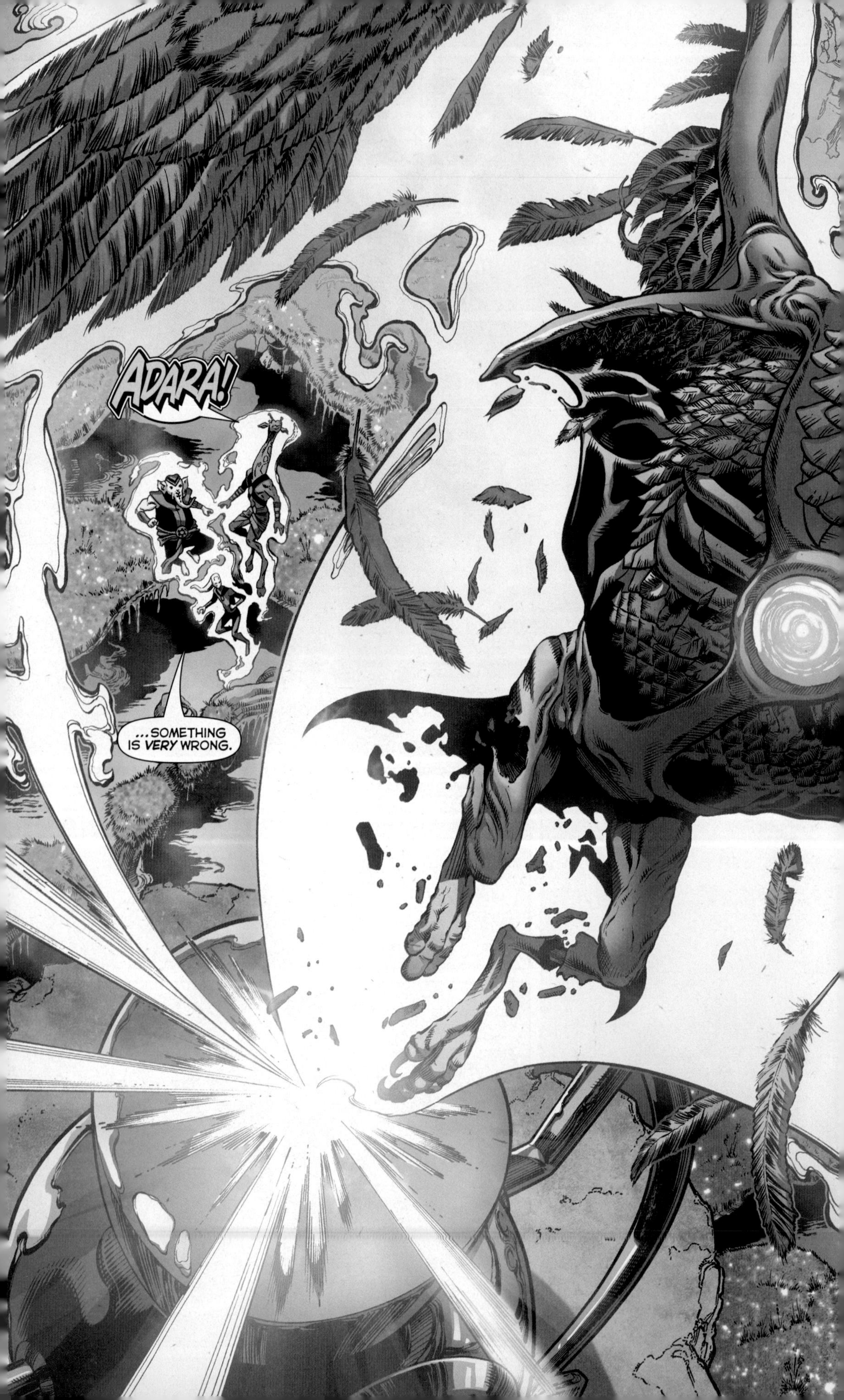
ADARA!
...SOMETHING IS VERY WRONG.

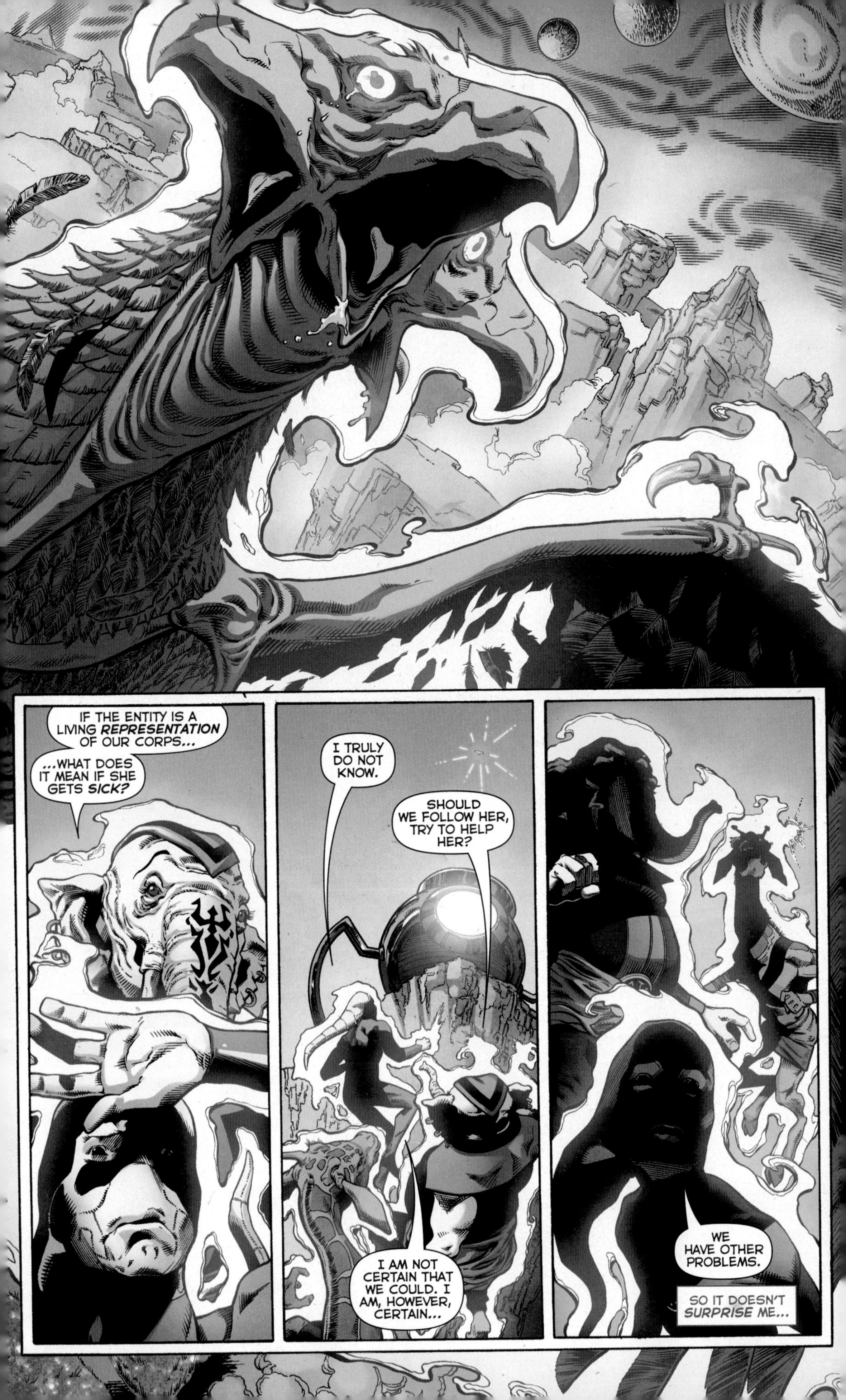
IF THE ENTITY IS A LIVING REPRESENTATION OF OUR CORPS...
...WHAT DOES IT MEAN IF SHE GETS SICK?
I TRULY DO NOT KNOW.
SHOULD WE FOLLOW HER, TRY TO HELP HER?
I AM NOT CERTAIN THAT WE COULD. I AM, HOWEVER, CERTAIN...
WE HAVE OTHER PROBLEMS.
SO IT DOESN'T SURPRISE ME...

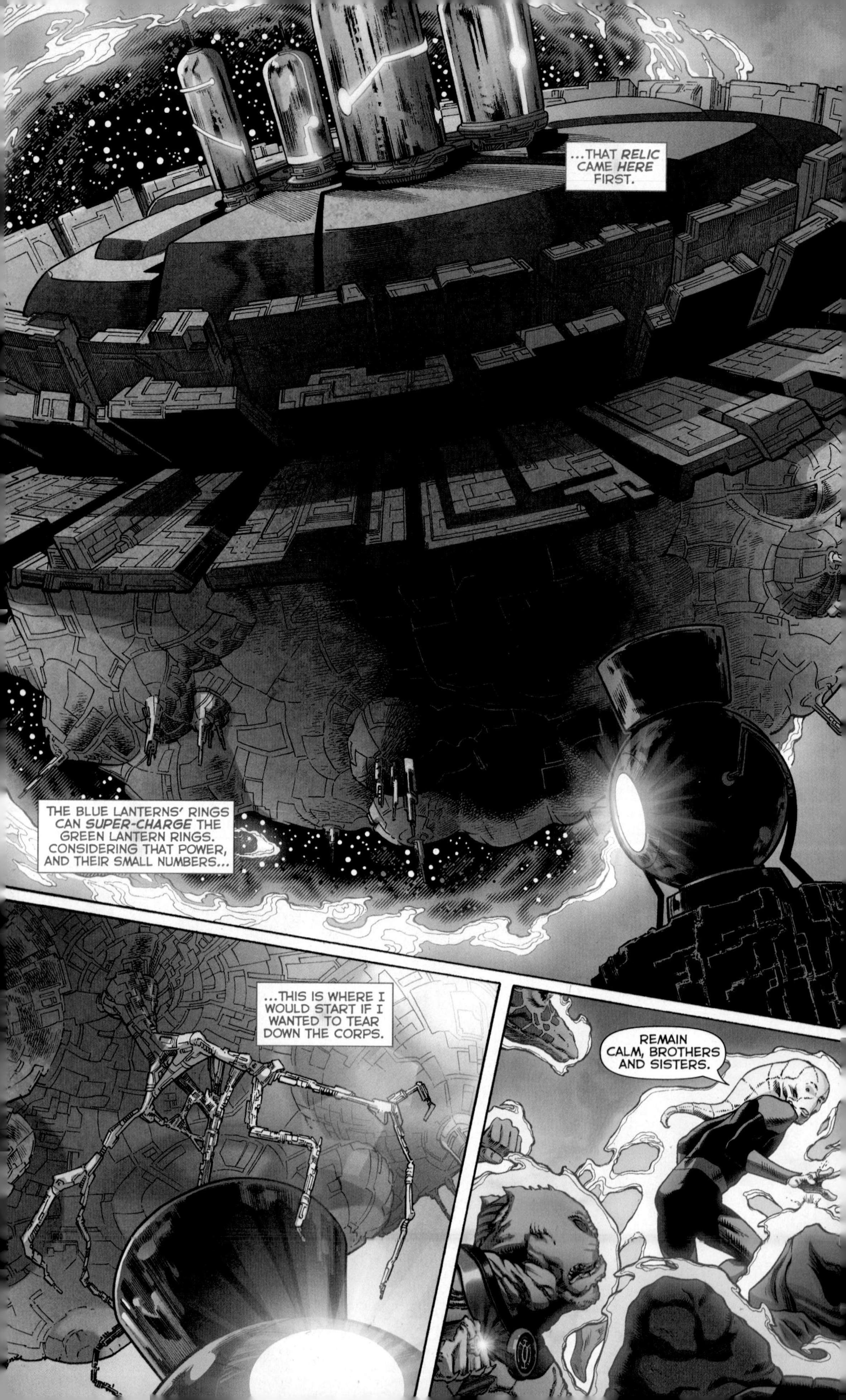
...THAT RELIC CAME HERE FIRST.
THE BLUE LANTERNS' RINGS CAN SUPER-CHARGE THE GREEN LANTERN RINGS. CONSIDERING THAT POWER, AND THEIR SMALL NUMBERS...
...THIS IS WHERE I WOULD START IF I WANTED TO TEAR DOWN THE CORPS.
REMAIN CALM, BROTHERS AND SISTERS.

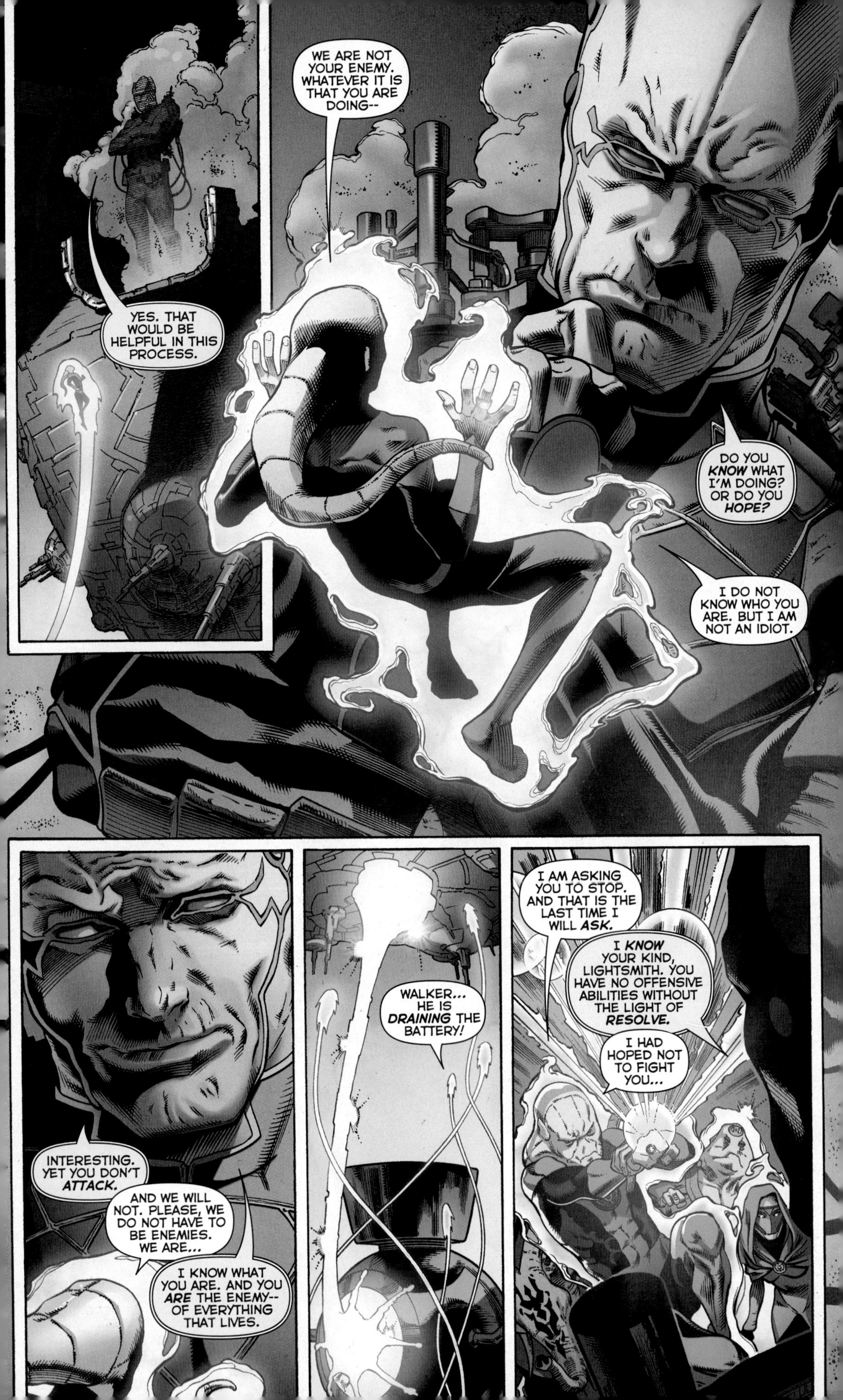

YES. THAT WOULD BE HELPFUL IN THIS PROCESS.
WE ARE NOT YOUR ENEMY. WHATEVER IT IS THAT YOU ARE DOING--
DO YOU KNOW WHAT I'M DOING? OR DO YOU HOPE?
I DO NOT KNOW WHO YOU ARE. BUT I AM NOT AN IDIOT.
INTERESTING. YET YOU DON'T ATTACK.
AND WE WILL NOT. PLEASE, WE DO NOT HAVE TO BE ENEMIES. WE ARE...
I KNOW WHAT YOU ARE. AND YOU ARE THE ENEMY-- OF EVERYTHING THAT LIVES.
WALKER... HE IS DRAINING THE BATTERY!
I AM ASKING YOU TO STOP. AND THAT IS THE LAST TIME I WILL ASK.
I KNOW YOUR KIND, LIGHTSMITH. YOU HAVE NO OFFENSIVE ABILITIES WITHOUT THE LIGHT OF RESOLVE.
I HAD HOPED NOT TO FIGHT YOU...

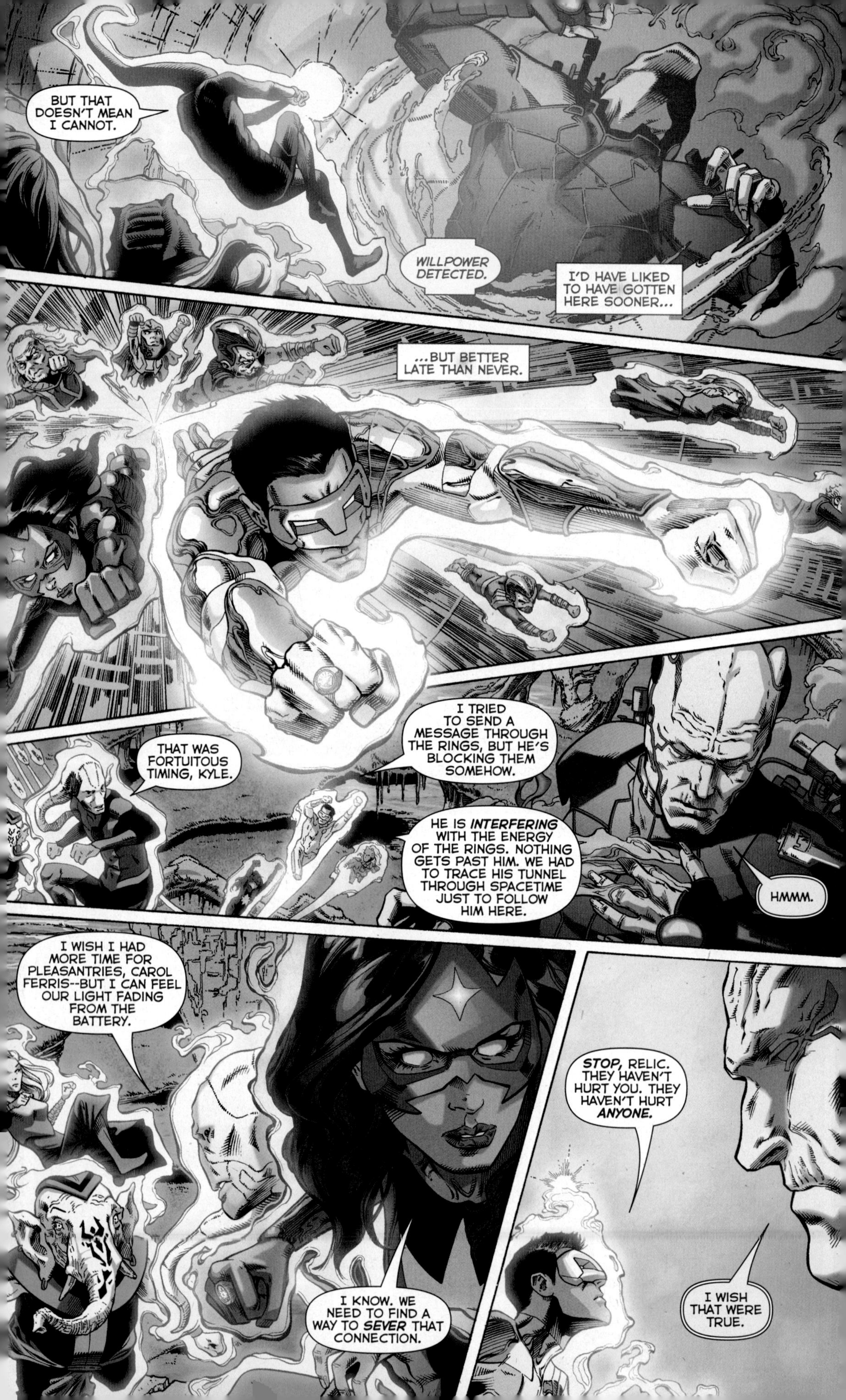
BUT THAT DOESN'T MEAN I CANNOT.
WILLPOWER DETECTED.
I'D HAVE LIKED TO HAVE GOTTEN HERE SOONER...
...BUT BETTER LATE THAN NEVER.
THAT WAS FORTUITOUS TIMING, KYLE.
I TRIED TO SEND A MESSAGE THROUGH THE RINGS, BUT HE'S BLOCKING THEM SOMEHOW.
HE IS INTERFERING WITH THE ENERGY OF THE RINGS. NOTHING GETS PAST HIM. WE HAD TO TRACE HIS TUNNEL THROUGH SPACETIME JUST TO FOLLOW HIM HERE.
HMMM.
I WISH I HAD MORE TIME FOR PLEASANTRIES, CAROL FERRIS--BUT I CAN FEEL OUR LIGHT FADING FROM THE BATTERY.
I KNOW. WE NEED TO FIND A WAY TO SEVER THAT CONNECTION.
STOP, RELIC. THEY HAVEN'T HURT YOU. THEY HAVEN'T HURT ANYONE.
I WISH THAT WERE TRUE.

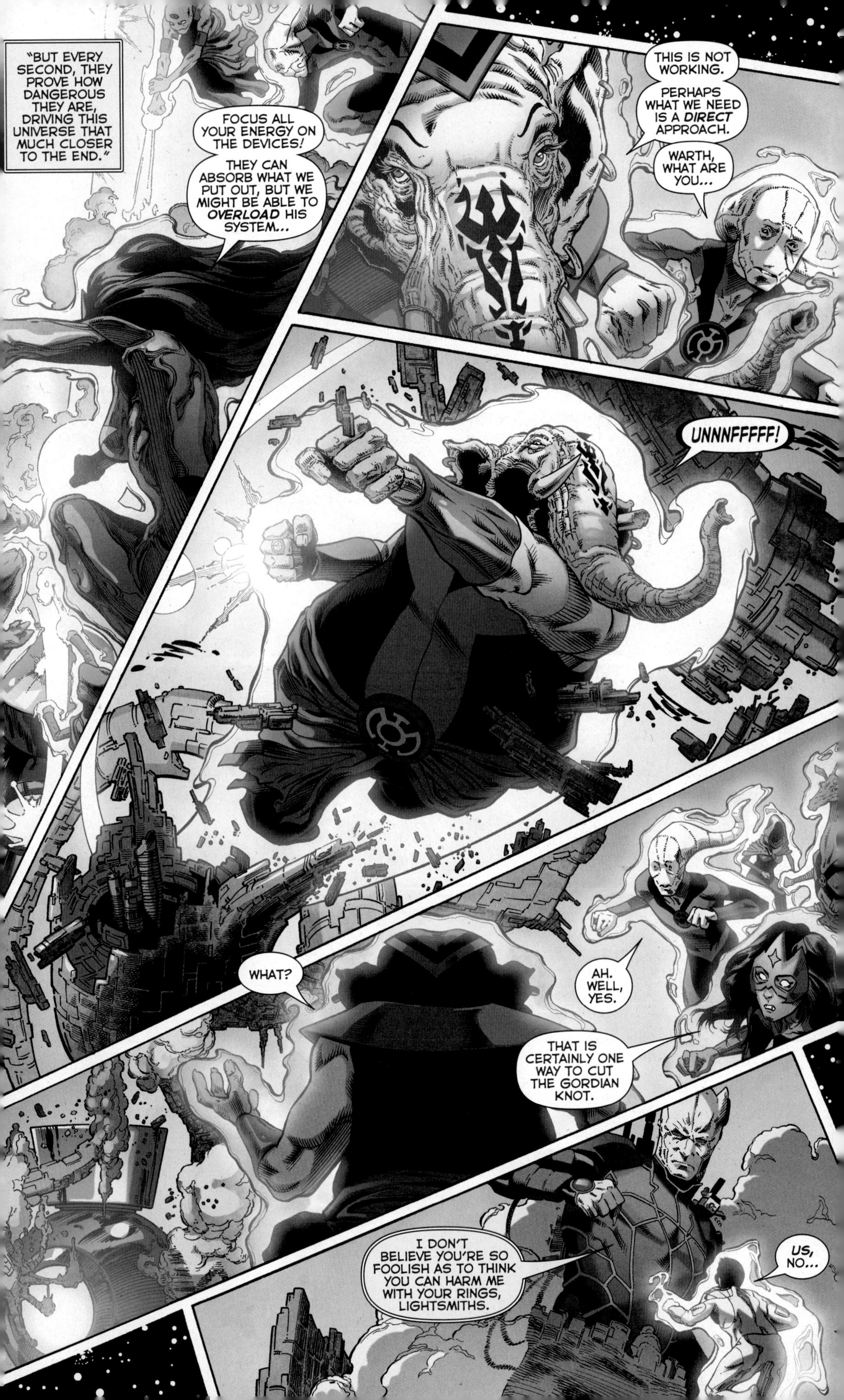

"BUT EVERY SECOND, THEY PROVE HOW DANGEROUS THEY ARE, DRIVING THIS UNIVERSE THAT MUCH CLOSER TO THE END."
FOCUS ALL YOUR ENERGY ON THE DEVICES!
THEY CAN ABSORB WHAT WE PUT OUT, BUT WE MIGHT BE ABLE TO OVERLOAD HIS SYSTEM...
THIS IS NOT WORKING.
PERHAPS WHAT WE NEED IS A DIRECT APPROACH.
WARTH, WHAT ARE YOU...
UNNNFFFFF!
WHAT?
AH. WELL, YES.
THAT IS CERTAINLY ONE WAY TO CUT THE GORDIAN KNOT.
I DON'T BELIEVE YOU'RE SO FOOLISH AS TO THINK YOU CAN HARM ME WITH YOUR RINGS, LIGHTSMITHS.
US, NO...

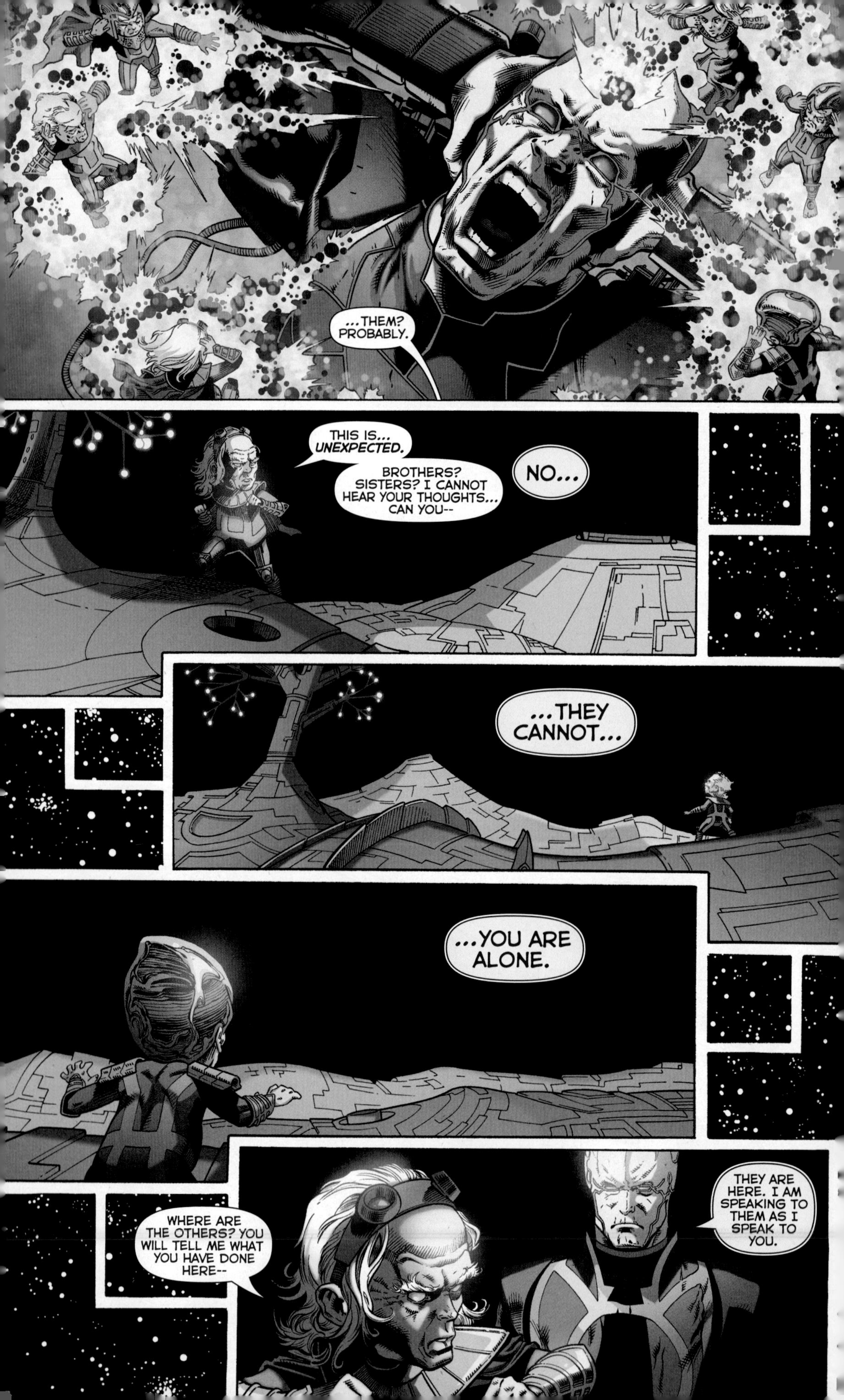
...THEM? PROBABLY.
THIS IS... UNEXPECTED.
BROTHERS? SISTERS? I CANNOT HEAR YOUR THOUGHTS... CAN YOU--
NO...
...THEY CANNOT...
...YOU ARE ALONE.
WHERE ARE THE OTHERS? YOU WILL TELL ME WHAT YOU HAVE DONE HERE--
THEY ARE HERE. I AM SPEAKING TO THEM AS I SPEAK TO YOU.

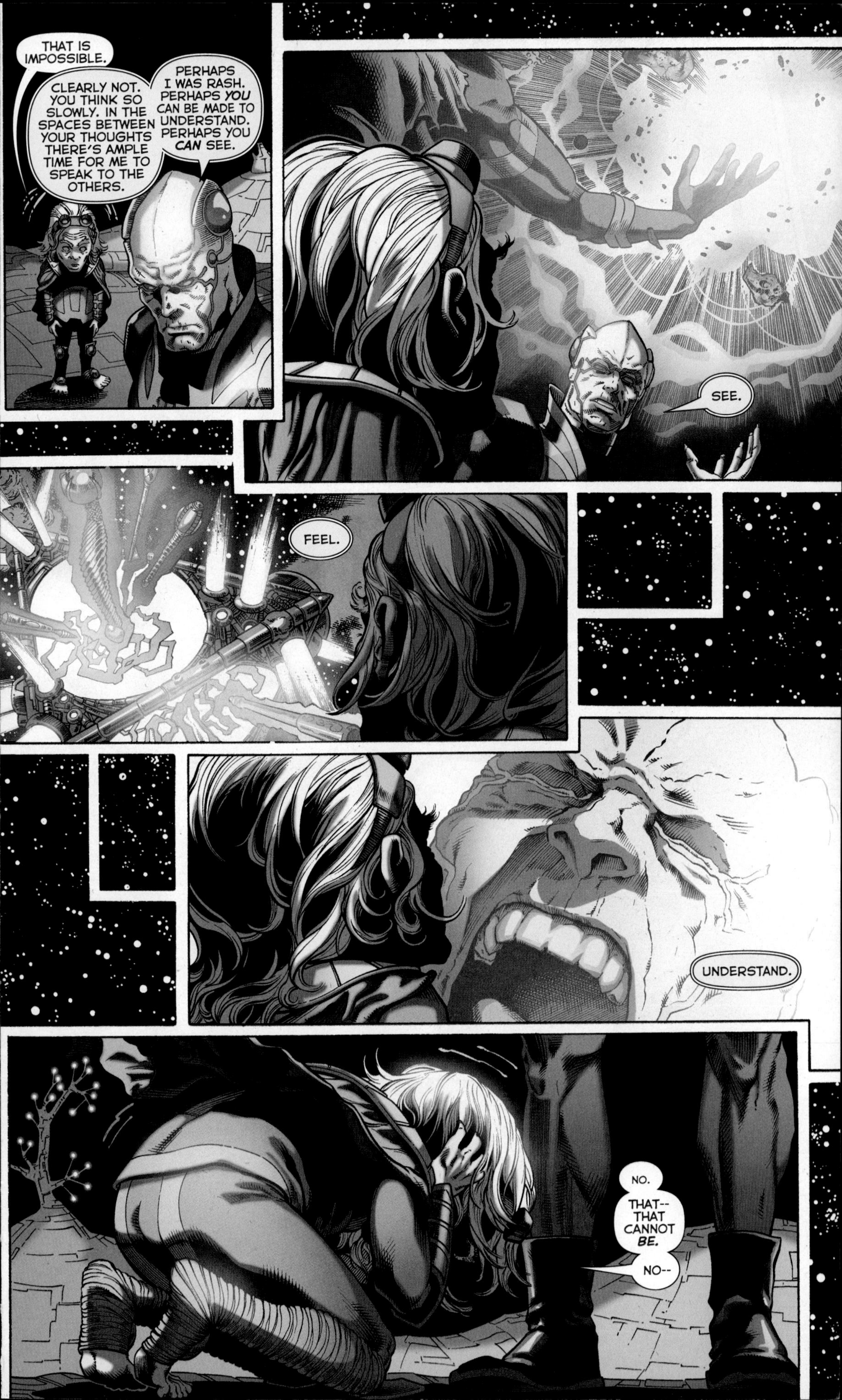
THAT IS IMPOSSIBLE.
CLEARLY NOT. YOU THINK SO SLOWLY. IN THE SPACES BETWEEN YOUR THOUGHTS THERE'S AMPLE TIME FOR ME TO SPEAK TO THE OTHERS.
PERHAPS I WAS RASH. PERHAPS *YOU* CAN BE MADE TO UNDERSTAND. PERHAPS YOU *CAN* SEE.
SEE.
FEEL.
UNDERSTAND.
NO.
THAT-- THAT CANNOT *BE.*
NO--

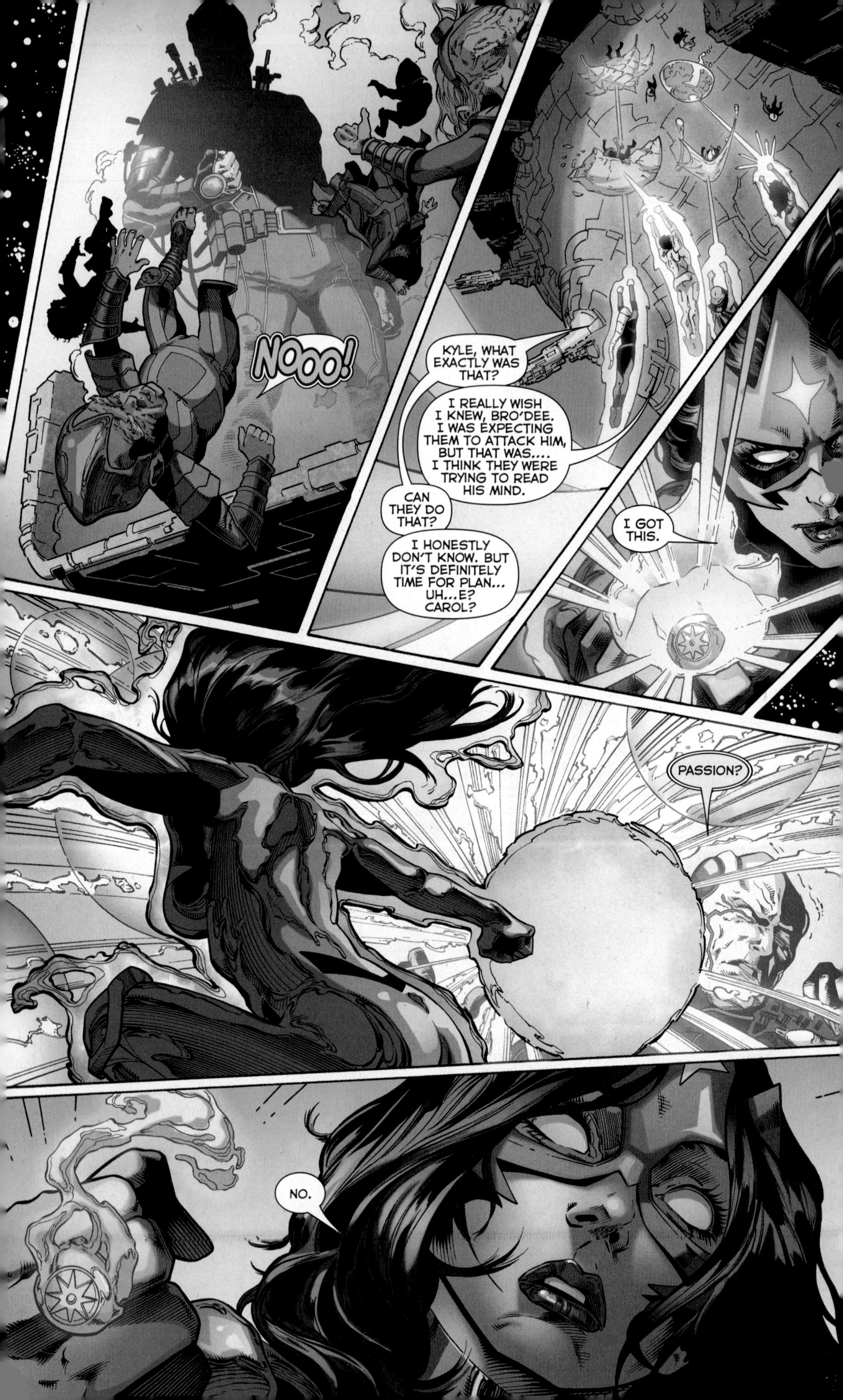
NOOO!
KYLE, WHAT EXACTLY WAS THAT?
I REALLY WISH I KNEW, BRO'DEE. I WAS EXPECTING THEM TO ATTACK HIM, BUT THAT WAS.... I THINK THEY WERE TRYING TO READ HIS MIND.
CAN THEY DO THAT?
I HONESTLY DON'T KNOW. BUT IT'S DEFINITELY TIME FOR PLAN... UH...E? CAROL?
I GOT THIS.
PASSION?
NO.

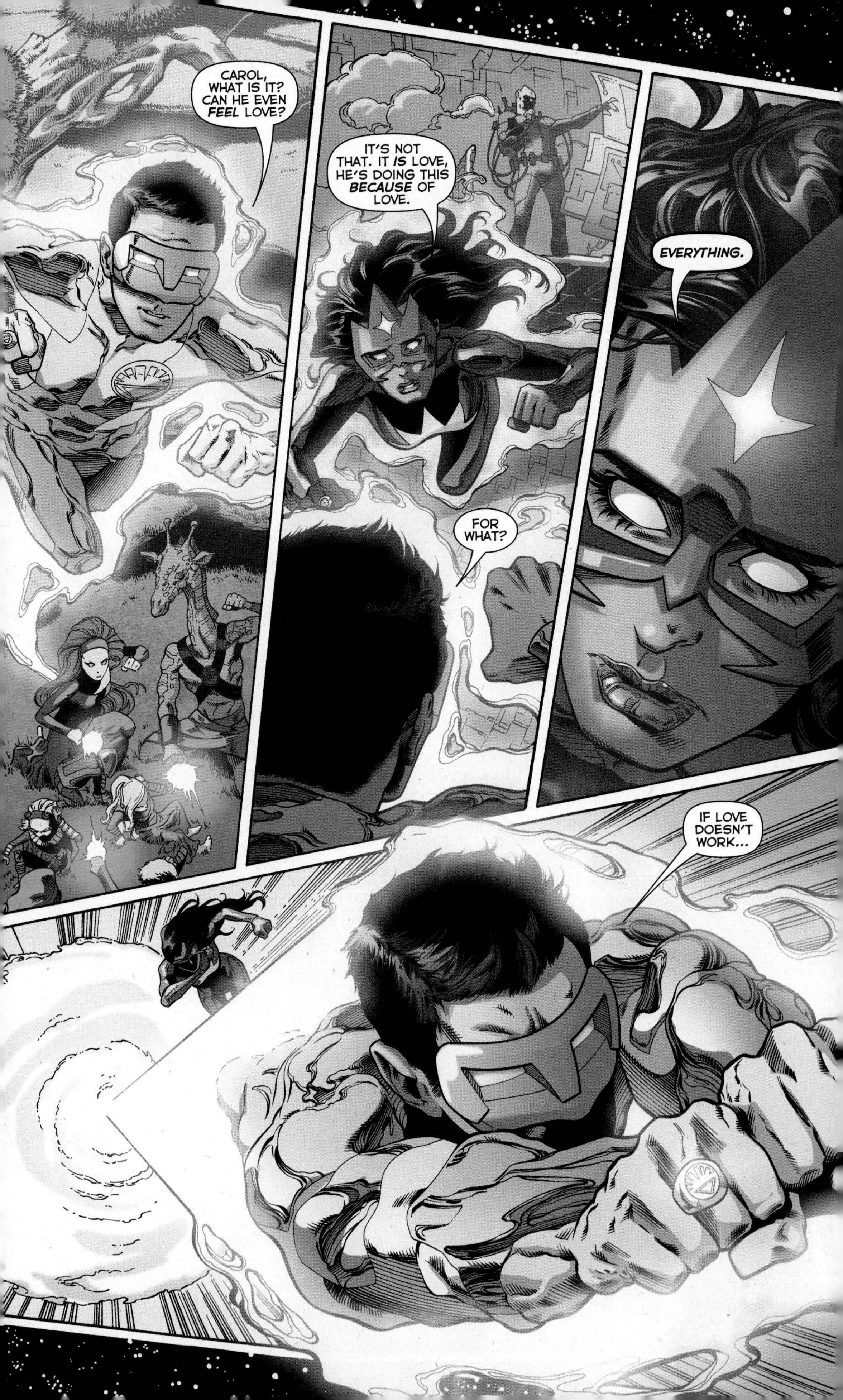
CAROL, WHAT IS IT? CAN HE EVEN FEEL LOVE?
IT'S NOT THAT. IT IS LOVE, HE'S DOING THIS BECAUSE OF LOVE.
FOR WHAT?
EVERYTHING.
IF LOVE DOESN'T WORK...

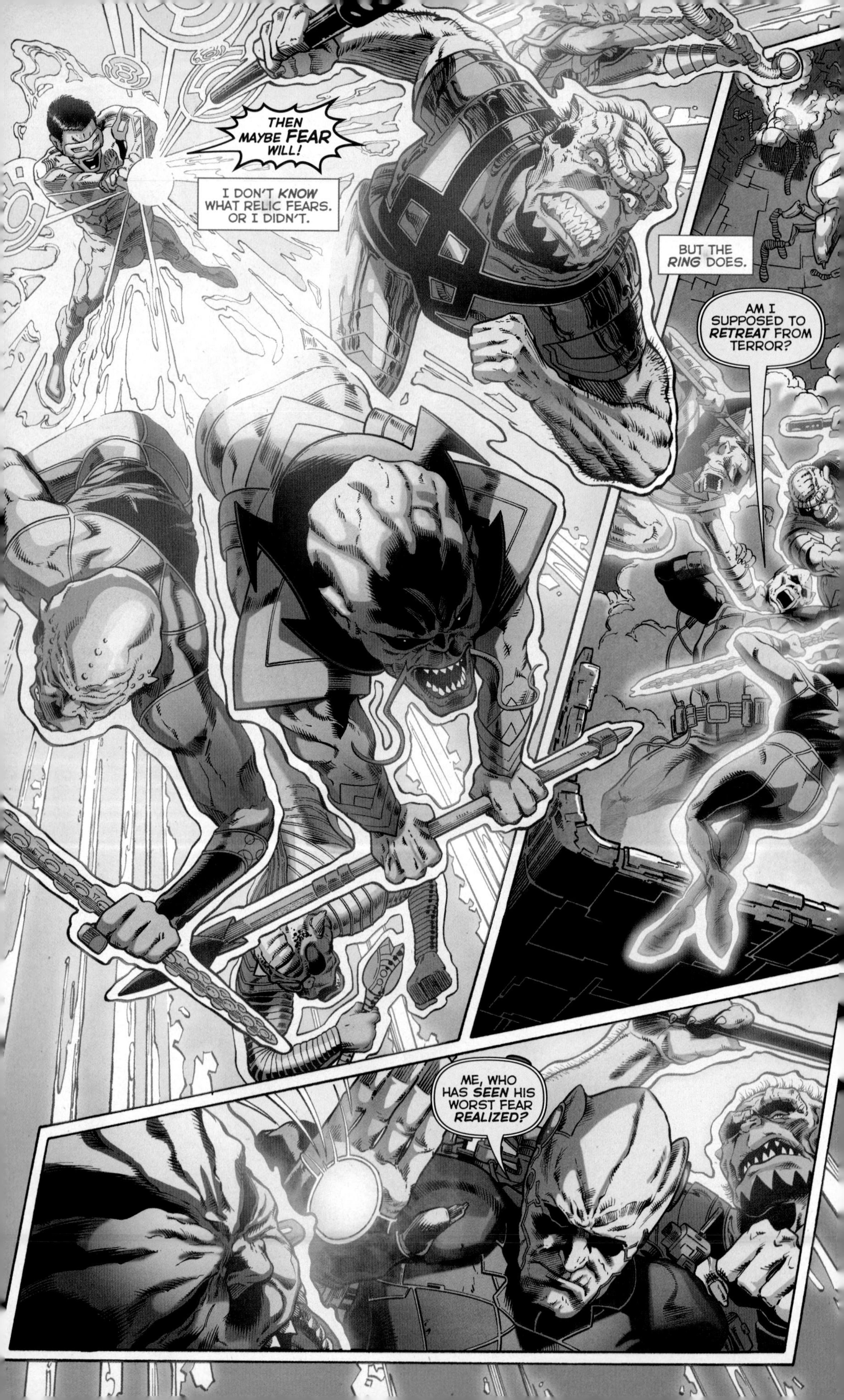
I DON'T *KNOW* WHAT RELIC FEARS. OR I DIDN'T.
THEN MAYBE *FEAR* WILL!
BUT THE *RING* DOES.
AM I SUPPOSED TO *RETREAT* FROM TERROR?
ME, WHO HAS *SEEN* HIS WORST FEAR *REALIZED?*

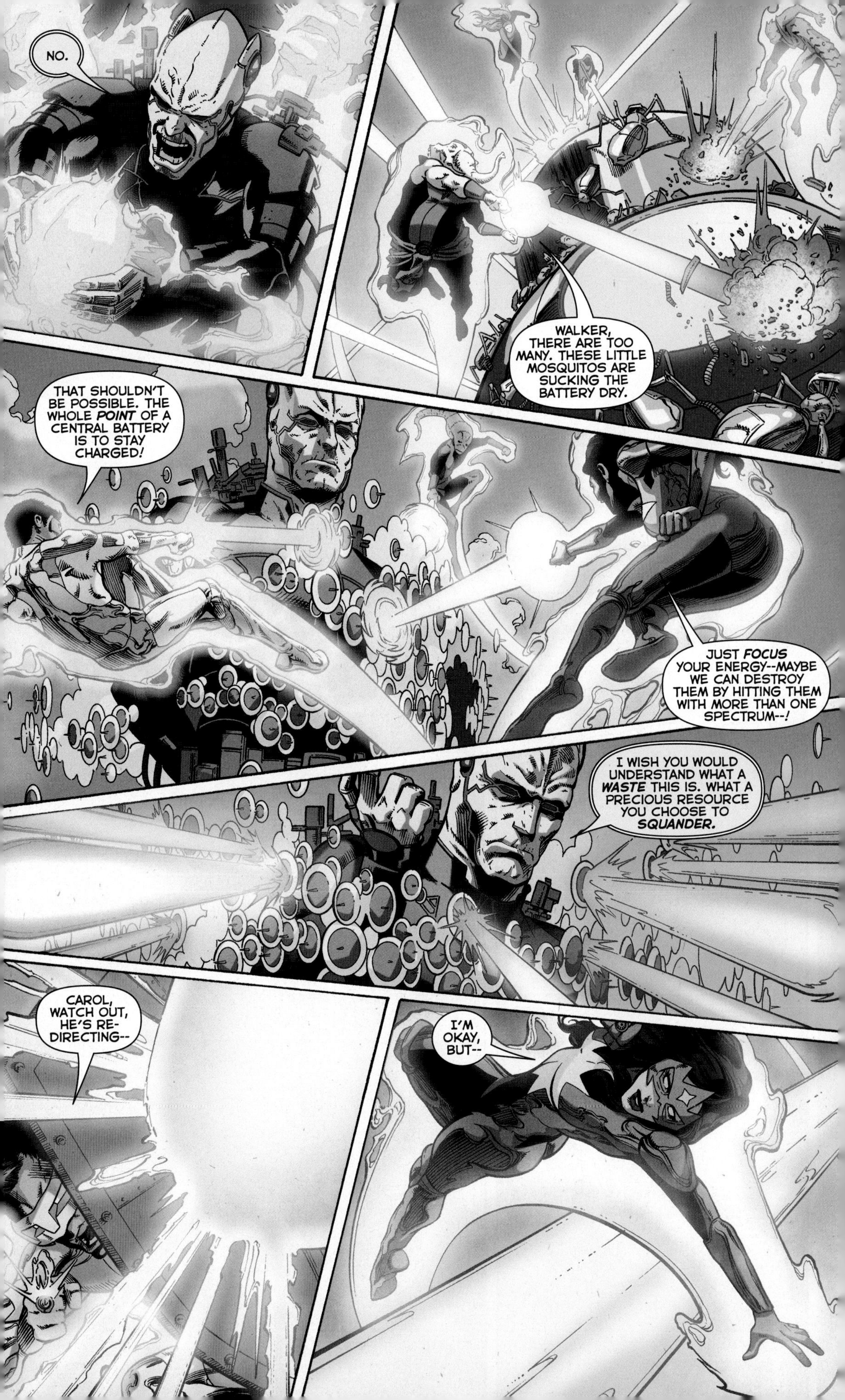

NO.
WALKER, THERE ARE TOO MANY. THESE LITTLE MOSQUITOS ARE SUCKING THE BATTERY DRY.
THAT SHOULDN'T BE POSSIBLE. THE WHOLE POINT OF A CENTRAL BATTERY IS TO STAY CHARGED!
JUST FOCUS YOUR ENERGY--MAYBE WE CAN DESTROY THEM BY HITTING THEM WITH MORE THAN ONE SPECTRUM--!
I WISH YOU WOULD UNDERSTAND WHAT A WASTE THIS IS. WHAT A PRECIOUS RESOURCE YOU CHOOSE TO SQUANDER.
CAROL, WATCH OUT, HE'S RE-DIRECTING--
I'M OKAY, BUT--

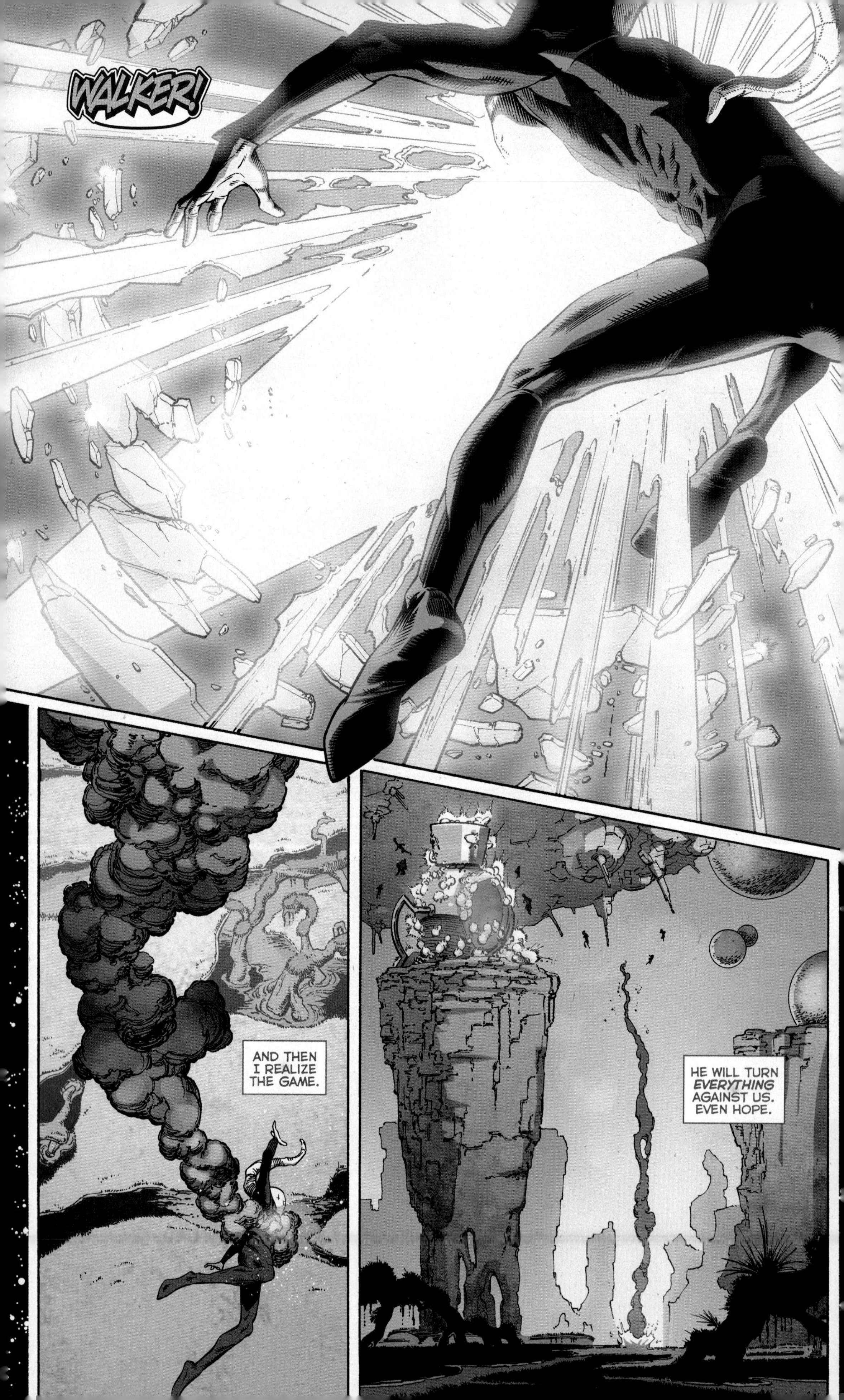
WALKER!
AND THEN I REALIZE THE GAME.
HE WILL TURN *EVERYTHING* AGAINST US. EVEN HOPE.

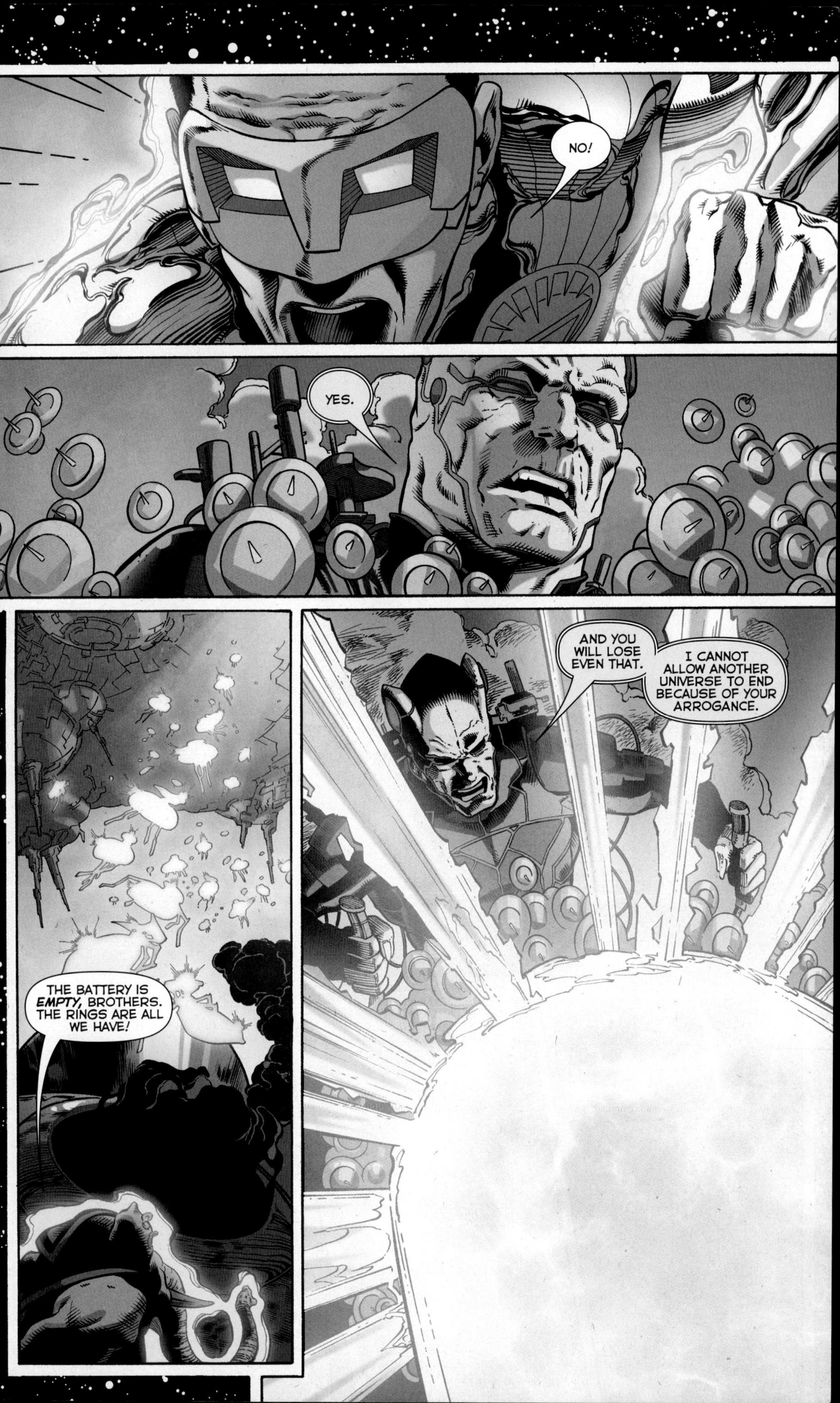
NO!
YES.
THE BATTERY IS *EMPTY*, BROTHERS. THE RINGS ARE ALL WE HAVE!
AND YOU WILL LOSE EVEN THAT.
I CANNOT ALLOW ANOTHER UNIVERSE TO END BECAUSE OF YOUR ARROGANCE.

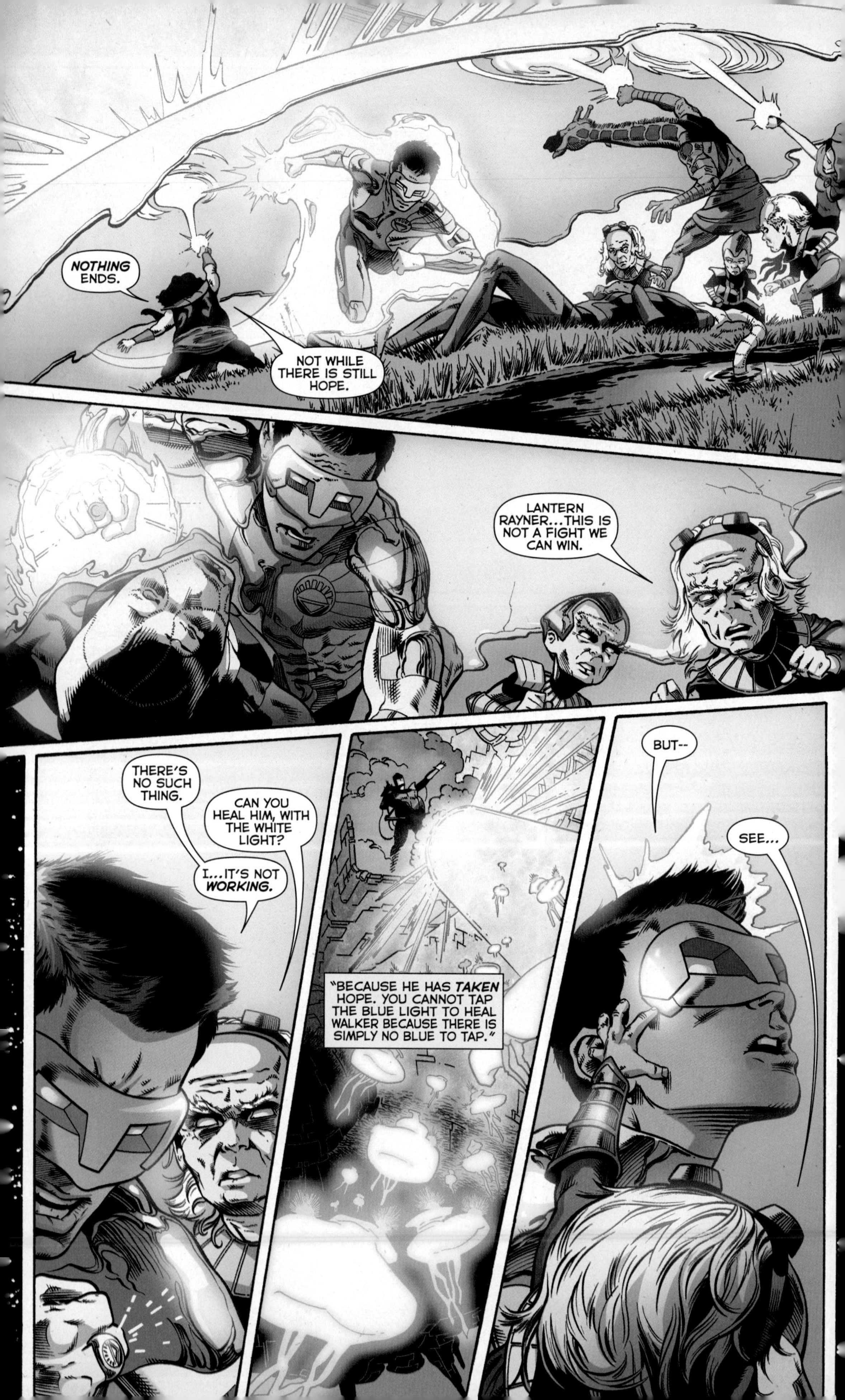
NOTHING ENDS.
NOT WHILE THERE IS STILL HOPE.
LANTERN RAYNER...THIS IS NOT A FIGHT WE CAN WIN.
THERE'S NO SUCH THING.
CAN YOU HEAL HIM, WITH THE WHITE LIGHT?
I...IT'S NOT WORKING.
"BECAUSE HE HAS TAKEN HOPE. YOU CANNOT TAP THE BLUE LIGHT TO HEAL WALKER BECAUSE THERE IS SIMPLY NO BLUE TO TAP."
BUT--
SEE...

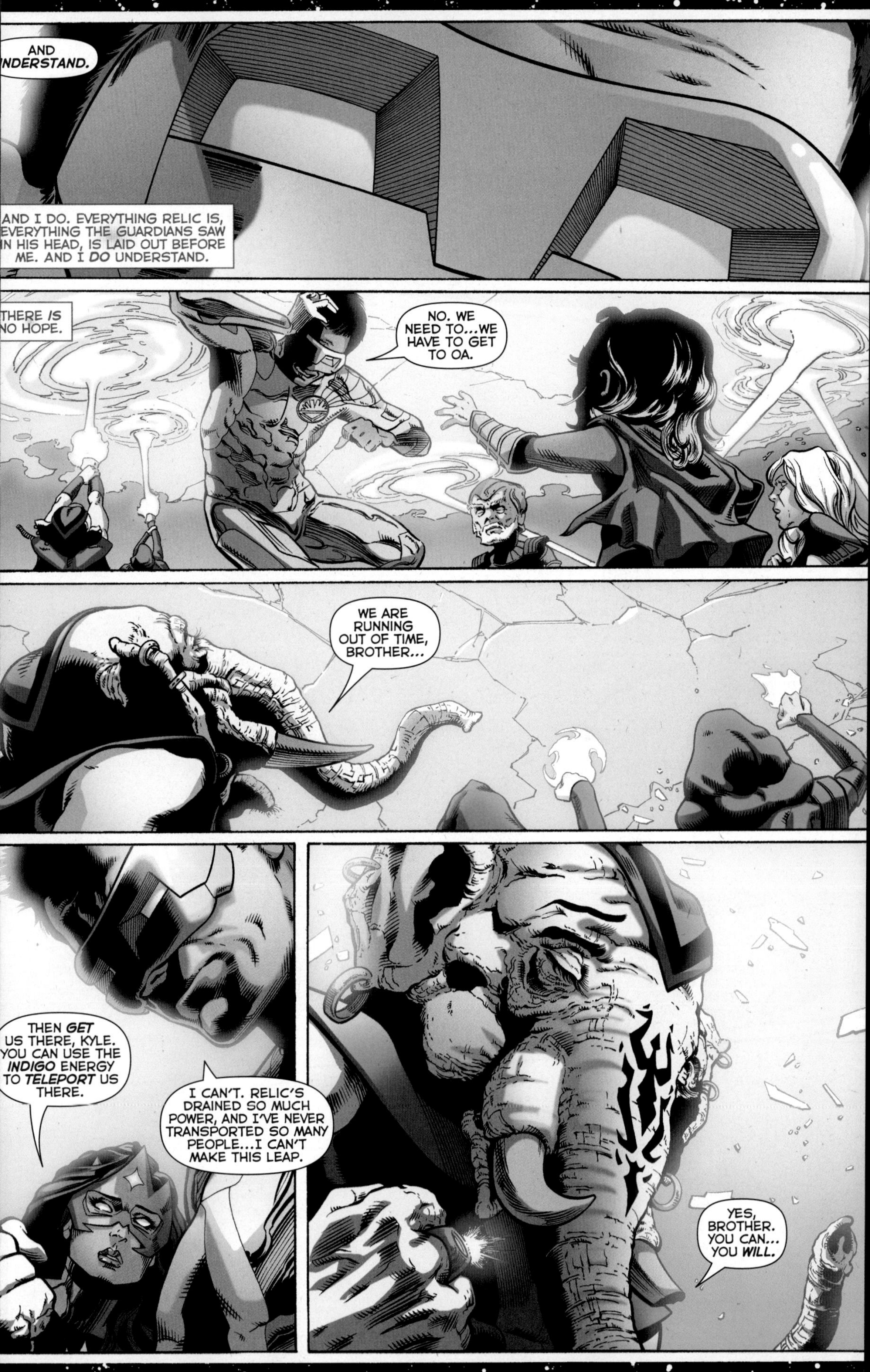
AND UNDERSTAND.
AND I DO. EVERYTHING RELIC IS, EVERYTHING THE GUARDIANS SAW IN HIS HEAD, IS LAID OUT BEFORE ME. AND I DO UNDERSTAND.
THERE IS NO HOPE.
NO. WE NEED TO...WE HAVE TO GET TO OA.
WE ARE RUNNING OUT OF TIME, BROTHER...
THEN GET US THERE, KYLE. YOU CAN USE THE INDIGO ENERGY TO TELEPORT US THERE.
I CAN'T. RELIC'S DRAINED SO MUCH POWER, AND I'VE NEVER TRANSPORTED SO MANY PEOPLE...I CAN'T MAKE THIS LEAP.
YES, BROTHER. YOU CAN... YOU WILL.

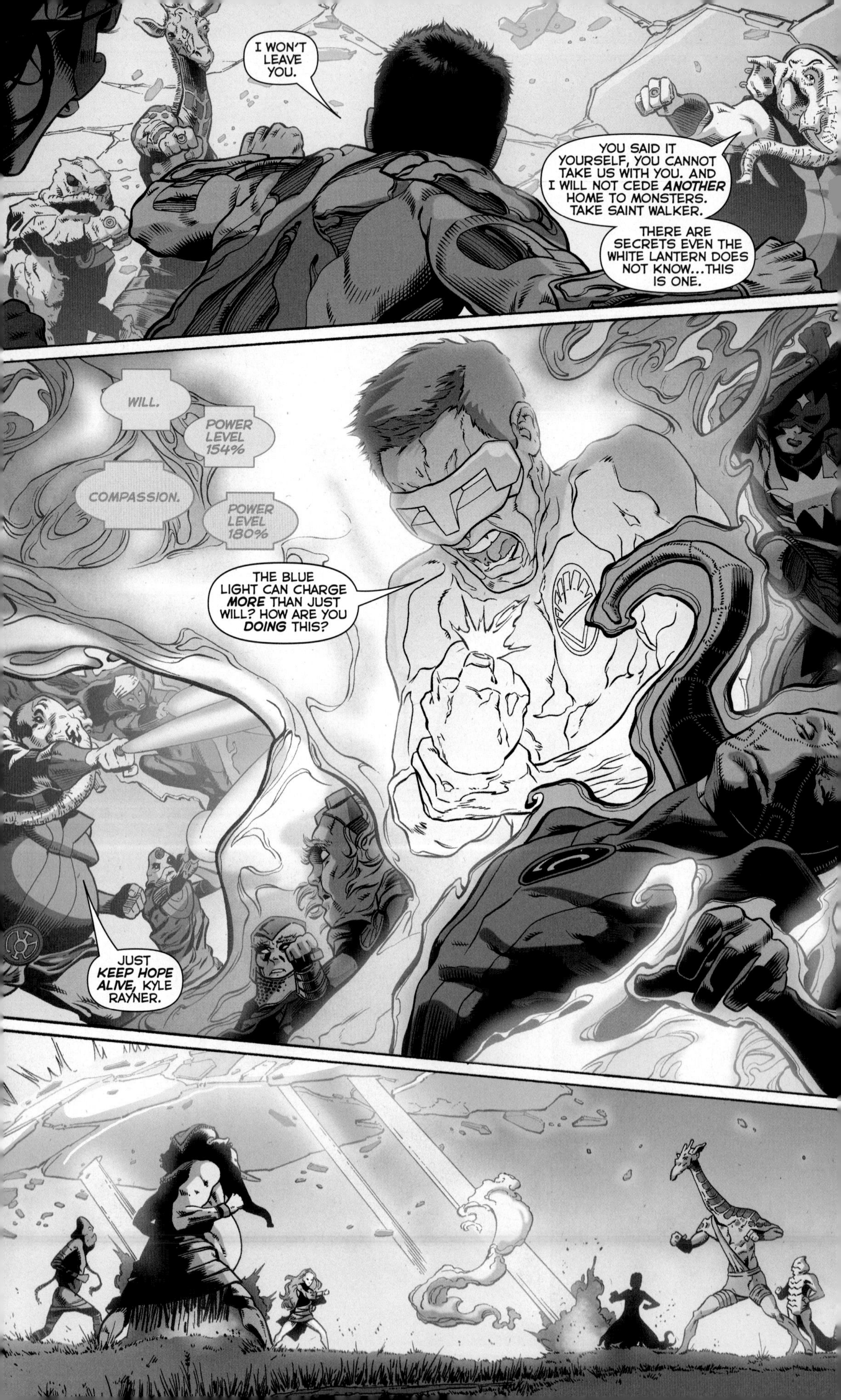
I WON'T LEAVE YOU.
YOU SAID IT YOURSELF, YOU CANNOT TAKE US WITH YOU. AND I WILL NOT CEDE ANOTHER HOME TO MONSTERS. TAKE SAINT WALKER.
THERE ARE SECRETS EVEN THE WHITE LANTERN DOES NOT KNOW...THIS IS ONE.
WILL.
POWER LEVEL 154%
COMPASSION.
POWER LEVEL 180%
THE BLUE LIGHT CAN CHARGE MORE THAN JUST WILL? HOW ARE YOU DOING THIS?
JUST KEEP HOPE ALIVE, KYLE RAYNER.

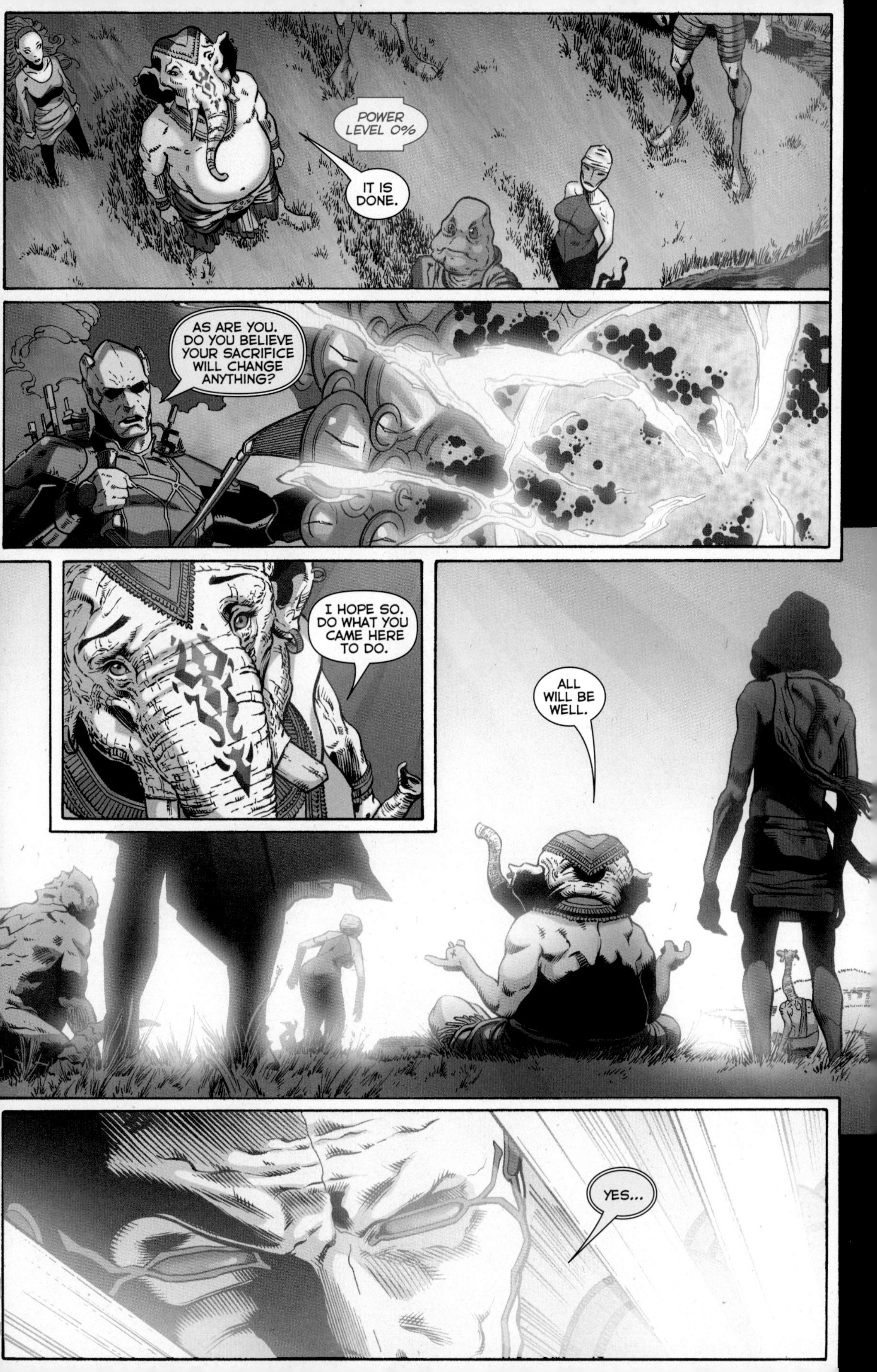
POWER LEVEL 0%
IT IS DONE.
AS ARE YOU. DO YOU BELIEVE YOUR SACRIFICE WILL CHANGE ANYTHING?
I HOPE SO. DO WHAT YOU CAME HERE TO DO.
ALL WILL BE WELL.
YES...

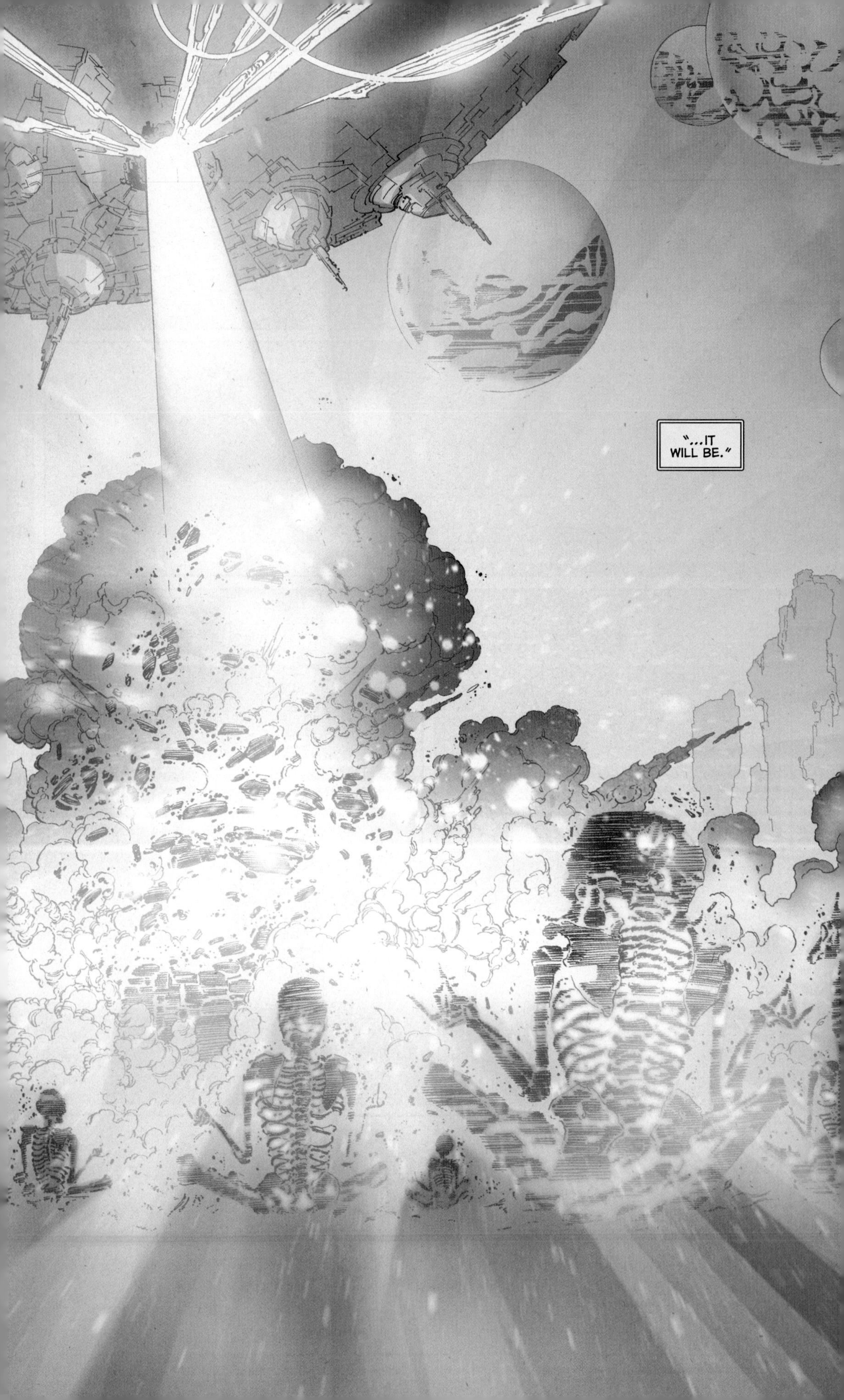
"...IT WILL BE."

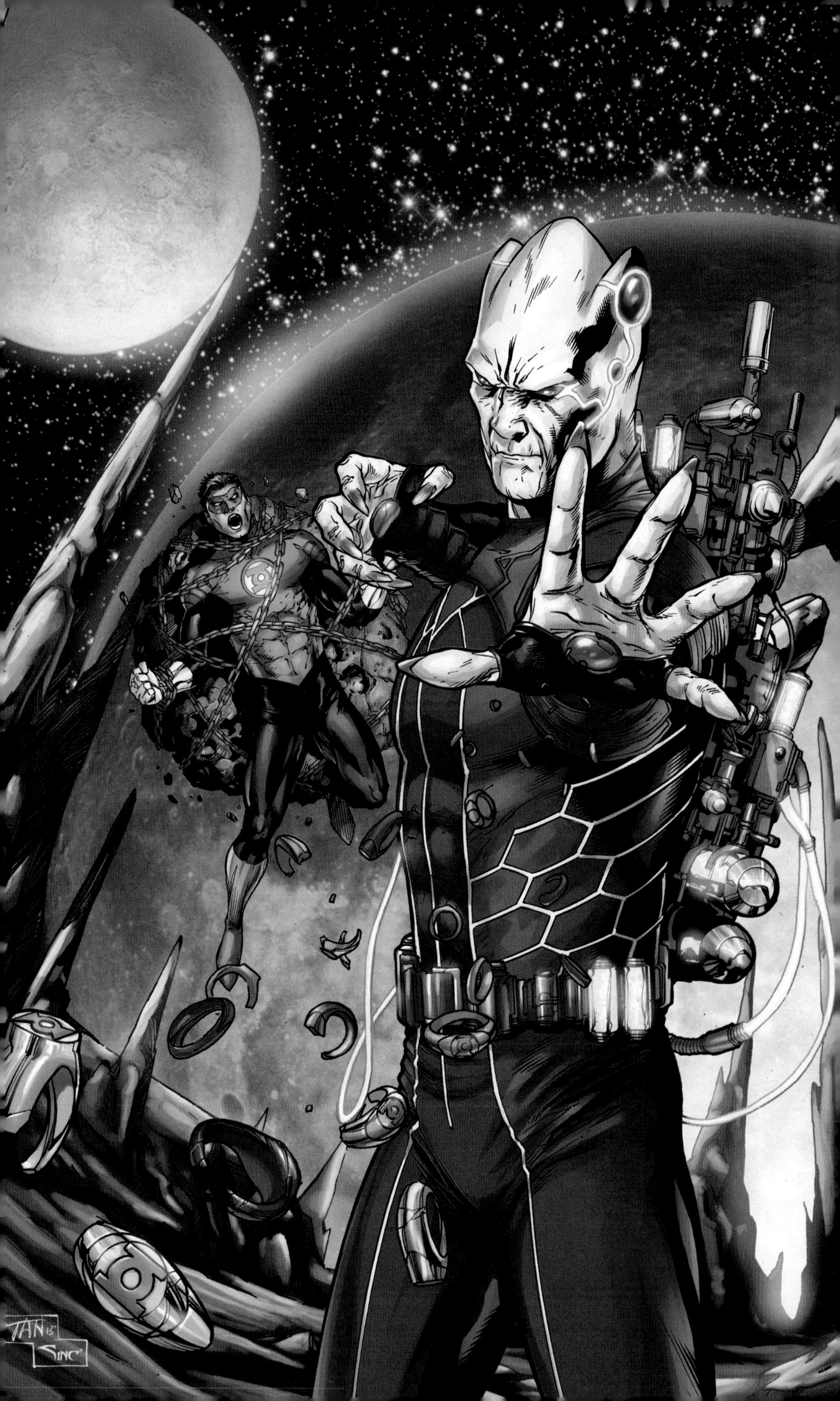
TAN 13
SINC

FALL OF THE LIGHTSMITHS

ROBERT VENDITTI writer RAGS MORALES penciller CAM SMITH with RAGS MORALES inkers ANDREW DALHOUSE colorist
BILLY TAN with ALEX SINCLAIR cover artists

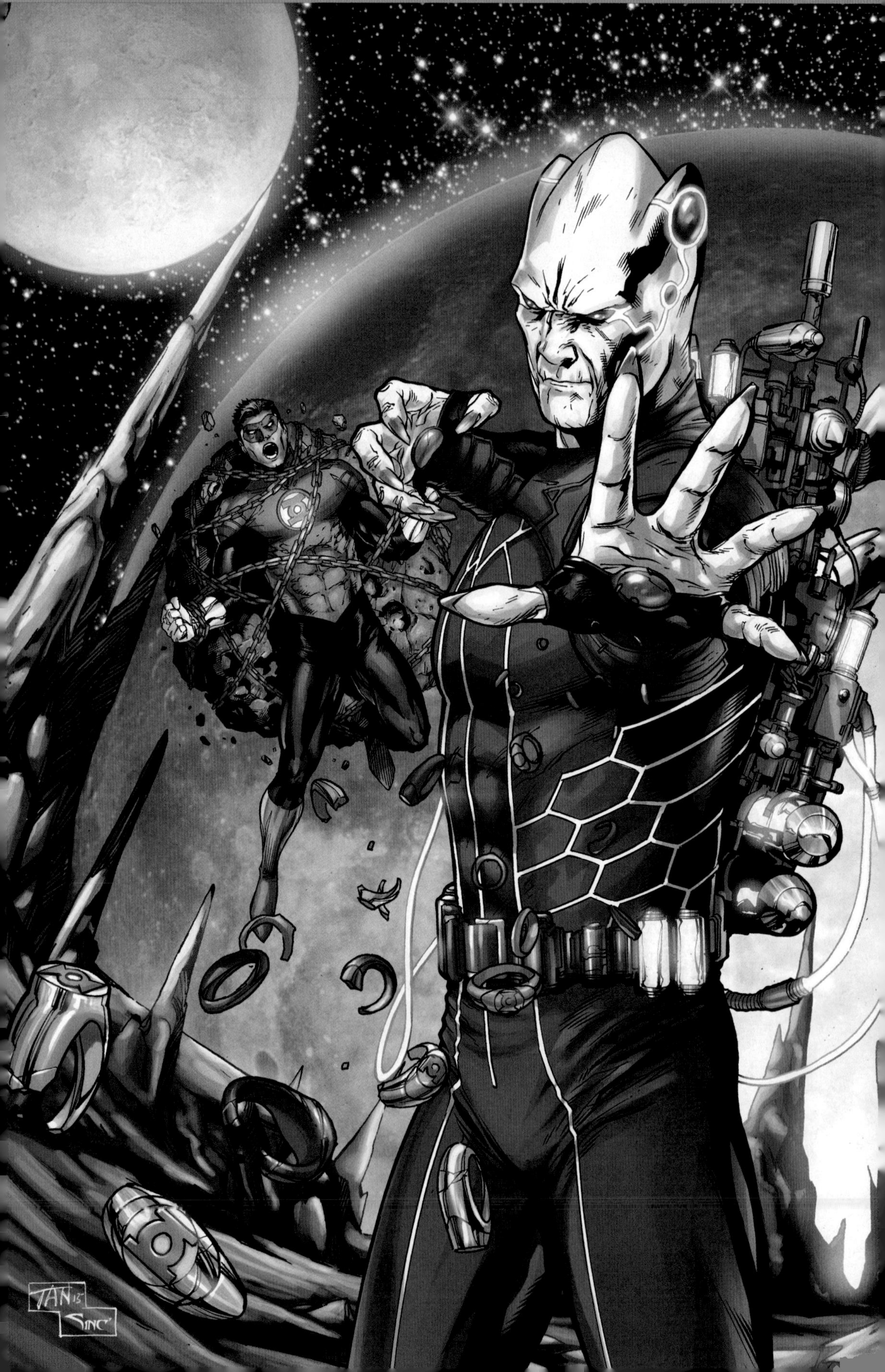

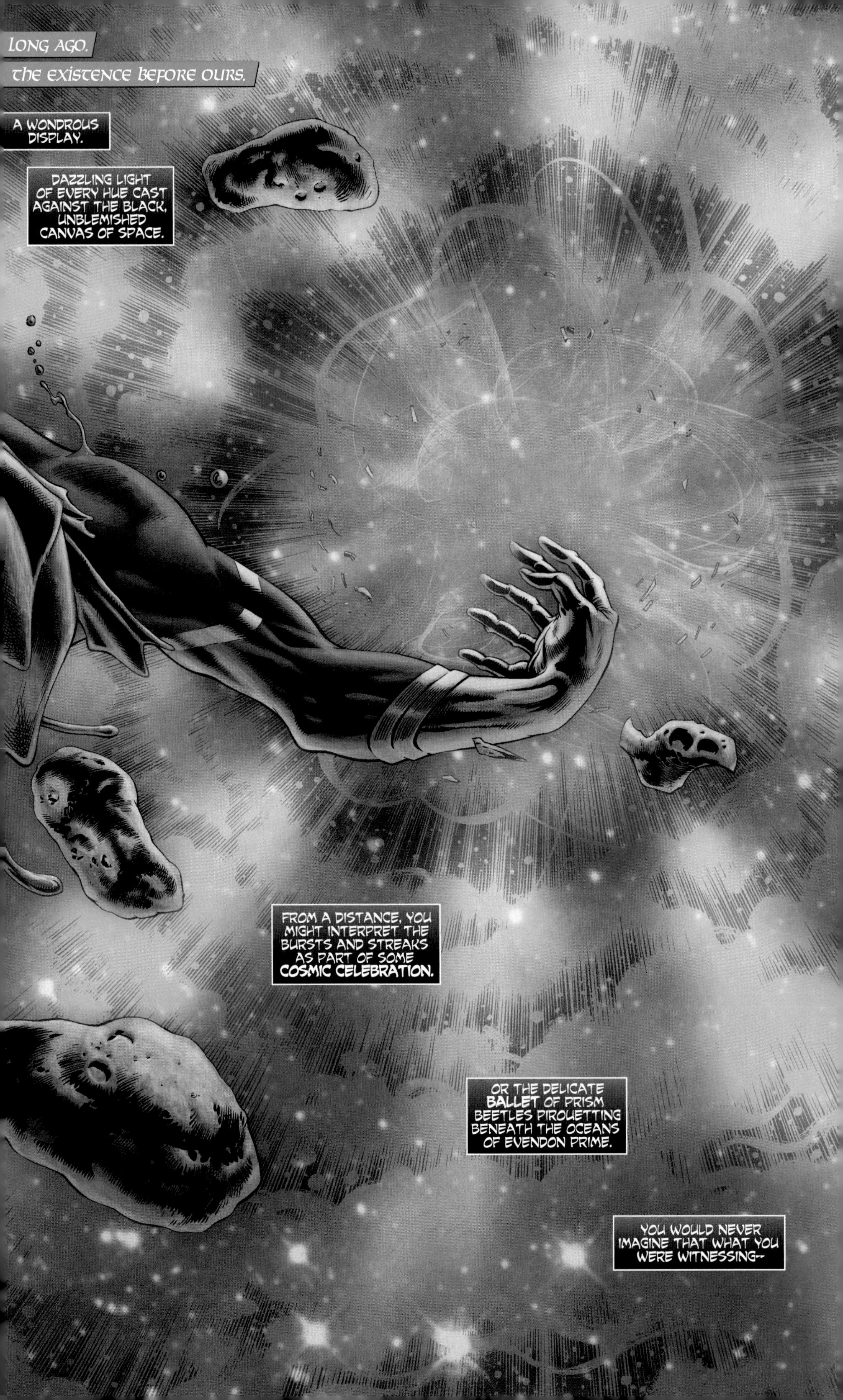
LONG AGO.
THE EXISTENCE BEFORE OURS.
A WONDROUS DISPLAY.
DAZZLING LIGHT OF EVERY HUE CAST AGAINST THE BLACK, UNBLEMISHED CANVAS OF SPACE.
FROM A DISTANCE, YOU MIGHT INTERPRET THE BURSTS AND STREAKS AS PART OF SOME COSMIC CELEBRATION.
OR THE DELICATE BALLET OF PRISM BEETLES PIROUETTING BENEATH THE OCEANS OF EVENDON PRIME.
YOU WOULD NEVER IMAGINE THAT WHAT YOU WERE WITNESSING--

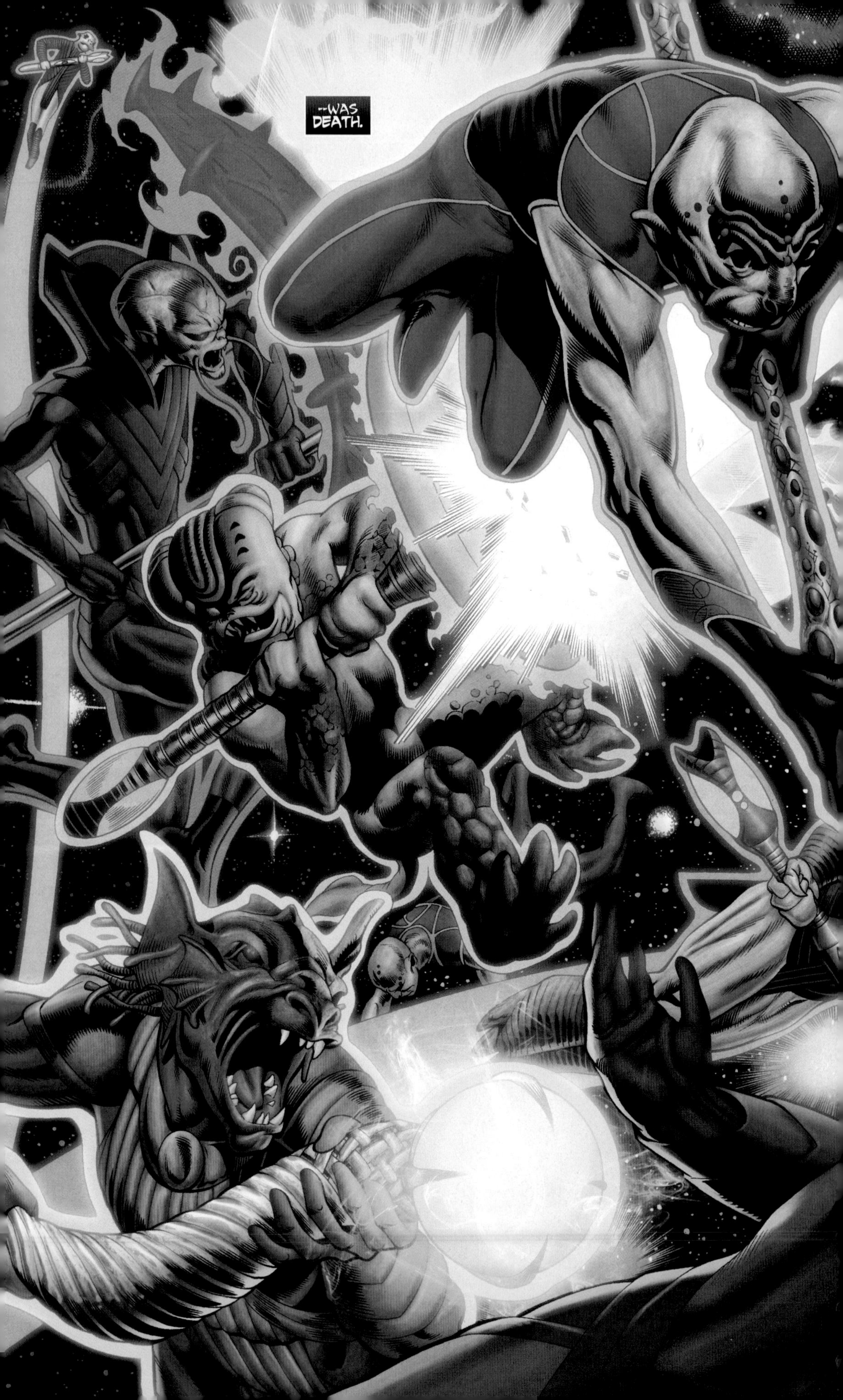
--WAS DEATH.

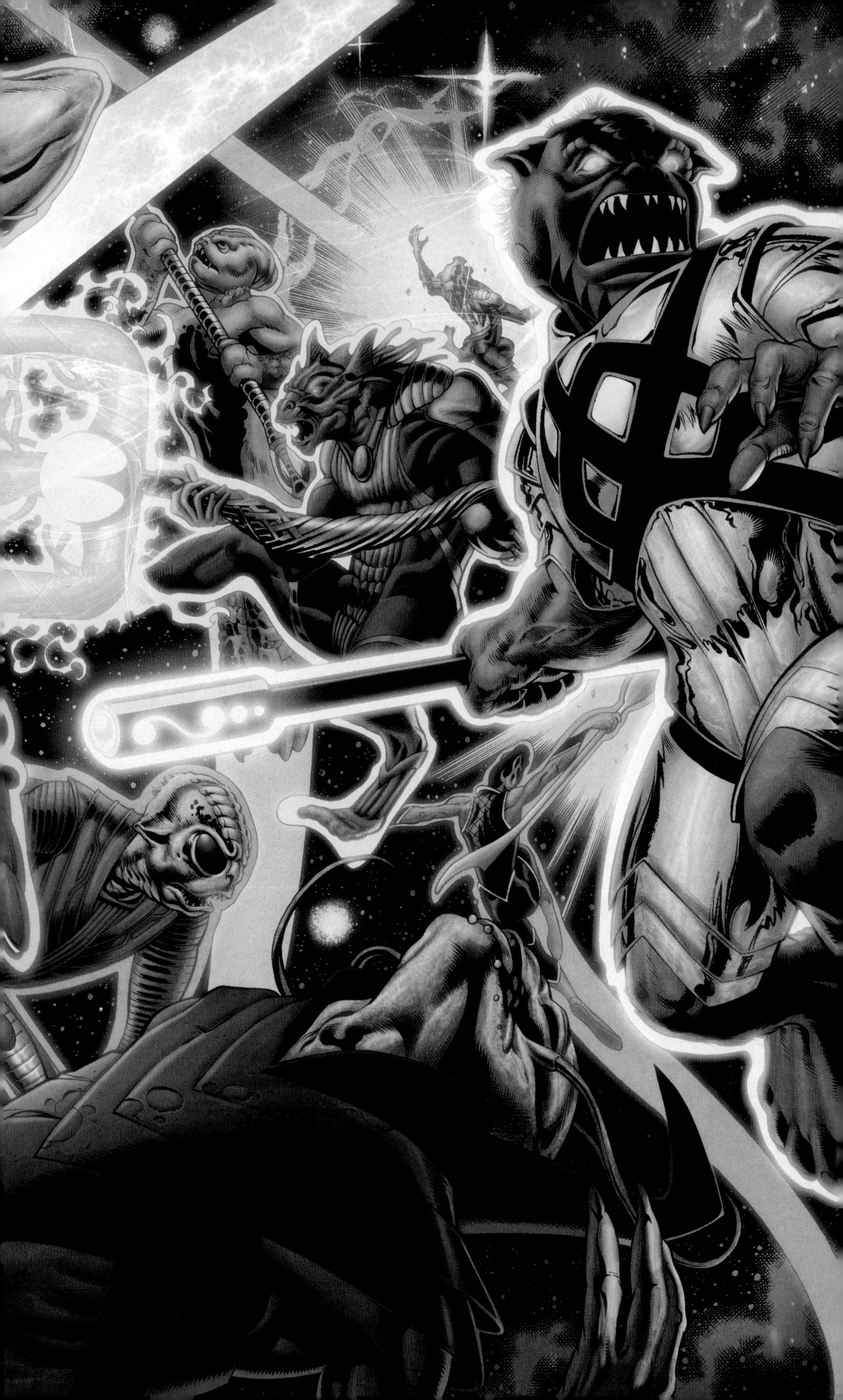

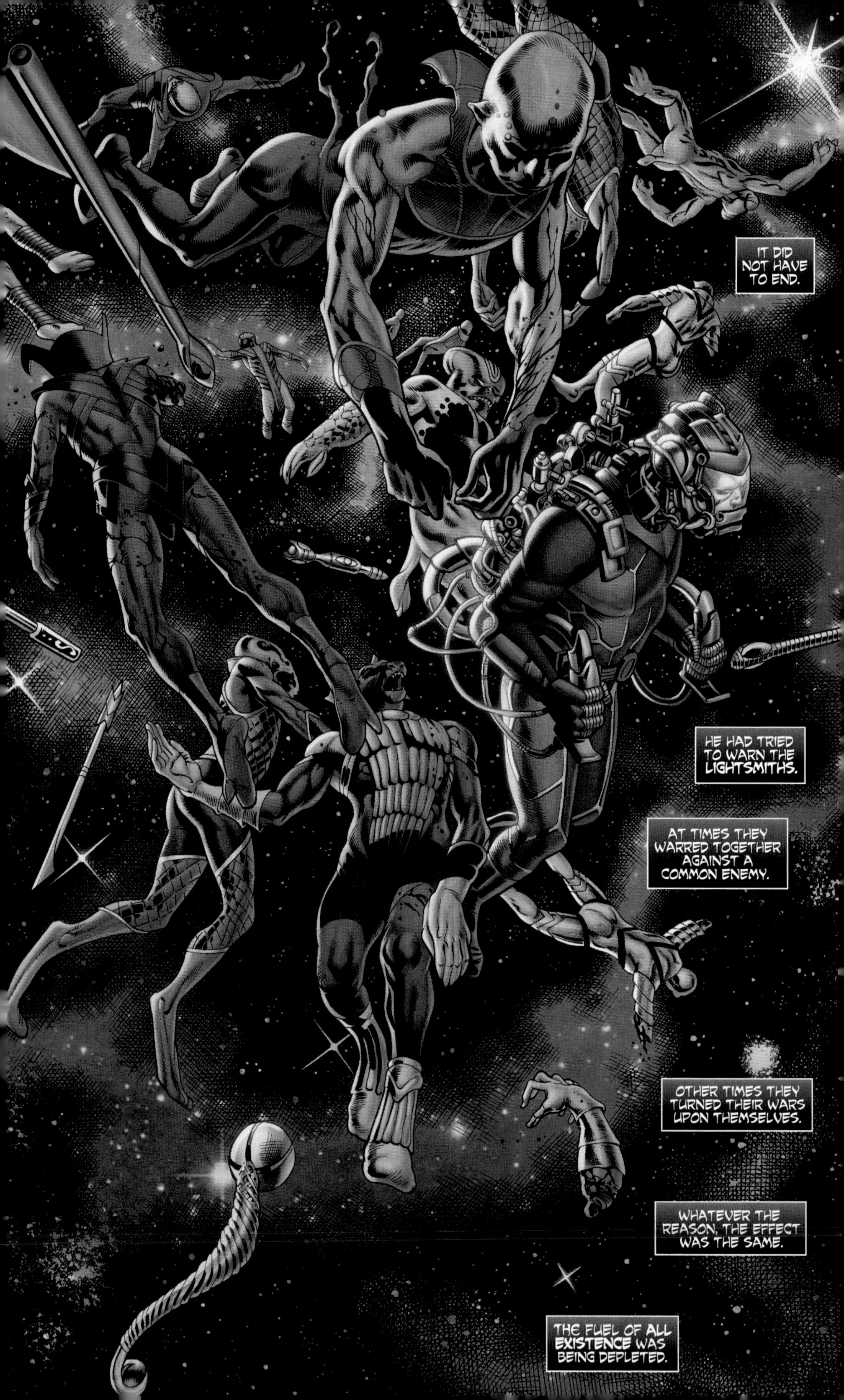
IT DID NOT HAVE TO END.
HE HAD TRIED TO WARN THE LIGHTSMITHS.
AT TIMES THEY WARRED TOGETHER AGAINST A COMMON ENEMY.
OTHER TIMES THEY TURNED THEIR WARS UPON THEMSELVES.
WHATEVER THE REASON, THE EFFECT WAS THE SAME.
THE FUEL OF ALL EXISTENCE WAS BEING DEPLETED.

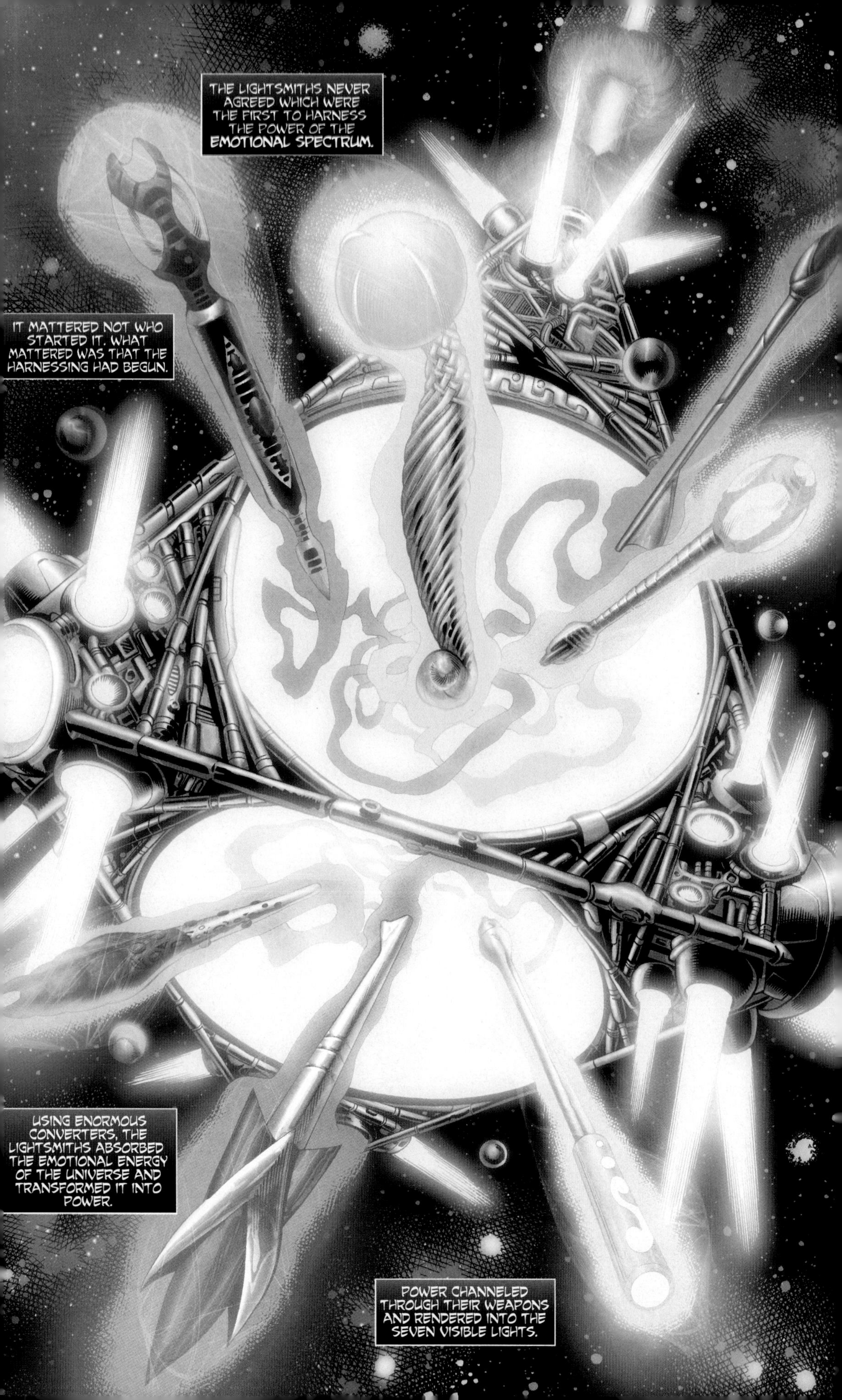
THE LIGHTSMITHS NEVER AGREED WHICH WERE THE FIRST TO HARNESS THE POWER OF THE EMOTIONAL SPECTRUM.
IT MATTERED NOT WHO STARTED IT. WHAT MATTERED WAS THAT THE HARNESSING HAD BEGUN.
USING ENORMOUS CONVERTERS, THE LIGHTSMITHS ABSORBED THE EMOTIONAL ENERGY OF THE UNIVERSE AND TRANSFORMED IT INTO POWER.
POWER CHANNELED THROUGH THEIR WEAPONS AND RENDERED INTO THE SEVEN VISIBLE LIGHTS.

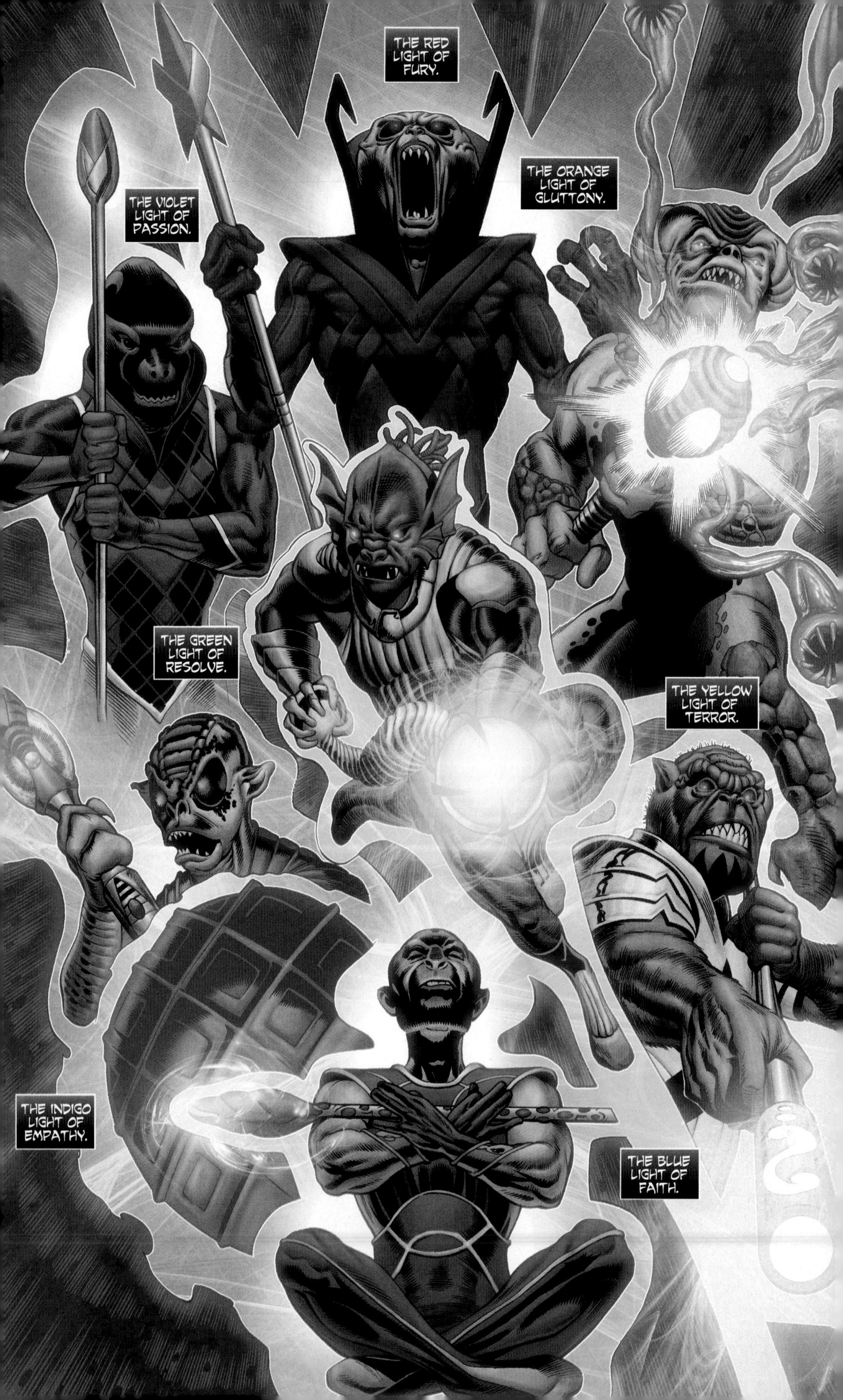
THE RED LIGHT OF FURY.
THE ORANGE LIGHT OF GLUTTONY.
THE VIOLET LIGHT OF PASSION.
THE GREEN LIGHT OF RESOLVE.
THE YELLOW LIGHT OF TERROR.
THE INDIGO LIGHT OF EMPATHY.
THE BLUE LIGHT OF FAITH.

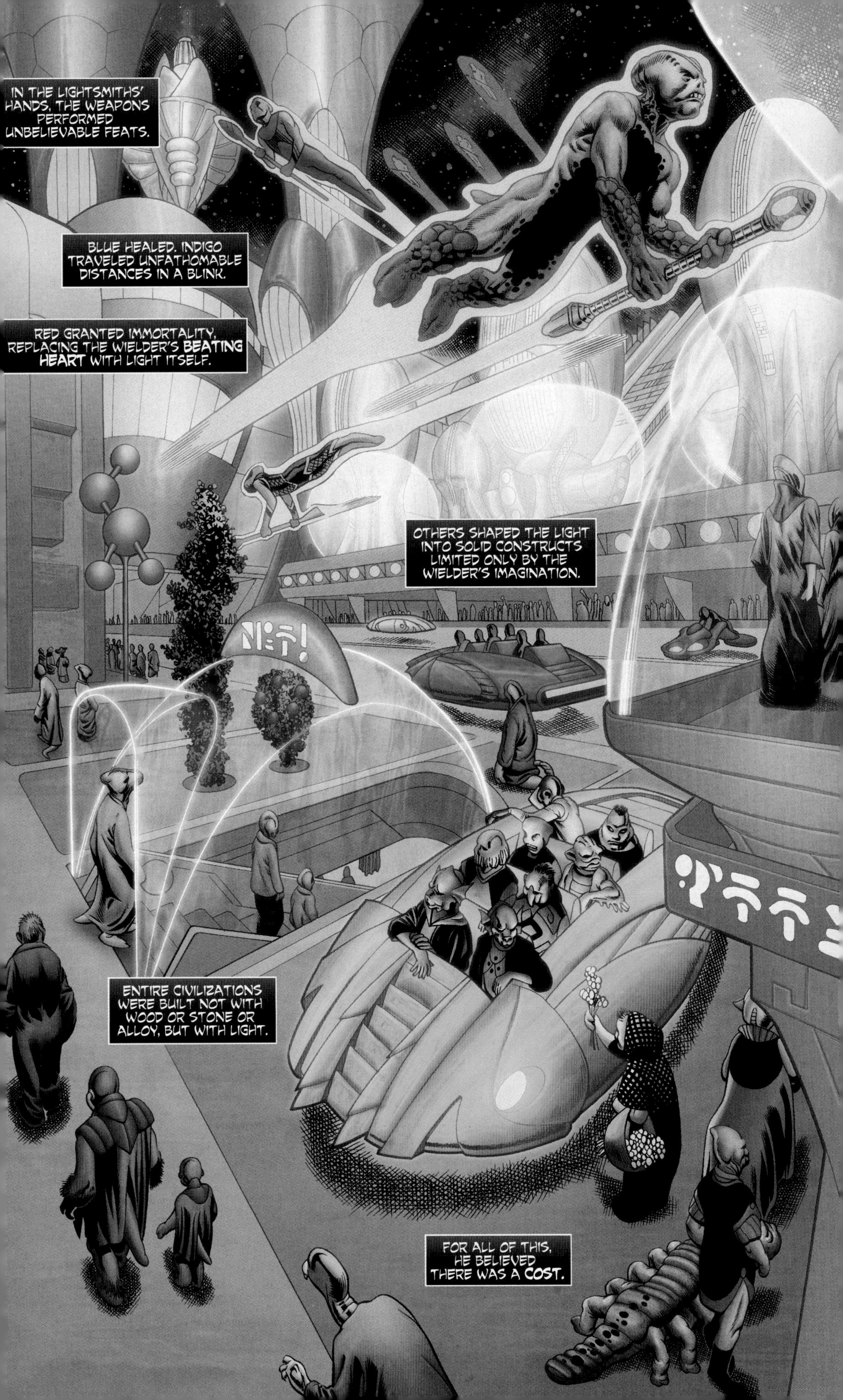
IN THE LIGHTSMITHS' HANDS, THE WEAPONS PERFORMED UNBELIEVABLE FEATS.
BLUE HEALED. INDIGO TRAVELED UNFATHOMABLE DISTANCES IN A BLINK.
RED GRANTED IMMORTALITY, REPLACING THE WIELDER'S **BEATING HEART** WITH LIGHT ITSELF.
OTHERS SHAPED THE LIGHT INTO SOLID CONSTRUCTS LIMITED ONLY BY THE WIELDER'S IMAGINATION.
ENTIRE CIVILIZATIONS WERE BUILT NOT WITH WOOD OR STONE OR ALLOY, BUT WITH LIGHT.
FOR ALL OF THIS, HE BELIEVED THERE WAS A **COST.**

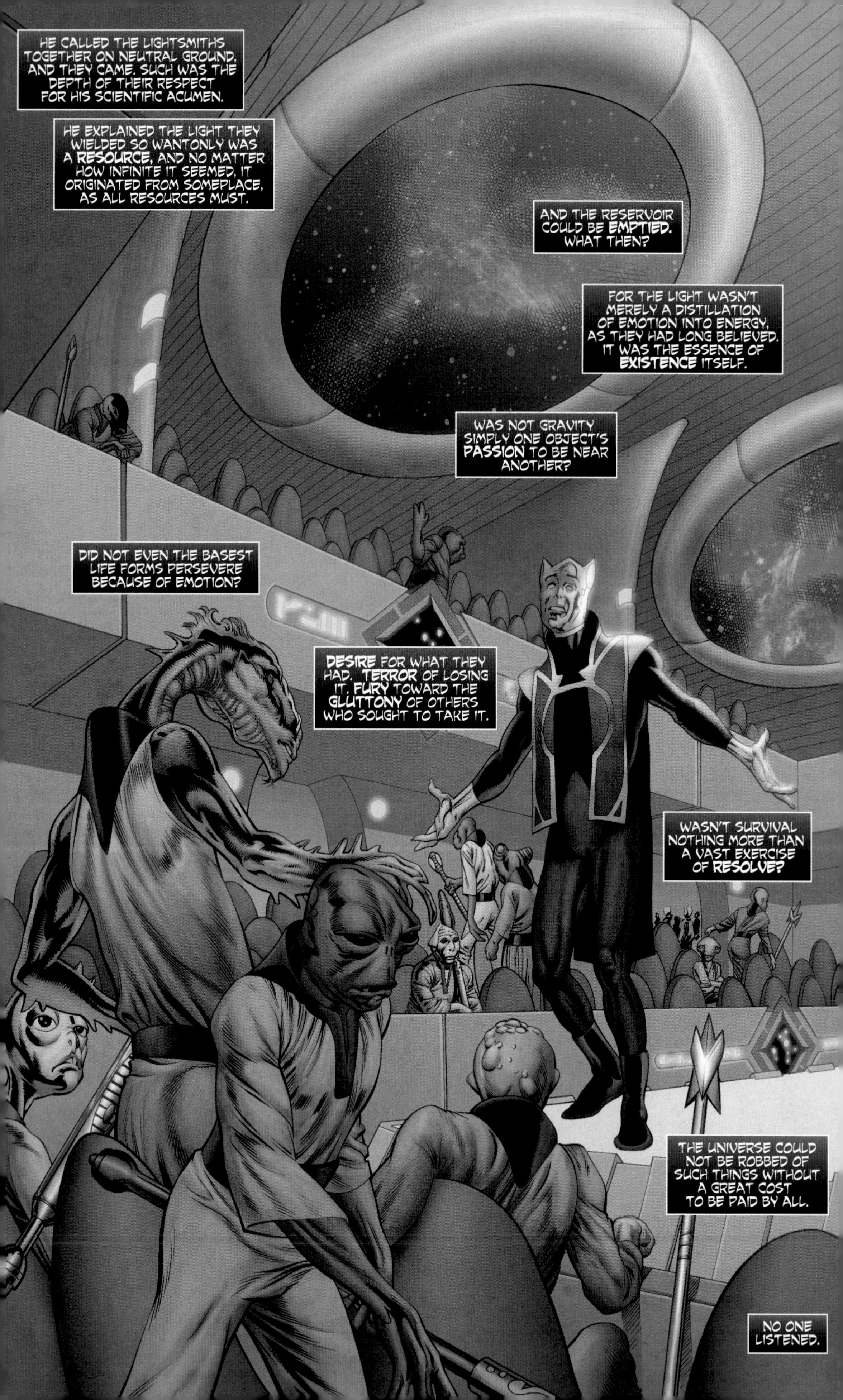
HE CALLED THE LIGHTSMITHS TOGETHER ON NEUTRAL GROUND, AND THEY CAME. SUCH WAS THE DEPTH OF THEIR RESPECT FOR HIS SCIENTIFIC ACUMEN.
HE EXPLAINED THE LIGHT THEY WIELDED SO WANTONLY WAS A RESOURCE, AND NO MATTER HOW INFINITE IT SEEMED, IT ORIGINATED FROM SOMEPLACE, AS ALL RESOURCES MUST.
AND THE RESERVOIR COULD BE EMPTIED. WHAT THEN?
FOR THE LIGHT WASN'T MERELY A DISTILLATION OF EMOTION INTO ENERGY, AS THEY HAD LONG BELIEVED. IT WAS THE ESSENCE OF EXISTENCE ITSELF.
WAS NOT GRAVITY SIMPLY ONE OBJECT'S PASSION TO BE NEAR ANOTHER?
DID NOT EVEN THE BASEST LIFE FORMS PERSEVERE BECAUSE OF EMOTION?
DESIRE FOR WHAT THEY HAD. TERROR OF LOSING IT. FURY TOWARD THE GLUTTONY OF OTHERS WHO SOUGHT TO TAKE IT.
WASN'T SURVIVAL NOTHING MORE THAN A VAST EXERCISE OF RESOLVE?
THE UNIVERSE COULD NOT BE ROBBED OF SUCH THINGS WITHOUT A GREAT COST TO BE PAID BY ALL.
NO ONE LISTENED.

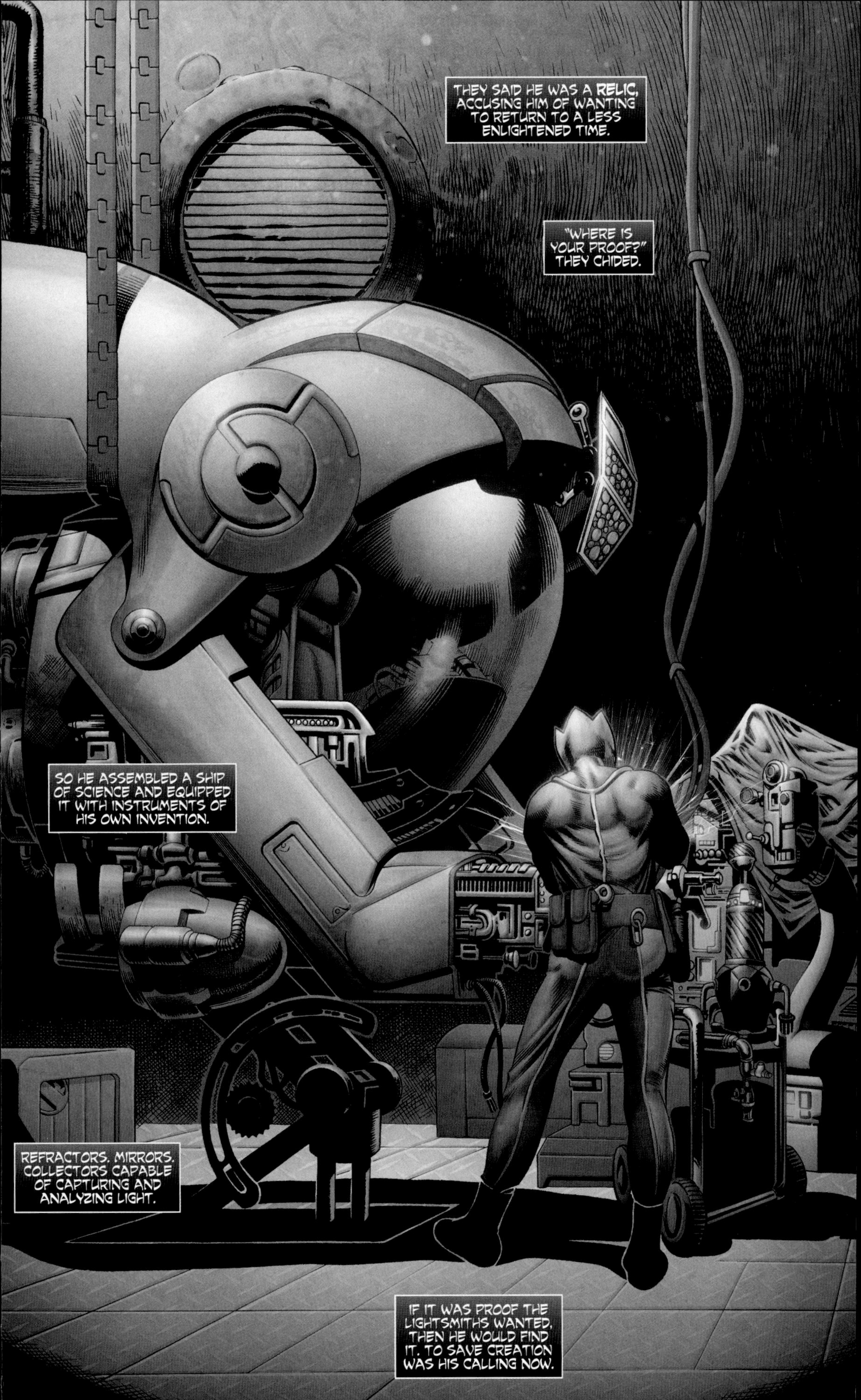
THEY SAID HE WAS A RELIC, ACCUSING HIM OF WANTING TO RETURN TO A LESS ENLIGHTENED TIME.
"WHERE IS YOUR PROOF?" THEY CHIDED.
SO HE ASSEMBLED A SHIP OF SCIENCE AND EQUIPPED IT WITH INSTRUMENTS OF HIS OWN INVENTION.
REFRACTORS. MIRRORS. COLLECTORS CAPABLE OF CAPTURING AND ANALYZING LIGHT.
IF IT WAS PROOF THE LIGHTSMITHS WANTED, THEN HE WOULD FIND IT. TO SAVE CREATION WAS HIS CALLING NOW.

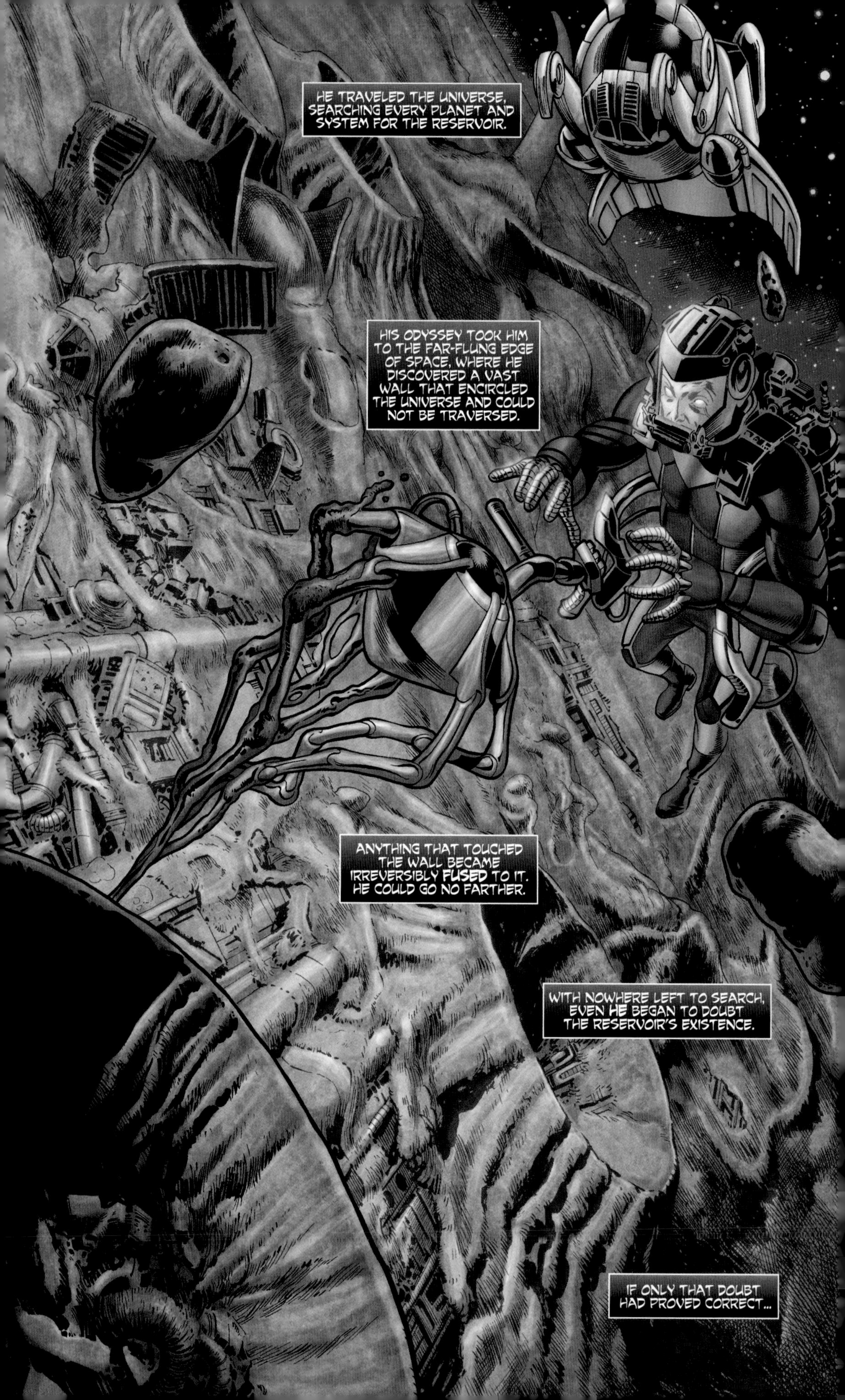
HE TRAVELED THE UNIVERSE, SEARCHING EVERY PLANET AND SYSTEM FOR THE RESERVOIR.
HIS ODYSSEY TOOK HIM TO THE FAR-FLUNG EDGE OF SPACE, WHERE HE DISCOVERED A VAST WALL THAT ENCIRCLED THE UNIVERSE AND COULD NOT BE TRAVERSED.
ANYTHING THAT TOUCHED THE WALL BECAME IRREVERSIBLY **FUSED** TO IT. HE COULD GO NO FARTHER.
WITH NOWHERE LEFT TO SEARCH, EVEN **HE** BEGAN TO DOUBT THE RESERVOIR'S EXISTENCE.
IF ONLY THAT DOUBT HAD PROVED CORRECT...

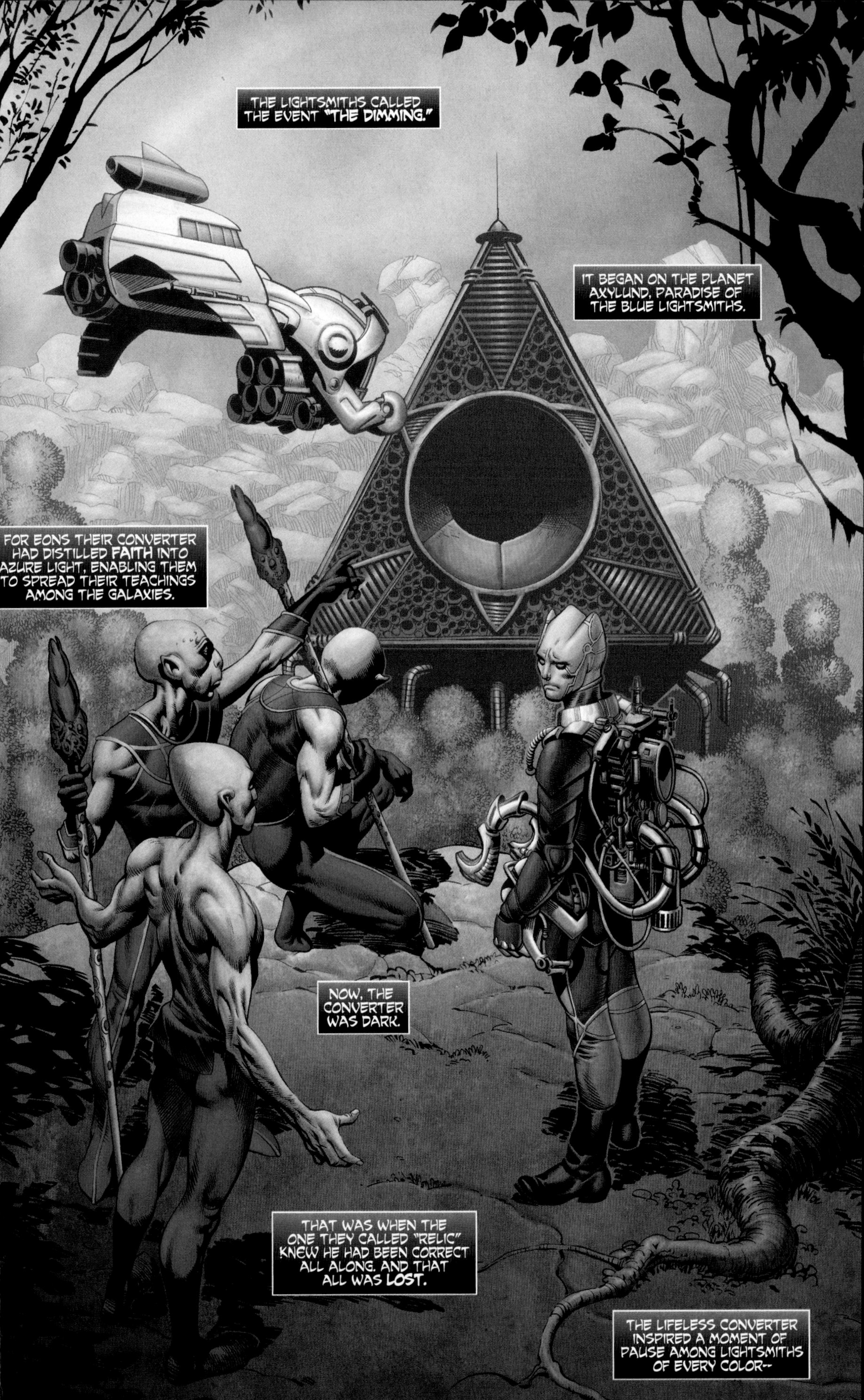
THE LIGHTSMITHS CALLED THE EVENT "THE DIMMING."
IT BEGAN ON THE PLANET AXYLUND, PARADISE OF THE BLUE LIGHTSMITHS.
FOR EONS THEIR CONVERTER HAD DISTILLED FAITH INTO AZURE LIGHT, ENABLING THEM TO SPREAD THEIR TEACHINGS AMONG THE GALAXIES.
NOW, THE CONVERTER WAS DARK.
THAT WAS WHEN THE ONE THEY CALLED "RELIC" KNEW HE HAD BEEN CORRECT ALL ALONG. AND THAT ALL WAS LOST.
THE LIFELESS CONVERTER INSPIRED A MOMENT OF PAUSE AMONG LIGHTSMITHS OF EVERY COLOR--

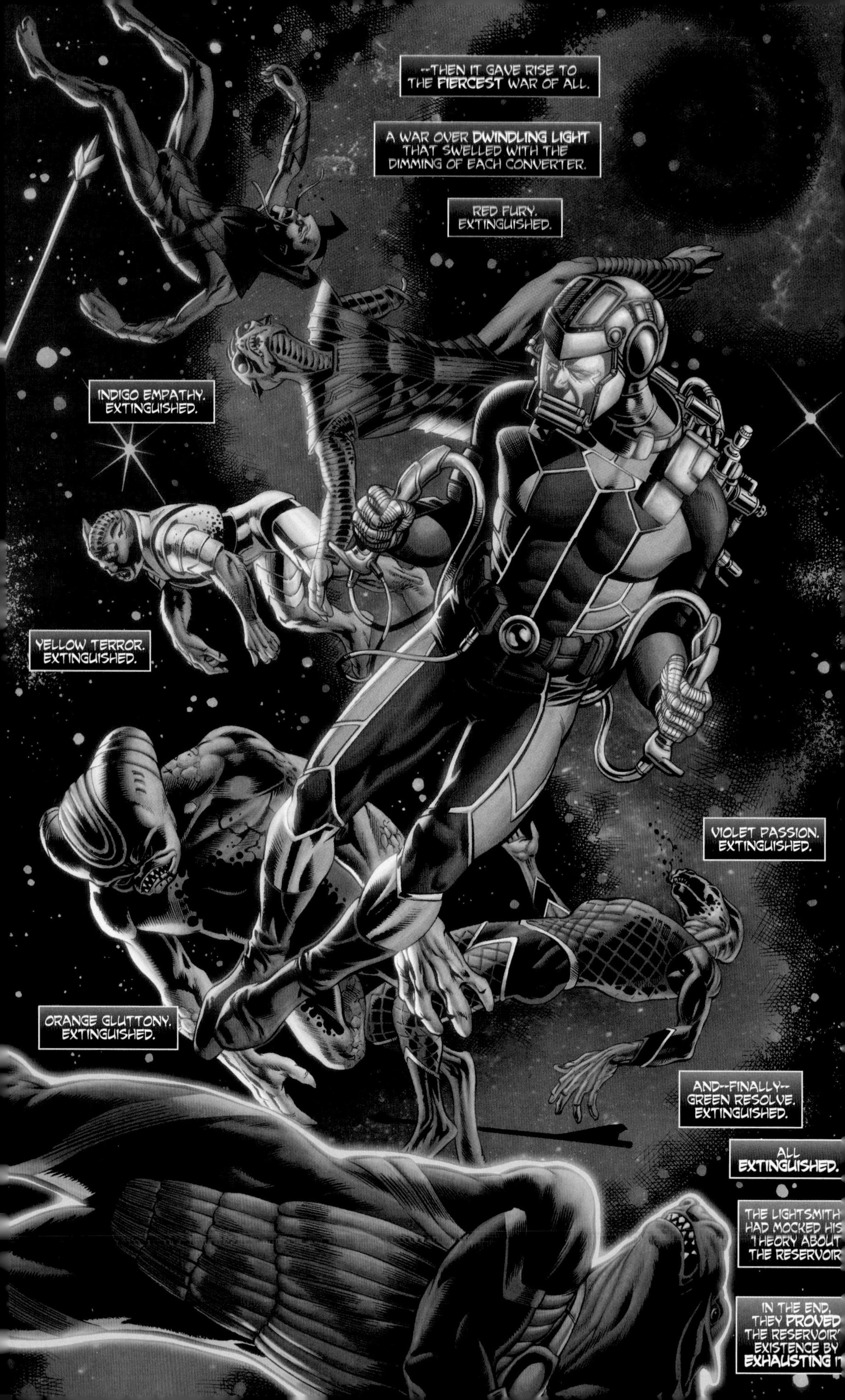
--THEN IT GAVE RISE TO THE FIERCEST WAR OF ALL.
A WAR OVER DWINDLING LIGHT THAT SWELLED WITH THE DIMMING OF EACH CONVERTER.
RED FURY. EXTINGUISHED.
INDIGO EMPATHY. EXTINGUISHED.
YELLOW TERROR. EXTINGUISHED.
VIOLET PASSION. EXTINGUISHED.
ORANGE GLUTTONY. EXTINGUISHED.
AND--FINALLY--GREEN RESOLVE. EXTINGUISHED.
ALL EXTINGUISHED.
THE LIGHTSMITH HAD MOCKED HIS THEORY ABOUT THE RESERVOIR
IN THE END, THEY PROVED THE RESERVOIR' EXISTENCE BY EXHAUSTING IT

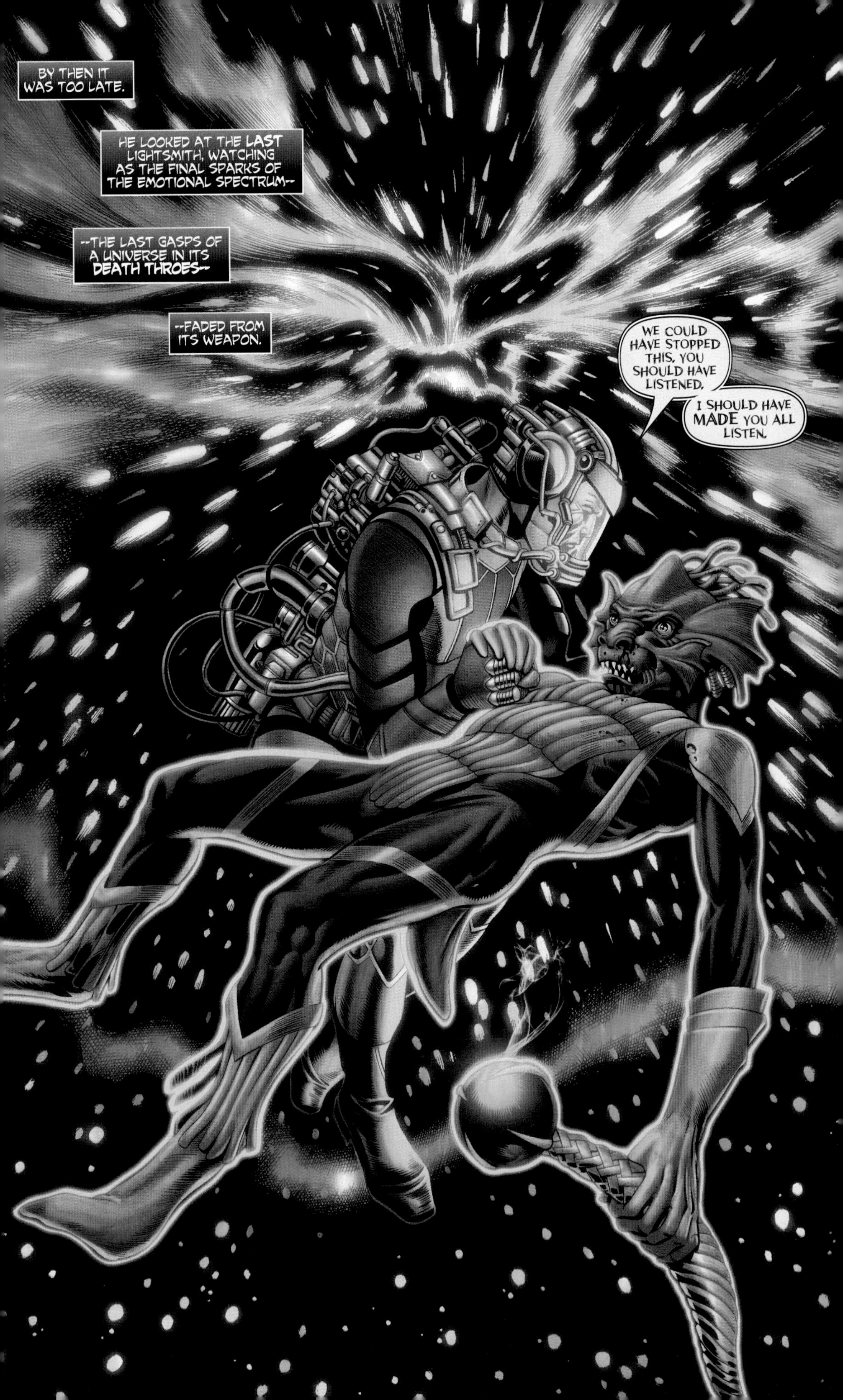
BY THEN IT WAS TOO LATE.
HE LOOKED AT THE LAST LIGHTSMITH, WATCHING AS THE FINAL SPARKS OF THE EMOTIONAL SPECTRUM--
--THE LAST GASPS OF A UNIVERSE IN ITS DEATH THROES--
--FADED FROM ITS WEAPON.
WE COULD HAVE STOPPED THIS. YOU SHOULD HAVE LISTENED.
I SHOULD HAVE MADE YOU ALL LISTEN.

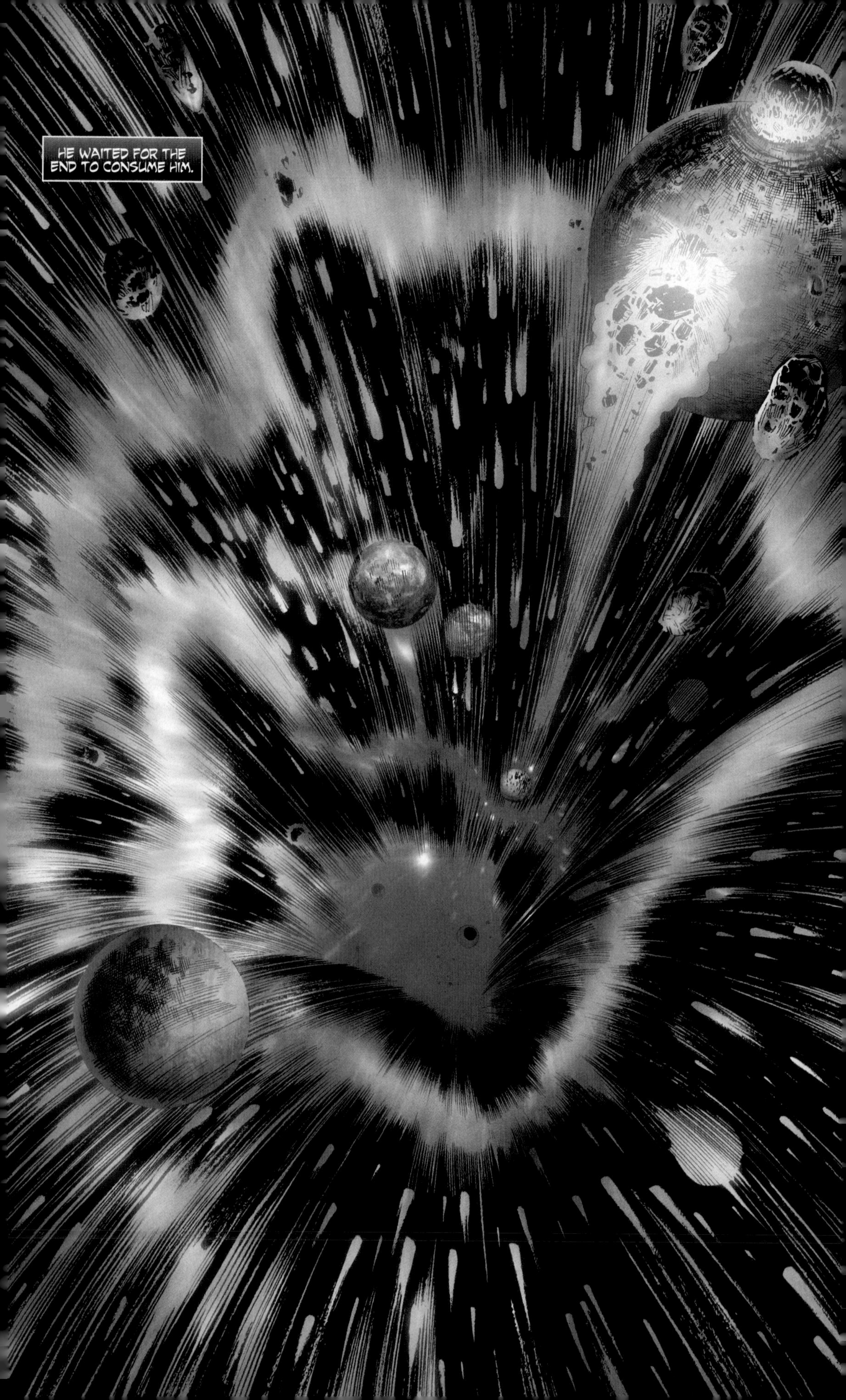
HE WAITED FOR THE END TO CONSUME HIM.

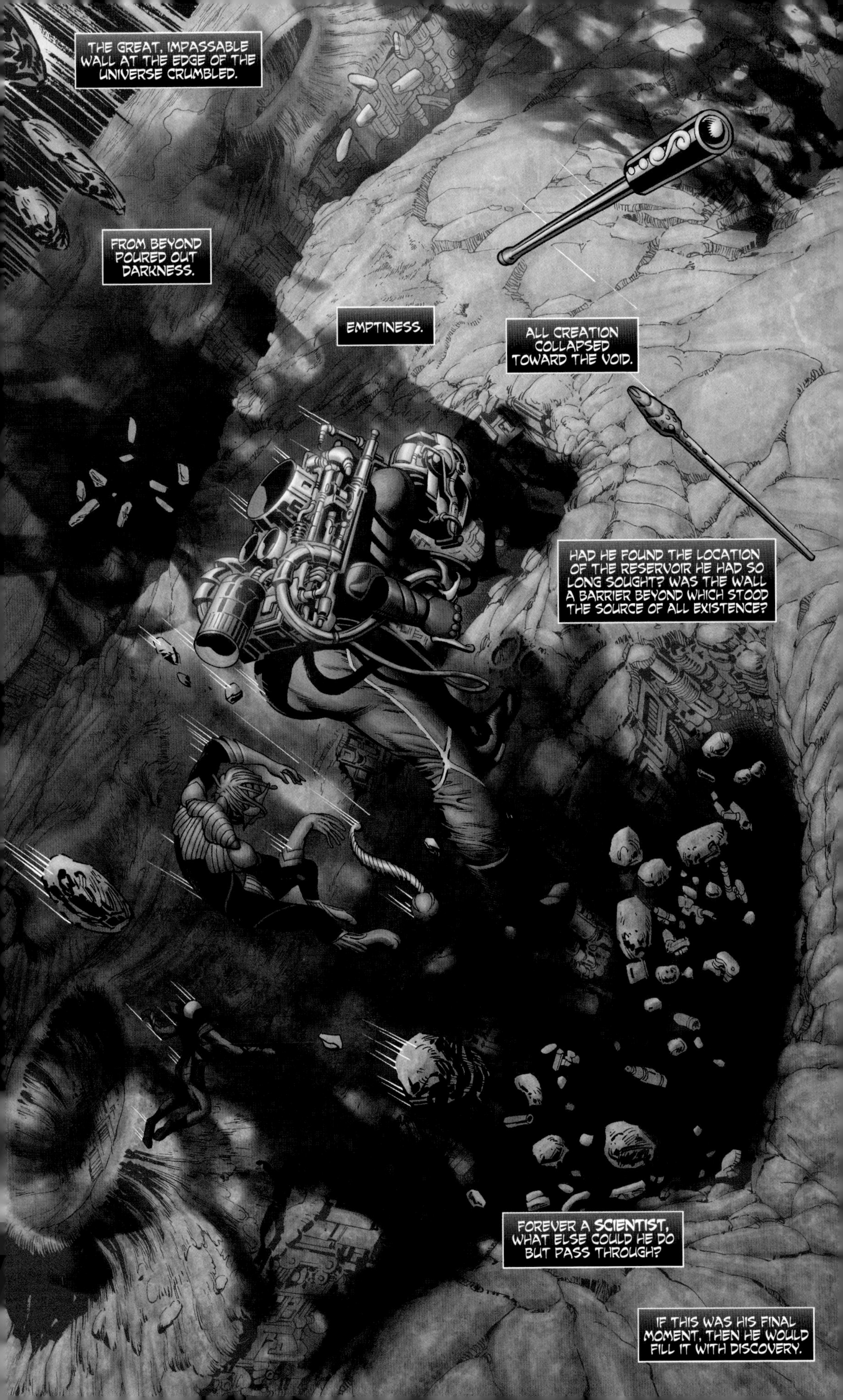
THE GREAT, IMPASSABLE WALL AT THE EDGE OF THE UNIVERSE CRUMBLED.
FROM BEYOND POURED OUT DARKNESS.
EMPTINESS.
ALL CREATION COLLAPSED TOWARD THE VOID.
HAD HE FOUND THE LOCATION OF THE RESERVOIR HE HAD SO LONG SOUGHT? WAS THE WALL A BARRIER BEYOND WHICH STOOD THE SOURCE OF ALL EXISTENCE?
FOREVER A SCIENTIST, WHAT ELSE COULD HE DO BUT PASS THROUGH?
IF THIS WAS HIS FINAL MOMENT, THEN HE WOULD FILL IT WITH DISCOVERY.

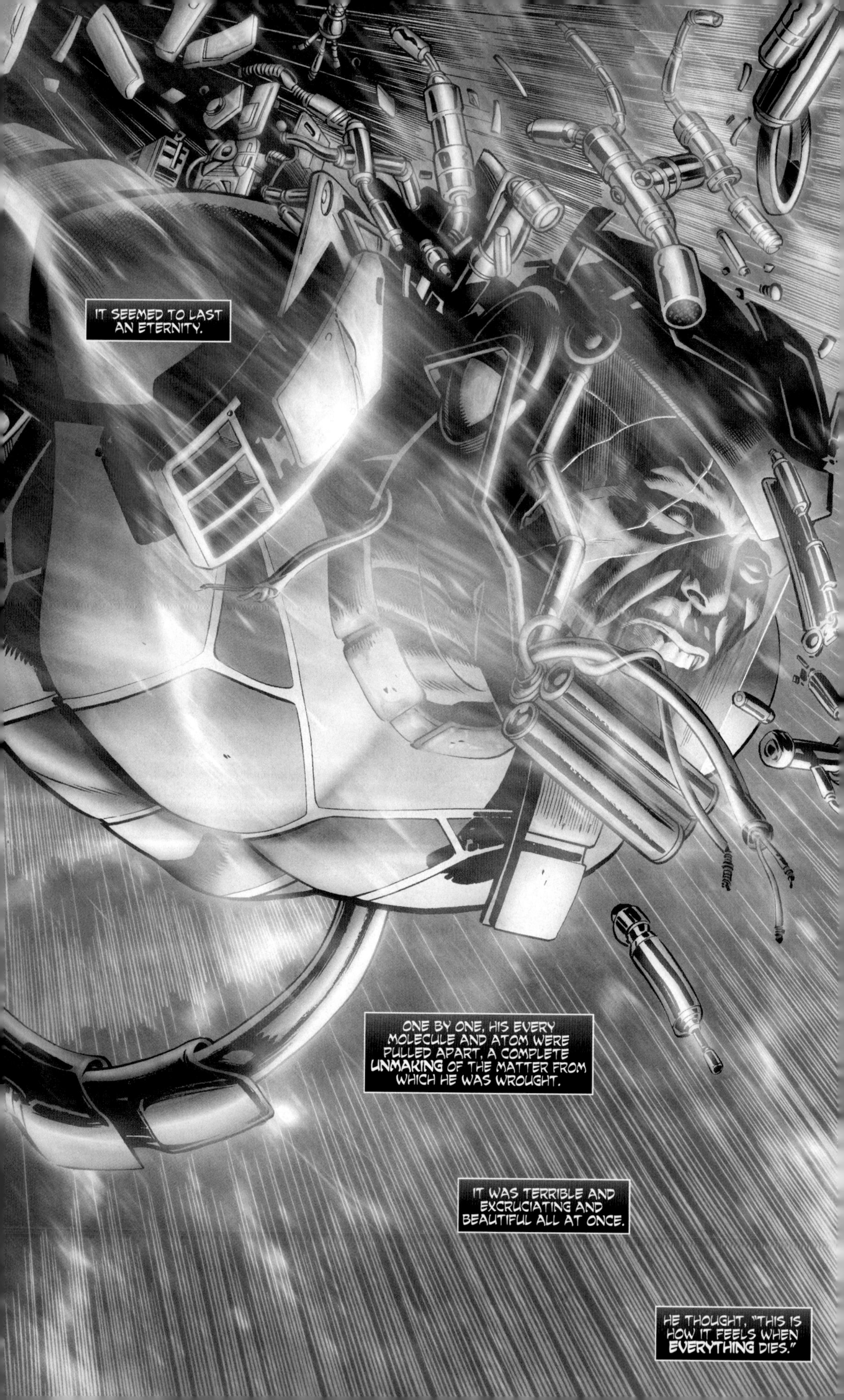
IT SEEMED TO LAST AN ETERNITY.
ONE BY ONE, HIS EVERY MOLECULE AND ATOM WERE PULLED APART, A COMPLETE **UNMAKING** OF THE MATTER FROM WHICH HE WAS WROUGHT.
IT WAS TERRIBLE AND EXCRUCIATING AND BEAUTIFUL ALL AT ONCE.
HE THOUGHT, "THIS IS HOW IT FEELS WHEN **EVERYTHING** DIES."

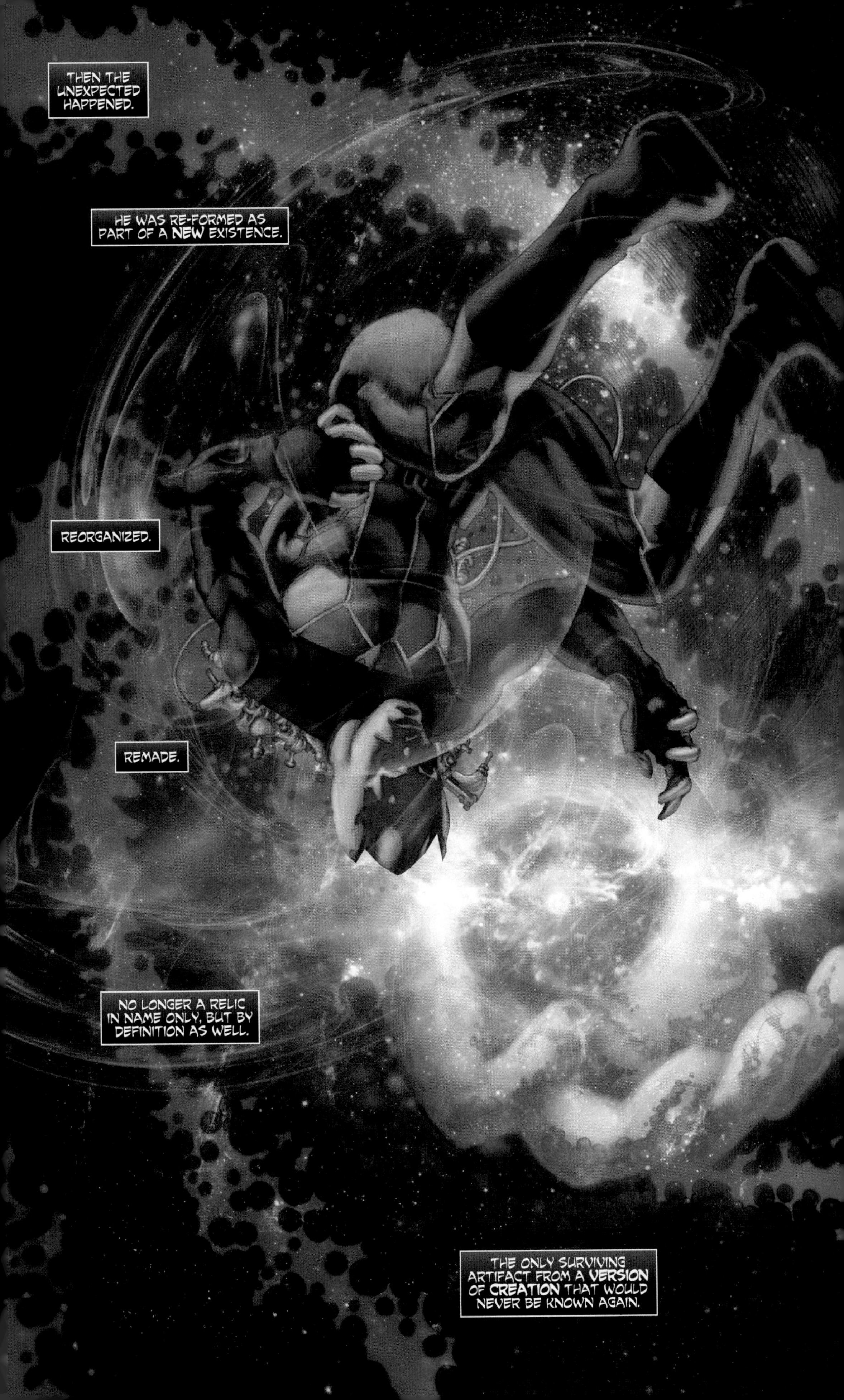
THEN THE UNEXPECTED HAPPENED.
HE WAS RE-FORMED AS PART OF A **NEW** EXISTENCE.
REORGANIZED.
REMADE.
NO LONGER A RELIC IN NAME ONLY, BUT BY DEFINITION AS WELL.
THE ONLY SURVIVING ARTIFACT FROM A **VERSION** OF **CREATION** THAT WOULD NEVER BE KNOWN AGAIN.

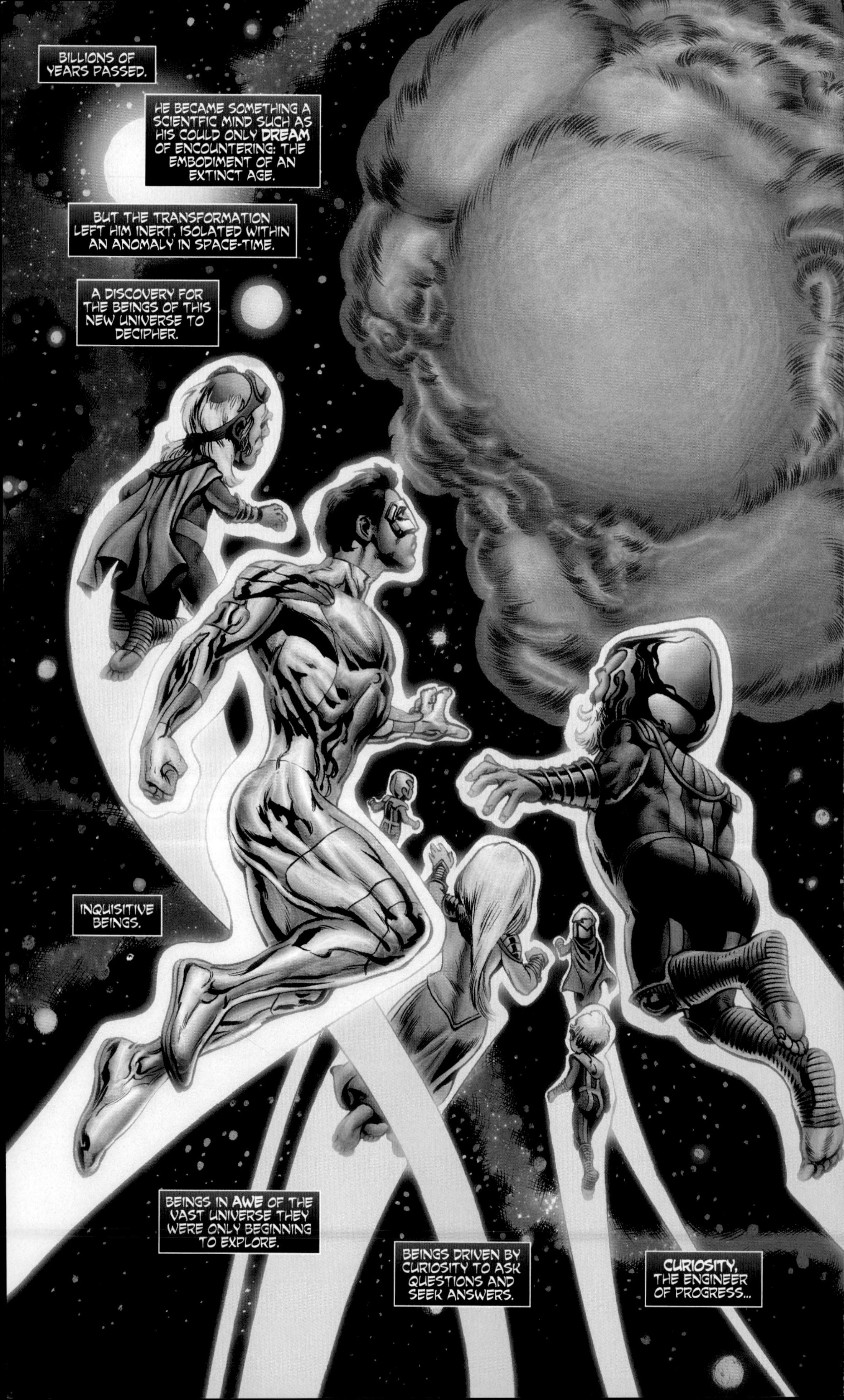
BILLIONS OF YEARS PASSED.
HE BECAME SOMETHING A SCIENTFIC MIND SUCH AS HIS COULD ONLY **DREAM** OF ENCOUNTERING: THE EMBODIMENT OF AN EXTINCT AGE.
BUT THE TRANSFORMATION LEFT HIM INERT, ISOLATED WITHIN AN ANOMALY IN SPACE-TIME.
A DISCOVERY FOR THE BEINGS OF THIS NEW UNIVERSE TO DECIPHER.
INQUISITIVE BEINGS.
BEINGS IN **AWE** OF THE VAST UNIVERSE THEY WERE ONLY BEGINNING TO EXPLORE.
BEINGS DRIVEN BY CURIOSITY TO ASK QUESTIONS AND SEEK ANSWERS.
CURIOSITY, THE ENGINEER OF PROGRESS...

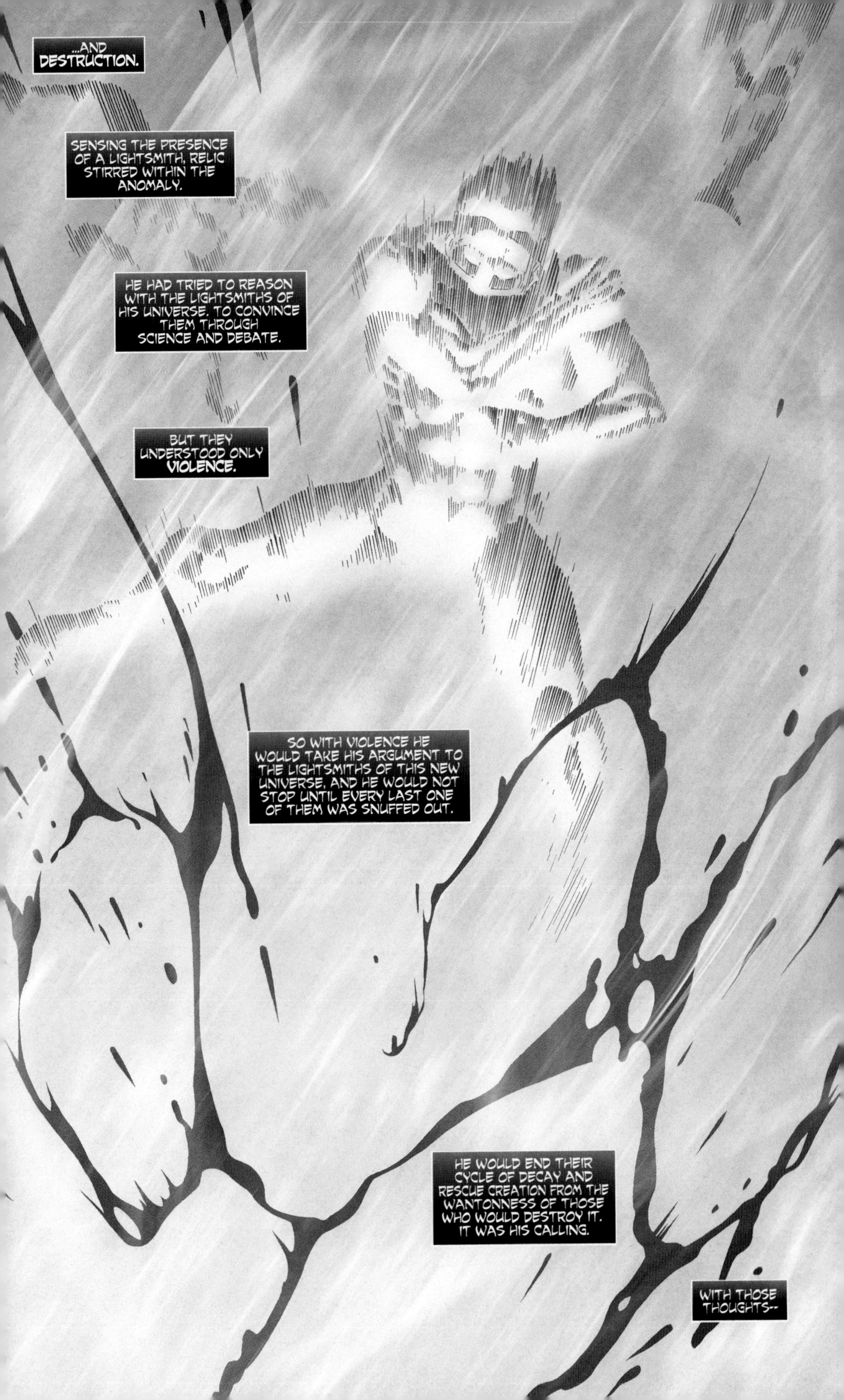
...AND DESTRUCTION.
SENSING THE PRESENCE OF A LIGHTSMITH, RELIC STIRRED WITHIN THE ANOMALY.
HE HAD TRIED TO REASON WITH THE LIGHTSMITHS OF HIS UNIVERSE. TO CONVINCE THEM THROUGH SCIENCE AND DEBATE.
BUT THEY UNDERSTOOD ONLY VIOLENCE.
SO WITH VIOLENCE HE WOULD TAKE HIS ARGUMENT TO THE LIGHTSMITHS OF THIS NEW UNIVERSE, AND HE WOULD NOT STOP UNTIL EVERY LAST ONE OF THEM WAS SNUFFED OUT.
HE WOULD END THEIR CYCLE OF DECAY AND RESCUE CREATION FROM THE WANTONNESS OF THOSE WHO WOULD DESTROY IT. IT WAS HIS CALLING.
WITH THOSE THOUGHTS--

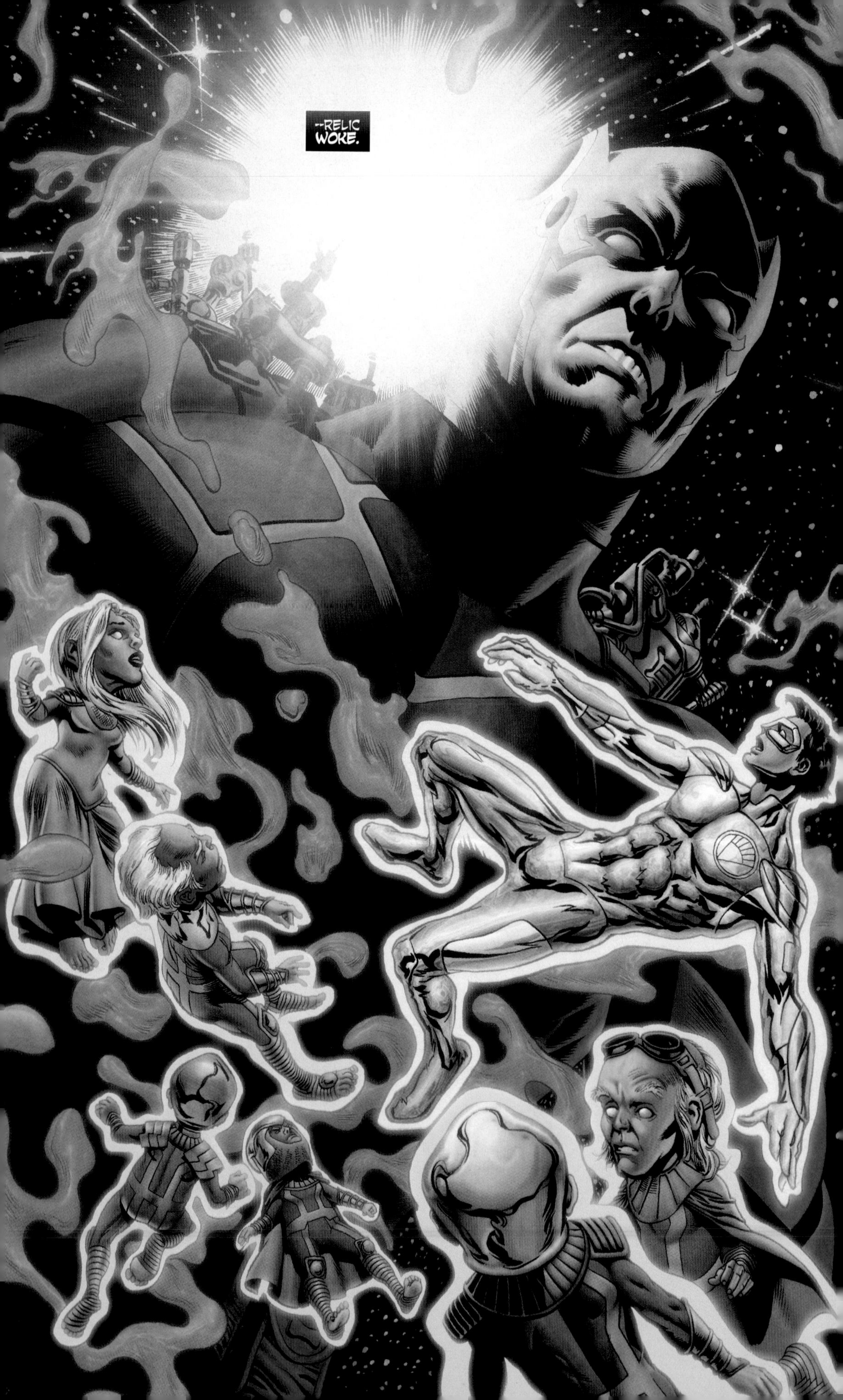
--RELIC WOKE.

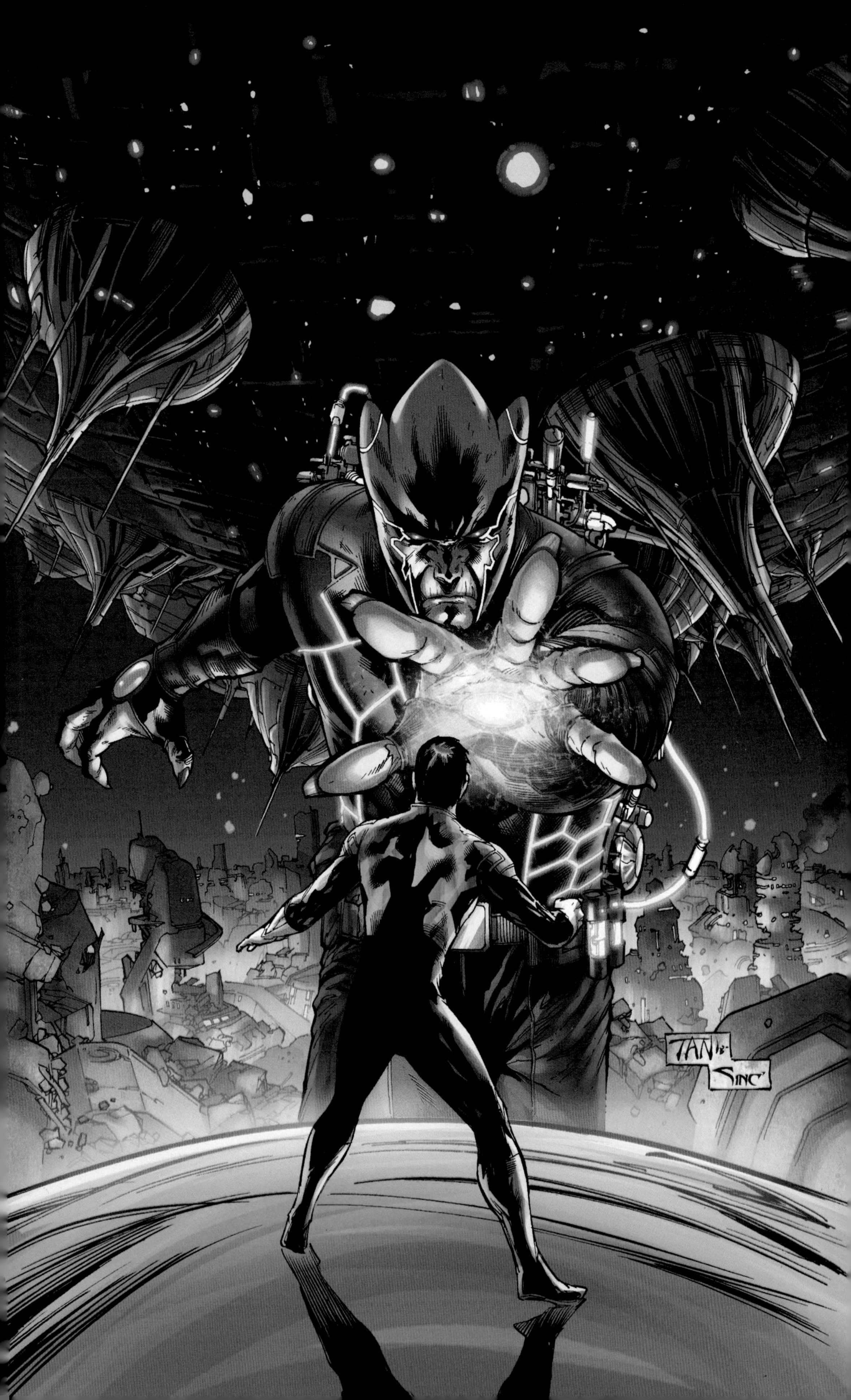

LIGHTS OUT part one: DARK DAYS

ROBERT VENDITTI writer BILLY TAN penciller ROB HUNTER inker ALEX SINCLAIR colorist
BILLY TAN with ALEX SINCLAIR cover artists

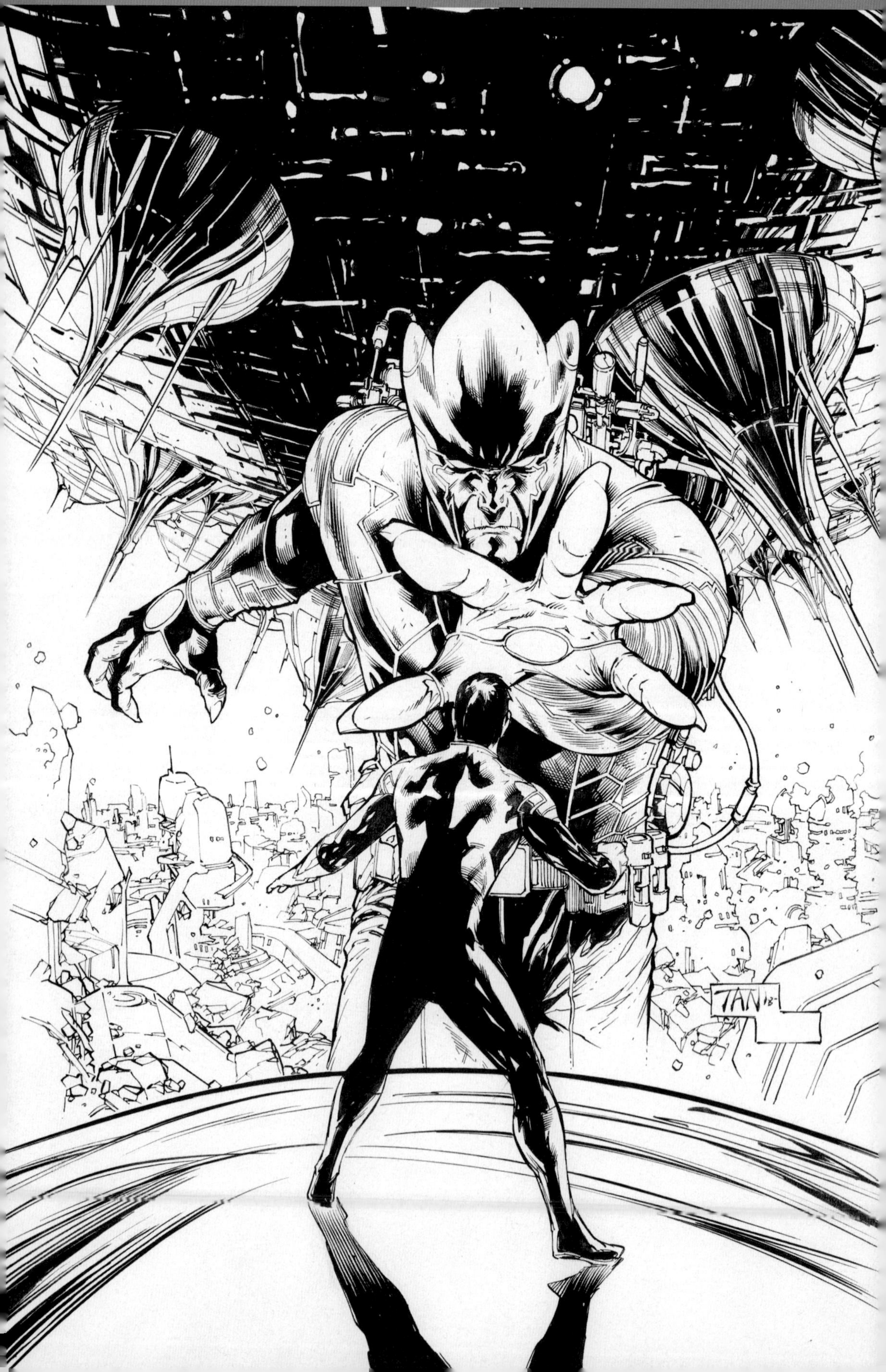

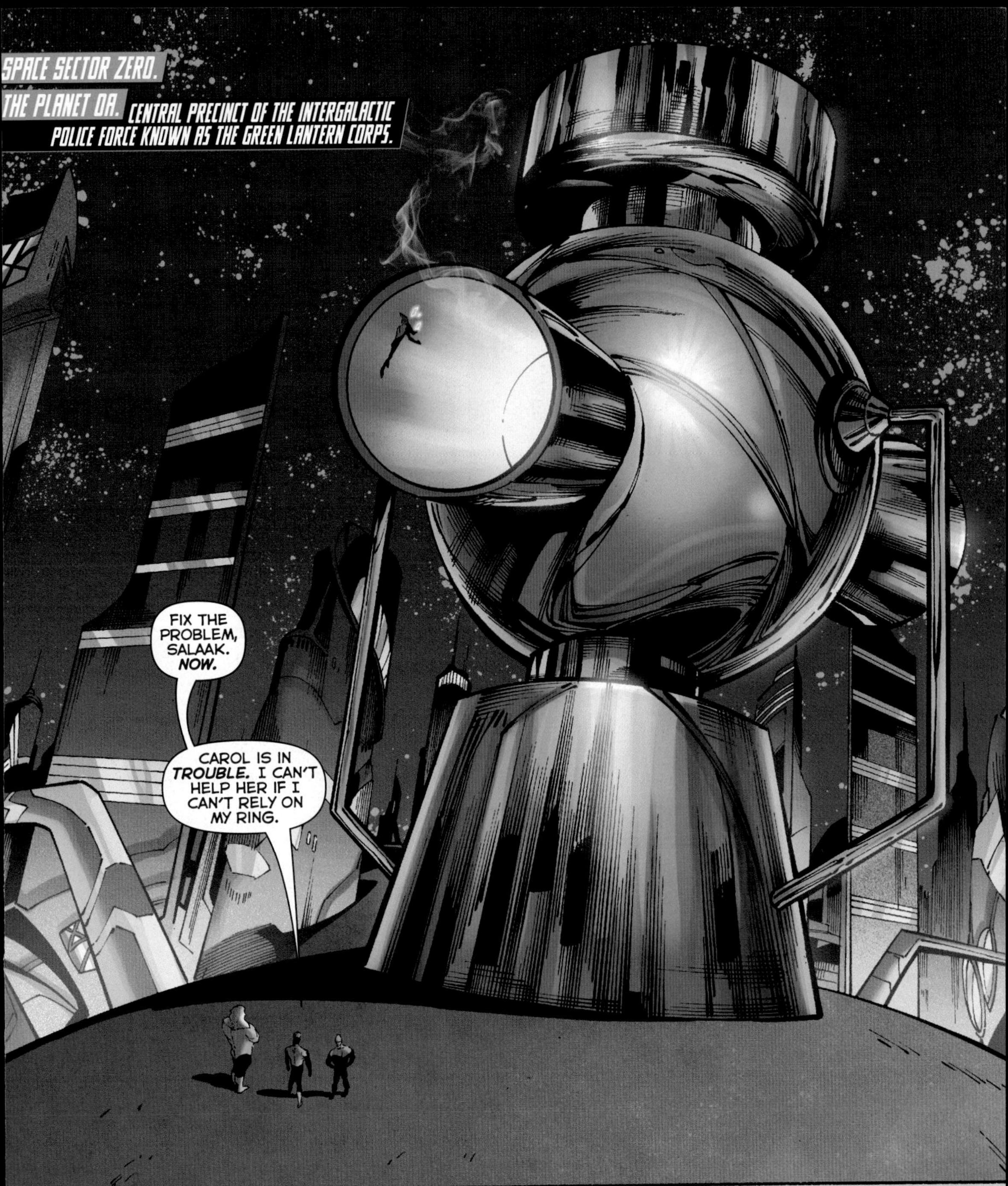
SPACE SECTOR ZERO.
THE PLANET OA. CENTRAL PRECINCT OF THE INTERGALACTIC POLICE FORCE KNOWN AS THE GREEN LANTERN CORPS.
FIX THE PROBLEM, SALAAK. NOW.
CAROL IS IN TROUBLE. I CAN'T HELP HER IF I CAN'T RELY ON MY RING.

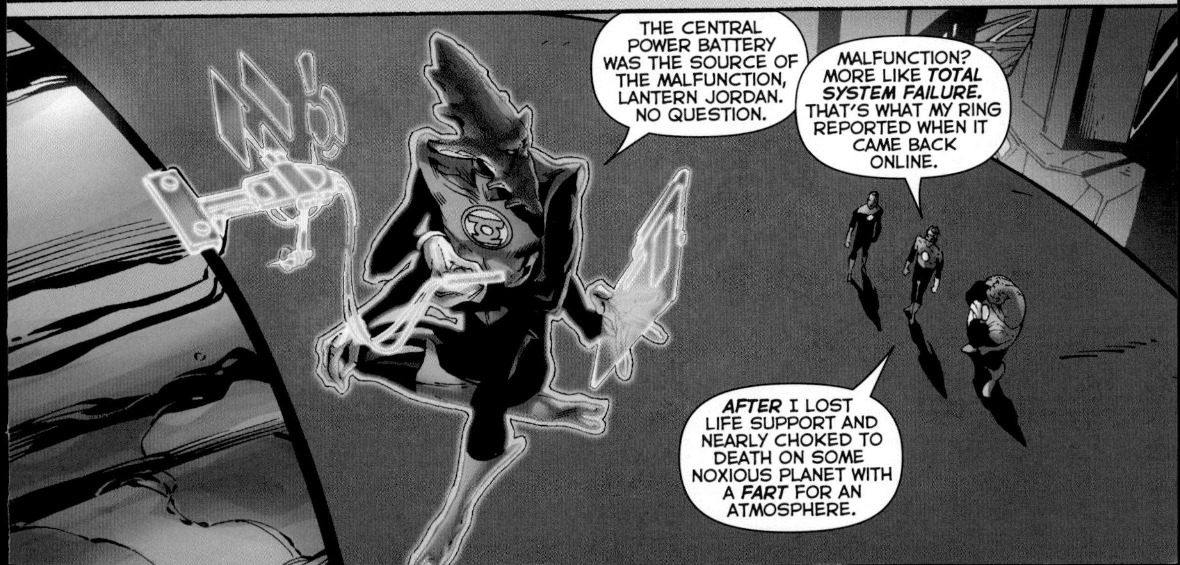
THE CENTRAL POWER BATTERY WAS THE SOURCE OF THE MALFUNCTION, LANTERN JORDAN. NO QUESTION.
MALFUNCTION? MORE LIKE TOTAL SYSTEM FAILURE. THAT'S WHAT MY RING REPORTED WHEN IT CAME BACK ONLINE.
AFTER I LOST LIFE SUPPORT AND NEARLY CHOKED TO DEATH ON SOME NOXIOUS PLANET WITH A FART FOR AN ATMOSPHERE.

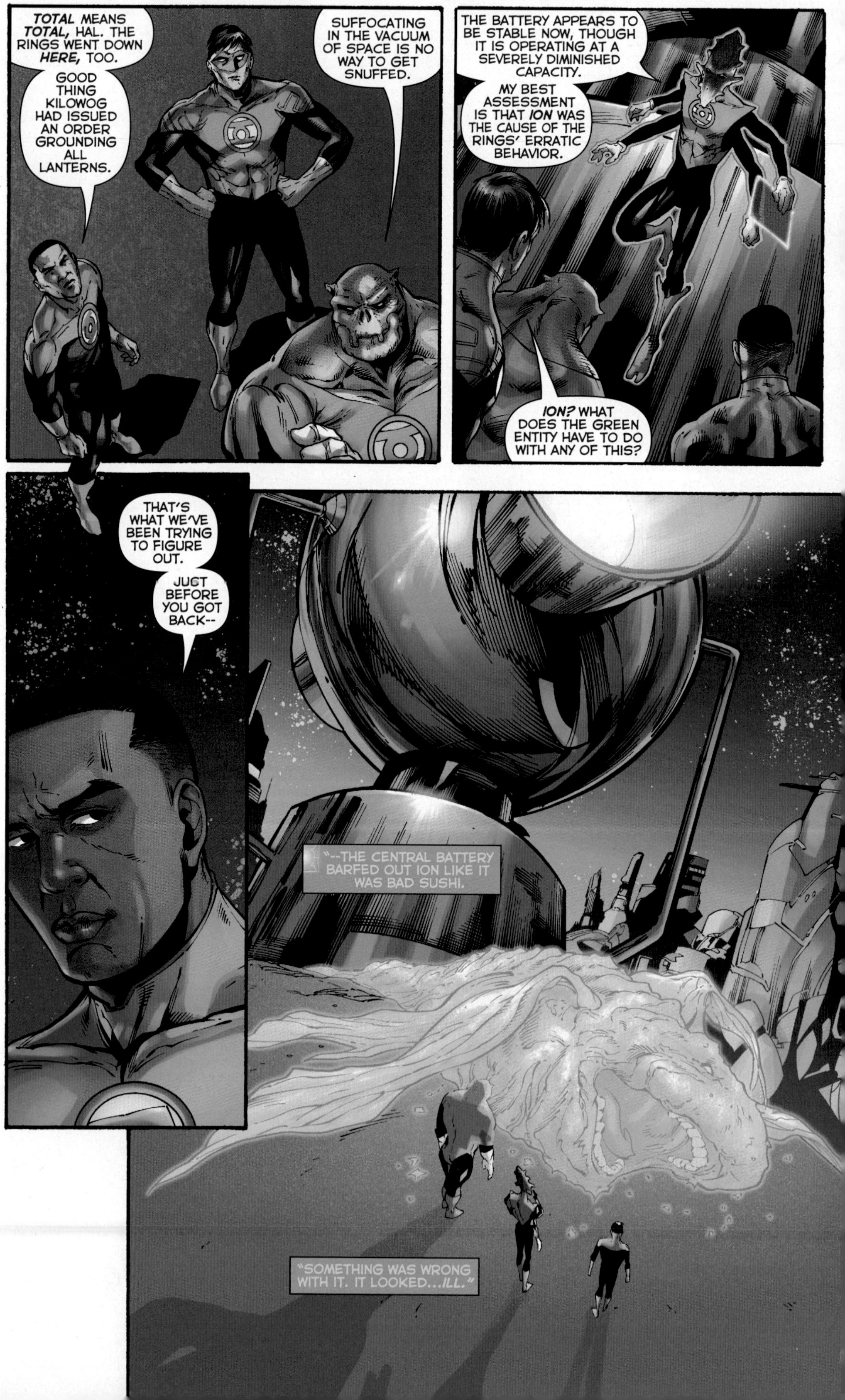
TOTAL MEANS TOTAL, HAL. THE RINGS WENT DOWN HERE, TOO.
GOOD THING KILOWOG HAD ISSUED AN ORDER GROUNDING ALL LANTERNS.
SUFFOCATING IN THE VACUUM OF SPACE IS NO WAY TO GET SNUFFED.
THE BATTERY APPEARS TO BE STABLE NOW, THOUGH IT IS OPERATING AT A SEVERELY DIMINISHED CAPACITY.
MY BEST ASSESSMENT IS THAT ION WAS THE CAUSE OF THE RINGS' ERRATIC BEHAVIOR.
ION? WHAT DOES THE GREEN ENTITY HAVE TO DO WITH ANY OF THIS?
THAT'S WHAT WE'VE BEEN TRYING TO FIGURE OUT.
JUST BEFORE YOU GOT BACK--
"--THE CENTRAL BATTERY BARFED OUT ION LIKE IT WAS BAD SUSHI.
"SOMETHING WAS WRONG WITH IT. IT LOOKED...ILL."

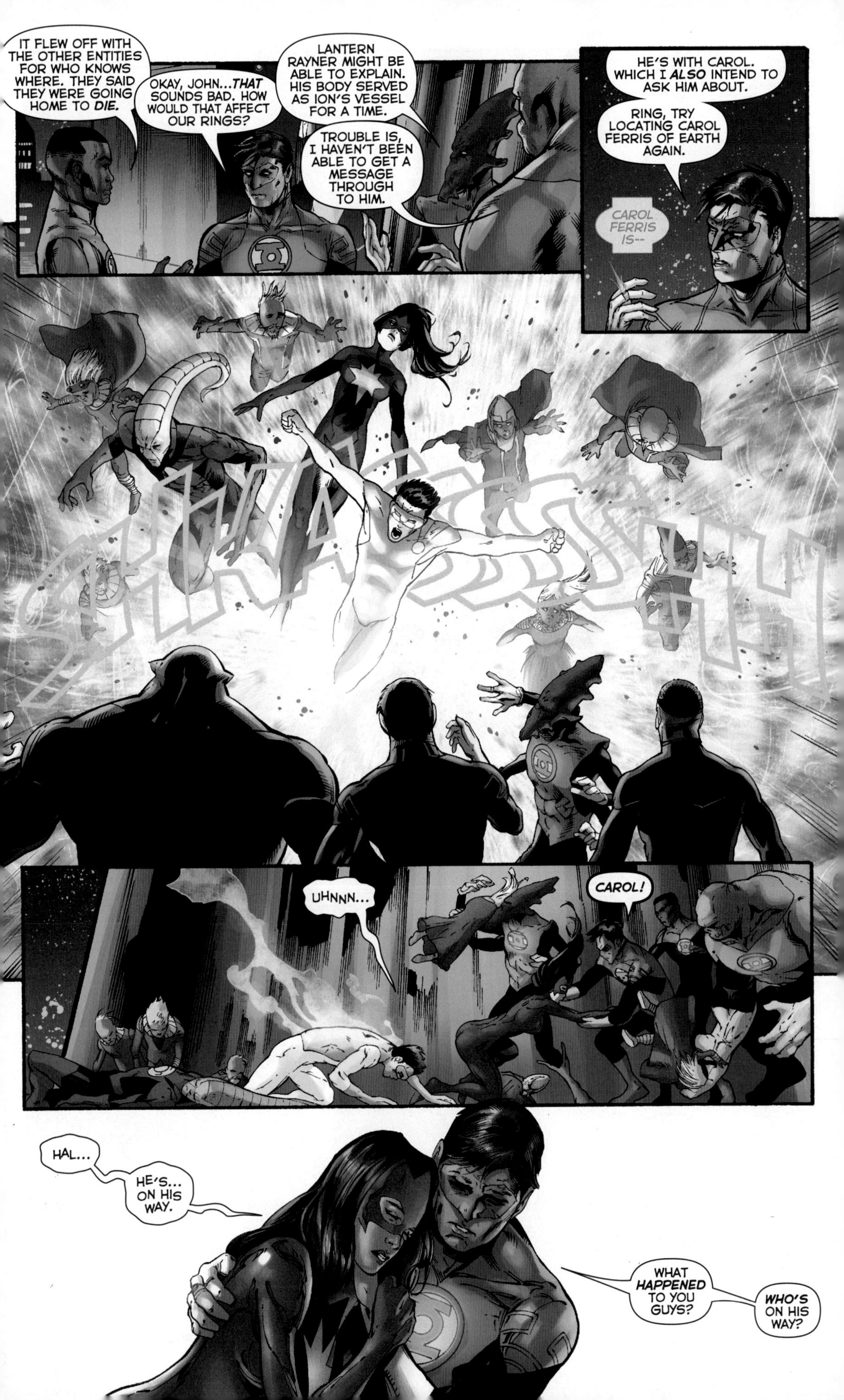

IT FLEW OFF WITH THE OTHER ENTITIES FOR WHO KNOWS WHERE. THEY SAID THEY WERE GOING HOME TO DIE.
OKAY, JOHN...THAT SOUNDS BAD. HOW WOULD THAT AFFECT OUR RINGS?
LANTERN RAYNER MIGHT BE ABLE TO EXPLAIN. HIS BODY SERVED AS ION'S VESSEL FOR A TIME.
TROUBLE IS, I HAVEN'T BEEN ABLE TO GET A MESSAGE THROUGH TO HIM.
HE'S WITH CAROL. WHICH I ALSO INTEND TO ASK HIM ABOUT.
RING, TRY LOCATING CAROL FERRIS OF EARTH AGAIN.
CAROL FERRIS IS--
SHWASHH
UHNNN...
CAROL!
HAL...
HE'S... ON HIS WAY.
WHAT HAPPENED TO YOU GUYS?
WHO'S ON HIS WAY?

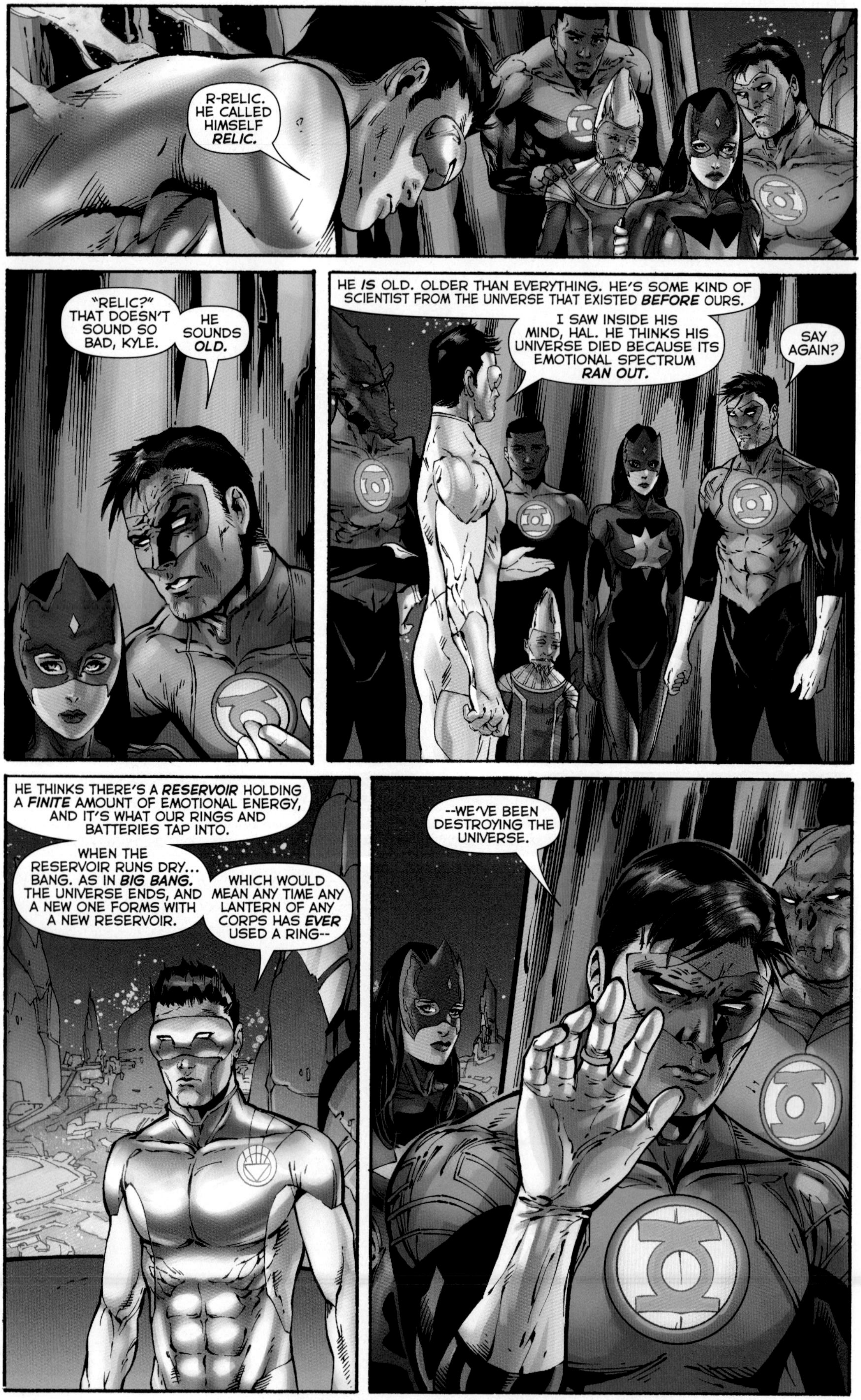
R-RELIC. HE CALLED HIMSELF RELIC.
"RELIC?" THAT DOESN'T SOUND SO BAD, KYLE.
HE SOUNDS OLD.
HE IS OLD. OLDER THAN EVERYTHING. HE'S SOME KIND OF SCIENTIST FROM THE UNIVERSE THAT EXISTED BEFORE OURS.
I SAW INSIDE HIS MIND, HAL. HE THINKS HIS UNIVERSE DIED BECAUSE ITS EMOTIONAL SPECTRUM RAN OUT.
SAY AGAIN?
HE THINKS THERE'S A RESERVOIR HOLDING A FINITE AMOUNT OF EMOTIONAL ENERGY, AND IT'S WHAT OUR RINGS AND BATTERIES TAP INTO.
WHEN THE RESERVOIR RUNS DRY... BANG. AS IN BIG BANG. THE UNIVERSE ENDS, AND A NEW ONE FORMS WITH A NEW RESERVOIR.
WHICH WOULD MEAN ANY TIME ANY LANTERN OF ANY CORPS HAS EVER USED A RING--
--WE'VE BEEN DESTROYING THE UNIVERSE.

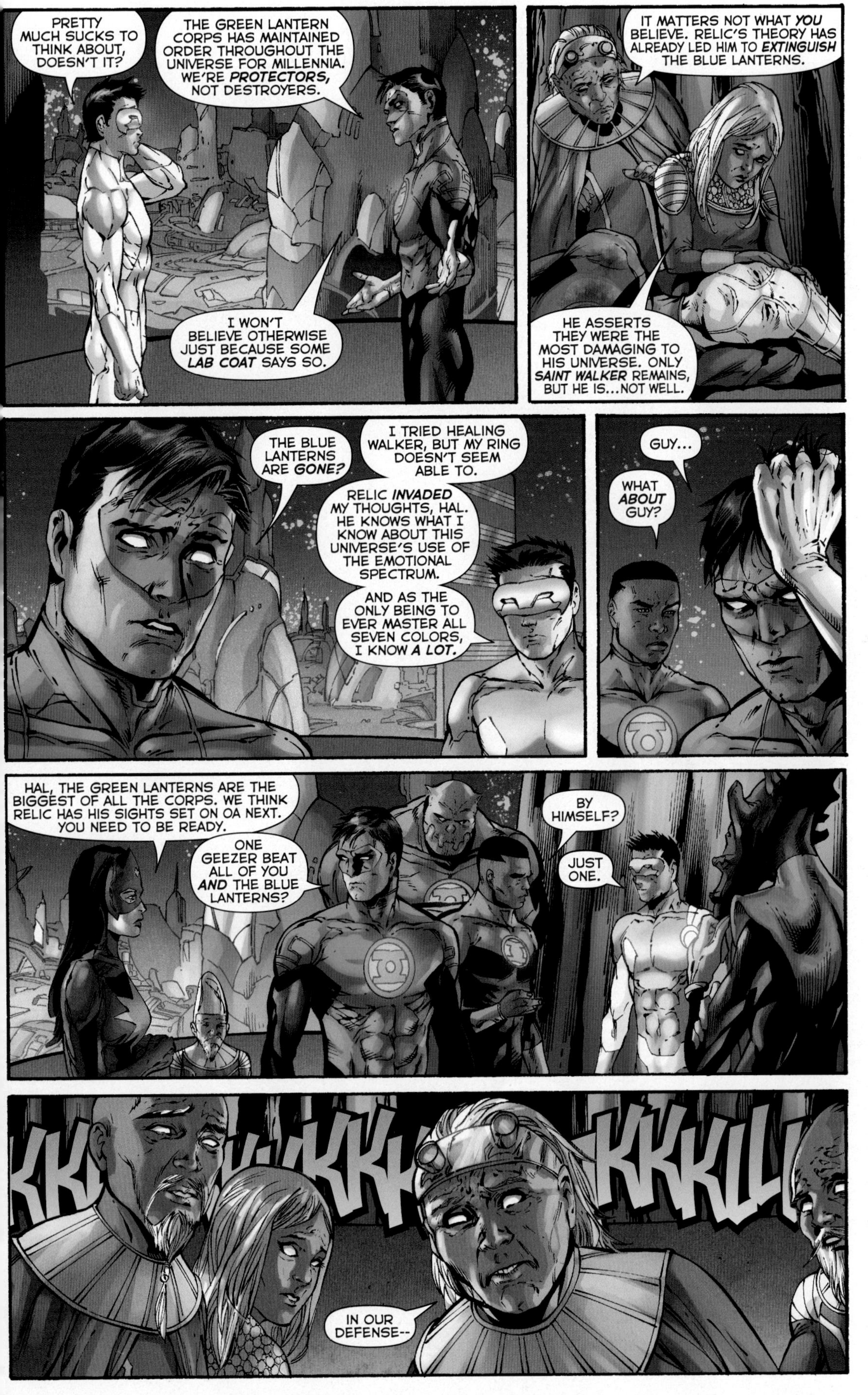
PRETTY MUCH SUCKS TO THINK ABOUT, DOESN'T IT?
THE GREEN LANTERN CORPS HAS MAINTAINED ORDER THROUGHOUT THE UNIVERSE FOR MILLENNIA. WE'RE PROTECTORS, NOT DESTROYERS.
I WON'T BELIEVE OTHERWISE JUST BECAUSE SOME LAB COAT SAYS SO.
IT MATTERS NOT WHAT YOU BELIEVE. RELIC'S THEORY HAS ALREADY LED HIM TO EXTINGUISH THE BLUE LANTERNS.
HE ASSERTS THEY WERE THE MOST DAMAGING TO HIS UNIVERSE. ONLY SAINT WALKER REMAINS, BUT HE IS...NOT WELL.
THE BLUE LANTERNS ARE GONE?
I TRIED HEALING WALKER, BUT MY RING DOESN'T SEEM ABLE TO.
RELIC INVADED MY THOUGHTS, HAL. HE KNOWS WHAT I KNOW ABOUT THIS UNIVERSE'S USE OF THE EMOTIONAL SPECTRUM.
AND AS THE ONLY BEING TO EVER MASTER ALL SEVEN COLORS, I KNOW A LOT.
GUY...
WHAT ABOUT GUY?
HAL, THE GREEN LANTERNS ARE THE BIGGEST OF ALL THE CORPS. WE THINK RELIC HAS HIS SIGHTS SET ON OA NEXT. YOU NEED TO BE READY.
ONE GEEZER BEAT ALL OF YOU AND THE BLUE LANTERNS?
BY HIMSELF?
JUST ONE.
IN OUR DEFENSE--

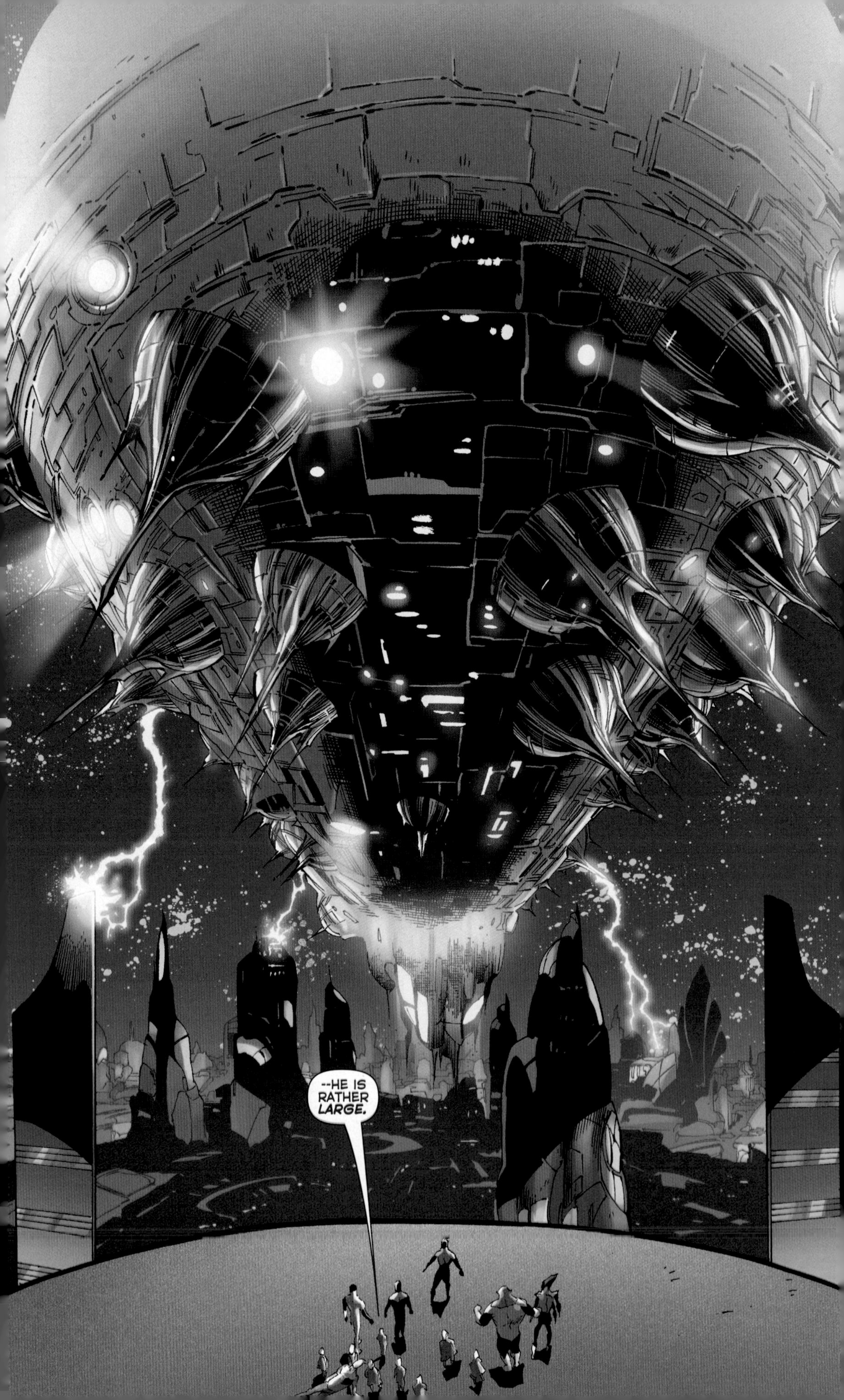
--HE IS RATHER LARGE.

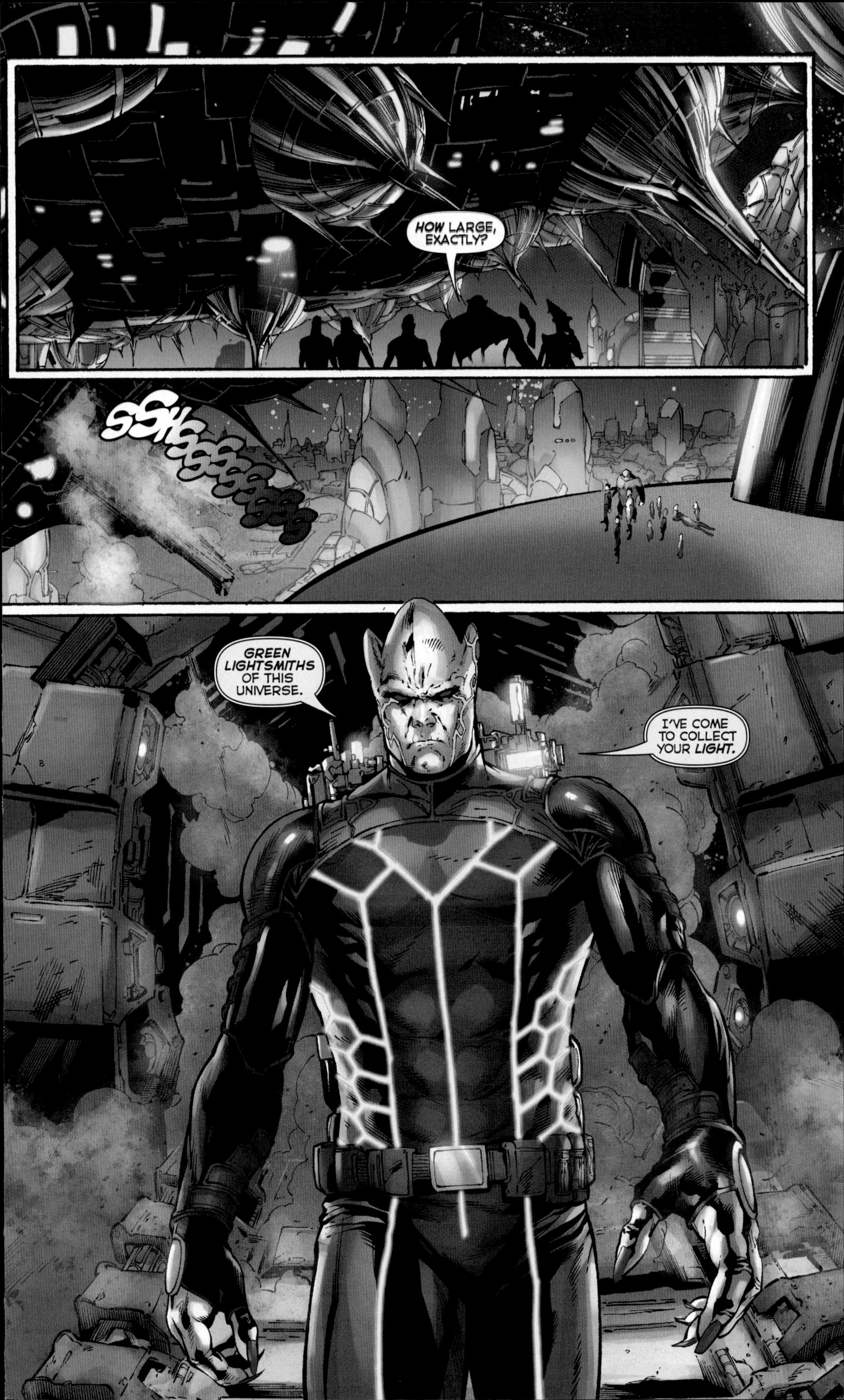
HOW LARGE, EXACTLY?
SSHSSSSSSSS
GREEN LIGHTSMITHS OF THIS UNIVERSE.
I'VE COME TO COLLECT YOUR LIGHT.

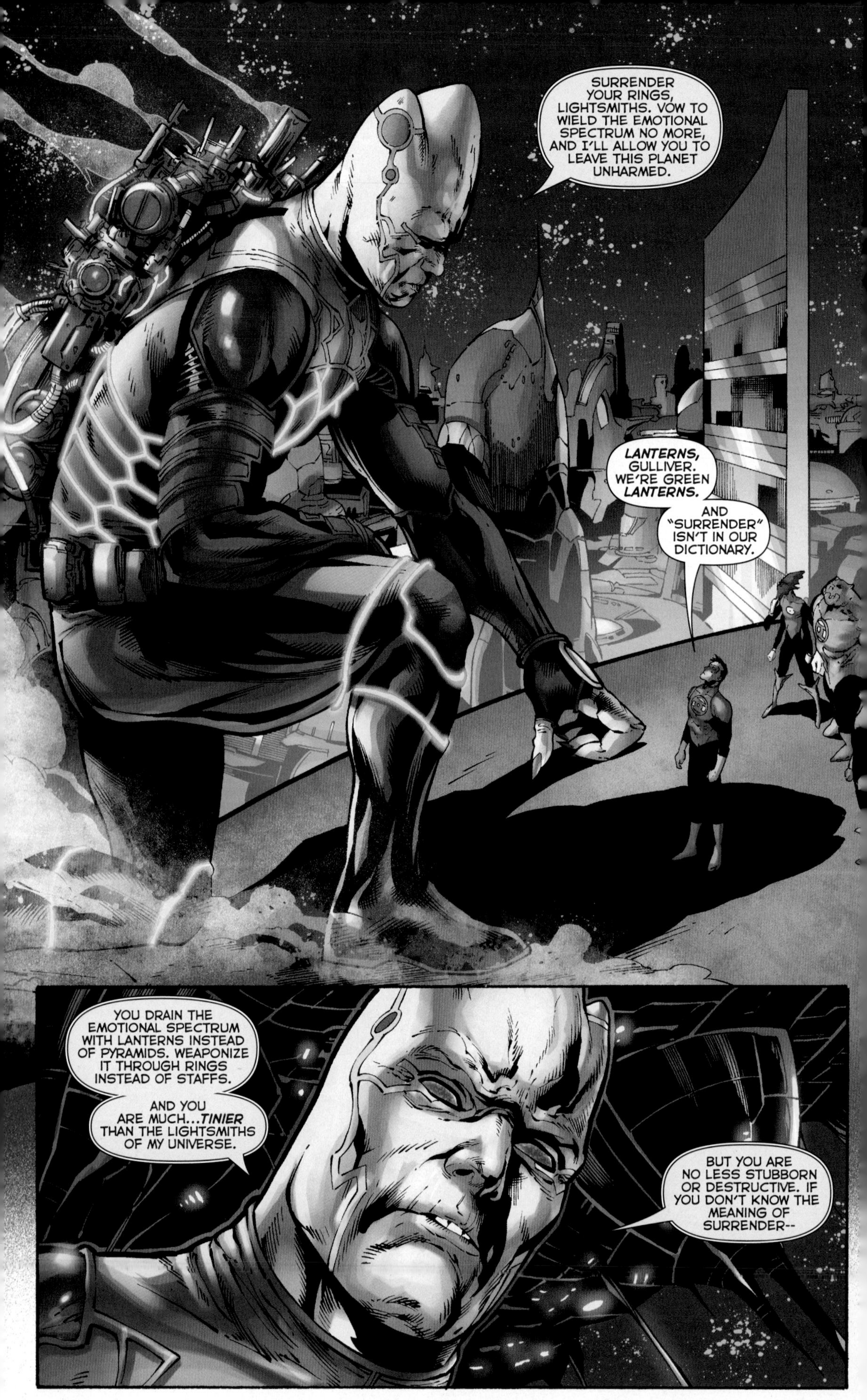
SURRENDER YOUR RINGS, LIGHTSMITHS. VOW TO WIELD THE EMOTIONAL SPECTRUM NO MORE, AND I'LL ALLOW YOU TO LEAVE THIS PLANET UNHARMED.
LANTERNS, GULLIVER. WE'RE GREEN *LANTERNS.*
AND "SURRENDER" ISN'T IN OUR DICTIONARY.
YOU DRAIN THE EMOTIONAL SPECTRUM WITH LANTERNS INSTEAD OF PYRAMIDS. WEAPONIZE IT THROUGH RINGS INSTEAD OF STAFFS.
AND YOU ARE MUCH...*TINIER* THAN THE LIGHTSMITHS OF MY UNIVERSE.
BUT YOU ARE NO LESS STUBBORN OR DESTRUCTIVE. IF YOU DON'T KNOW THE MEANING OF SURRENDER--

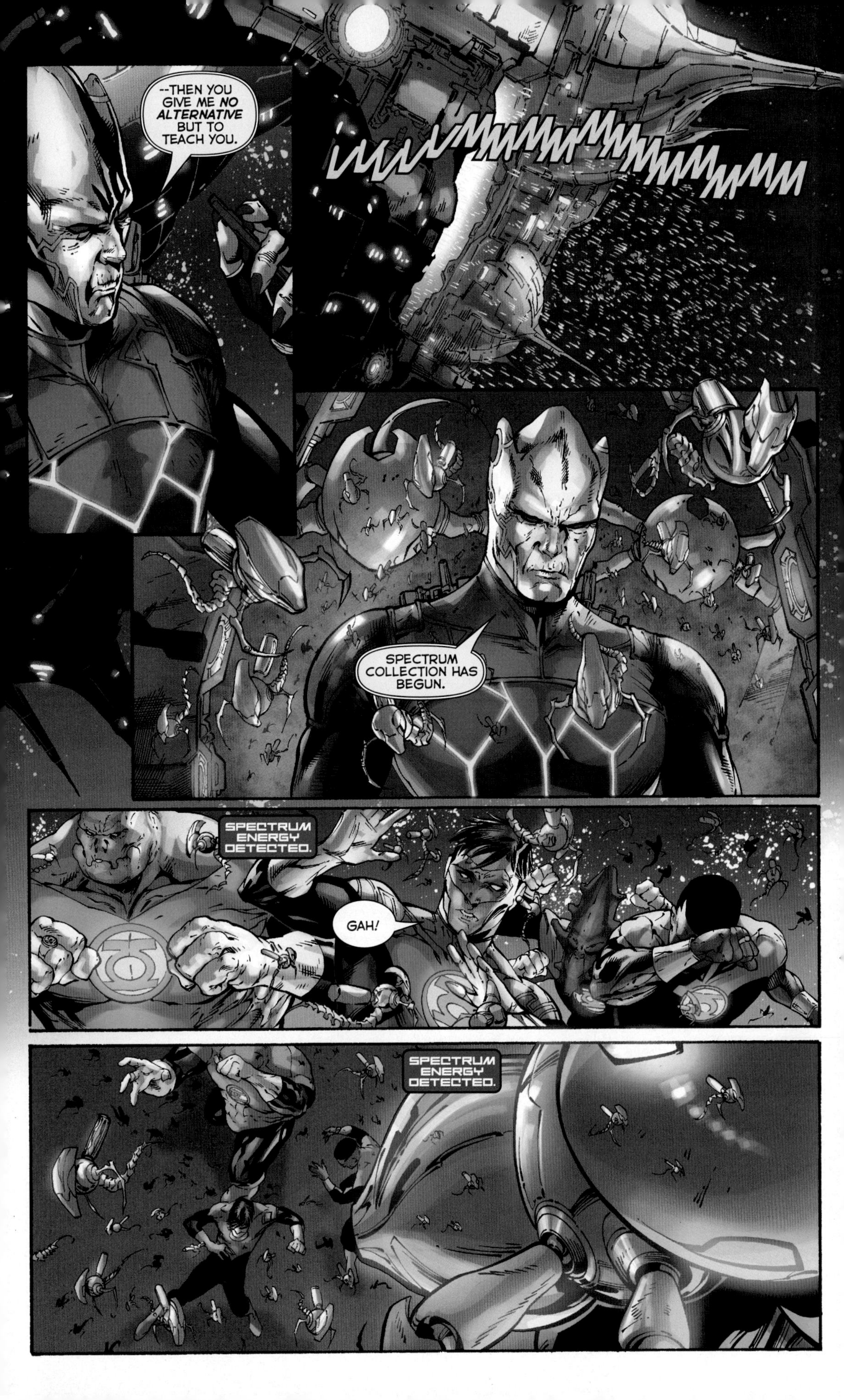
--THEN YOU GIVE ME NO ALTERNATIVE BUT TO TEACH YOU.
VVVVVMMMMMMMMMMMMMMMMMM
SPECTRUM COLLECTION HAS BEGUN.
SPECTRUM ENERGY DETECTED.
GAH!
SPECTRUM ENERGY DETECTED.

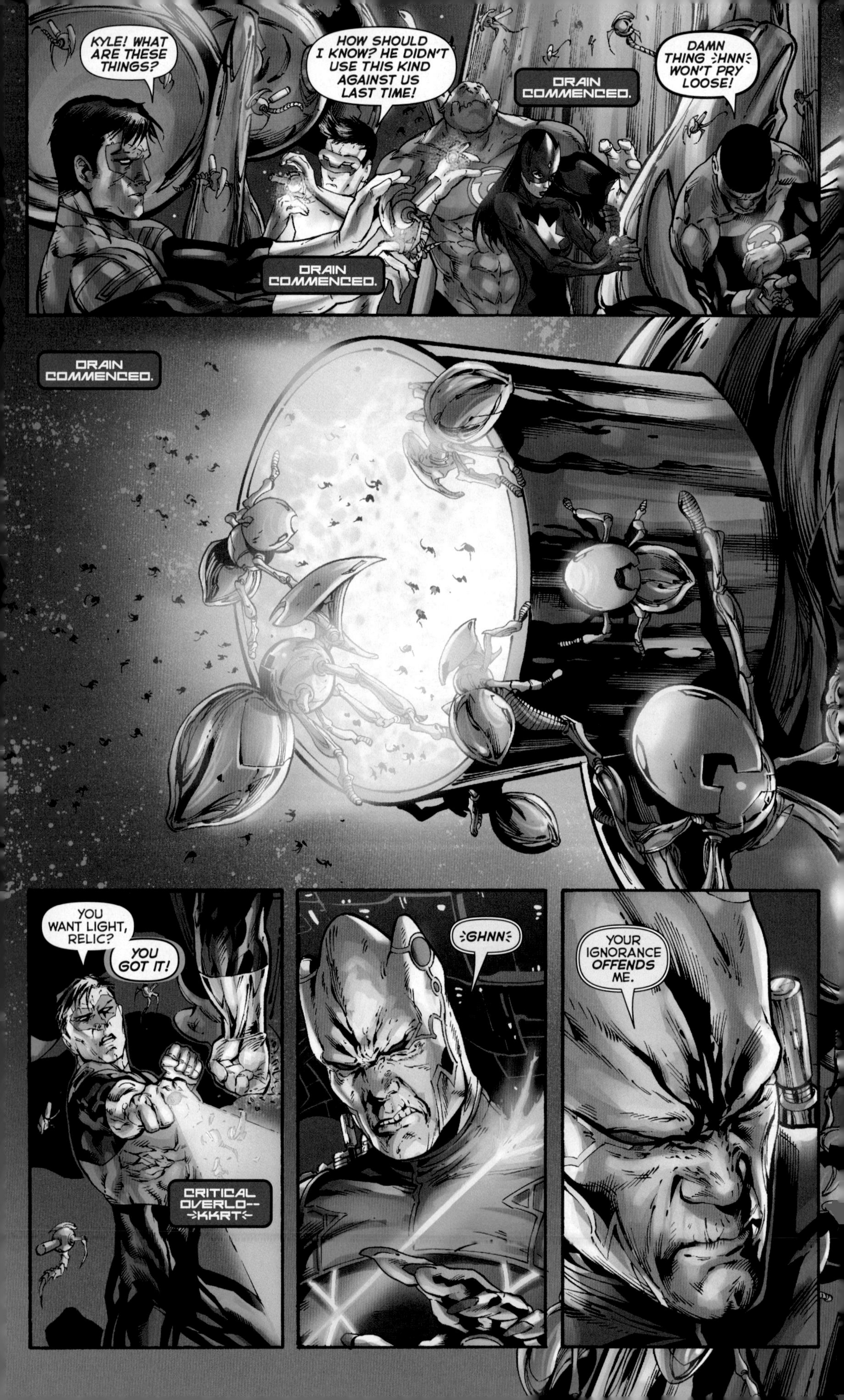

KYLE! WHAT ARE THESE THINGS?
HOW SHOULD I KNOW? HE DIDN'T USE THIS KIND AGAINST US LAST TIME!
DRAIN COMMENCED.
DAMN THING -HNN- WON'T PRY LOOSE!
DRAIN COMMENCED.
DRAIN COMMENCED.
YOU WANT LIGHT, RELIC?
YOU GOT IT!
CRITICAL OVERLO-- -KKRT-
-GHNN-
YOUR IGNORANCE OFFENDS ME.

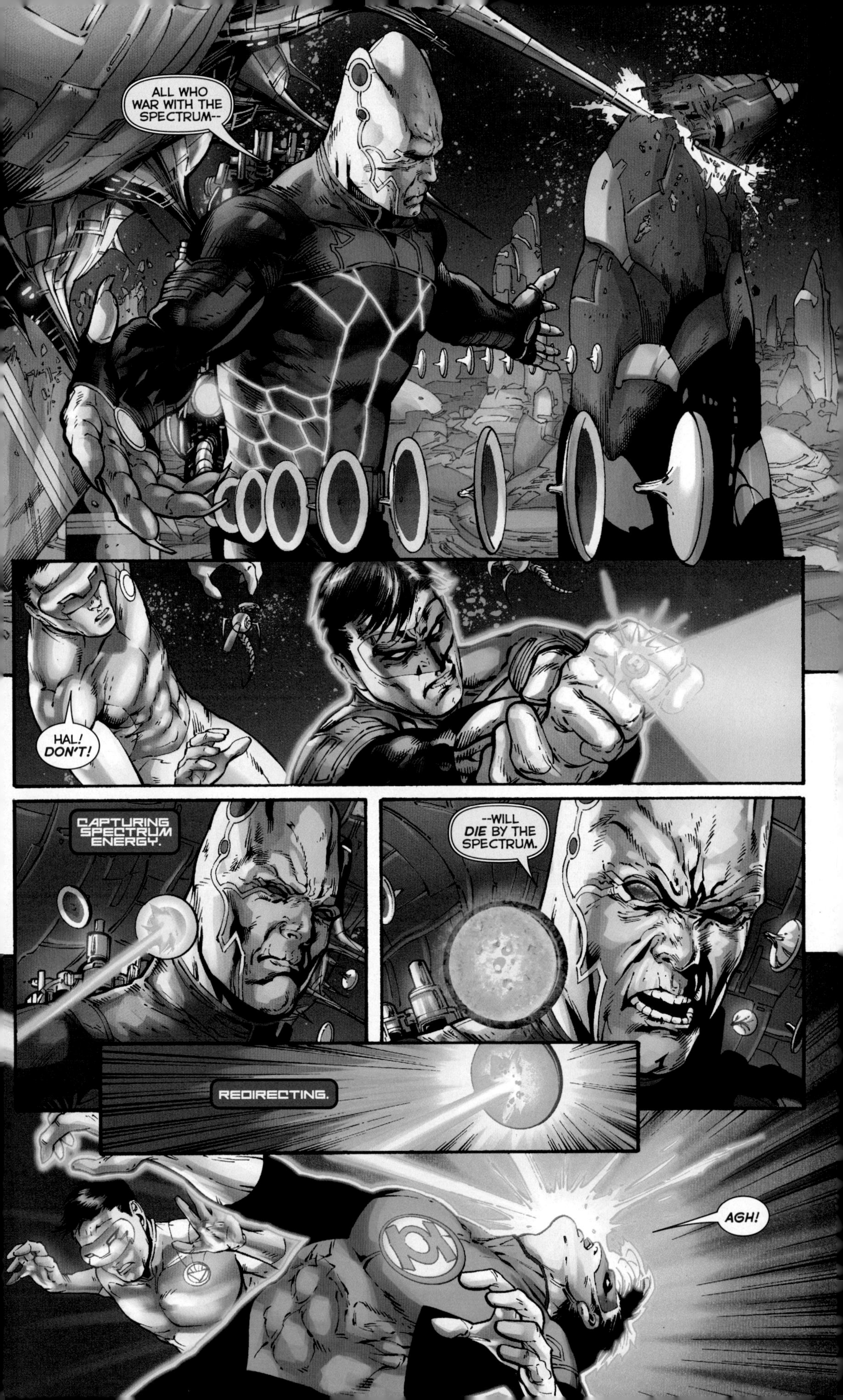
ALL WHO WAR WITH THE SPECTRUM--
HAL! DON'T!
CAPTURING SPECTRUM ENERGY.
--WILL DIE BY THE SPECTRUM.
REDIRECTING.
AGH!

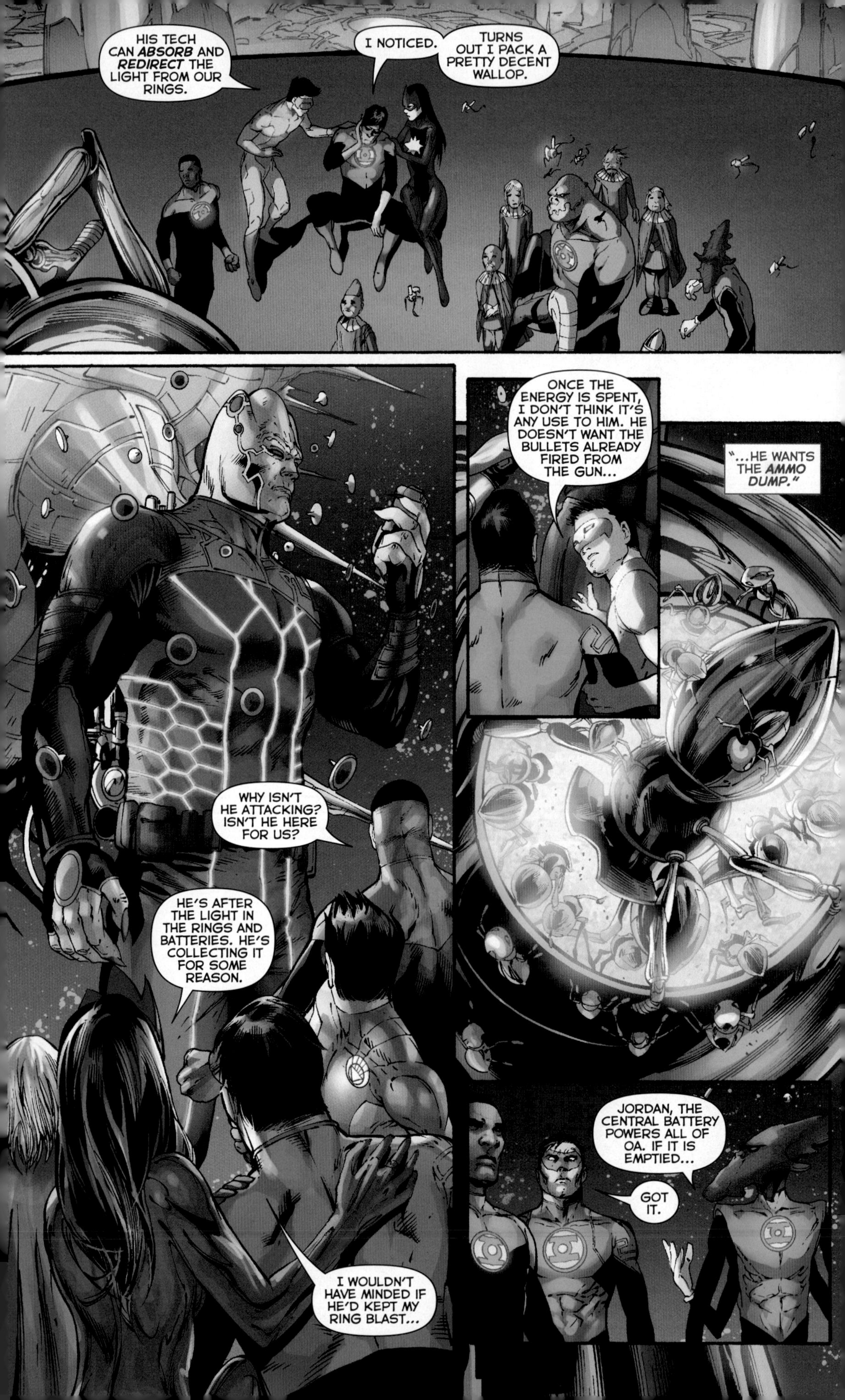
HIS TECH CAN ABSORB AND REDIRECT THE LIGHT FROM OUR RINGS.
I NOTICED.
TURNS OUT I PACK A PRETTY DECENT WALLOP.
WHY ISN'T HE ATTACKING? ISN'T HE HERE FOR US?
HE'S AFTER THE LIGHT IN THE RINGS AND BATTERIES. HE'S COLLECTING IT FOR SOME REASON.
I WOULDN'T HAVE MINDED IF HE'D KEPT MY RING BLAST...
ONCE THE ENERGY IS SPENT, I DON'T THINK IT'S ANY USE TO HIM. HE DOESN'T WANT THE BULLETS ALREADY FIRED FROM THE GUN...
"...HE WANTS THE AMMO DUMP."
JORDAN, THE CENTRAL BATTERY POWERS ALL OF OA. IF IT IS EMPTIED...
GOT IT.

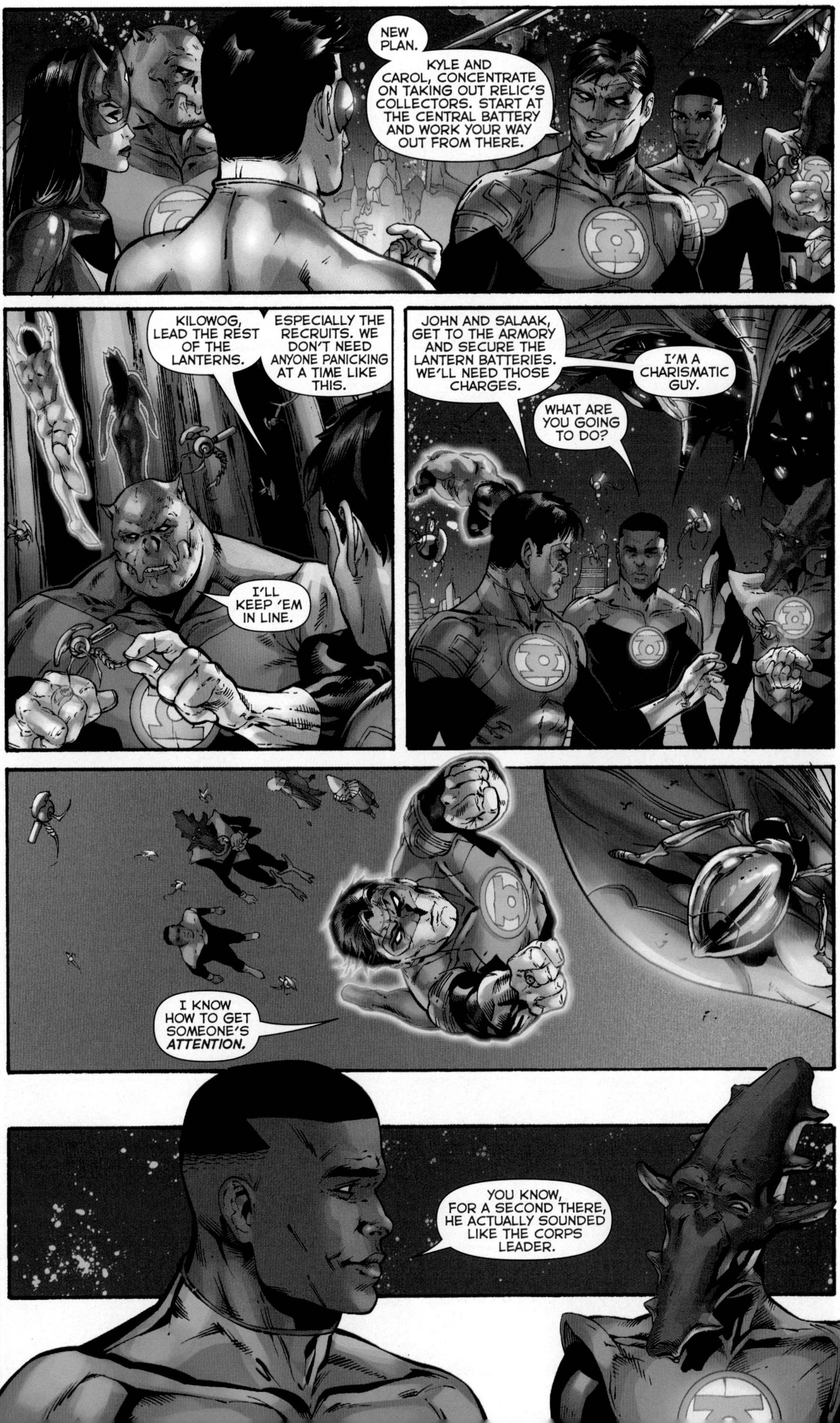
NEW PLAN.
KYLE AND CAROL, CONCENTRATE ON TAKING OUT RELIC'S COLLECTORS. START AT THE CENTRAL BATTERY AND WORK YOUR WAY OUT FROM THERE.
KILOWOG, LEAD THE REST OF THE LANTERNS.
ESPECIALLY THE RECRUITS. WE DON'T NEED ANYONE PANICKING AT A TIME LIKE THIS.
I'LL KEEP 'EM IN LINE.
JOHN AND SALAAK, GET TO THE ARMORY AND SECURE THE LANTERN BATTERIES. WE'LL NEED THOSE CHARGES.
WHAT ARE YOU GOING TO DO?
I'M A CHARISMATIC GUY.
I KNOW HOW TO GET SOMEONE'S *ATTENTION.*
YOU KNOW, FOR A SECOND THERE, HE ACTUALLY SOUNDED LIKE THE CORPS LEADER.

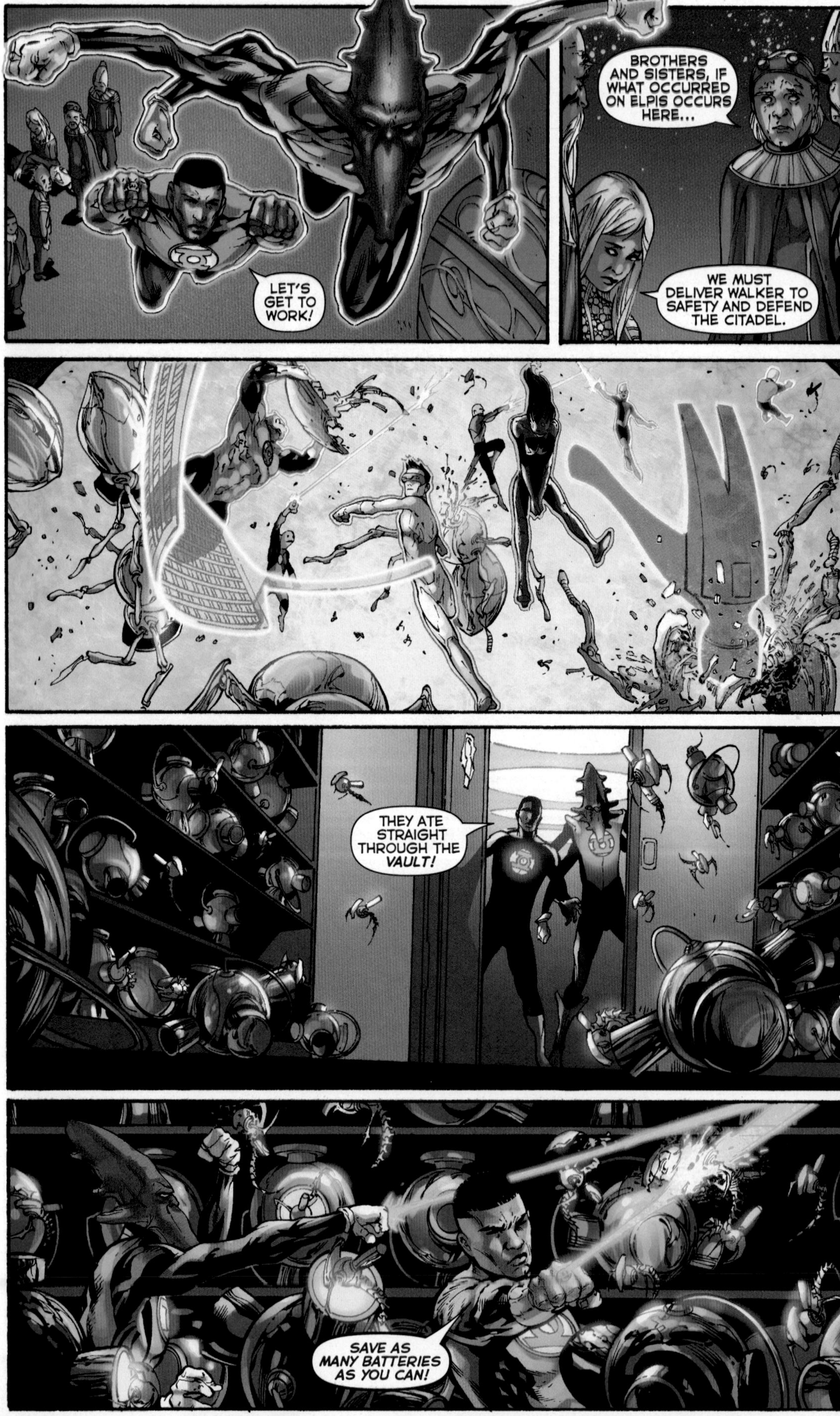
LET'S GET TO WORK!
BROTHERS AND SISTERS, IF WHAT OCCURRED ON ELPIS OCCURS HERE...
WE MUST DELIVER WALKER TO SAFETY AND DEFEND THE CITADEL.
THEY ATE STRAIGHT THROUGH THE VAULT!
SAVE AS MANY BATTERIES AS YOU CAN!

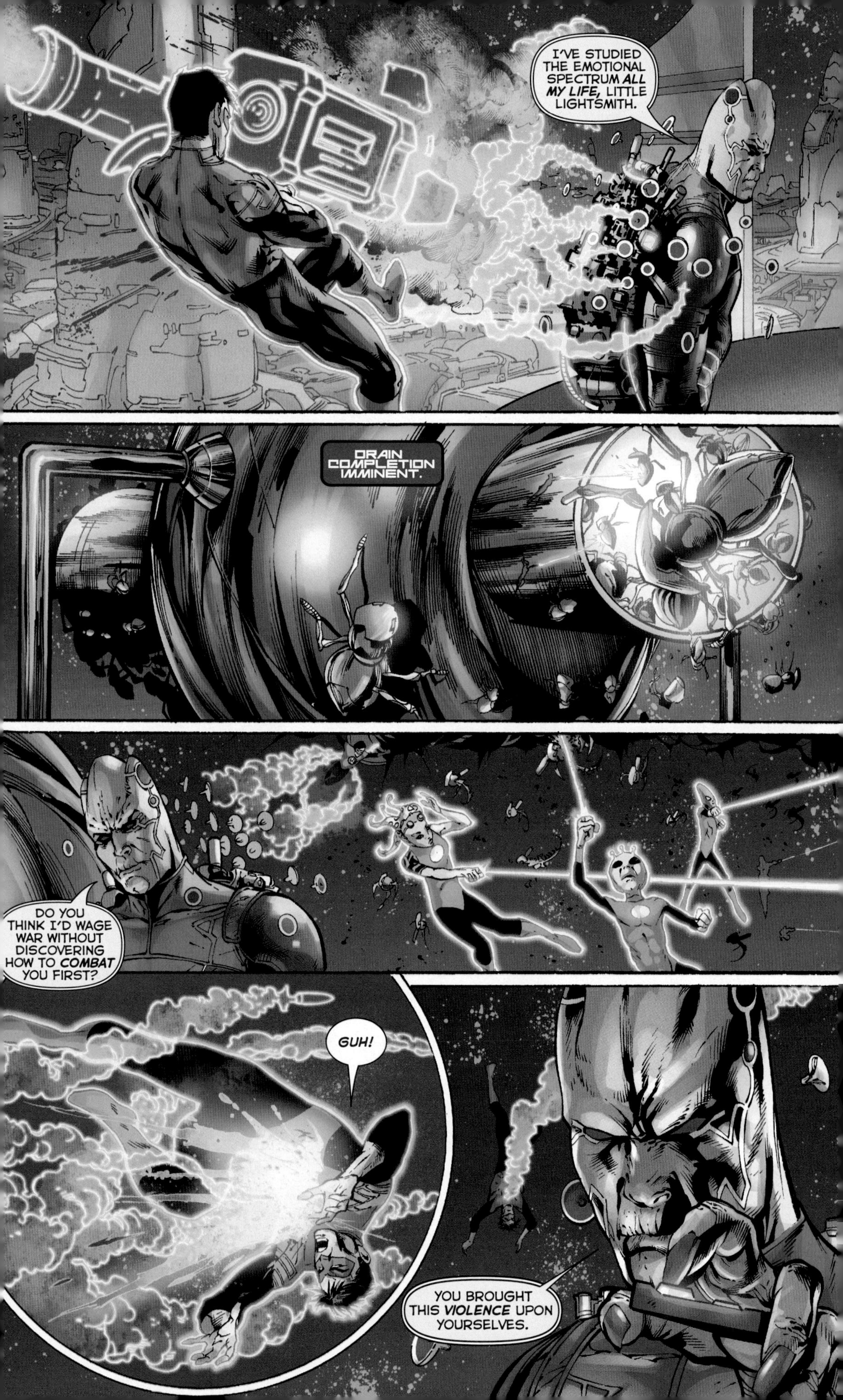
I'VE STUDIED THE EMOTIONAL SPECTRUM ALL MY LIFE, LITTLE LIGHTSMITH.
DRAIN COMPLETION IMMINENT.
DO YOU THINK I'D WAGE WAR WITHOUT DISCOVERING HOW TO COMBAT YOU FIRST?
GUH!
YOU BROUGHT THIS VIOLENCE UPON YOURSELVES.

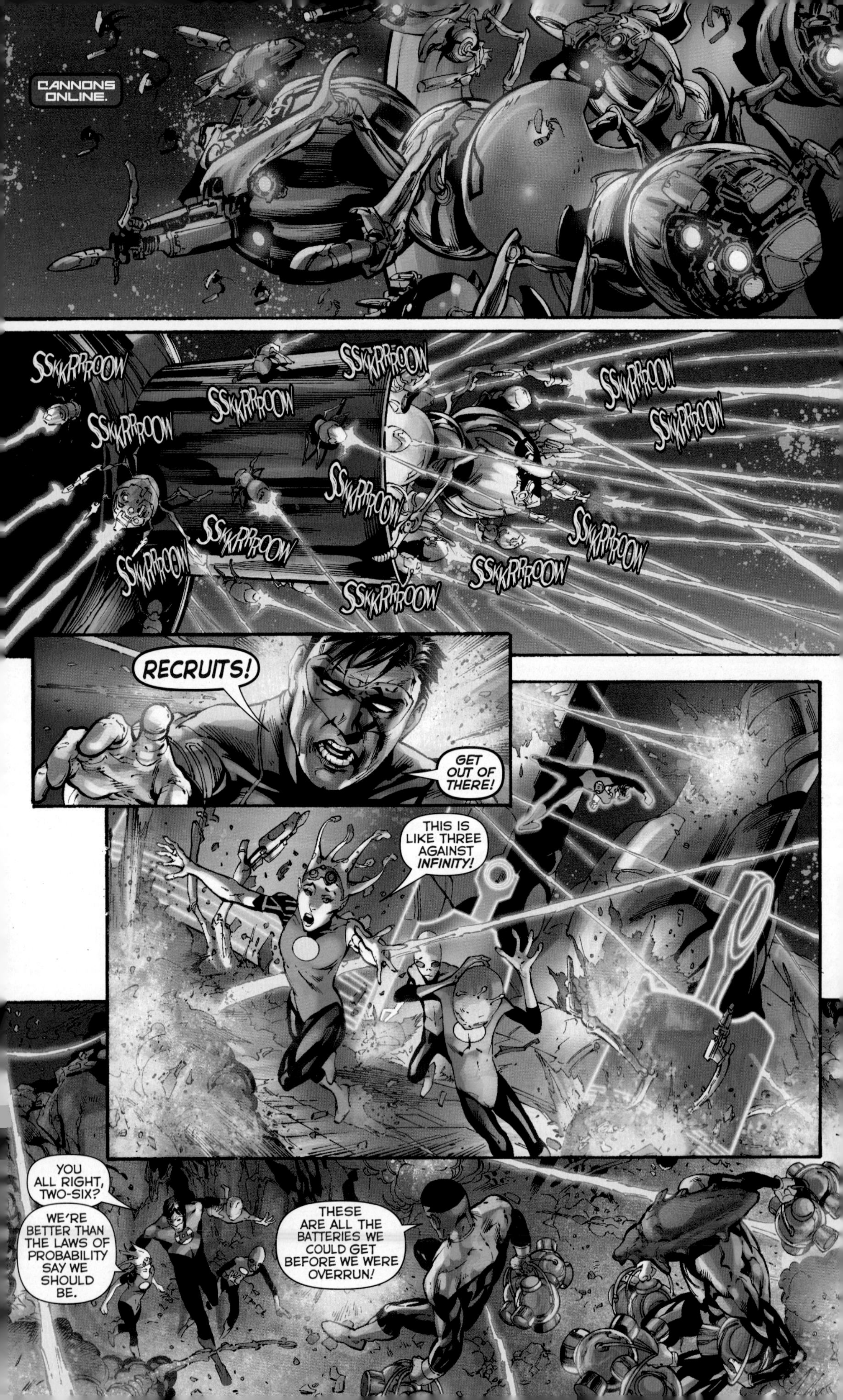
CANNONS ONLINE.
SSKKRRROOW
SSKKRRROOW
SSKKRRROOW
SSKKRRROOW
SSKKRRROOW
SSKKRRROOW
SSKKRRROOW
SSKKRRROOW
SSKKRRROOW
SSKKRRROOW
SSKKRRROOW
SSKKRRROOW
RECRUITS!
GET OUT OF THERE!
THIS IS LIKE THREE AGAINST INFINITY!
YOU ALL RIGHT, TWO-SIX?
WE'RE BETTER THAN THE LAWS OF PROBABILITY SAY WE SHOULD BE.
THESE ARE ALL THE BATTERIES WE COULD GET BEFORE WE WERE OVERRUN!

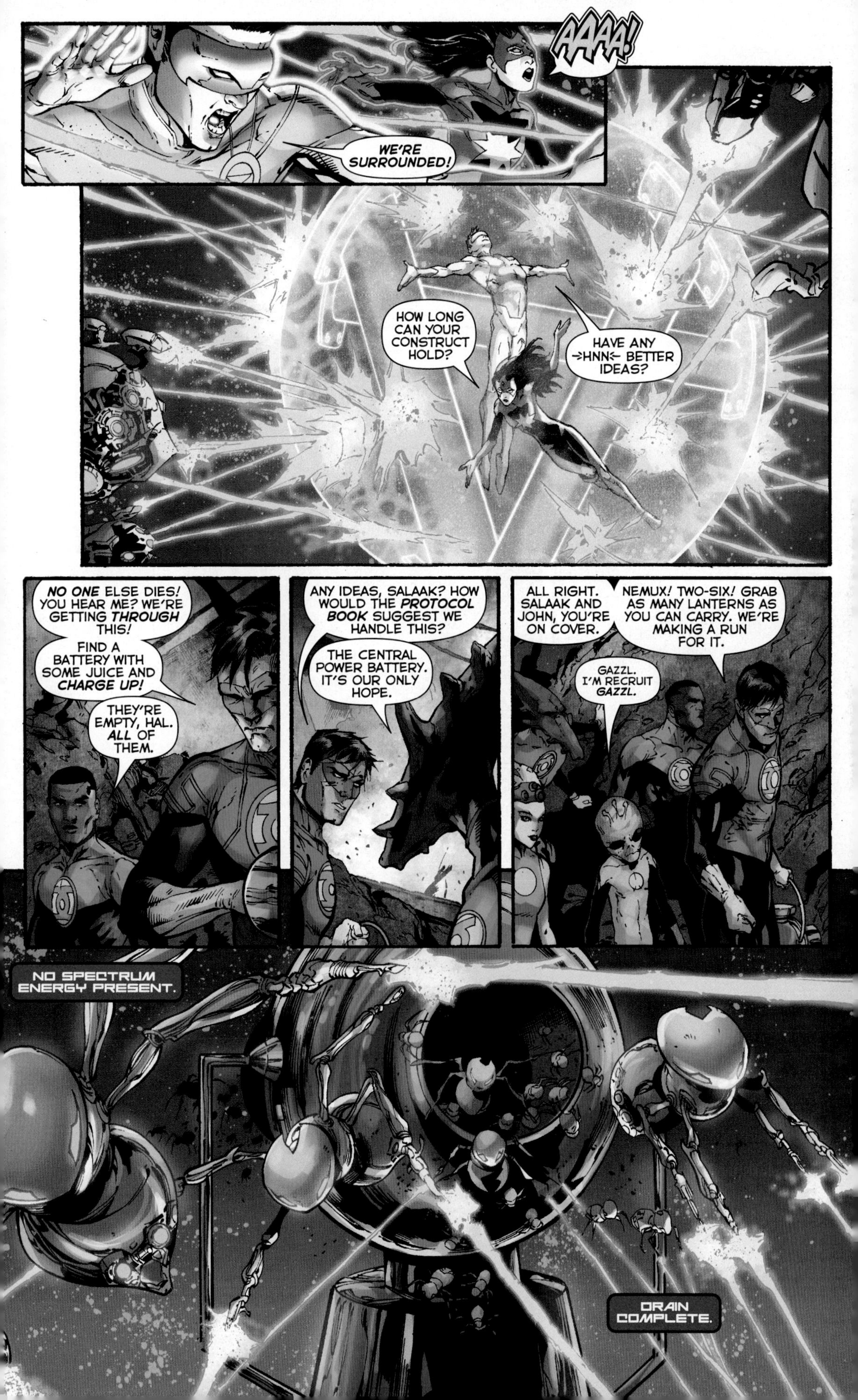
AAAA!
WE'RE SURROUNDED!
HOW LONG CAN YOUR CONSTRUCT HOLD?
HAVE ANY ➔HNN⬅ BETTER IDEAS?
NO ONE ELSE DIES! YOU HEAR ME? WE'RE GETTING THROUGH THIS!
FIND A BATTERY WITH SOME JUICE AND CHARGE UP!
THEY'RE EMPTY, HAL. ALL OF THEM.
ANY IDEAS, SALAAK? HOW WOULD THE PROTOCOL BOOK SUGGEST WE HANDLE THIS?
THE CENTRAL POWER BATTERY. IT'S OUR ONLY HOPE.
ALL RIGHT. SALAAK AND JOHN, YOU'RE ON COVER.
NEMUX! TWO-SIX! GRAB AS MANY LANTERNS AS YOU CAN CARRY. WE'RE MAKING A RUN FOR IT.
GAZZL. I'M RECRUIT GAZZL.
NO SPECTRUM ENERGY PRESENT.
DRAIN COMPLETE.

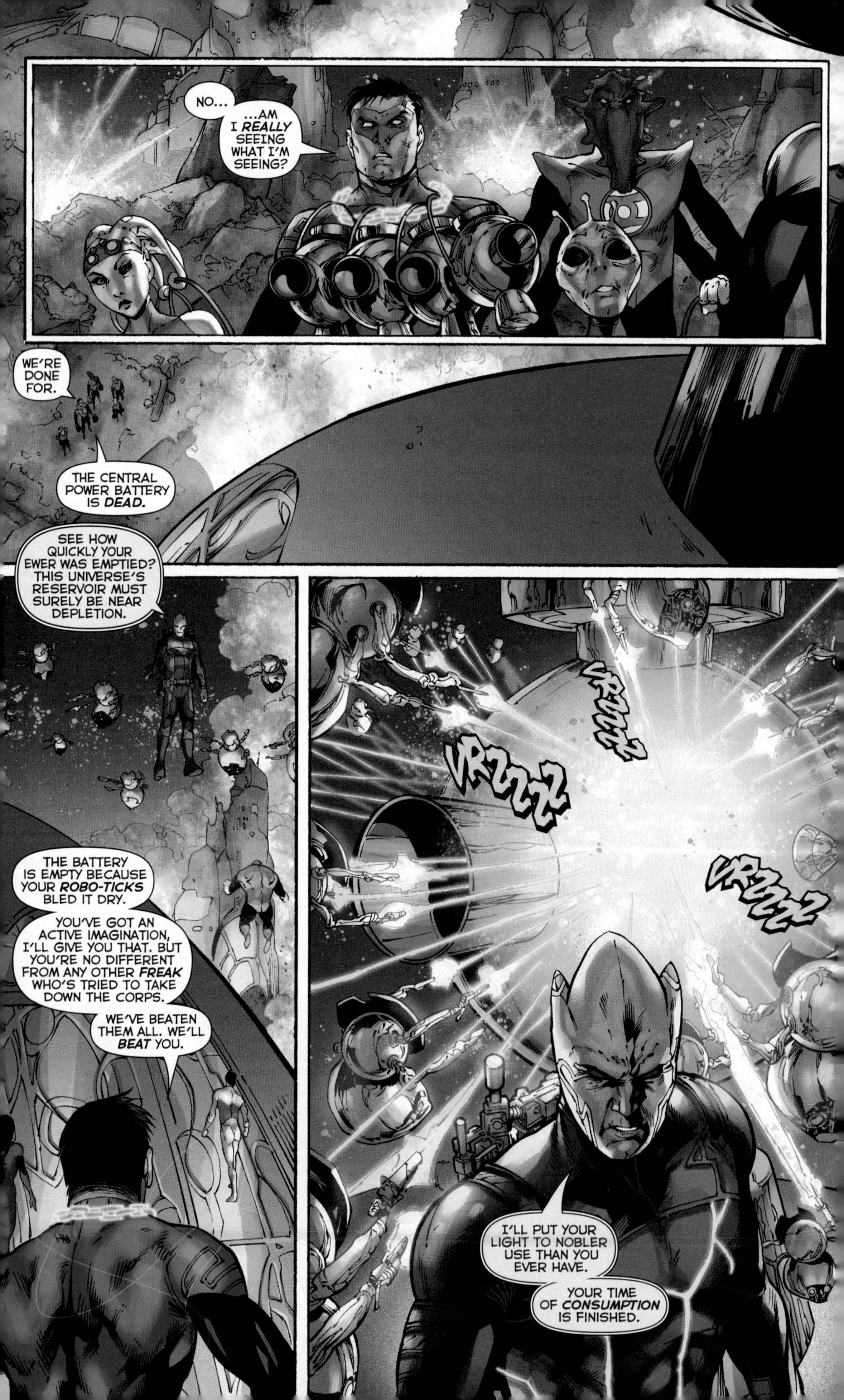
NO...
...AM I REALLY SEEING WHAT I'M SEEING?
WE'RE DONE FOR.
THE CENTRAL POWER BATTERY IS DEAD.
SEE HOW QUICKLY YOUR EWER WAS EMPTIED? THIS UNIVERSE'S RESERVOIR MUST SURELY BE NEAR DEPLETION.
THE BATTERY IS EMPTY BECAUSE YOUR ROBO-TICKS BLED IT DRY.
YOU'VE GOT AN ACTIVE IMAGINATION, I'LL GIVE YOU THAT. BUT YOU'RE NO DIFFERENT FROM ANY OTHER FREAK WHO'S TRIED TO TAKE DOWN THE CORPS.
WE'VE BEATEN THEM ALL. WE'LL BEAT YOU.
VRZZZ
VRZZZZ
VRZZZZ
I'LL PUT YOUR LIGHT TO NOBLER USE THAN YOU EVER HAVE.
YOUR TIME OF CONSUMPTION IS FINISHED.

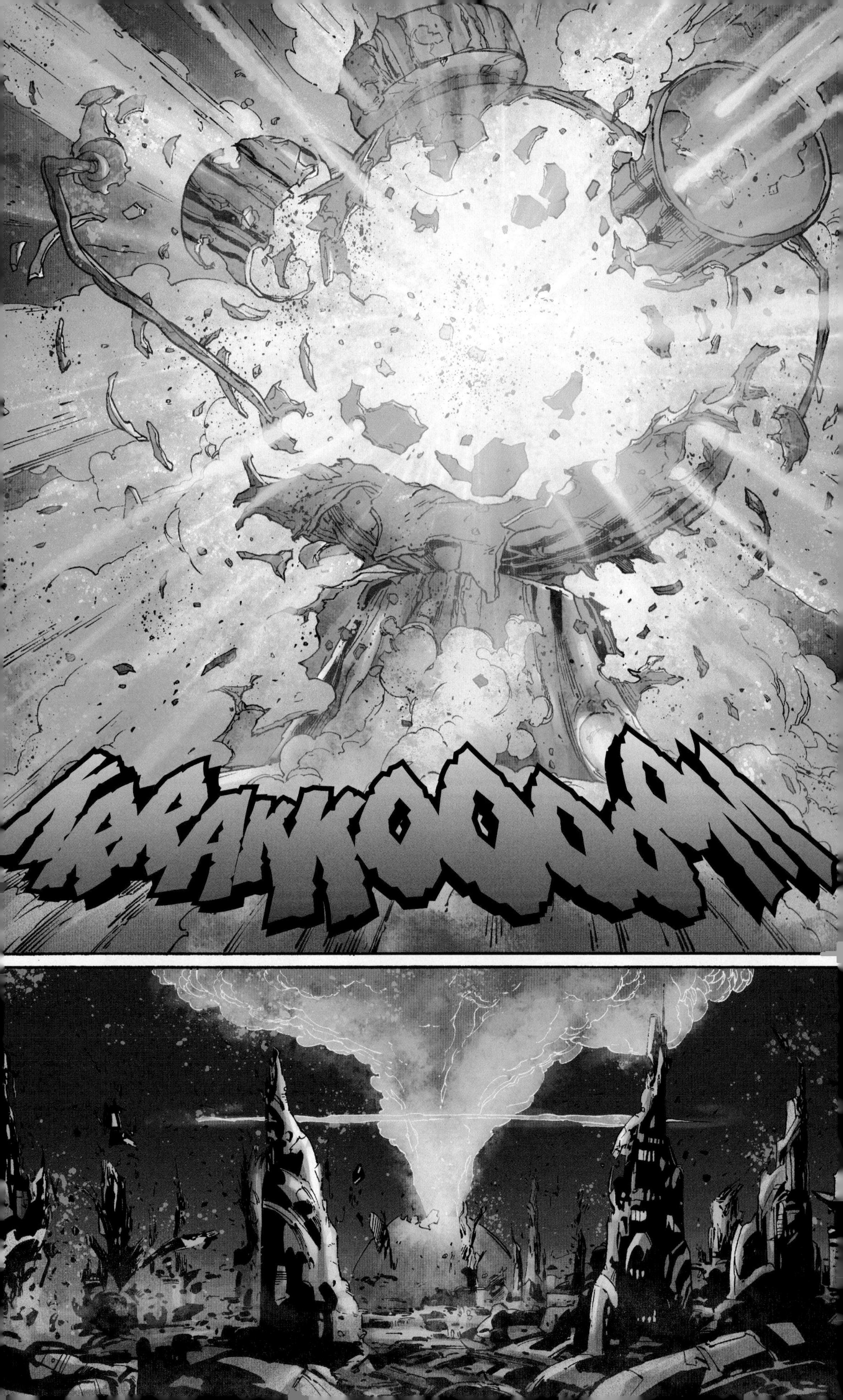
KRAKOOOM

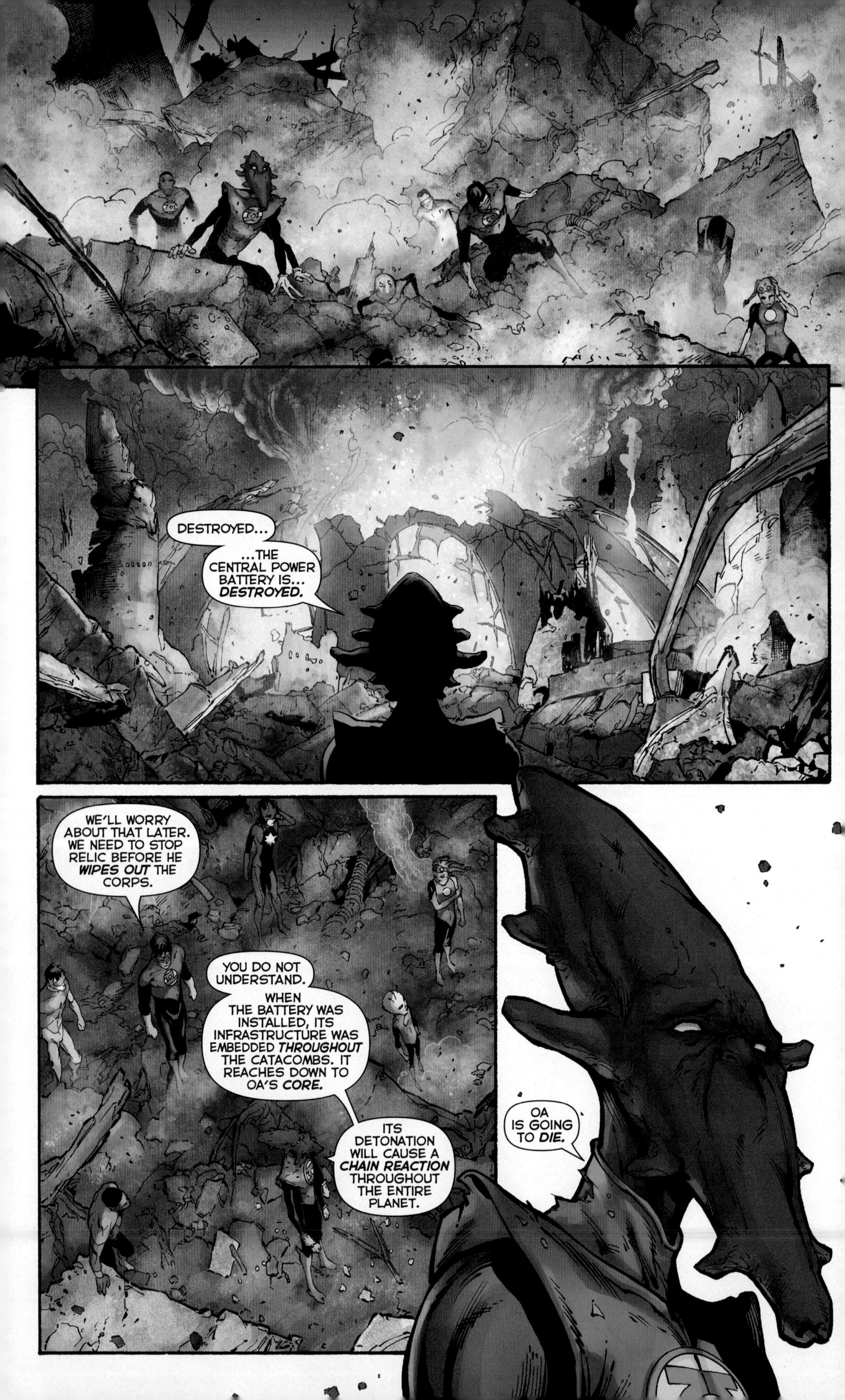
DESTROYED...
...THE CENTRAL POWER BATTERY IS... *DESTROYED.*
WE'LL WORRY ABOUT THAT LATER. WE NEED TO STOP RELIC BEFORE HE *WIPES OUT* THE CORPS.
YOU DO NOT UNDERSTAND.
WHEN THE BATTERY WAS INSTALLED, ITS INFRASTRUCTURE WAS EMBEDDED *THROUGHOUT* THE CATACOMBS. IT REACHES DOWN TO OA'S *CORE.*
ITS DETONATION WILL CAUSE A *CHAIN REACTION* THROUGHOUT THE ENTIRE PLANET.
OA IS GOING TO *DIE.*

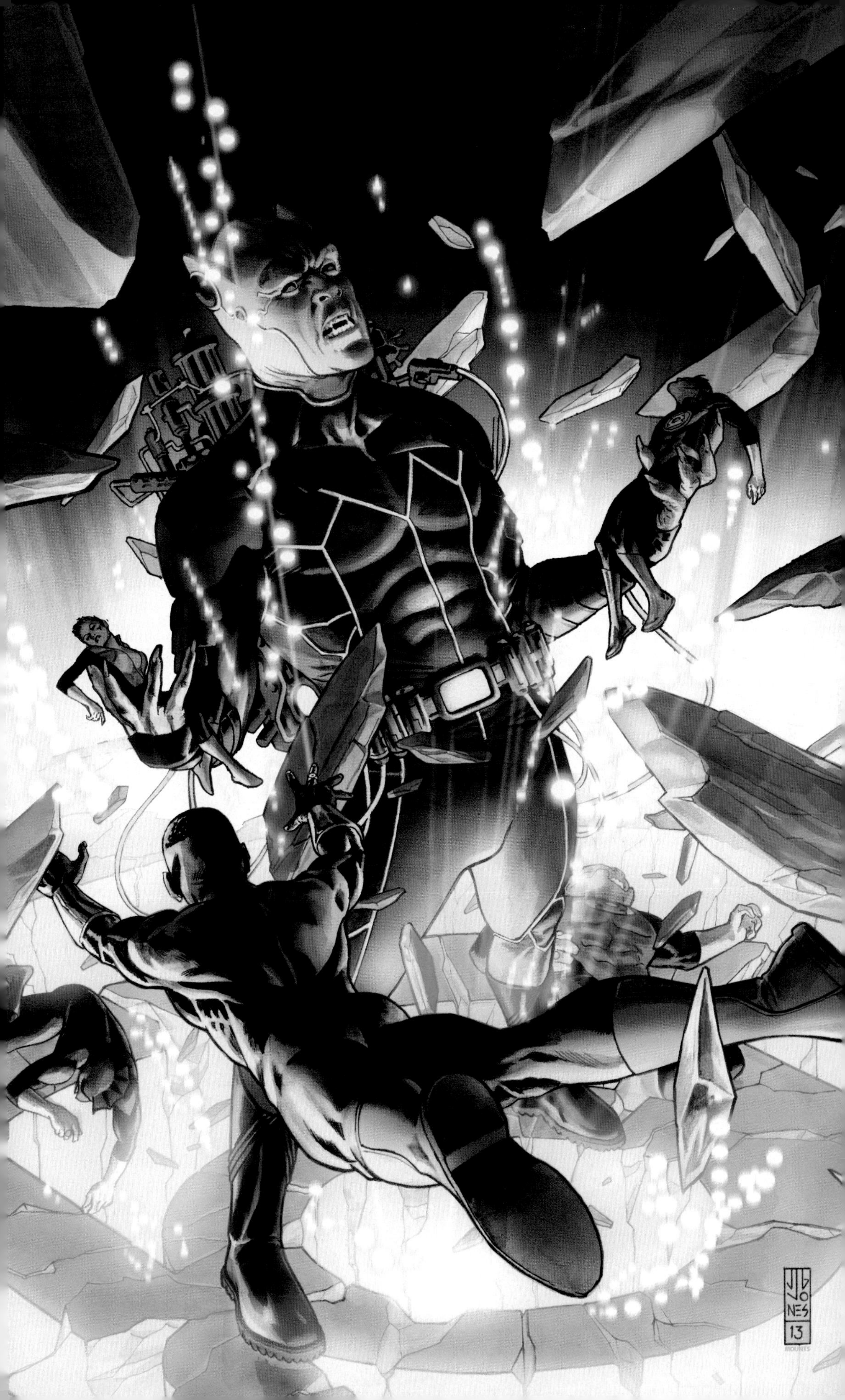
JG JONES
13
MOUNTS

LIGHTS OUT part two: OA'S LAST STAND

VAN JENSEN scripter **ROBERT VENDITTI** co-plotter **BERNARD CHANG** artist **MARCELO MAIOLO** colorist
J.G. JONES with **PAUL MOUNTS** cover artists

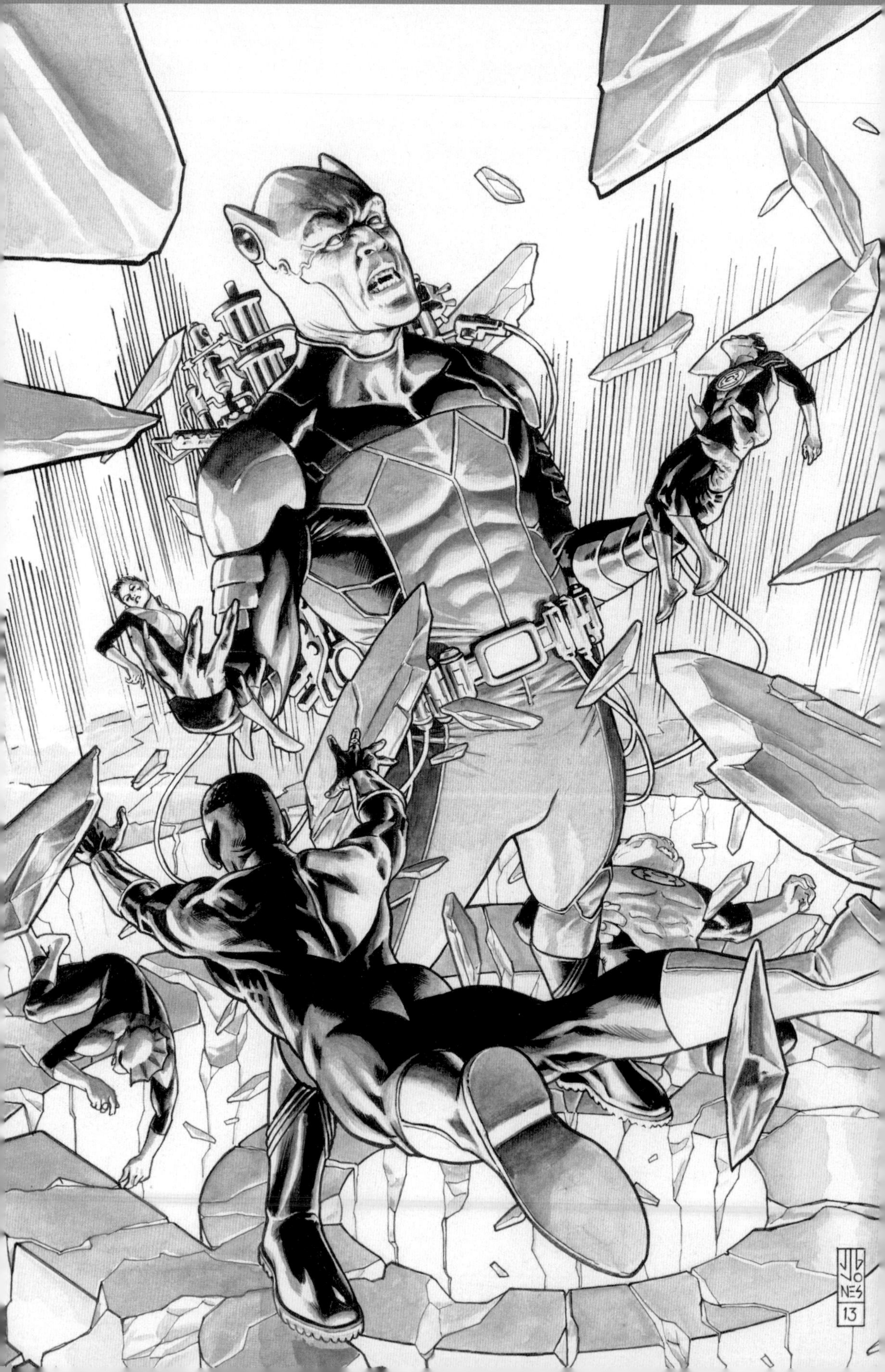

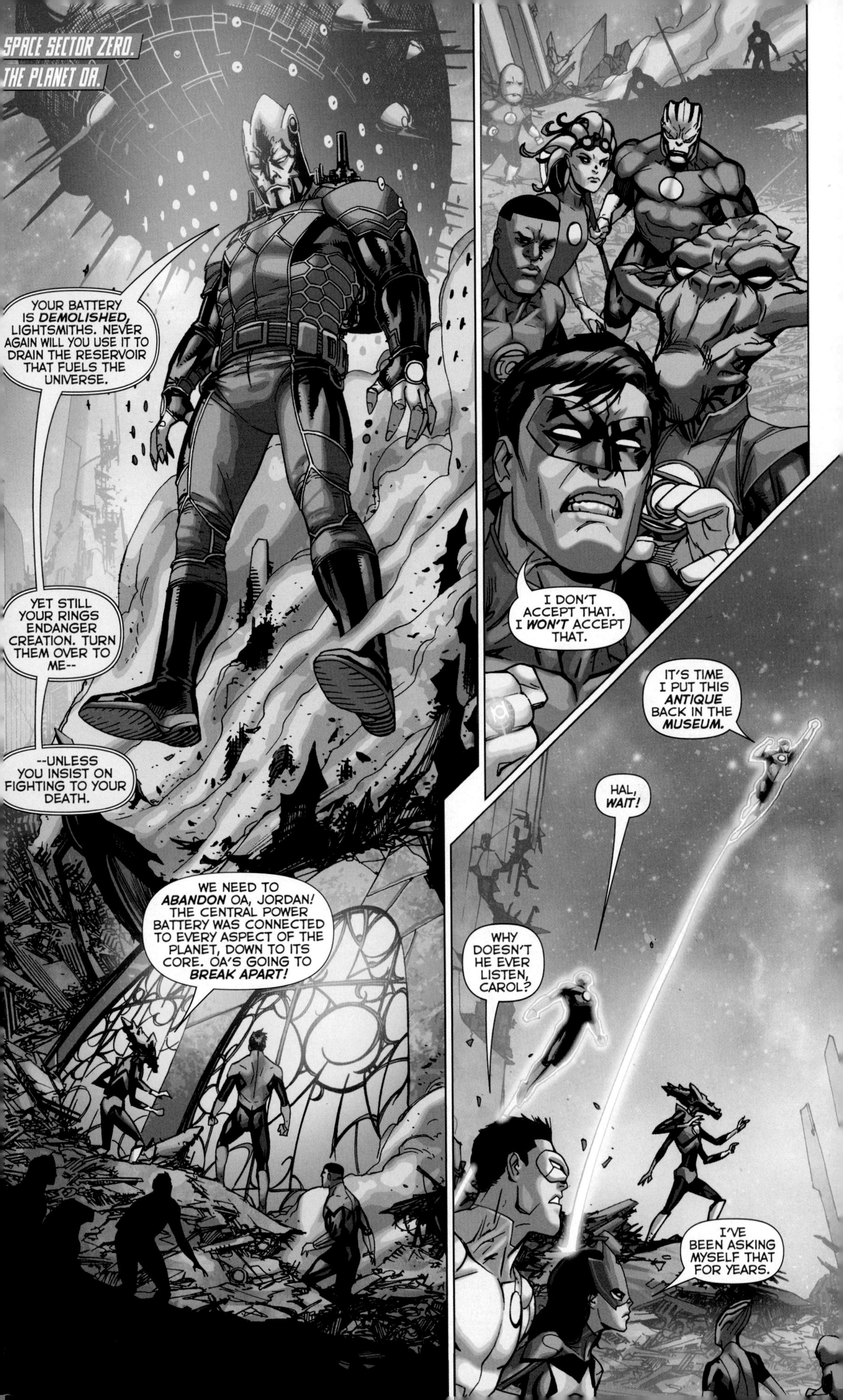
SPACE SECTOR ZERO.
THE PLANET OA.
YOUR BATTERY IS DEMOLISHED, LIGHTSMITHS. NEVER AGAIN WILL YOU USE IT TO DRAIN THE RESERVOIR THAT FUELS THE UNIVERSE.
YET STILL YOUR RINGS ENDANGER CREATION. TURN THEM OVER TO ME--
--UNLESS YOU INSIST ON FIGHTING TO YOUR DEATH.
WE NEED TO ABANDON OA, JORDAN! THE CENTRAL POWER BATTERY WAS CONNECTED TO EVERY ASPECT OF THE PLANET, DOWN TO ITS CORE. OA'S GOING TO BREAK APART!
I DON'T ACCEPT THAT. I WON'T ACCEPT THAT.
IT'S TIME I PUT THIS ANTIQUE BACK IN THE MUSEUM.
HAL, WAIT!
WHY DOESN'T HE EVER LISTEN, CAROL?
I'VE BEEN ASKING MYSELF THAT FOR YEARS.

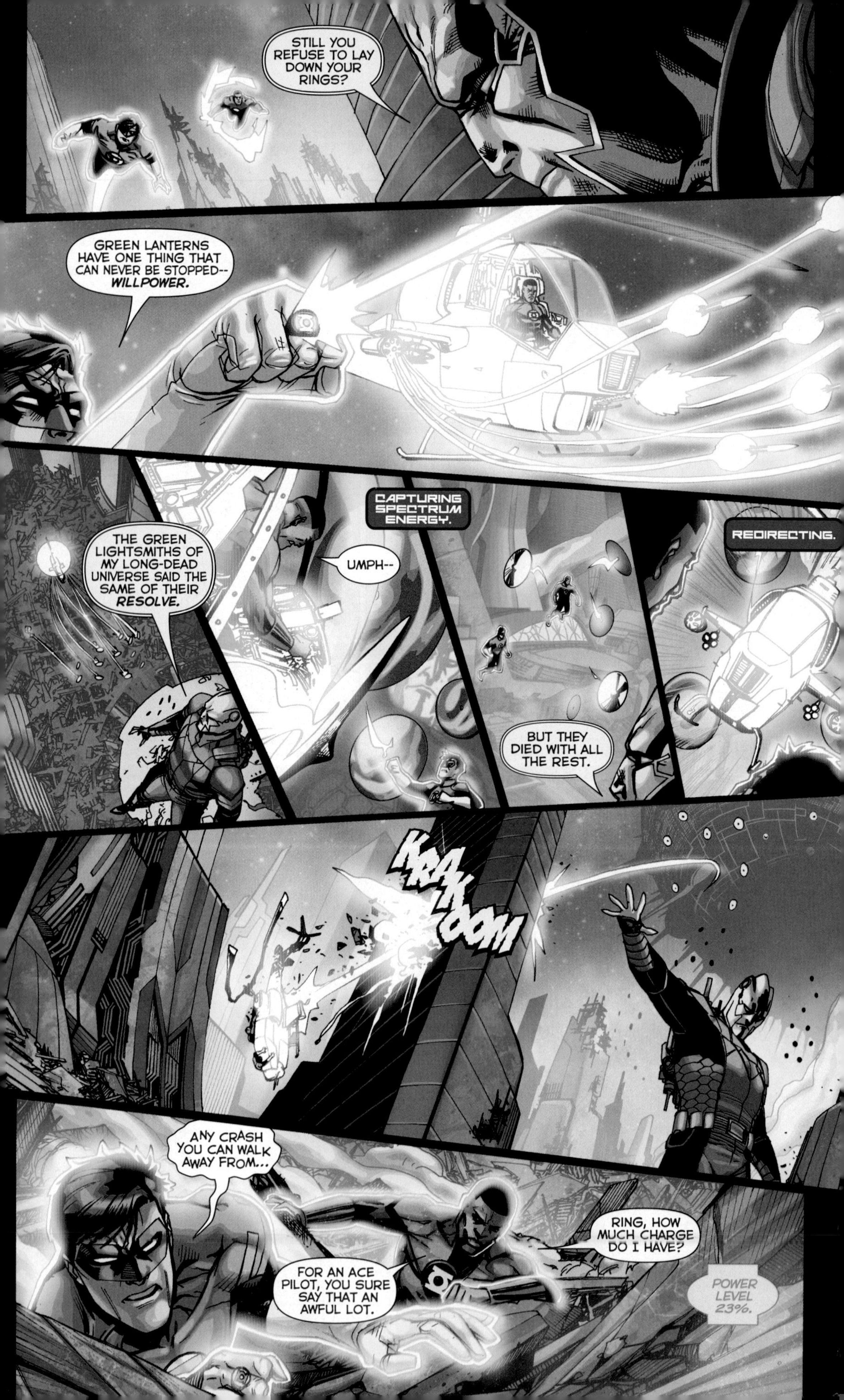
STILL YOU REFUSE TO LAY DOWN YOUR RINGS?
GREEN LANTERNS HAVE ONE THING THAT CAN NEVER BE STOPPED-- WILLPOWER.
THE GREEN LIGHTSMITHS OF MY LONG-DEAD UNIVERSE SAID THE SAME OF THEIR RESOLVE.
UMPH--
CAPTURING SPECTRUM ENERGY.
BUT THEY DIED WITH ALL THE REST.
REDIRECTING.
KRAKOOM
ANY CRASH YOU CAN WALK AWAY FROM...
FOR AN ACE PILOT, YOU SURE SAY THAT AN AWFUL LOT.
RING, HOW MUCH CHARGE DO I HAVE?
POWER LEVEL 23%.

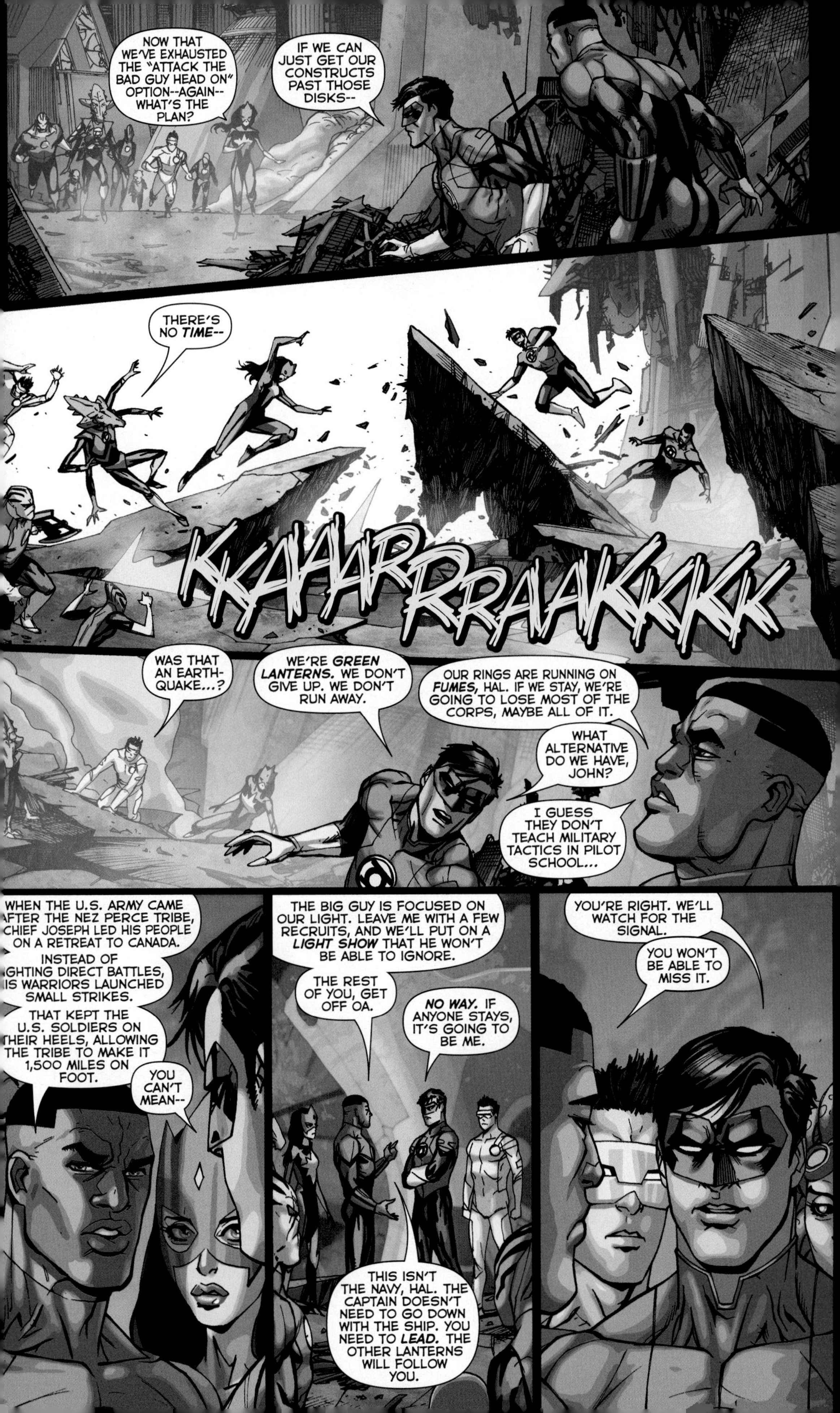
NOW THAT WE'VE EXHAUSTED THE "ATTACK THE BAD GUY HEAD ON" OPTION--AGAIN--WHAT'S THE PLAN?
IF WE CAN JUST GET OUR CONSTRUCTS PAST THOSE DISKS--
THERE'S NO TIME--
KKAAARRRAAKKKK
WAS THAT AN EARTH-QUAKE...?
WE'RE GREEN LANTERNS. WE DON'T GIVE UP. WE DON'T RUN AWAY.
OUR RINGS ARE RUNNING ON FUMES, HAL. IF WE STAY, WE'RE GOING TO LOSE MOST OF THE CORPS, MAYBE ALL OF IT.
WHAT ALTERNATIVE DO WE HAVE, JOHN?
I GUESS THEY DON'T TEACH MILITARY TACTICS IN PILOT SCHOOL...
WHEN THE U.S. ARMY CAME AFTER THE NEZ PERCE TRIBE, CHIEF JOSEPH LED HIS PEOPLE ON A RETREAT TO CANADA.
INSTEAD OF FIGHTING DIRECT BATTLES, HIS WARRIORS LAUNCHED SMALL STRIKES.
THAT KEPT THE U.S. SOLDIERS ON THEIR HEELS, ALLOWING THE TRIBE TO MAKE IT 1,500 MILES ON FOOT.
YOU CAN'T MEAN--
THE BIG GUY IS FOCUSED ON OUR LIGHT. LEAVE ME WITH A FEW RECRUITS, AND WE'LL PUT ON A LIGHT SHOW THAT HE WON'T BE ABLE TO IGNORE.
THE REST OF YOU, GET OFF OA.
NO WAY. IF ANYONE STAYS, IT'S GOING TO BE ME.
THIS ISN'T THE NAVY, HAL. THE CAPTAIN DOESN'T NEED TO GO DOWN WITH THE SHIP. YOU NEED TO LEAD. THE OTHER LANTERNS WILL FOLLOW YOU.
YOU'RE RIGHT. WE'LL WATCH FOR THE SIGNAL.
YOU WON'T BE ABLE TO MISS IT.

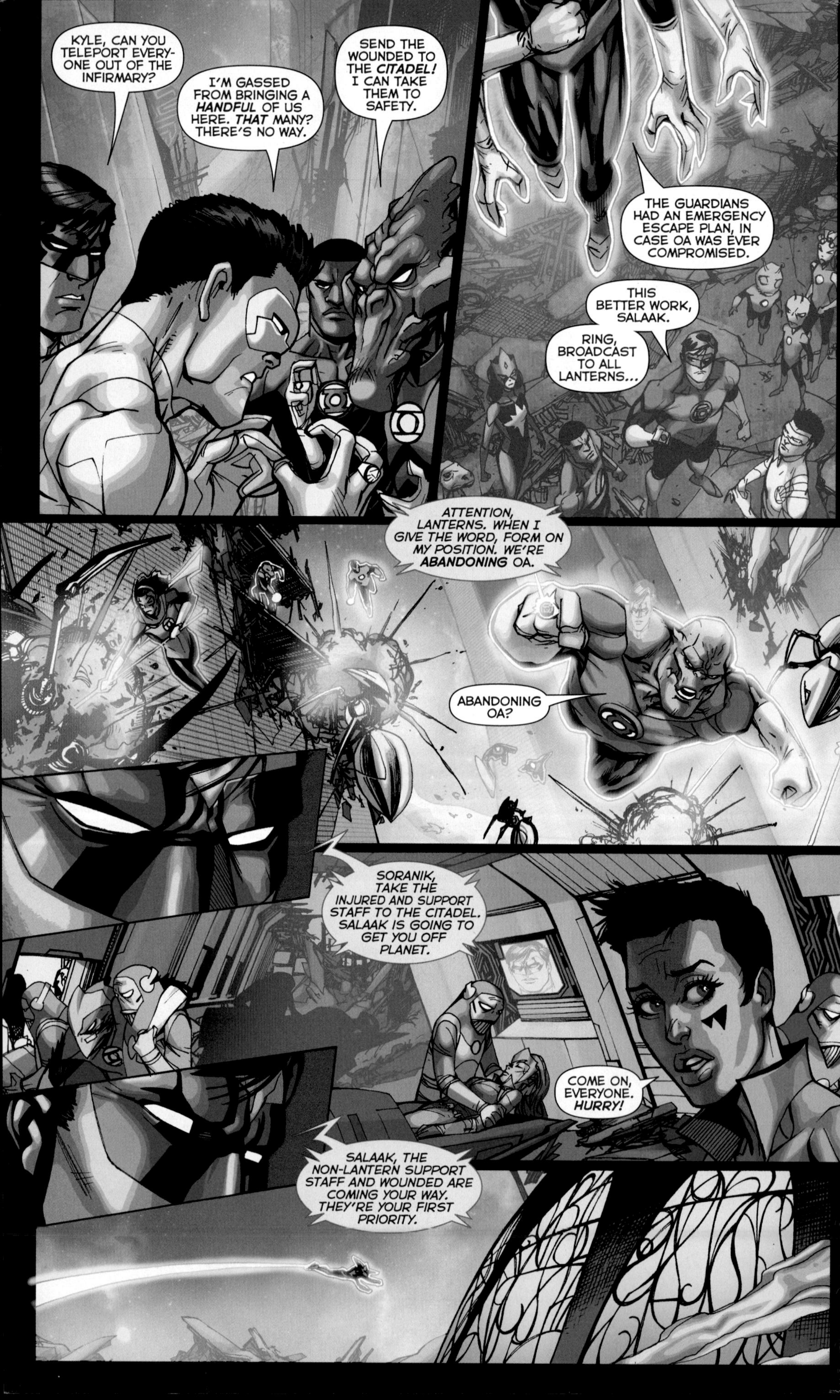
KYLE, CAN YOU TELEPORT EVERY-ONE OUT OF THE INFIRMARY?
I'M GASSED FROM BRINGING A *HANDFUL* OF US HERE. *THAT* MANY? THERE'S NO WAY.
SEND THE WOUNDED TO THE *CITADEL!* I CAN TAKE THEM TO SAFETY.
THE GUARDIANS HAD AN EMERGENCY ESCAPE PLAN, IN CASE OA WAS EVER COMPROMISED.
THIS BETTER WORK, SALAAK.
RING, BROADCAST TO ALL LANTERNS...
ATTENTION, LANTERNS. WHEN I GIVE THE WORD, FORM ON MY POSITION. WE'RE *ABANDONING* OA.
ABANDONING OA?
SORANIK, TAKE THE INJURED AND SUPPORT STAFF TO THE CITADEL. SALAAK IS GOING TO GET YOU OFF PLANET.
COME ON, EVERYONE. *HURRY!*
SALAAK, THE NON-LANTERN SUPPORT STAFF AND WOUNDED ARE COMING YOUR WAY. THEY'RE YOUR FIRST PRIORITY.

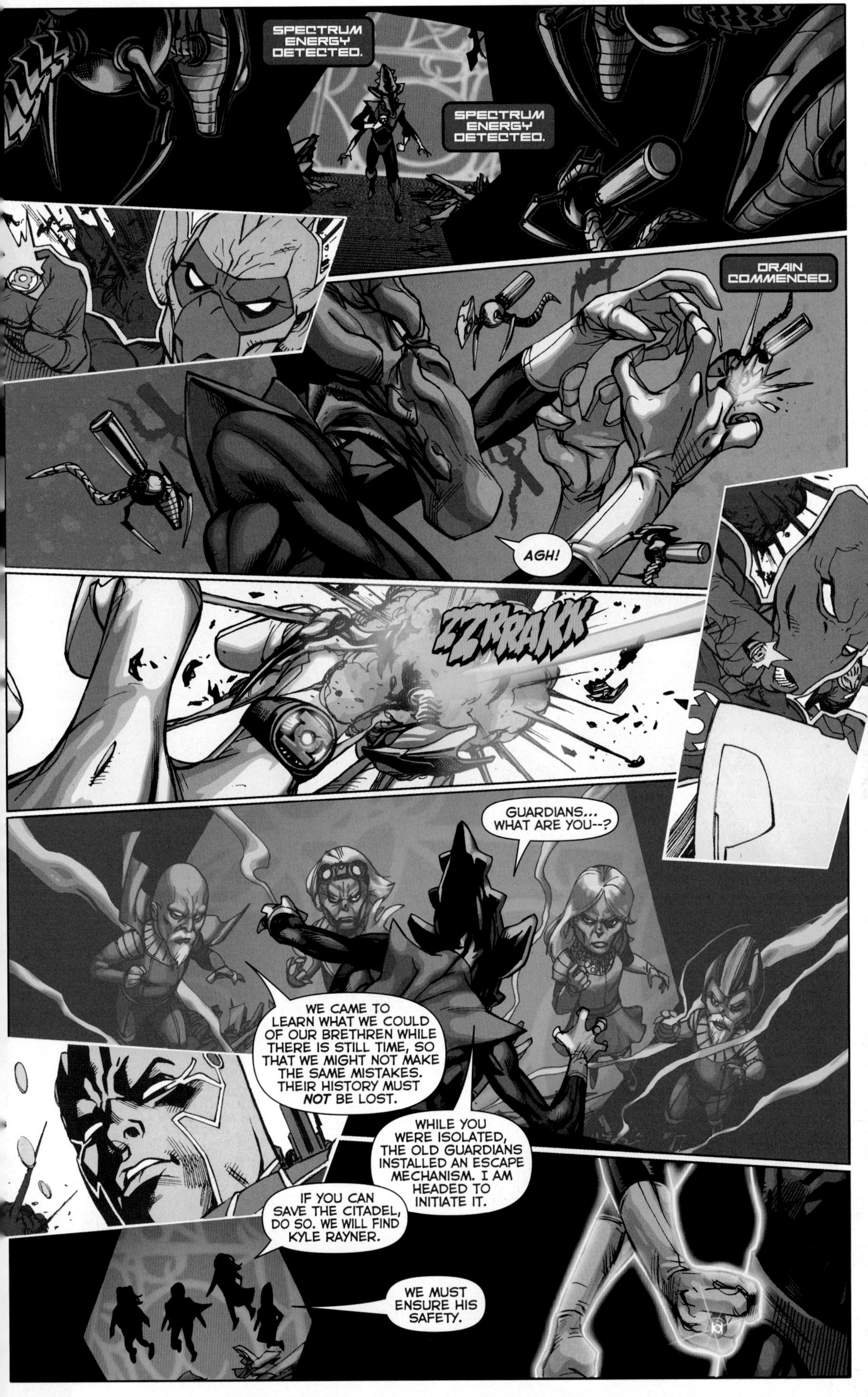

SPECTRUM ENERGY DETECTED.
SPECTRUM ENERGY DETECTED.
DRAIN COMMENCED.
AGH!
ZZRRAKK
GUARDIANS... WHAT ARE YOU--?
WE CAME TO LEARN WHAT WE COULD OF OUR BRETHREN WHILE THERE IS STILL TIME, SO THAT WE MIGHT NOT MAKE THE SAME MISTAKES. THEIR HISTORY MUST NOT BE LOST.
WHILE YOU WERE ISOLATED, THE OLD GUARDIANS INSTALLED AN ESCAPE MECHANISM. I AM HEADED TO INITIATE IT.
IF YOU CAN SAVE THE CITADEL, DO SO. WE WILL FIND KYLE RAYNER.
WE MUST ENSURE HIS SAFETY.

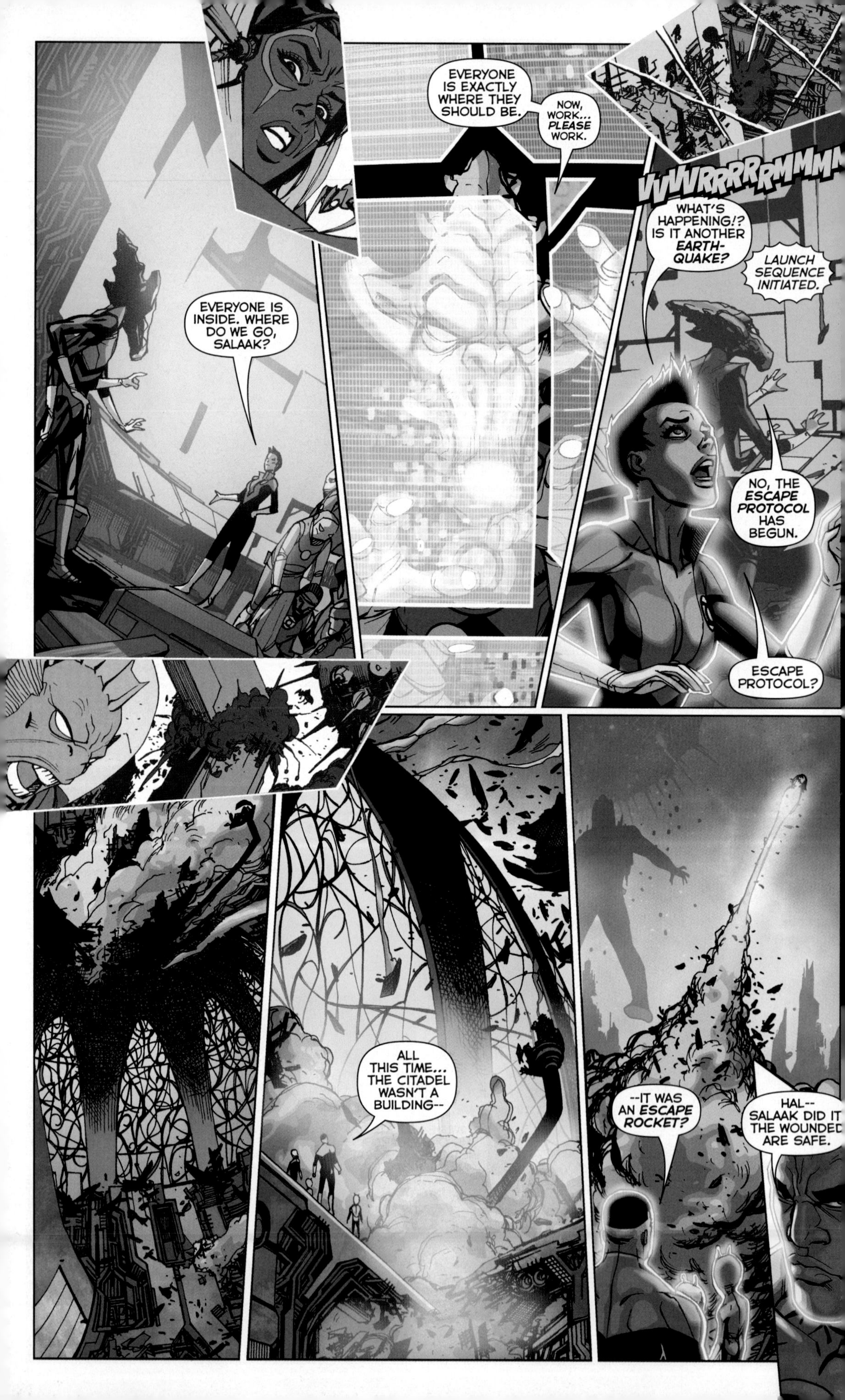
EVERYONE IS INSIDE. WHERE DO WE GO, SALAAK?
EVERYONE IS EXACTLY WHERE THEY SHOULD BE.
NOW, WORK... PLEASE WORK.
VVVVRRRRRMMMM
WHAT'S HAPPENING!? IS IT ANOTHER EARTH-QUAKE?
LAUNCH SEQUENCE INITIATED.
NO, THE ESCAPE PROTOCOL HAS BEGUN.
ESCAPE PROTOCOL?
ALL THIS TIME... THE CITADEL WASN'T A BUILDING--
--IT WAS AN ESCAPE ROCKET?
HAL-- SALAAK DID IT THE WOUNDED ARE SAFE.

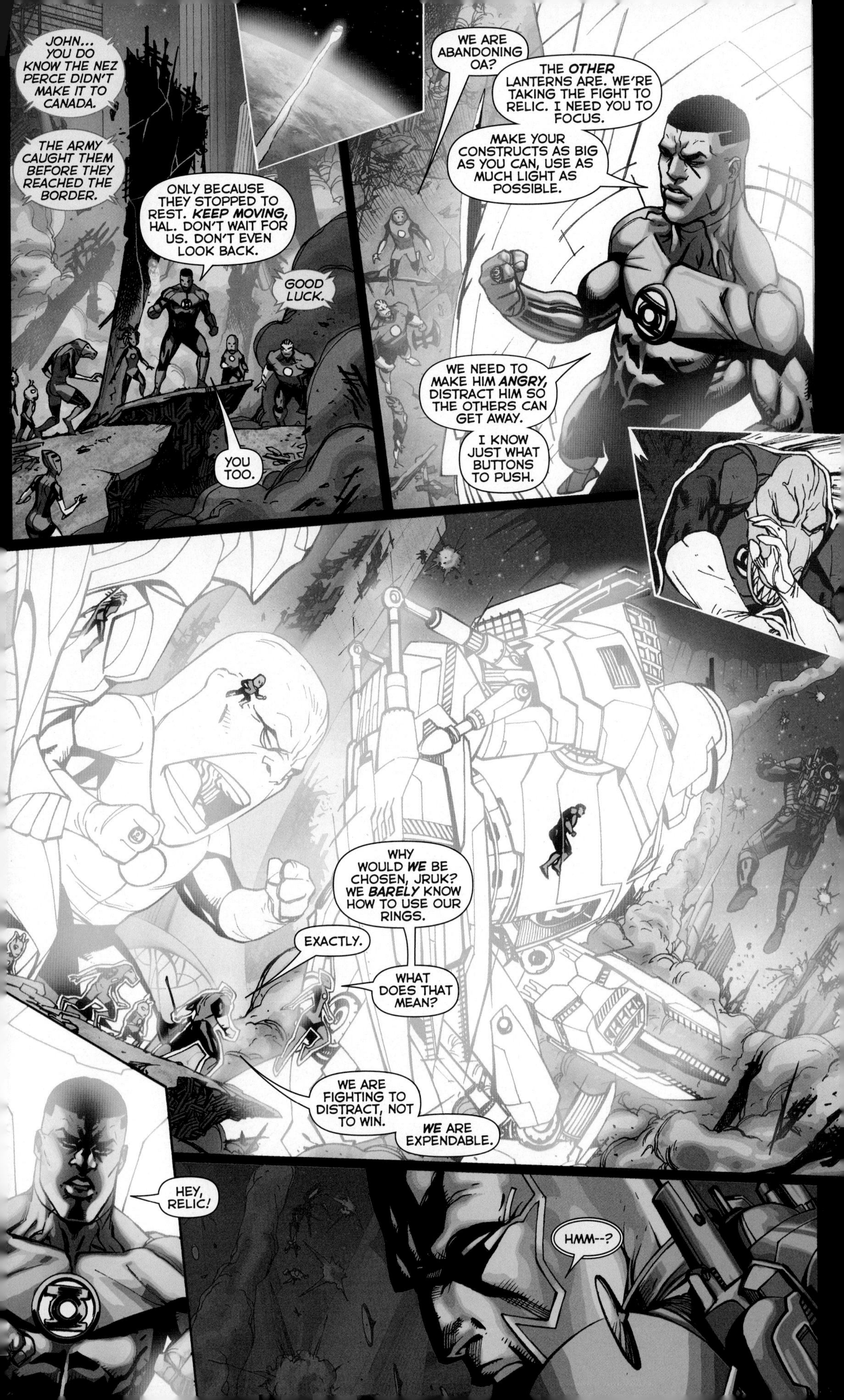
JOHN... YOU DO KNOW THE NEZ PERCE DIDN'T MAKE IT TO CANADA.
THE ARMY CAUGHT THEM BEFORE THEY REACHED THE BORDER.
ONLY BECAUSE THEY STOPPED TO REST. KEEP MOVING, HAL. DON'T WAIT FOR US. DON'T EVEN LOOK BACK.
GOOD LUCK.
YOU TOO.
WE ARE ABANDONING OA?
THE OTHER LANTERNS ARE. WE'RE TAKING THE FIGHT TO RELIC. I NEED YOU TO FOCUS.
MAKE YOUR CONSTRUCTS AS BIG AS YOU CAN, USE AS MUCH LIGHT AS POSSIBLE.
WE NEED TO MAKE HIM ANGRY, DISTRACT HIM SO THE OTHERS CAN GET AWAY.
I KNOW JUST WHAT BUTTONS TO PUSH.
WHY WOULD WE BE CHOSEN, JRUK? WE BARELY KNOW HOW TO USE OUR RINGS.
EXACTLY.
WHAT DOES THAT MEAN?
WE ARE FIGHTING TO DISTRACT, NOT TO WIN.
WE ARE EXPENDABLE.
HEY, RELIC!
HMM--?

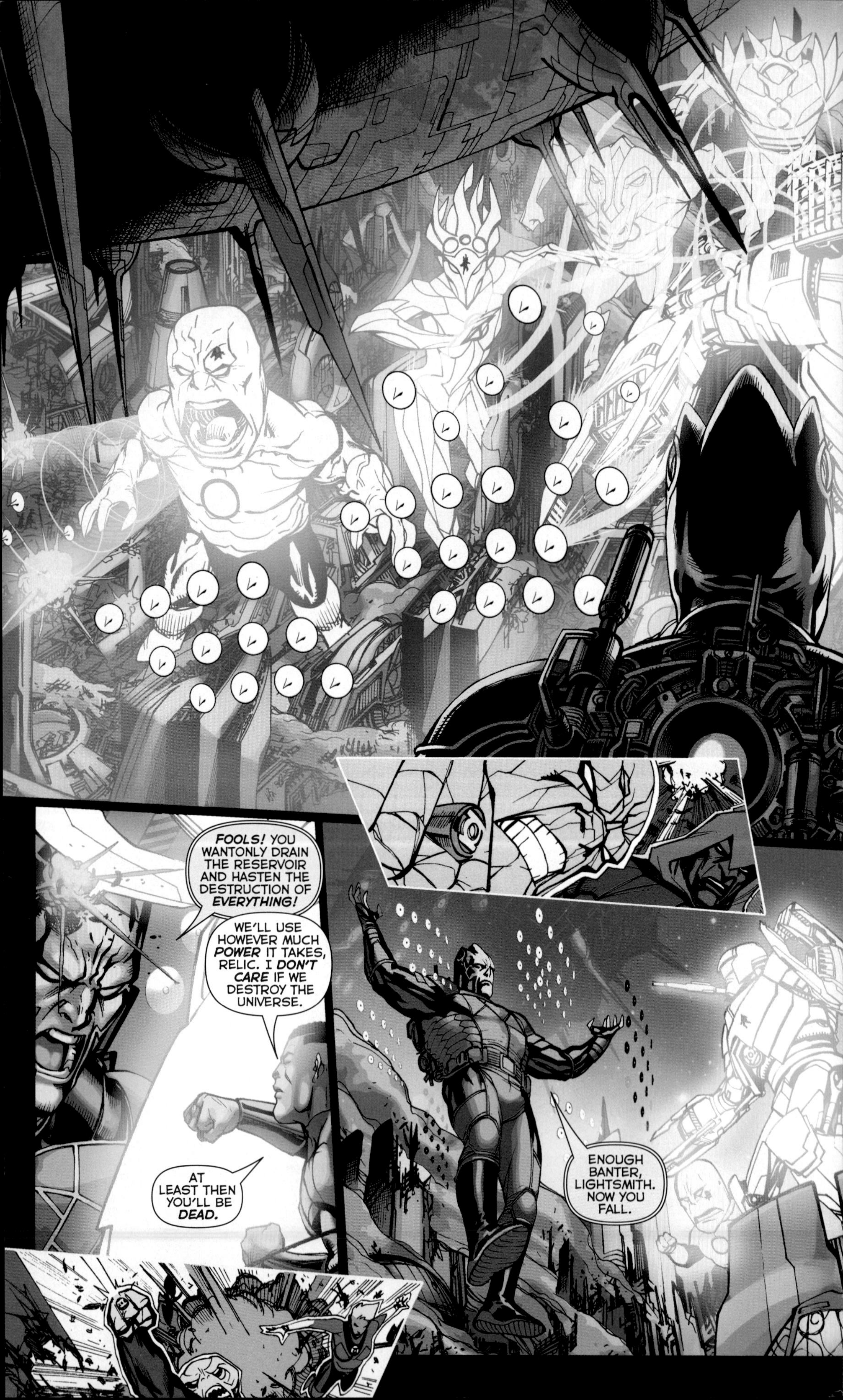
FOOLS! YOU WANTONLY DRAIN THE RESERVOIR AND HASTEN THE DESTRUCTION OF EVERYTHING!
WE'LL USE HOWEVER MUCH POWER IT TAKES, RELIC. I DON'T CARE IF WE DESTROY THE UNIVERSE.
AT LEAST THEN YOU'LL BE DEAD.
ENOUGH BANTER, LIGHTSMITH. NOW YOU FALL.

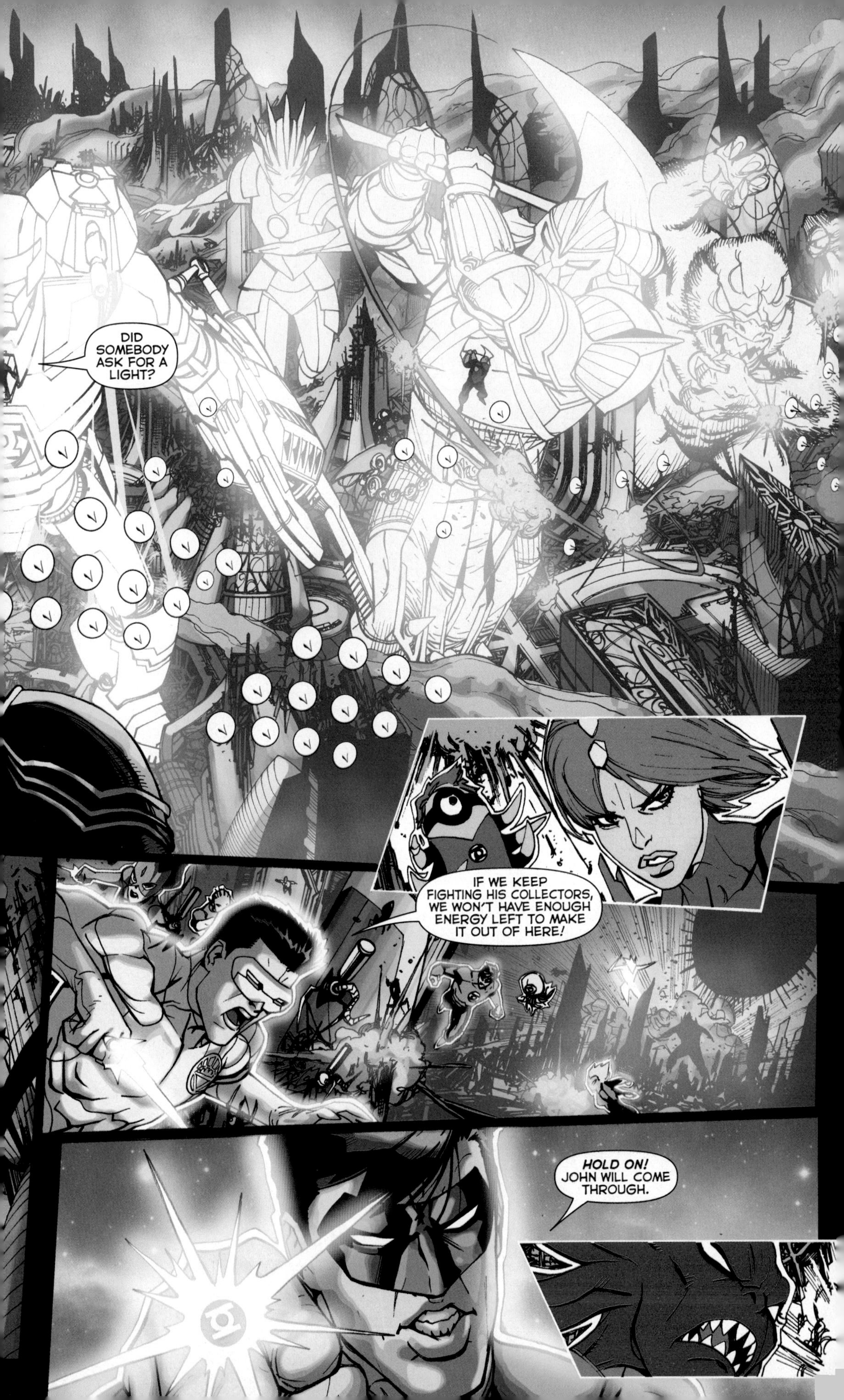
DID SOMEBODY ASK FOR A LIGHT?
IF WE KEEP FIGHTING HIS COLLECTORS, WE WON'T HAVE ENOUGH ENERGY LEFT TO MAKE IT OUT OF HERE!
HOLD ON! JOHN WILL COME THROUGH.

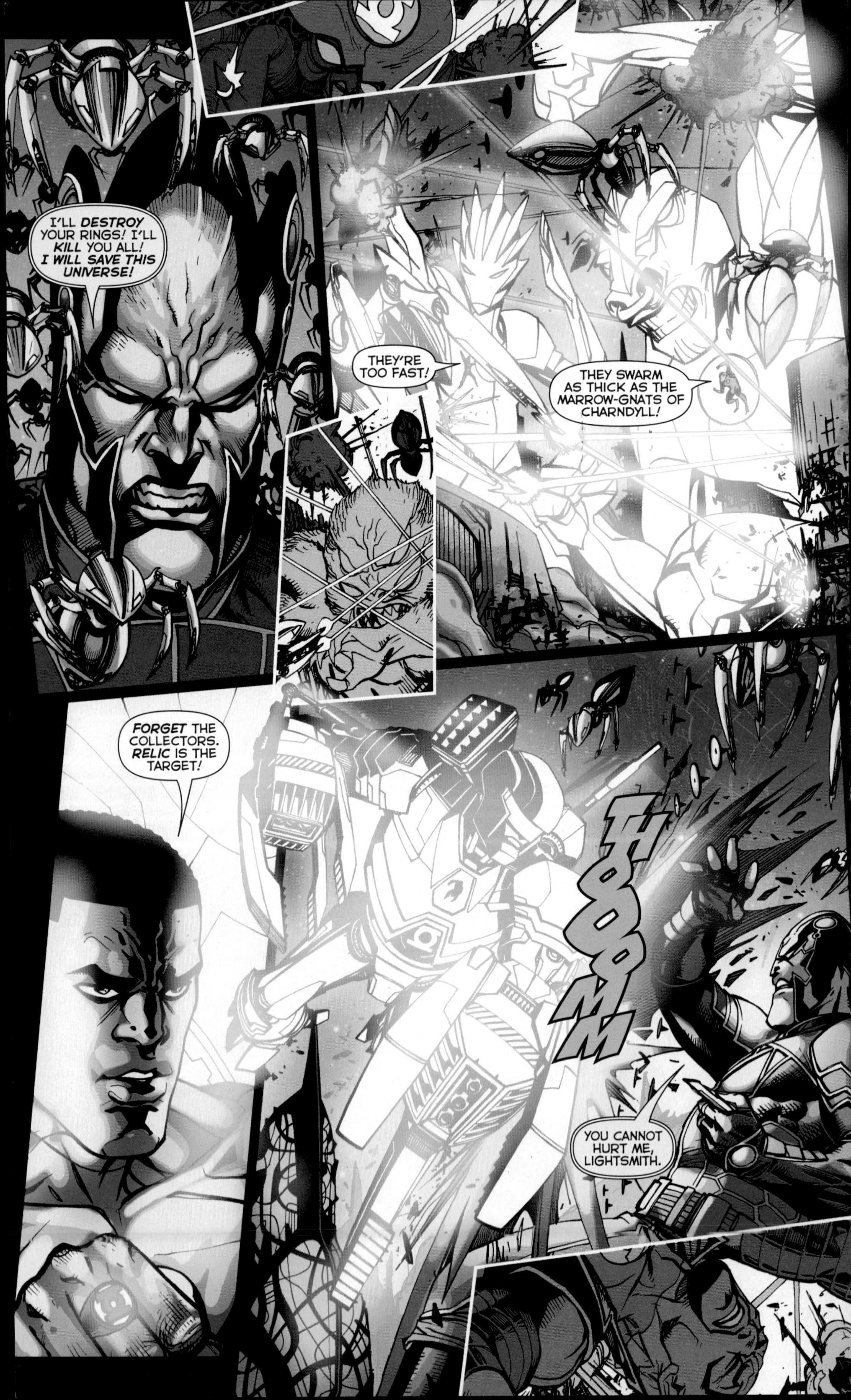
I'LL DESTROY YOUR RINGS! I'LL KILL YOU ALL! I WILL SAVE THIS UNIVERSE!
THEY'RE TOO FAST!
THEY SWARM AS THICK AS THE MARROW-GNATS OF CHARNDYLL!
FORGET THE COLLECTORS. RELIC IS THE TARGET!
THOOOMM
YOU CANNOT HURT ME, LIGHTSMITH.

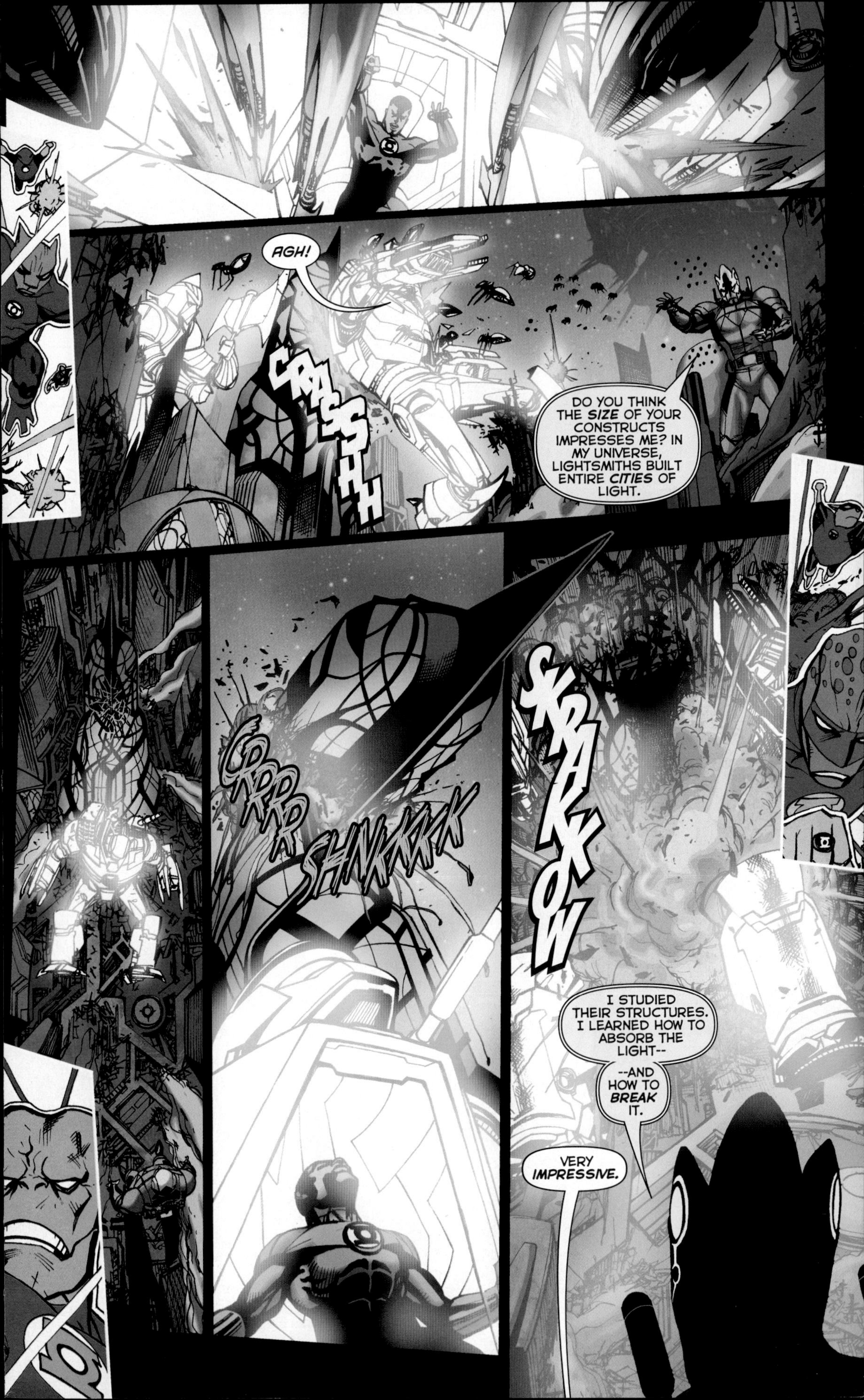
AGH!
CRASSHH
DO YOU THINK THE SIZE OF YOUR CONSTRUCTS IMPRESSES ME? IN MY UNIVERSE, LIGHTSMITHS BUILT ENTIRE CITIES OF LIGHT.
CRRRR SHNKKKKK
SKRAKOW
I STUDIED THEIR STRUCTURES. I LEARNED HOW TO ABSORB THE LIGHT--
--AND HOW TO BREAK IT.
VERY IMPRESSIVE.

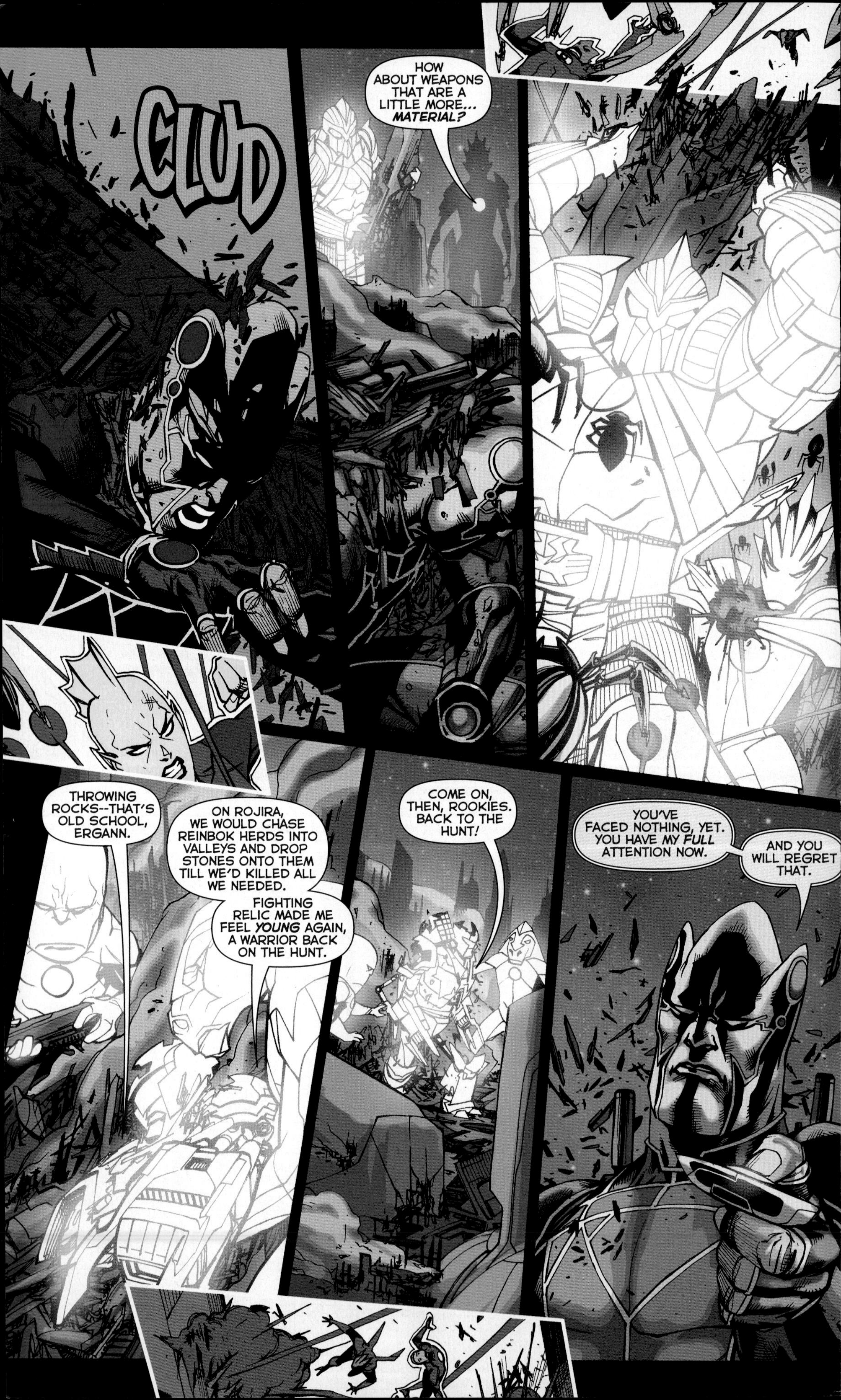
CLUD
HOW ABOUT WEAPONS THAT ARE A LITTLE MORE... *MATERIAL?*
THROWING ROCKS--THAT'S OLD SCHOOL, ERGANN.
ON ROJIRA, WE WOULD CHASE REINBOK HERDS INTO VALLEYS AND DROP STONES ONTO THEM TILL WE'D KILLED ALL WE NEEDED.
FIGHTING RELIC MADE ME FEEL *YOUNG* AGAIN, A WARRIOR BACK ON THE HUNT.
COME ON, THEN, ROOKIES. BACK TO THE HUNT!
YOU'VE FACED NOTHING, YET. YOU HAVE *MY FULL* ATTENTION NOW.
AND YOU WILL REGRET THAT.

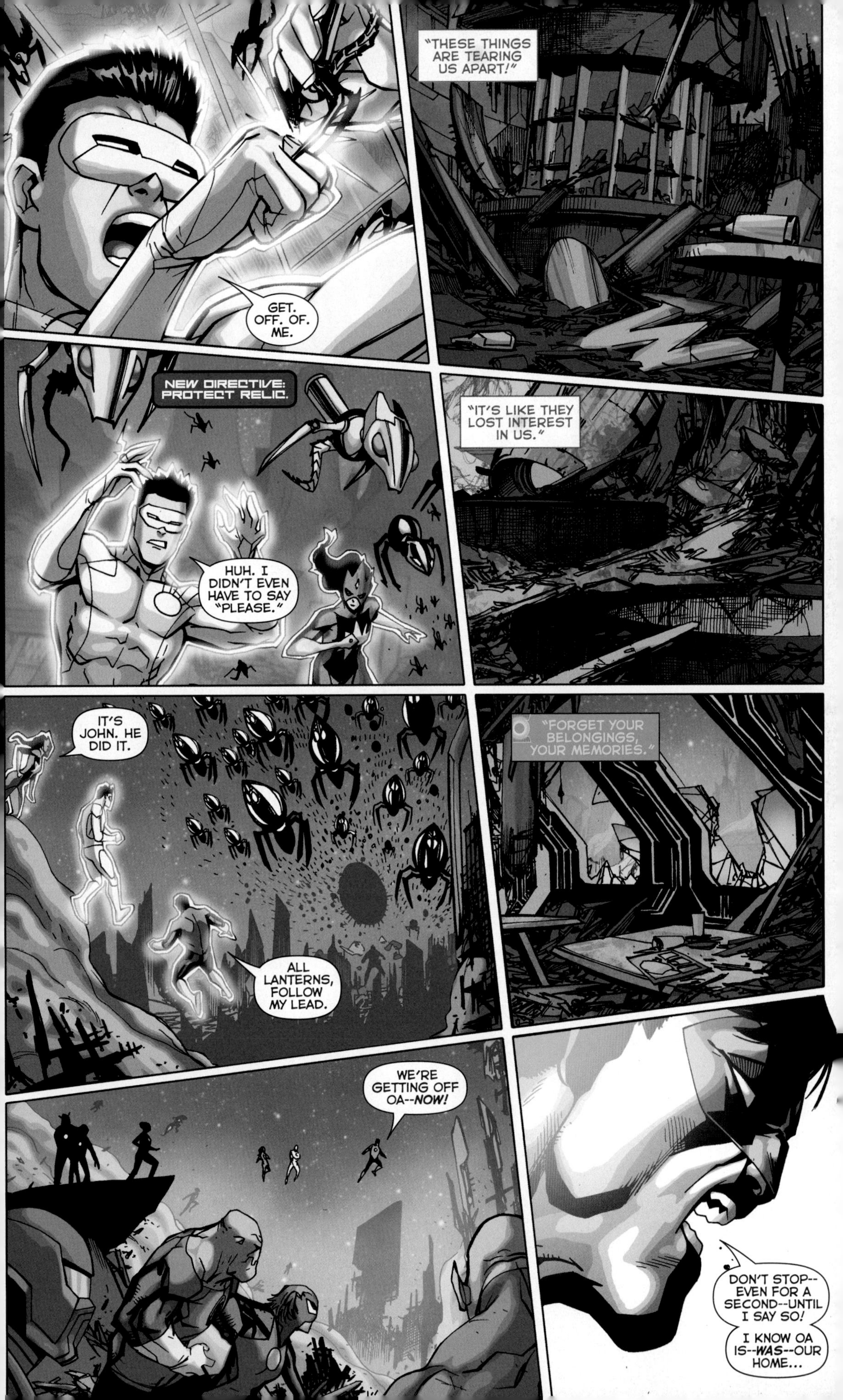
"THESE THINGS ARE TEARING US APART!"
GET. OFF. OF. ME.
NEW DIRECTIVE: PROTECT RELIC.
"IT'S LIKE THEY LOST INTEREST IN US."
HUH. I DIDN'T EVEN HAVE TO SAY "PLEASE."
IT'S JOHN. HE DID IT.
"FORGET YOUR BELONGINGS, YOUR MEMORIES."
ALL LANTERNS, FOLLOW MY LEAD.
WE'RE GETTING OFF OA--*NOW!*
DON'T STOP--EVEN FOR A SECOND--UNTIL I SAY SO!
I KNOW OA IS--*WAS*--OUR HOME...

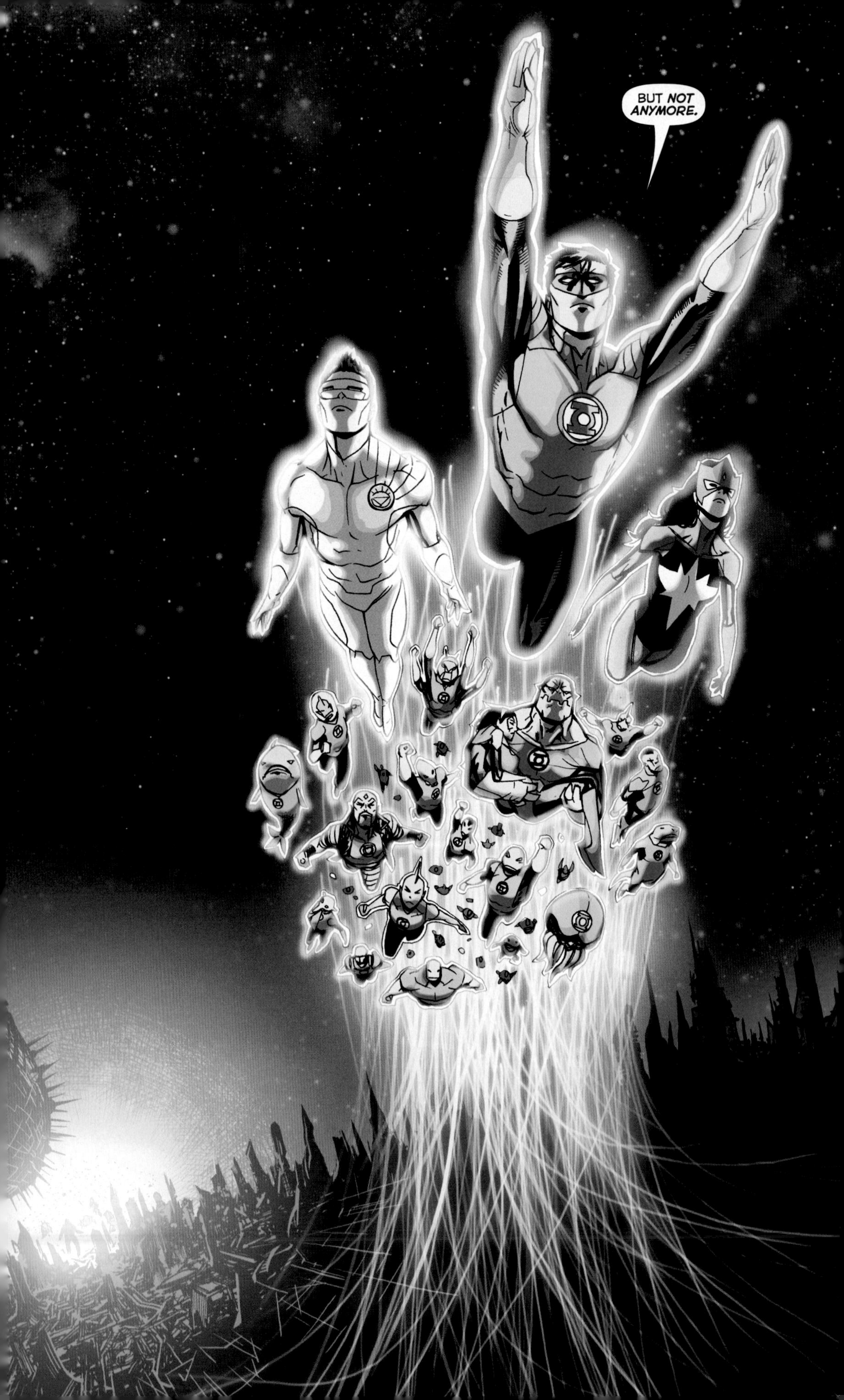
BUT *NOT* *ANYMORE.*

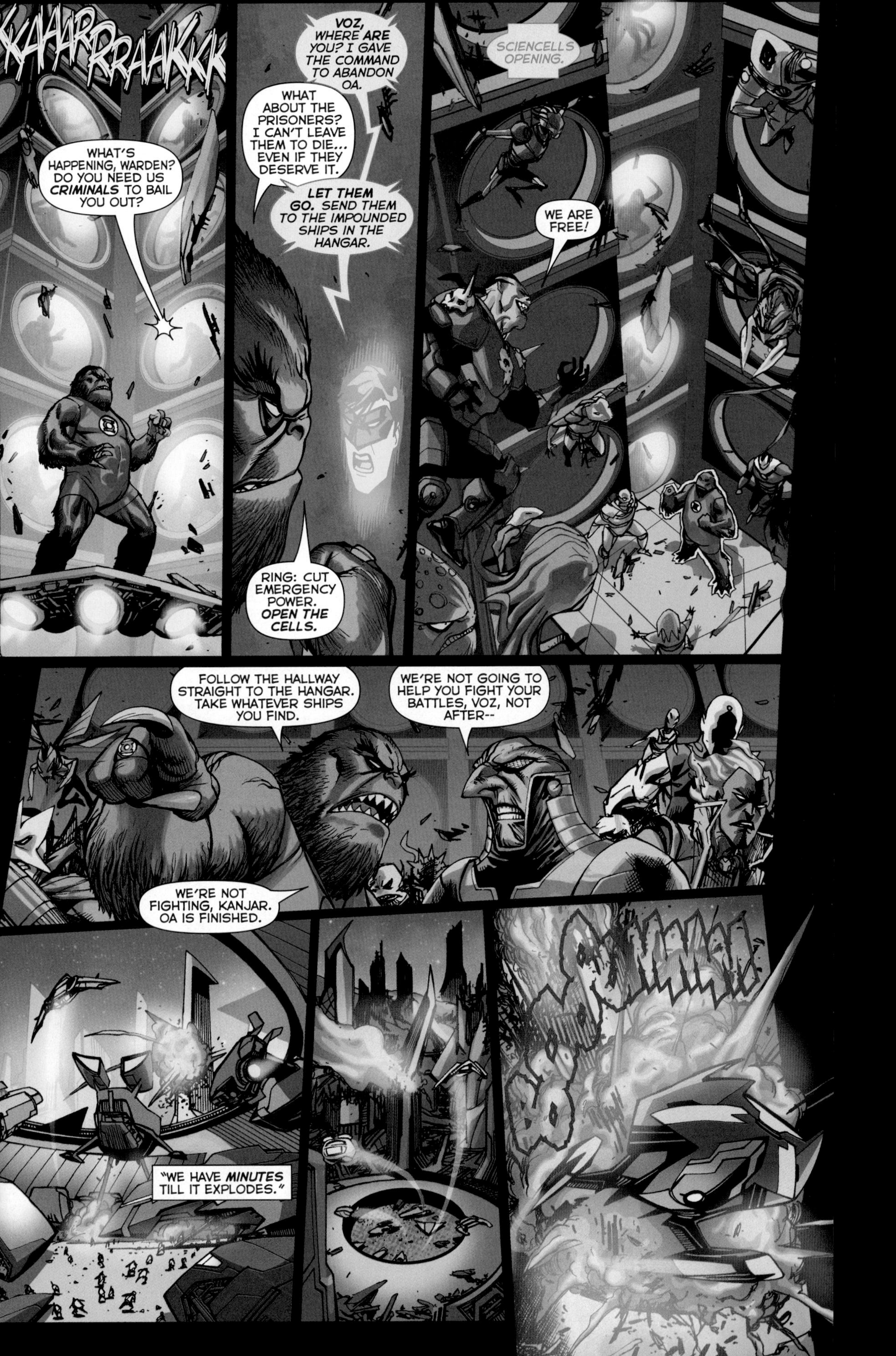
KKAAARRRAAKKK
WHAT'S HAPPENING, WARDEN? DO YOU NEED US CRIMINALS TO BAIL YOU OUT?
VOZ, WHERE ARE YOU? I GAVE THE COMMAND TO ABANDON OA.
WHAT ABOUT THE PRISONERS? I CAN'T LEAVE THEM TO DIE... EVEN IF THEY DESERVE IT.
LET THEM GO. SEND THEM TO THE IMPOUNDED SHIPS IN THE HANGAR.
RING: CUT EMERGENCY POWER. OPEN THE CELLS.
SCIENCELLS OPENING.
WE ARE FREE!
FOLLOW THE HALLWAY STRAIGHT TO THE HANGAR. TAKE WHATEVER SHIPS YOU FIND.
WE'RE NOT GOING TO HELP YOU FIGHT YOUR BATTLES, VOZ, NOT AFTER--
WE'RE NOT FIGHTING, KANJAR. OA IS FINISHED.
"WE HAVE MINUTES TILL IT EXPLODES."

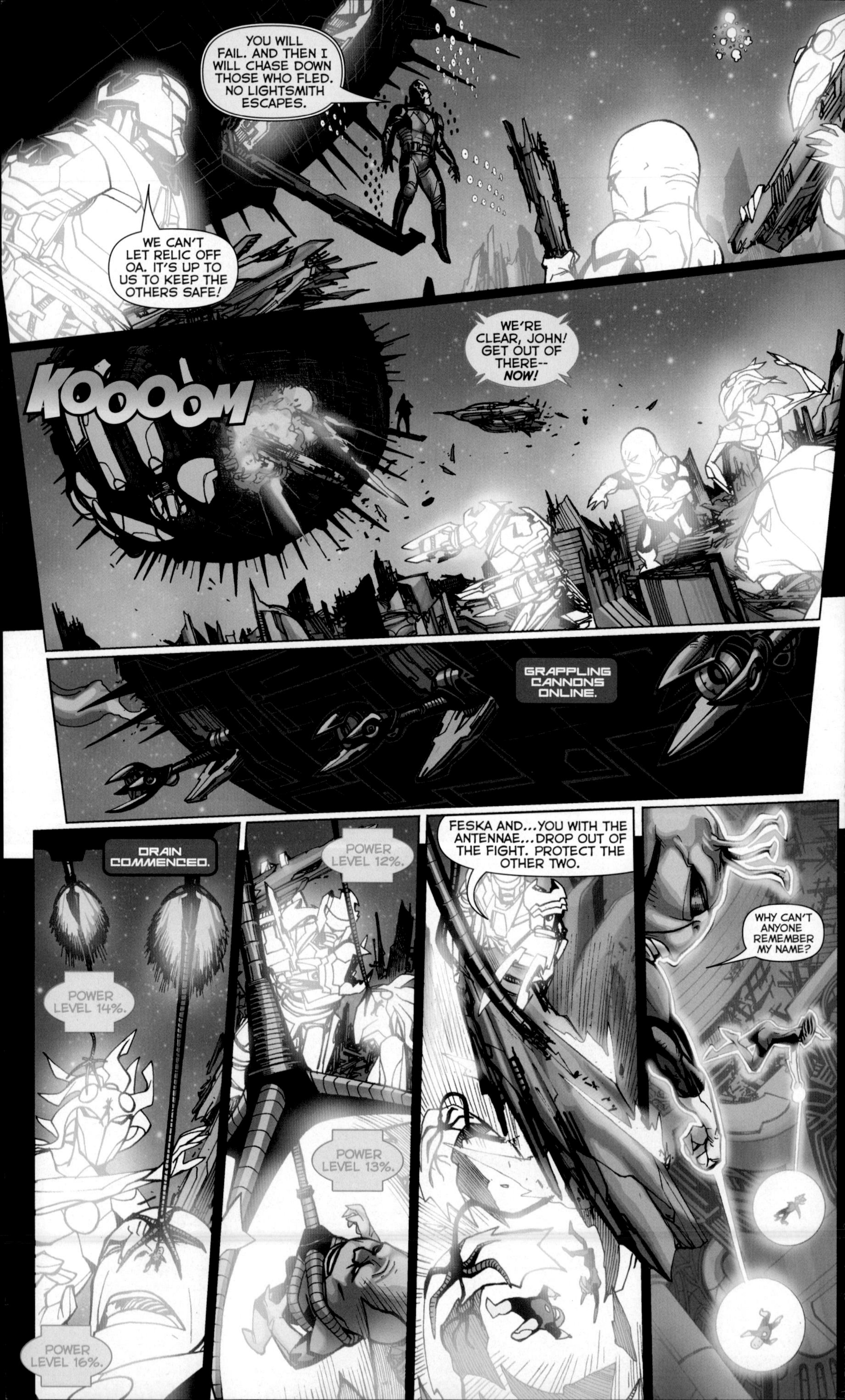

YOU WILL FAIL. AND THEN I WILL CHASE DOWN THOSE WHO FLED. NO LIGHTSMITH ESCAPES.
WE CAN'T LET RELIC OFF OA. IT'S UP TO US TO KEEP THE OTHERS SAFE!
KOOOOOM
WE'RE CLEAR, JOHN! GET OUT OF THERE-- NOW!
GRAPPLING CANNONS ONLINE.
DRAIN COMMENCED.
POWER LEVEL 14%.
POWER LEVEL 16%.
POWER LEVEL 12%.
POWER LEVEL 13%.
FESKA AND...YOU WITH THE ANTENNAE...DROP OUT OF THE FIGHT. PROTECT THE OTHER TWO.
WHY CAN'T ANYONE REMEMBER MY NAME?

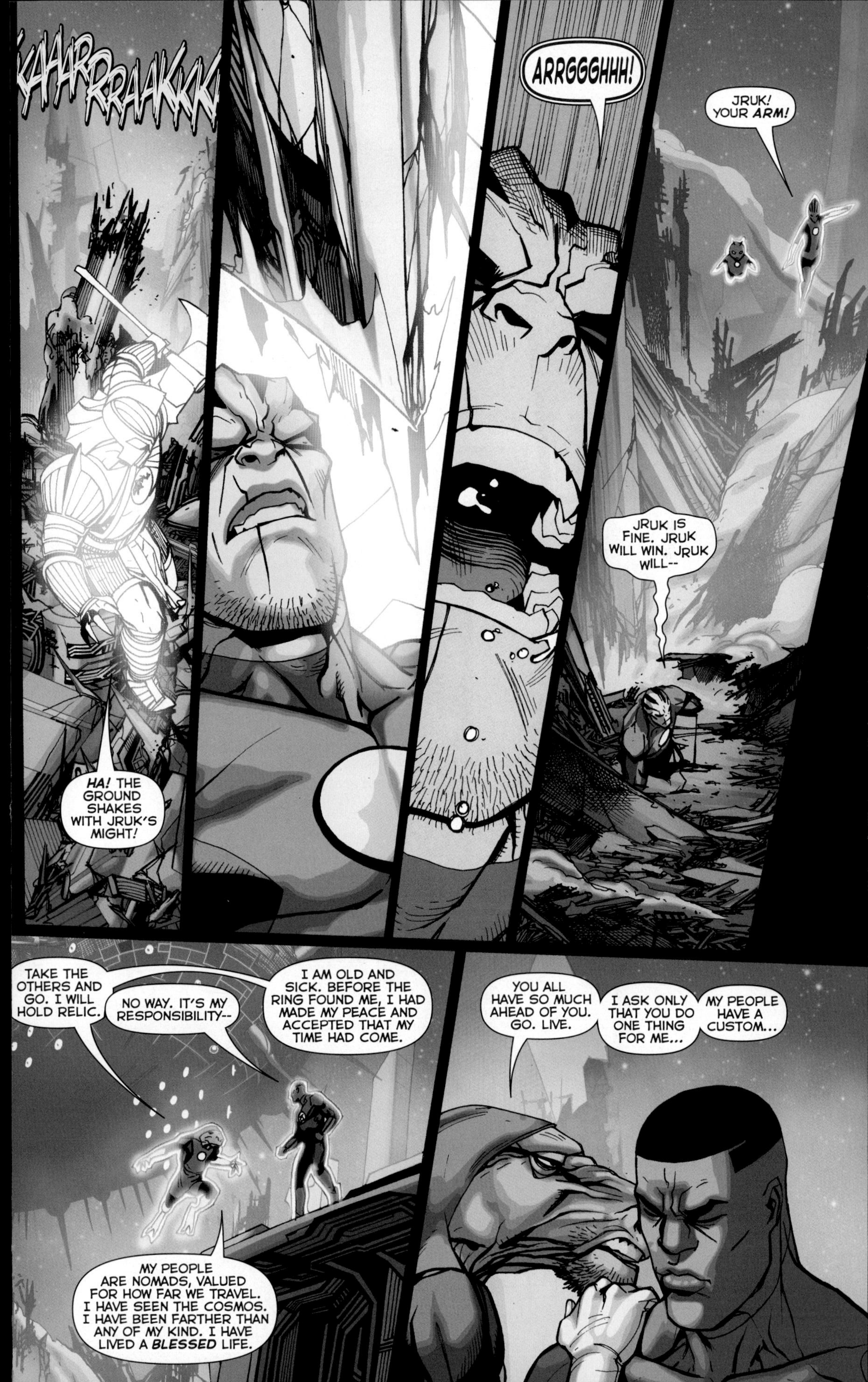
KAAARRRAAKKK
HA! THE GROUND SHAKES WITH JRUK'S MIGHT!
ARRGGGHHH!
JRUK! YOUR ARM!
JRUK IS FINE. JRUK WILL WIN. JRUK WILL--
TAKE THE OTHERS AND GO. I WILL HOLD RELIC.
NO WAY. IT'S MY RESPONSIBILITY--
I AM OLD AND SICK. BEFORE THE RING FOUND ME, I HAD MADE MY PEACE AND ACCEPTED THAT MY TIME HAD COME.
MY PEOPLE ARE NOMADS, VALUED FOR HOW FAR WE TRAVEL. I HAVE SEEN THE COSMOS. I HAVE BEEN FARTHER THAN ANY OF MY KIND. I HAVE LIVED A BLESSED LIFE.
YOU ALL HAVE SO MUCH AHEAD OF YOU. GO. LIVE.
I ASK ONLY THAT YOU DO ONE THING FOR ME...
MY PEOPLE HAVE A CUSTOM...

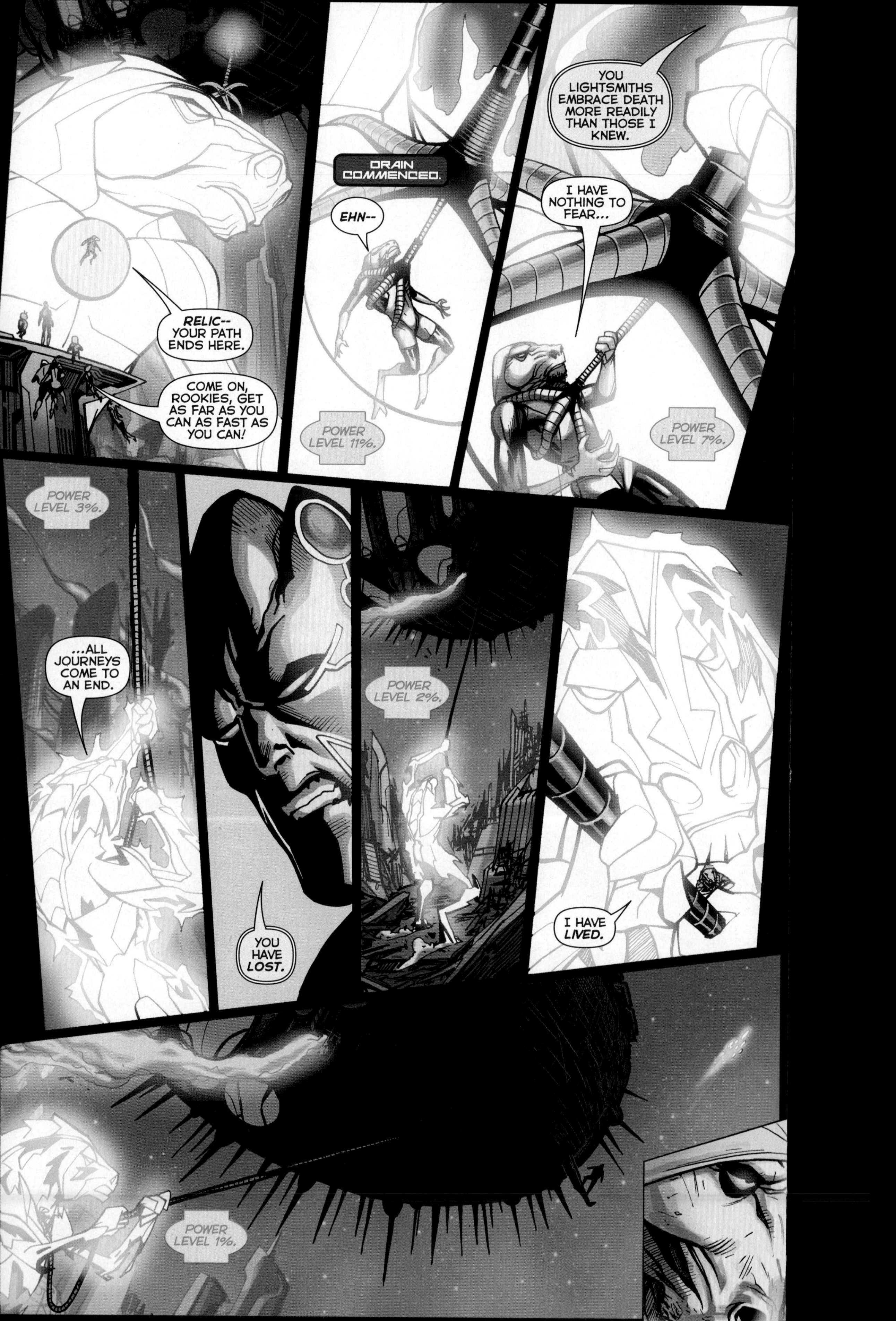
RELIC--
YOUR PATH ENDS HERE.
COME ON, ROOKIES, GET AS FAR AS YOU CAN AS FAST AS YOU CAN!
DRAIN COMMENCED.
EHN--
POWER LEVEL 11%.
YOU LIGHTSMITHS EMBRACE DEATH MORE READILY THAN THOSE I KNEW.
I HAVE NOTHING TO FEAR...
POWER LEVEL 7%.
POWER LEVEL 3%.
...ALL JOURNEYS COME TO AN END.
YOU HAVE LOST.
POWER LEVEL 2%.
I HAVE LIVED.
POWER LEVEL 1%.

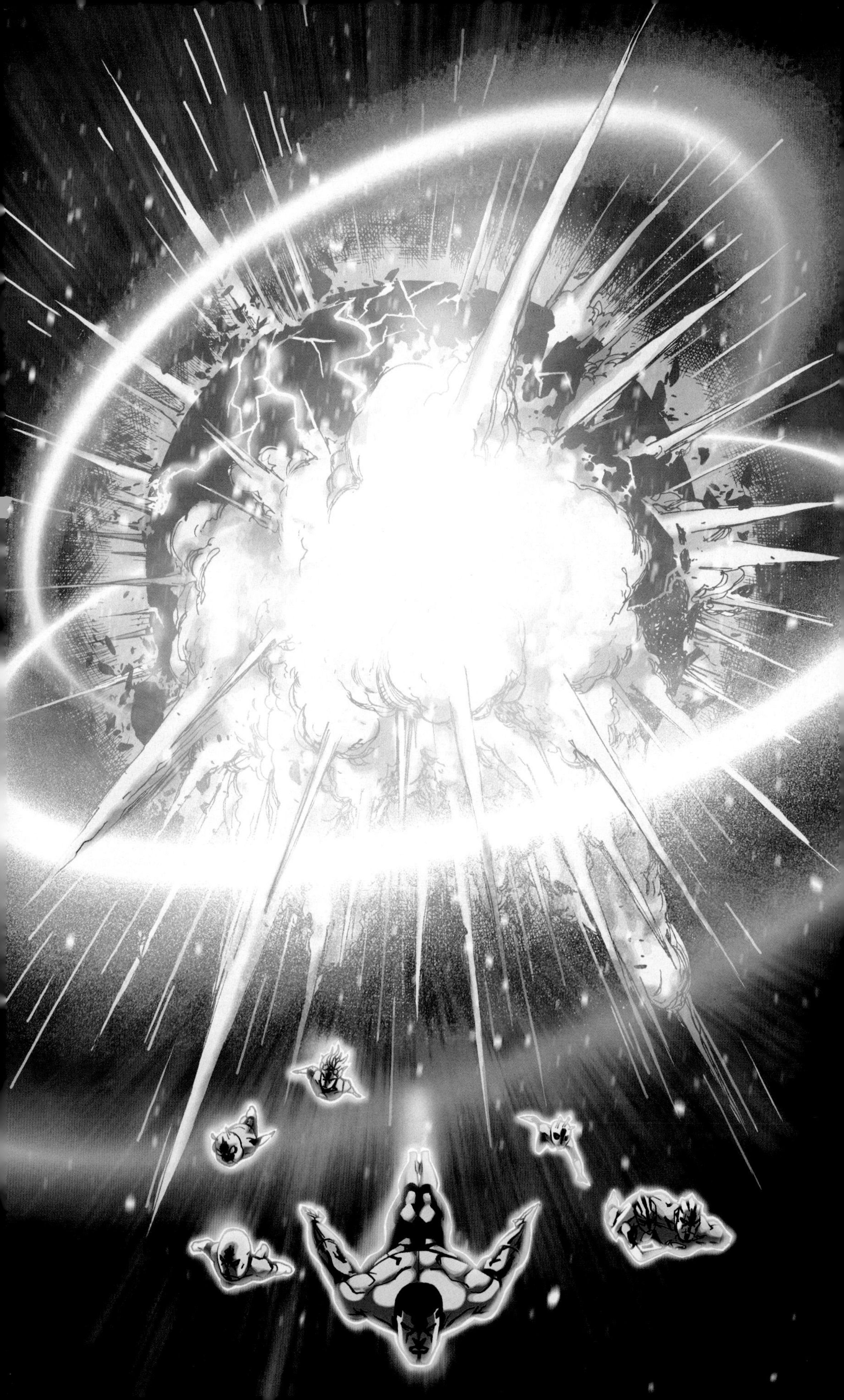

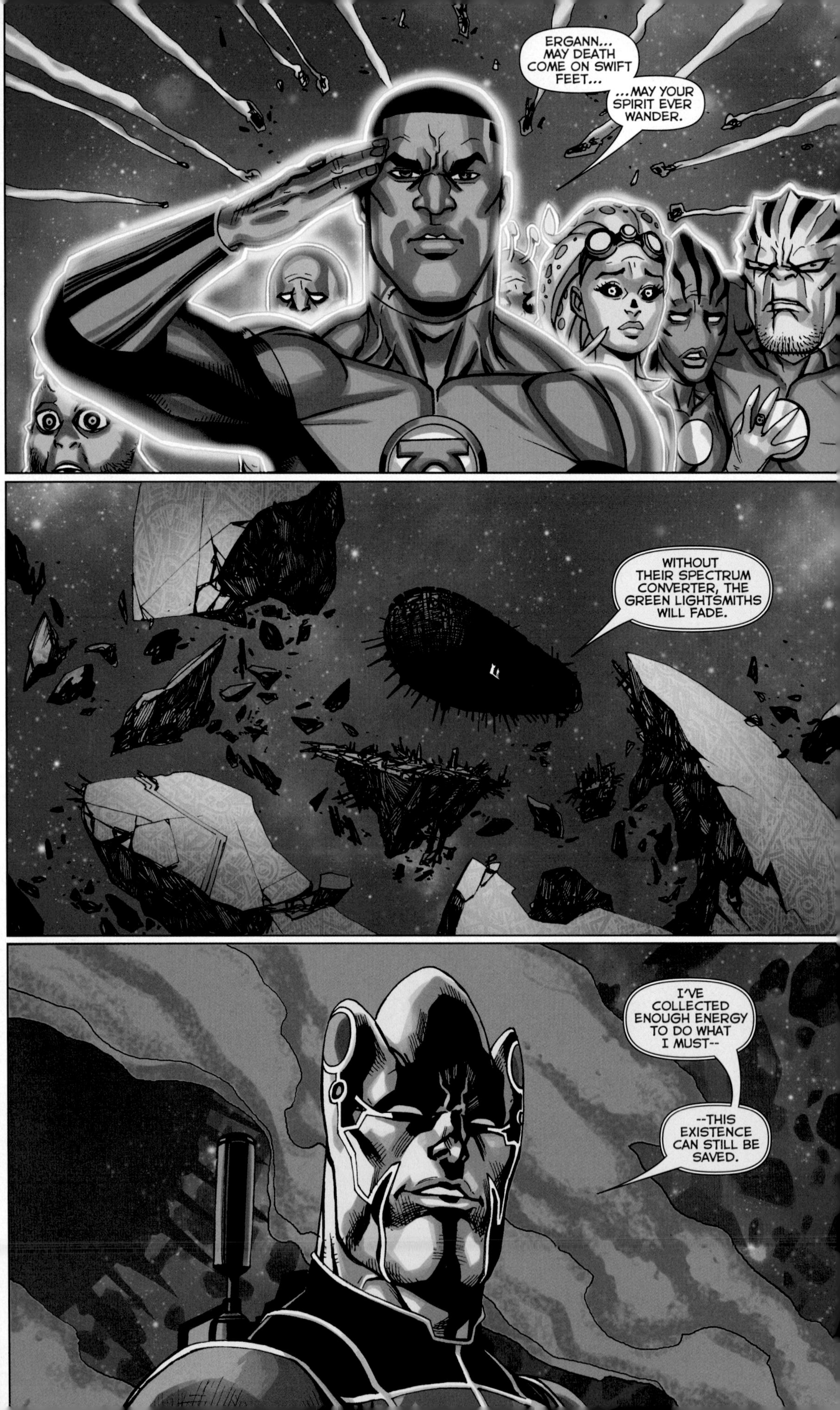
ERGANN... MAY DEATH COME ON SWIFT FEET...
...MAY YOUR SPIRIT EVER WANDER.
WITHOUT THEIR SPECTRUM CONVERTER, THE GREEN LIGHTSMITHS WILL FADE.
I'VE COLLECTED ENOUGH ENERGY TO DO WHAT I MUST--
--THIS EXISTENCE CAN STILL BE SAVED.

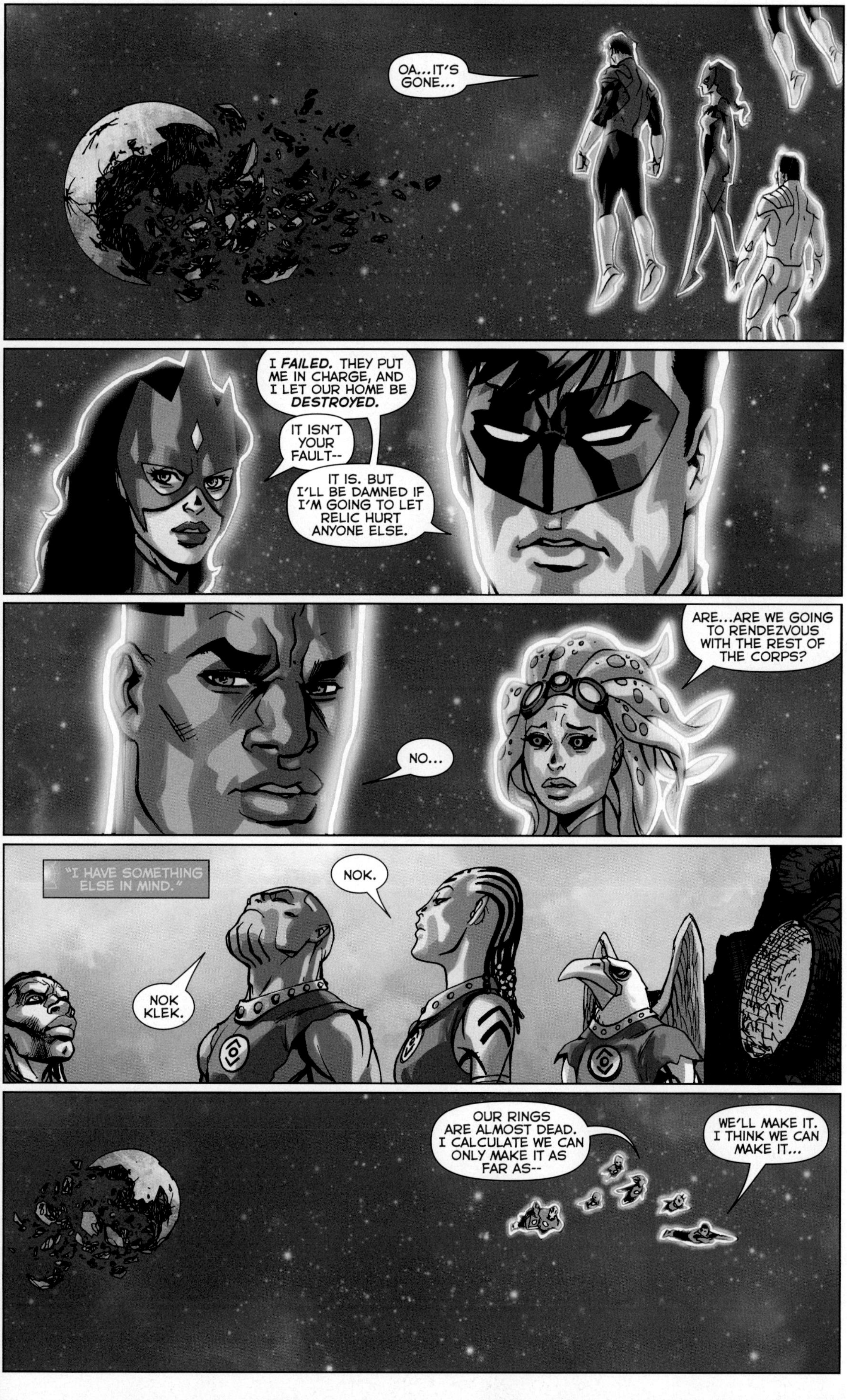
OA...IT'S GONE...
I FAILED. THEY PUT ME IN CHARGE, AND I LET OUR HOME BE DESTROYED.
IT ISN'T YOUR FAULT--
IT IS. BUT I'LL BE DAMNED IF I'M GOING TO LET RELIC HURT ANYONE ELSE.
ARE...ARE WE GOING TO RENDEZVOUS WITH THE REST OF THE CORPS?
NO...
"I HAVE SOMETHING ELSE IN MIND."
NOK.
NOK KLEK.
OUR RINGS ARE ALMOST DEAD. I CALCULATE WE CAN ONLY MAKE IT AS FAR AS--
WE'LL MAKE IT. I THINK WE CAN MAKE IT...

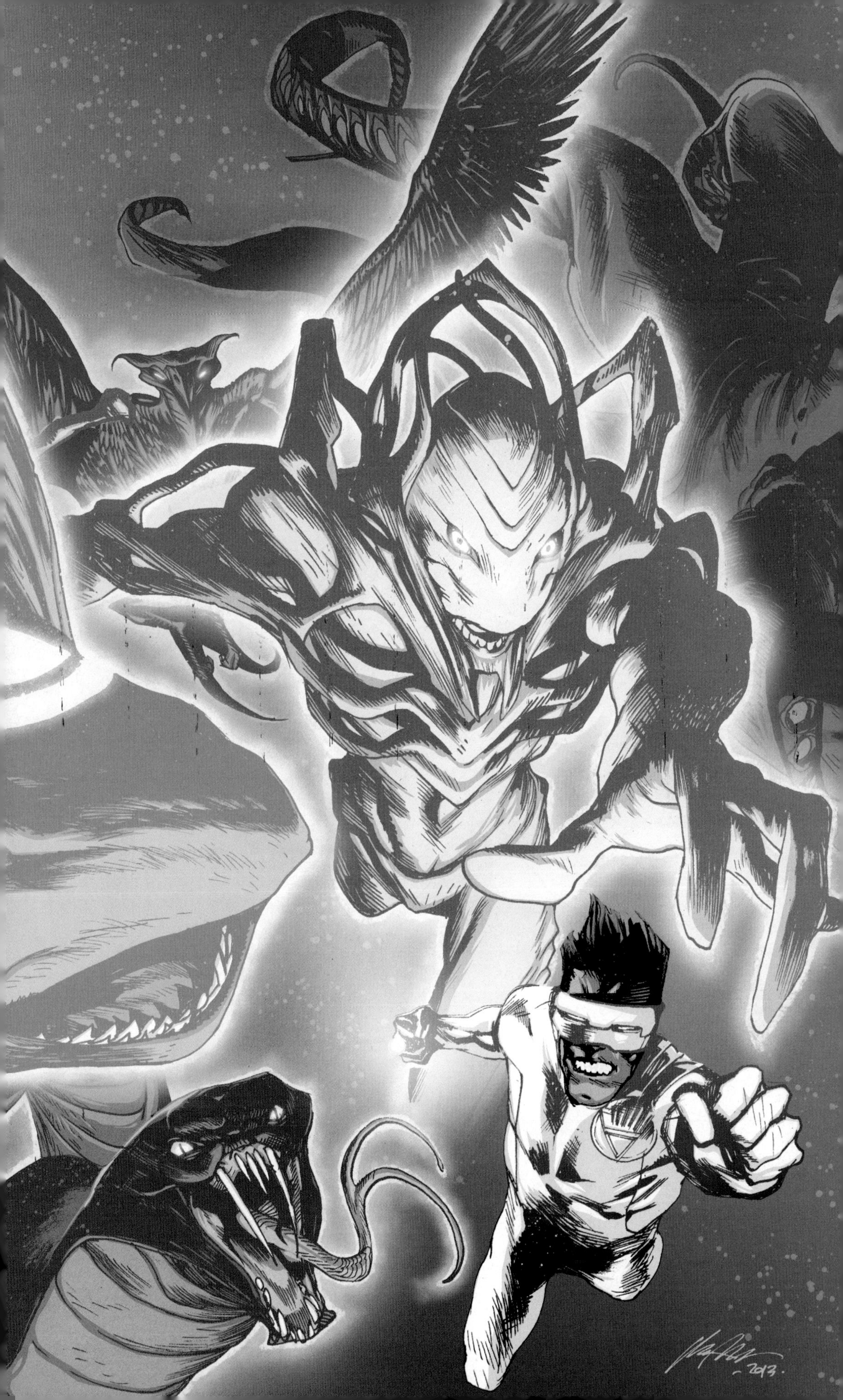

LIGHTS OUT part three: GODS AND MONSTERS

JUSTIN JORDAN writer BRAD WALKER penciller DREW HENNESSY with MARC DEERING and RYAN WINN inkers WIL QUINTANA colorist
RAFAEL ALBUQUERQUE with DAVE McCAIG cover artists

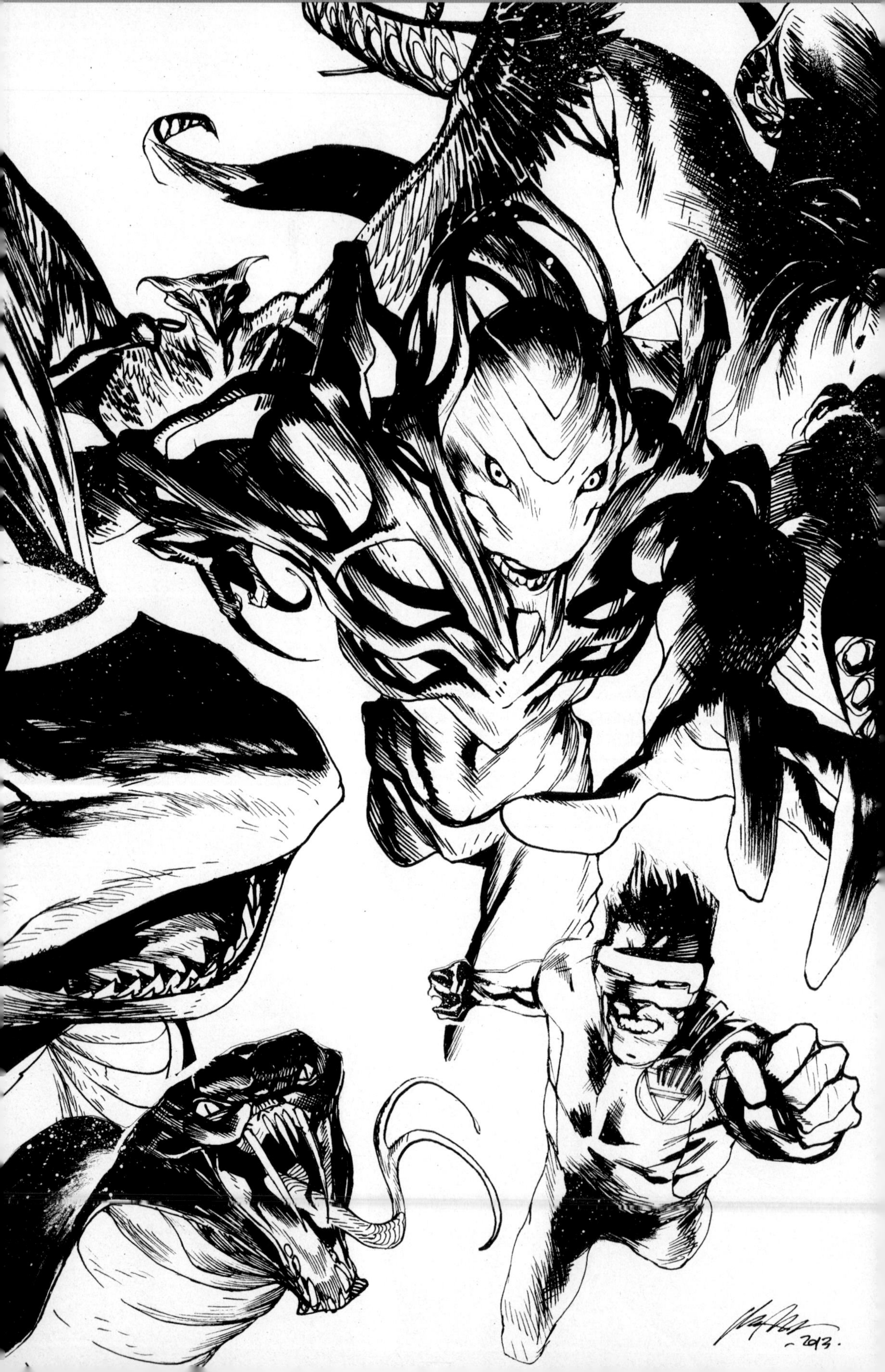

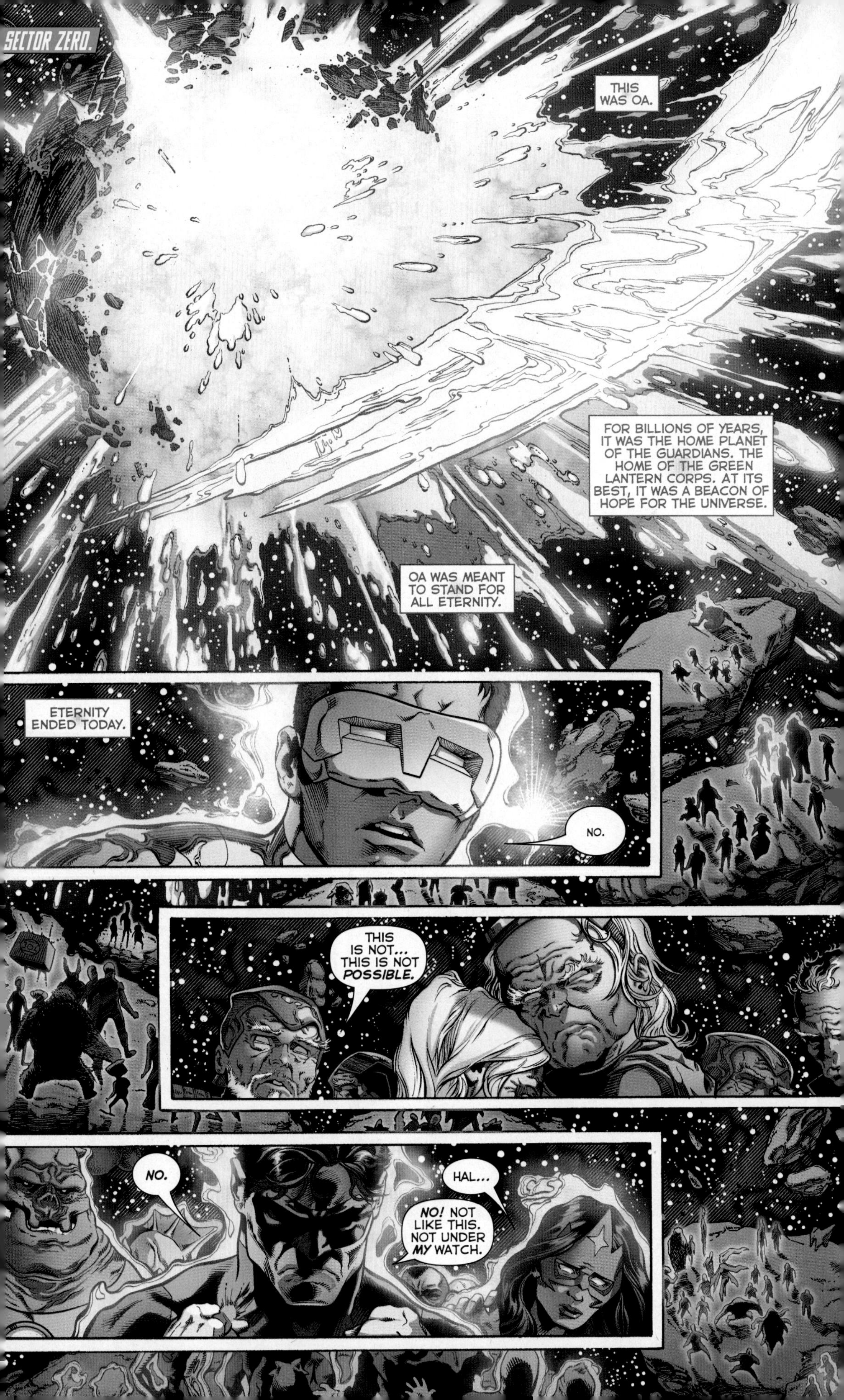
SECTOR ZERO.
THIS WAS OA.
FOR BILLIONS OF YEARS, IT WAS THE HOME PLANET OF THE GUARDIANS. THE HOME OF THE GREEN LANTERN CORPS. AT ITS BEST, IT WAS A BEACON OF HOPE FOR THE UNIVERSE.
OA WAS MEANT TO STAND FOR ALL ETERNITY.
ETERNITY ENDED TODAY.
NO.
THIS IS NOT... THIS IS NOT *POSSIBLE.*
NO.
HAL...
NO! NOT LIKE THIS. NOT UNDER *MY* WATCH.

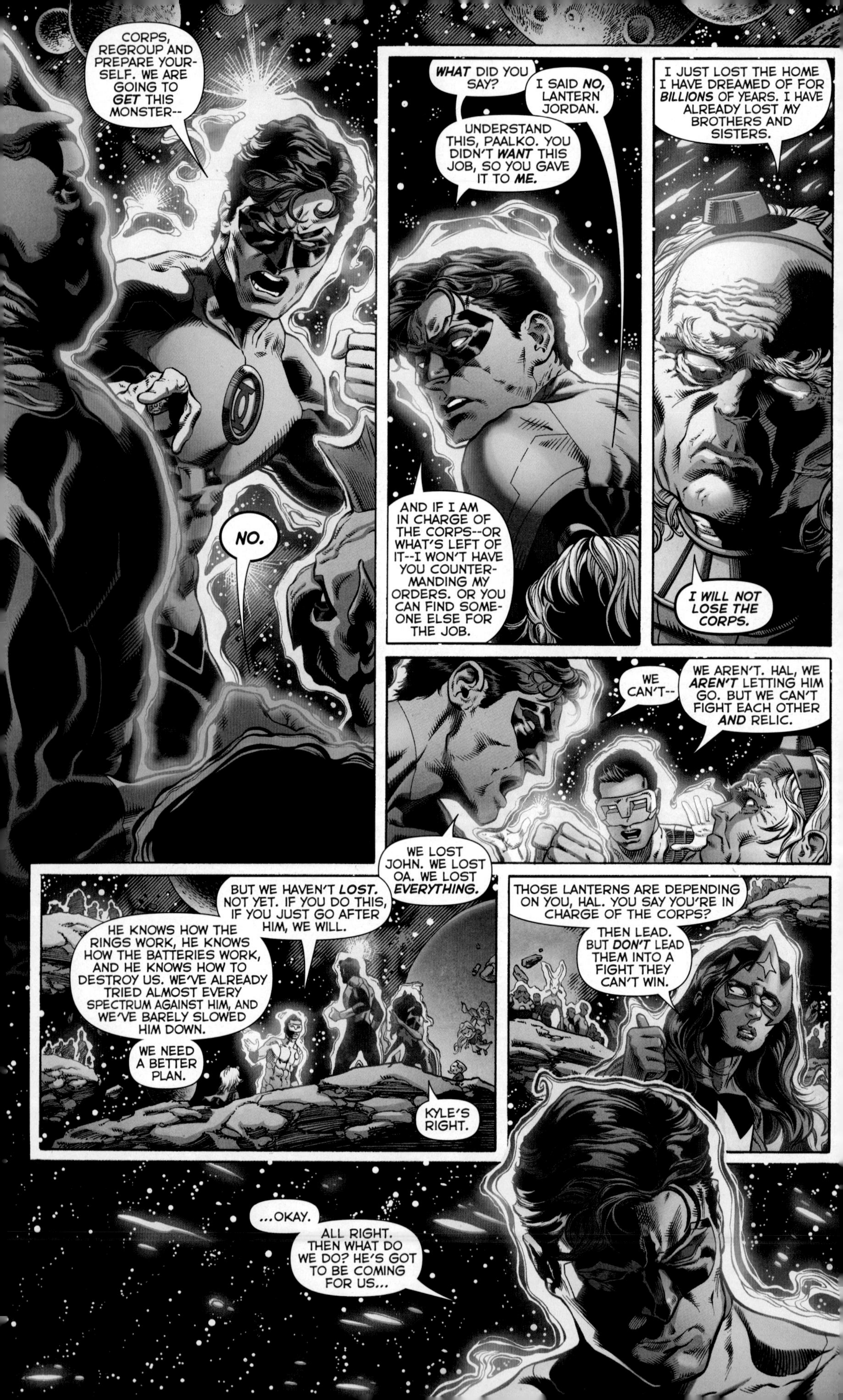
CORPS, REGROUP AND PREPARE YOURSELF. WE ARE GOING TO **GET** THIS MONSTER--
NO.
WHAT DID YOU SAY?
I SAID **NO,** LANTERN JORDAN.
UNDERSTAND THIS, PAALKO. YOU DIDN'T **WANT** THIS JOB, SO YOU GAVE IT TO **ME.**
AND IF I AM IN CHARGE OF THE CORPS--OR WHAT'S LEFT OF IT--I WON'T HAVE YOU COUNTERMANDING MY ORDERS. OR YOU CAN FIND SOMEONE ELSE FOR THE JOB.
I JUST LOST THE HOME I HAVE DREAMED OF FOR **BILLIONS** OF YEARS. I HAVE ALREADY LOST MY BROTHERS AND SISTERS.
I WILL NOT LOSE THE CORPS.
WE CAN'T--
WE AREN'T. HAL, WE **AREN'T** LETTING HIM GO. BUT WE CAN'T FIGHT EACH OTHER **AND** RELIC.
WE LOST JOHN. WE LOST OA. WE LOST **EVERYTHING.**
BUT WE HAVEN'T **LOST.** NOT YET. IF YOU DO THIS, IF YOU JUST GO AFTER HIM, WE WILL.
HE KNOWS HOW THE RINGS WORK, HE KNOWS HOW THE BATTERIES WORK, AND HE KNOWS HOW TO DESTROY US. WE'VE ALREADY TRIED ALMOST EVERY SPECTRUM AGAINST HIM, AND WE'VE BARELY SLOWED HIM DOWN.
WE NEED A BETTER PLAN.
KYLE'S RIGHT.
THOSE LANTERNS ARE DEPENDING ON YOU, HAL. YOU SAY YOU'RE IN CHARGE OF THE CORPS?
THEN LEAD. BUT **DON'T** LEAD THEM INTO A FIGHT THEY CAN'T WIN.
...OKAY.
ALL RIGHT. THEN WHAT DO WE DO? HE'S GOT TO BE COMING FOR US...

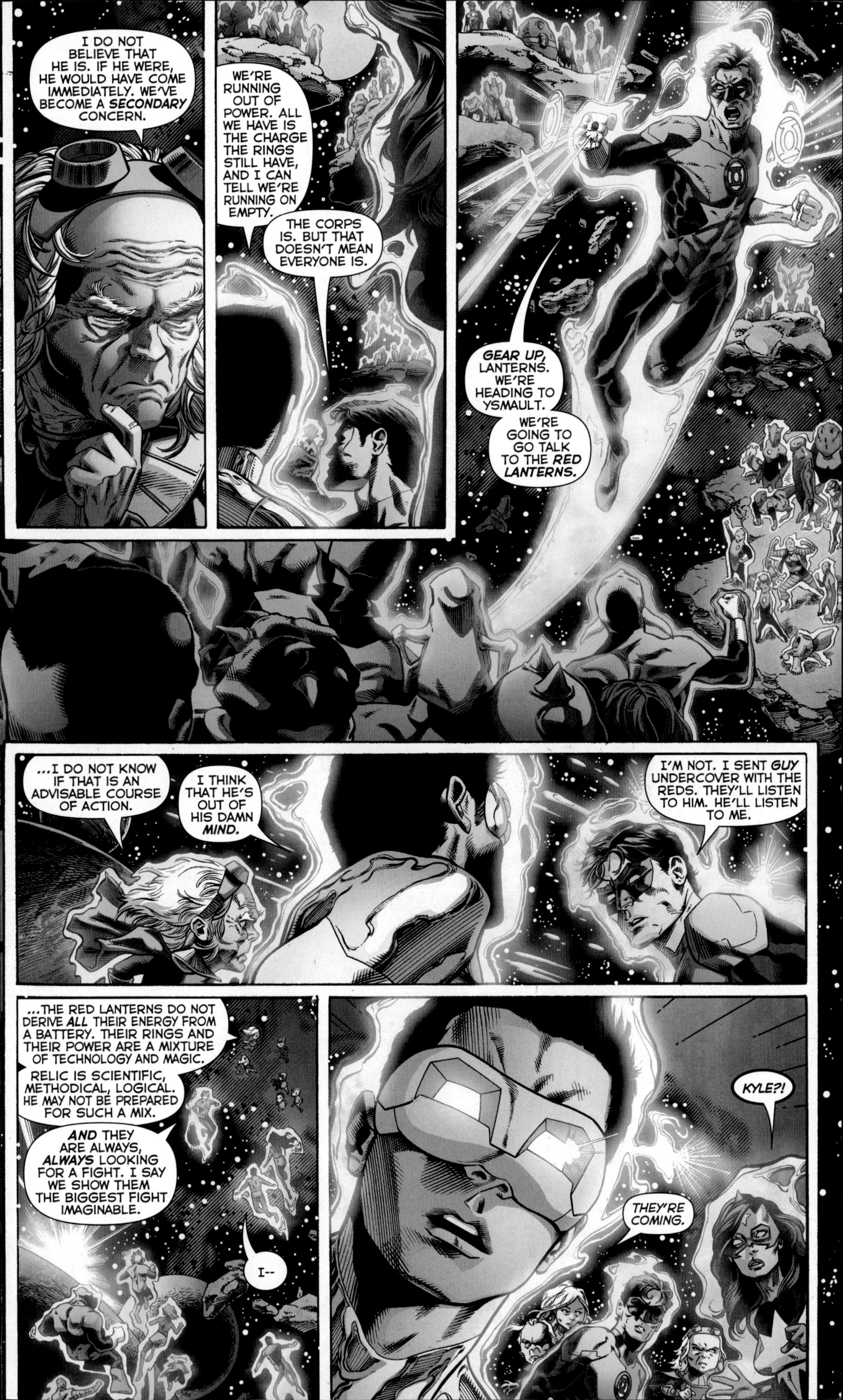
I DO NOT BELIEVE THAT HE IS. IF HE WERE, HE WOULD HAVE COME IMMEDIATELY. WE'VE BECOME A SECONDARY CONCERN.
WE'RE RUNNING OUT OF POWER. ALL WE HAVE IS THE CHARGE THE RINGS STILL HAVE, AND I CAN TELL WE'RE RUNNING ON EMPTY.
THE CORPS IS. BUT THAT DOESN'T MEAN EVERYONE IS.
GEAR UP, LANTERNS. WE'RE HEADING TO YSMAULT.
WE'RE GOING TO GO TALK TO THE RED LANTERNS.
...I DO NOT KNOW IF THAT IS AN ADVISABLE COURSE OF ACTION.
I THINK THAT HE'S OUT OF HIS DAMN MIND.
I'M NOT. I SENT GUY UNDERCOVER WITH THE REDS. THEY'LL LISTEN TO HIM. HE'LL LISTEN TO ME.
...THE RED LANTERNS DO NOT DERIVE ALL THEIR ENERGY FROM A BATTERY. THEIR RINGS AND THEIR POWER ARE A MIXTURE OF TECHNOLOGY AND MAGIC.
RELIC IS SCIENTIFIC, METHODICAL, LOGICAL. HE MAY NOT BE PREPARED FOR SUCH A MIX.
AND THEY ARE ALWAYS, ALWAYS LOOKING FOR A FIGHT. I SAY WE SHOW THEM THE BIGGEST FIGHT IMAGINABLE.
I--
KYLE?!
THEY'RE COMING.

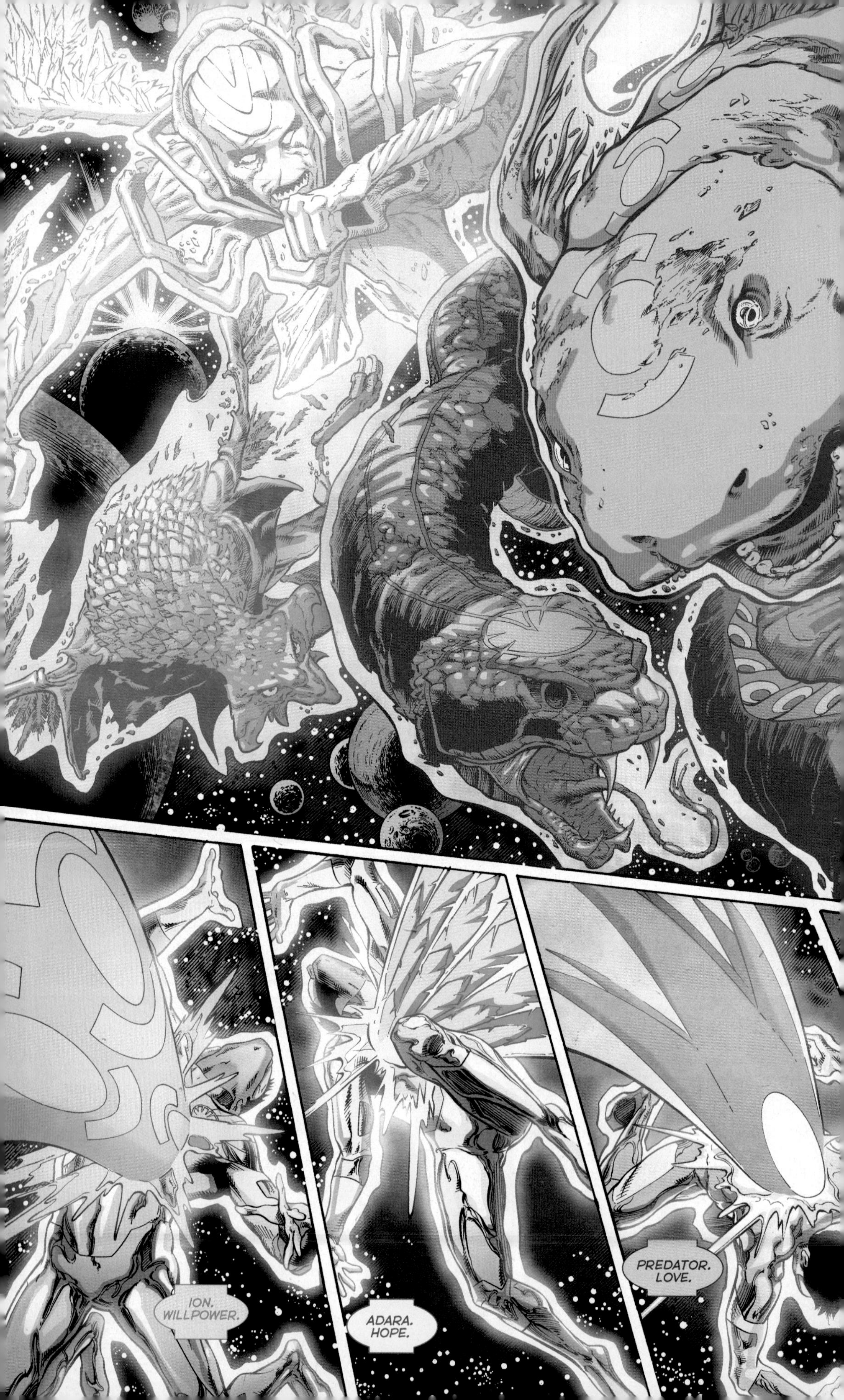
ION. WILLPOWER.
ADARA. HOPE.
PREDATOR. LOVE.

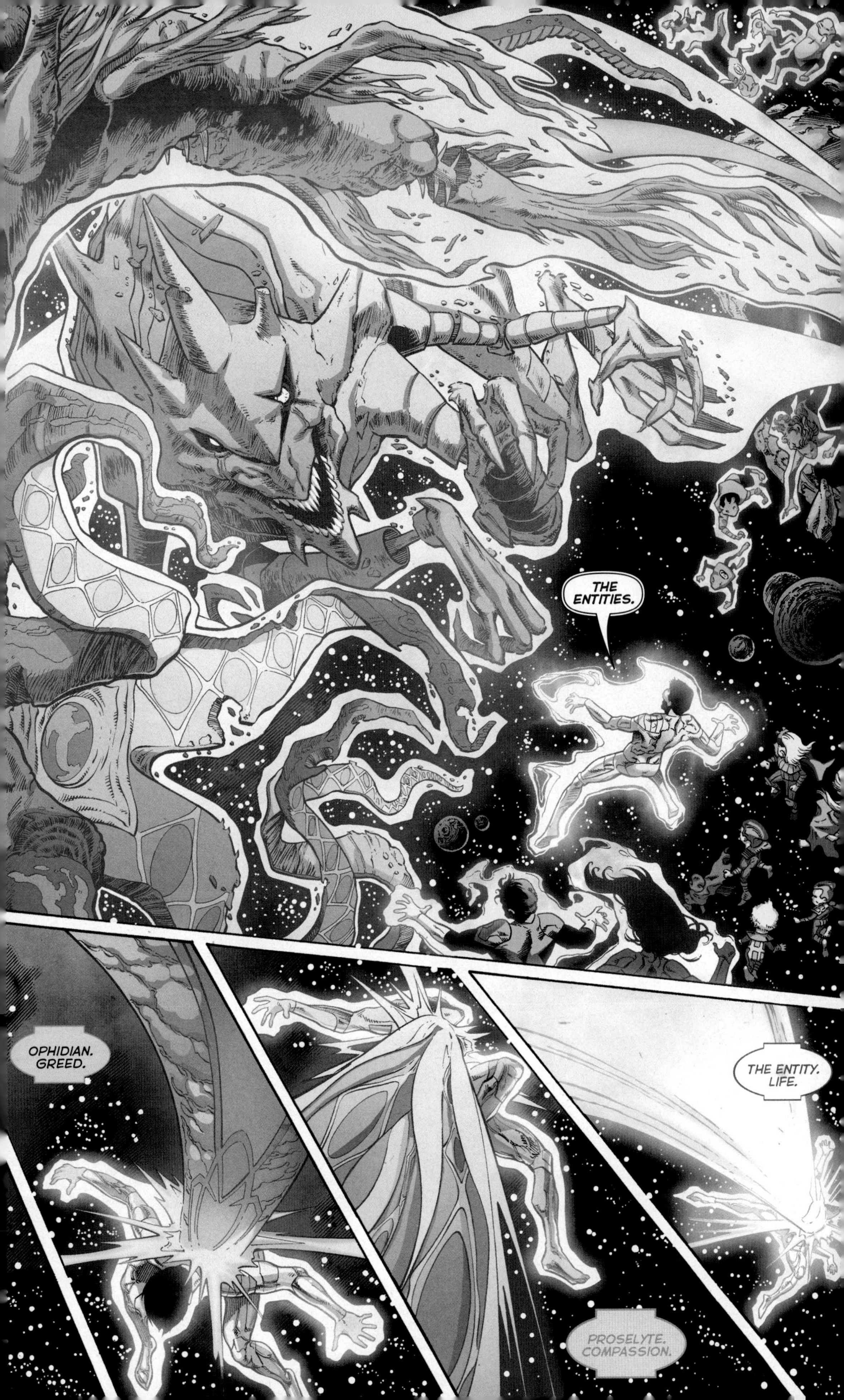
THE ENTITIES.
OPHIDIAN. GREED.
PROSELYTE. COMPASSION.
THE ENTITY. LIFE.

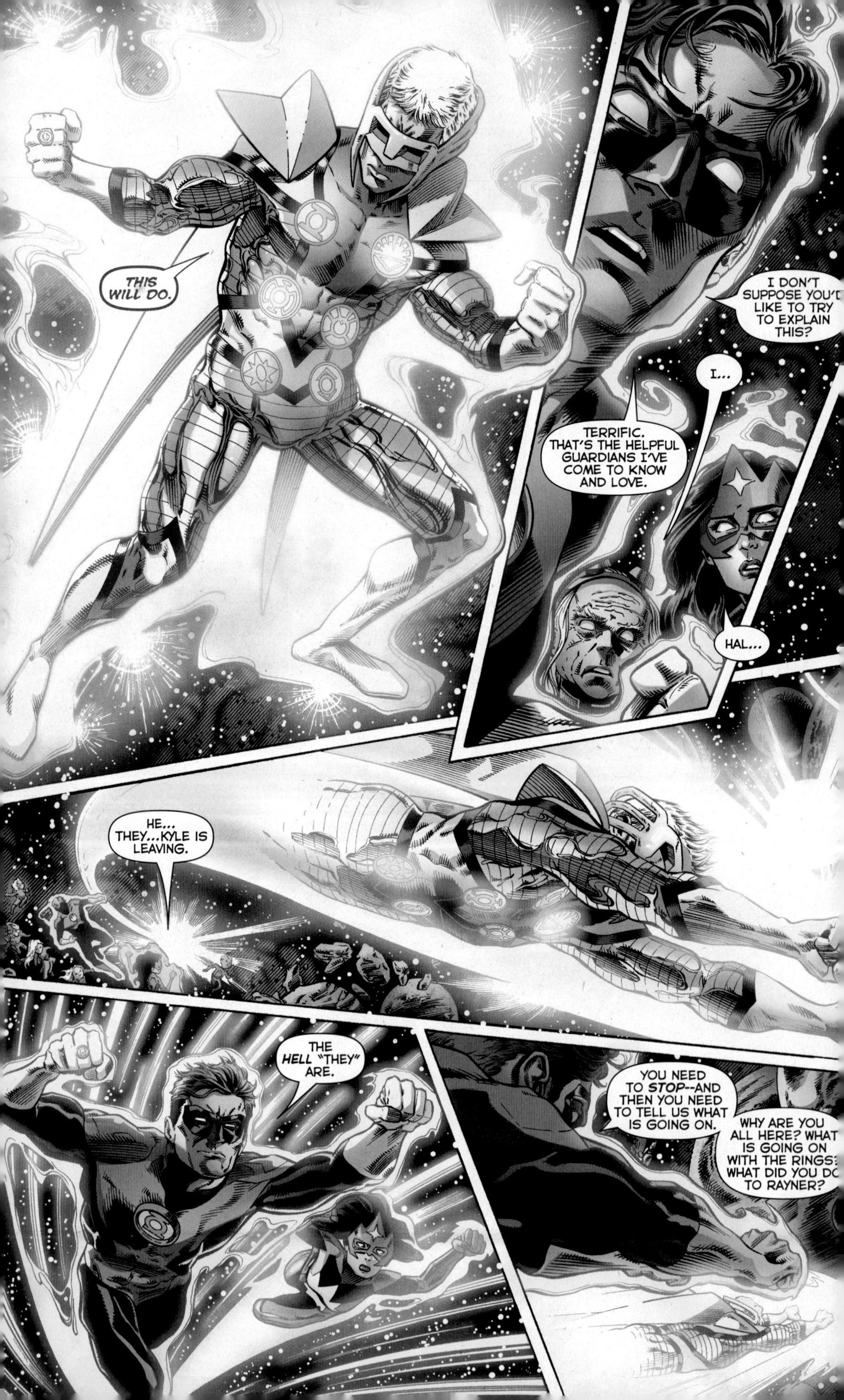
THIS WILL DO.
I DON'T SUPPOSE YOU'D LIKE TO TRY TO EXPLAIN THIS?
I...
TERRIFIC. THAT'S THE HELPFUL GUARDIANS I'VE COME TO KNOW AND LOVE.
HAL...
HE... THEY...KYLE IS LEAVING.
THE HELL "THEY" ARE.
YOU NEED TO STOP--AND THEN YOU NEED TO TELL US WHAT IS GOING ON.
WHY ARE YOU ALL HERE? WHAT IS GOING ON WITH THE RINGS? WHAT DID YOU DO TO RAYNER?

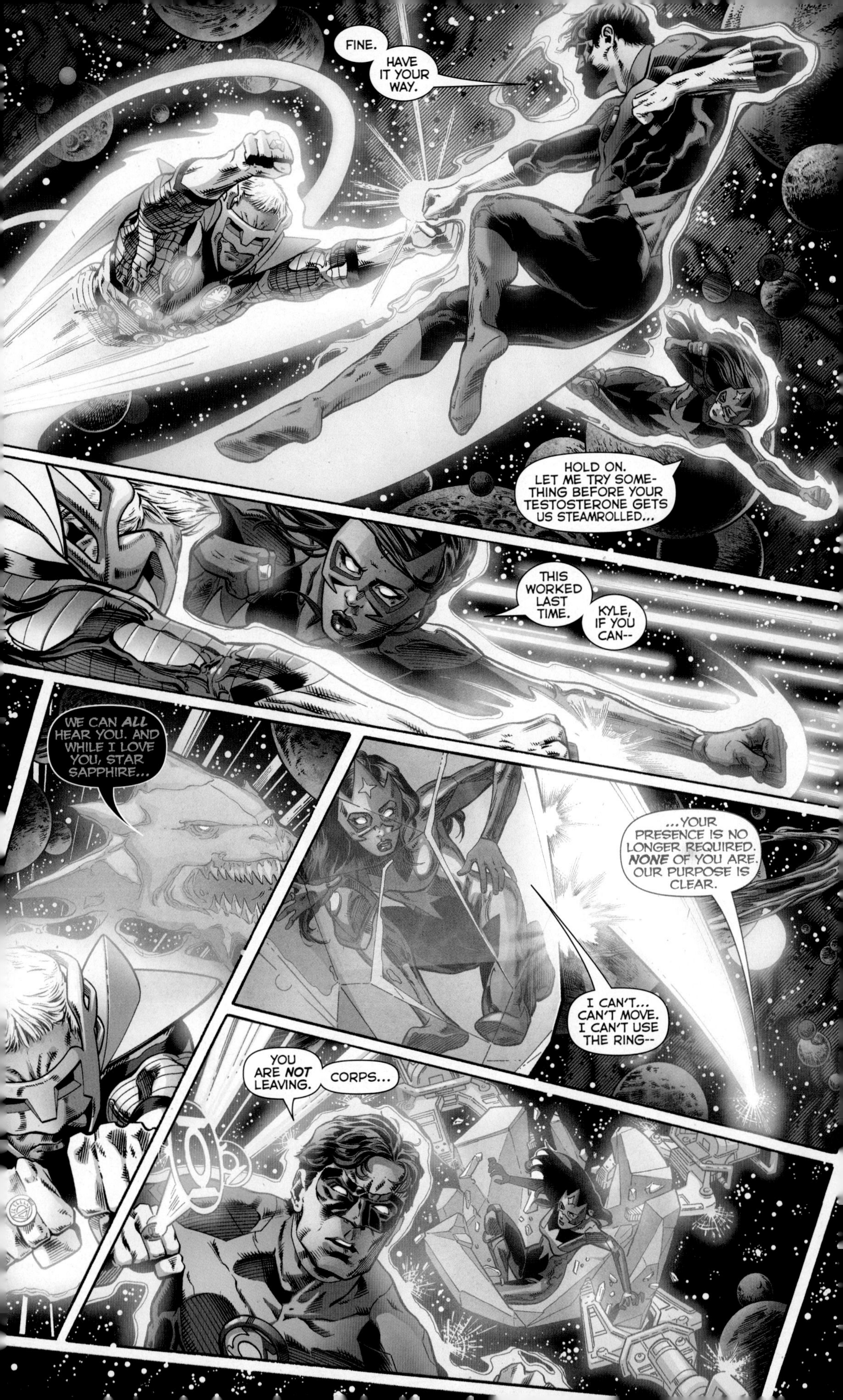
FINE.
HAVE IT YOUR WAY.
HOLD ON. LET ME TRY SOMETHING BEFORE YOUR TESTOSTERONE GETS US STEAMROLLED...
THIS WORKED LAST TIME.
KYLE, IF YOU CAN--
WE CAN ALL HEAR YOU. AND WHILE I LOVE YOU, STAR SAPPHIRE...
...YOUR PRESENCE IS NO LONGER REQUIRED. NONE OF YOU ARE. OUR PURPOSE IS CLEAR.
I CAN'T... CAN'T MOVE. I CAN'T USE THE RING--
YOU ARE NOT LEAVING.
CORPS...

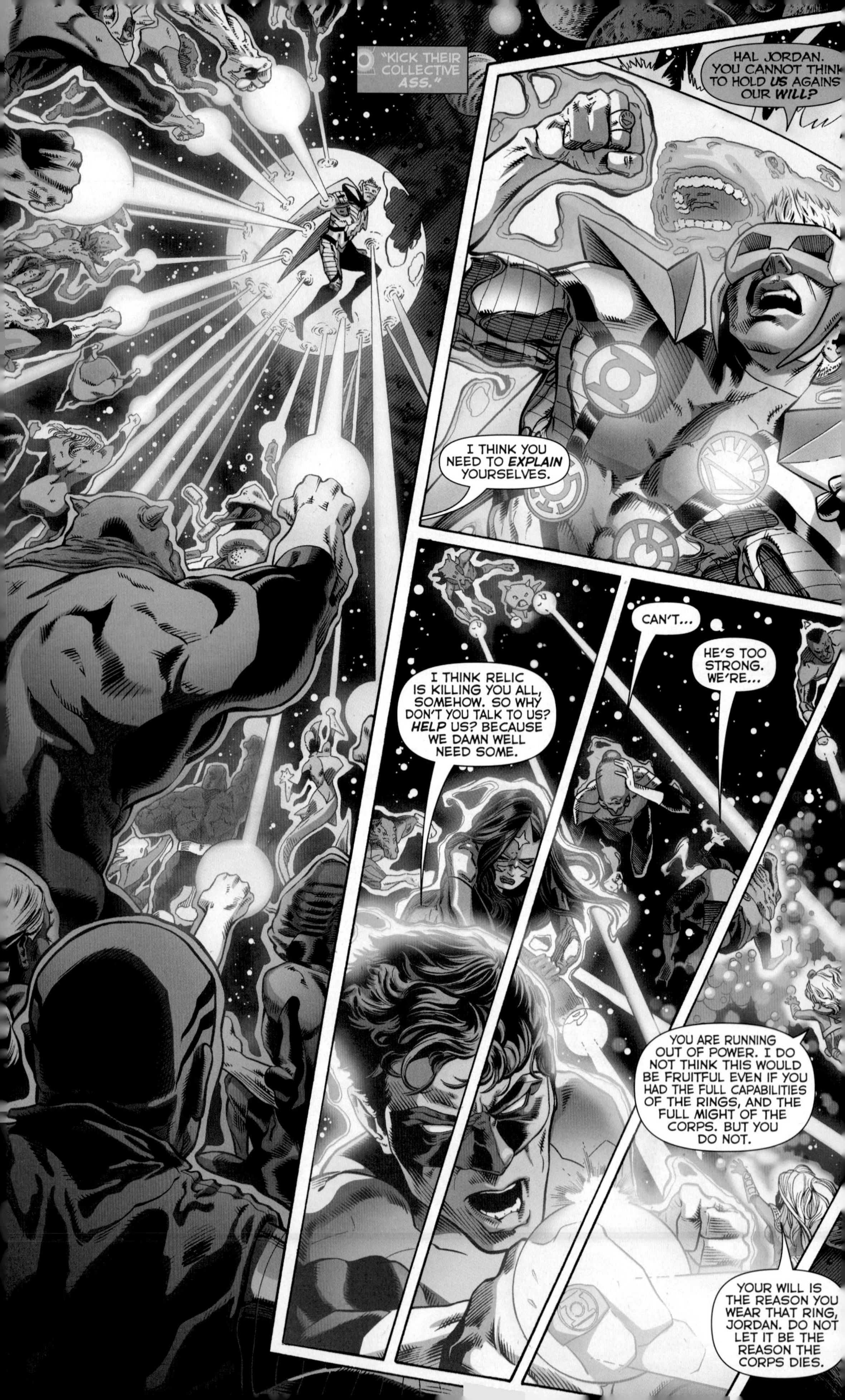
"KICK THEIR COLLECTIVE ASS."
HAL JORDAN. YOU CANNOT THINK TO HOLD US AGAINST OUR WILL?
I THINK YOU NEED TO EXPLAIN YOURSELVES.
I THINK RELIC IS KILLING YOU ALL, SOMEHOW. SO WHY DON'T YOU TALK TO US? HELP US? BECAUSE WE DAMN WELL NEED SOME.
CAN'T...
HE'S TOO STRONG. WE'RE...
YOU ARE RUNNING OUT OF POWER. I DO NOT THINK THIS WOULD BE FRUITFUL EVEN IF YOU HAD THE FULL CAPABILITIES OF THE RINGS, AND THE FULL MIGHT OF THE CORPS. BUT YOU DO NOT.
YOUR WILL IS THE REASON YOU WEAR THAT RING, JORDAN. DO NOT LET IT BE THE REASON THE CORPS DIES.

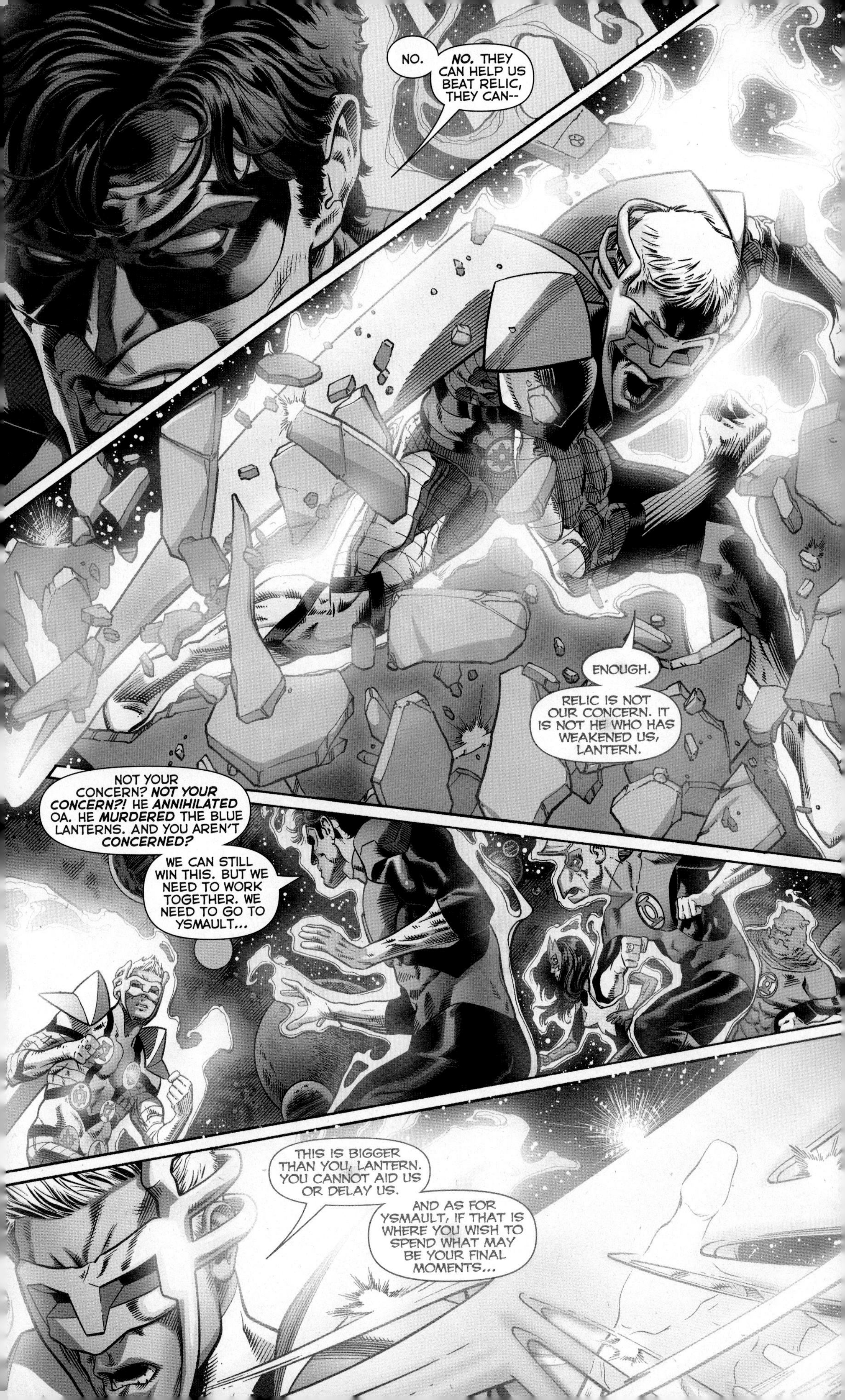
NO.
NO. THEY CAN HELP US BEAT RELIC, THEY CAN--
ENOUGH.
RELIC IS NOT OUR CONCERN. IT IS NOT HE WHO HAS WEAKENED US, LANTERN.
NOT YOUR CONCERN? NOT YOUR CONCERN?! HE ANNIHILATED OA. HE MURDERED THE BLUE LANTERNS. AND YOU AREN'T CONCERNED?
WE CAN STILL WIN THIS. BUT WE NEED TO WORK TOGETHER. WE NEED TO GO TO YSMAULT...
THIS IS BIGGER THAN YOU, LANTERN. YOU CANNOT AID US OR DELAY US.
AND AS FOR YSMAULT, IF THAT IS WHERE YOU WISH TO SPEND WHAT MAY BE YOUR FINAL MOMENTS...

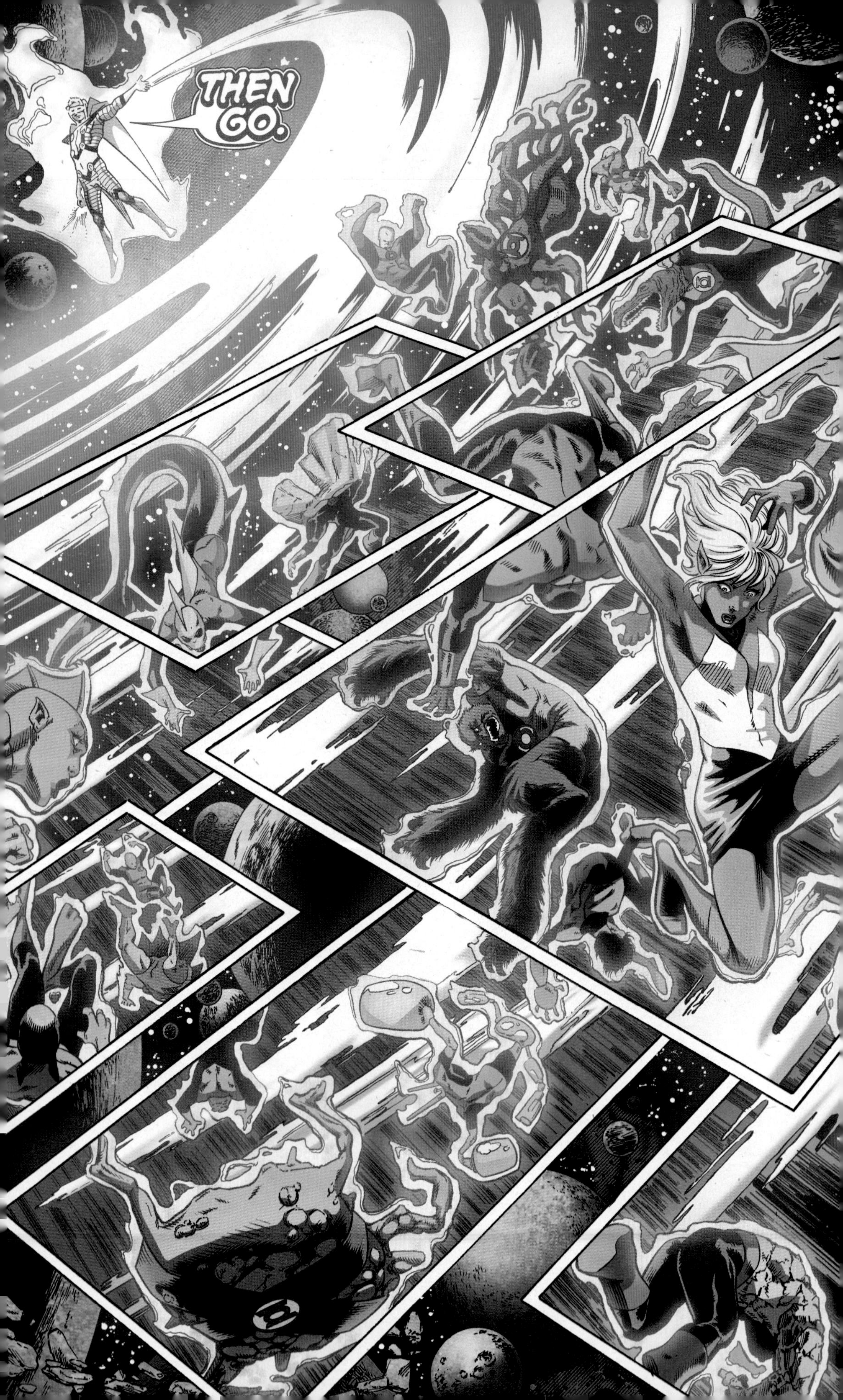
THEN GO.

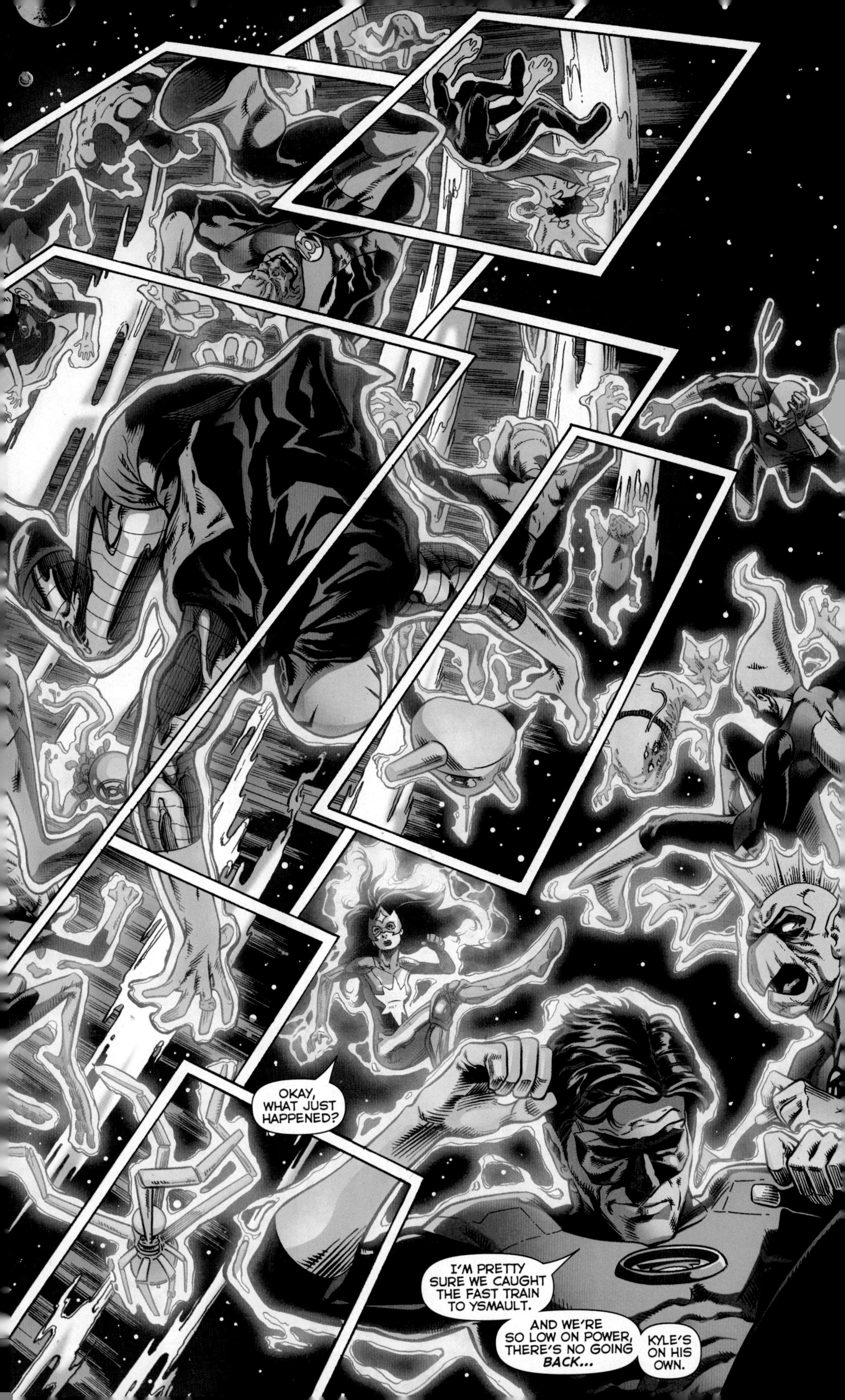
OKAY, WHAT JUST HAPPENED?
I'M PRETTY SURE WE CAUGHT THE FAST TRAIN TO YSMAULT.
AND WE'RE SO LOW ON POWER, THERE'S NO GOING BACK...
KYLE'S ON HIS OWN.

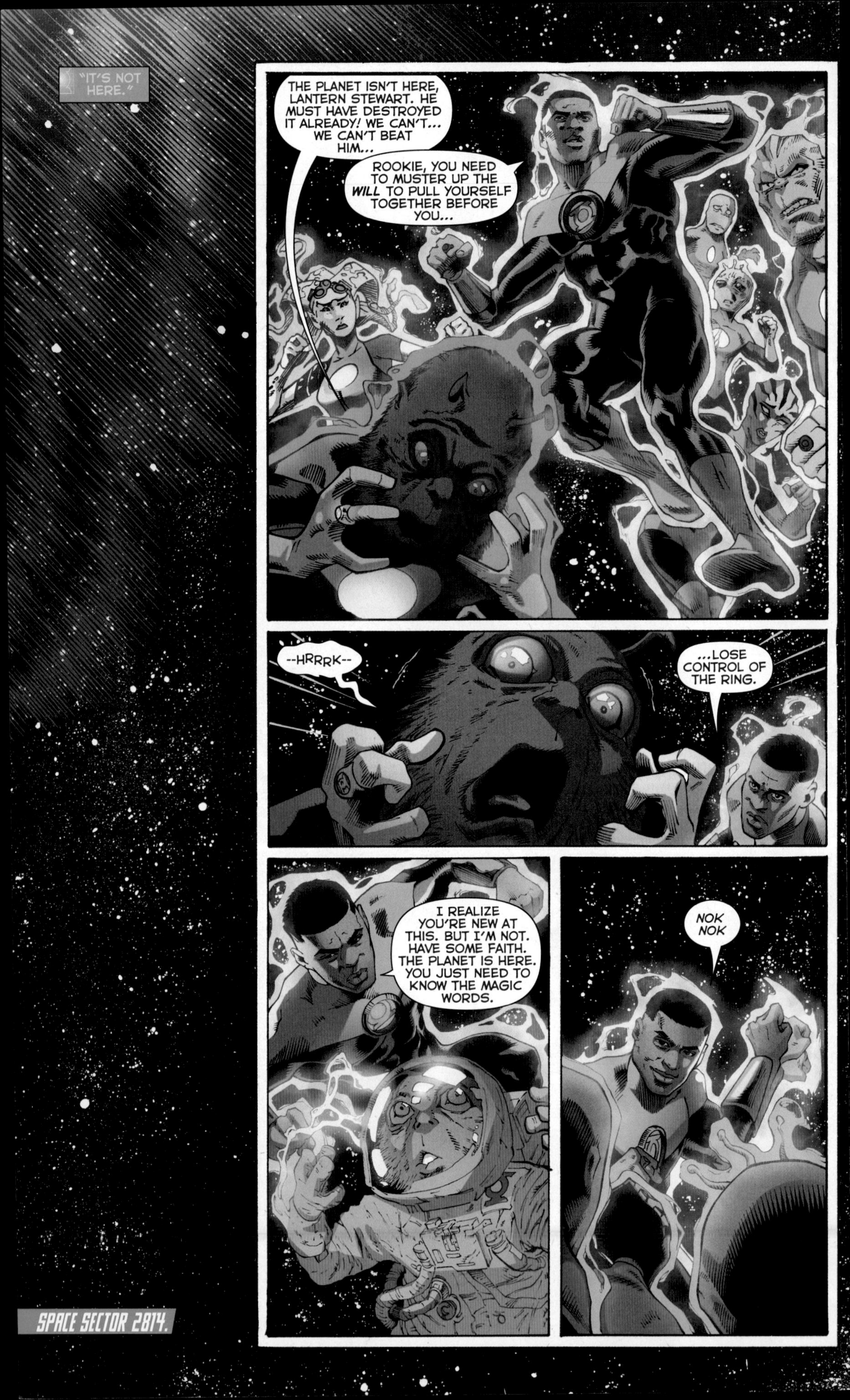
"IT'S NOT HERE."
THE PLANET ISN'T HERE, LANTERN STEWART. HE MUST HAVE DESTROYED IT ALREADY! WE CAN'T... WE CAN'T BEAT HIM...
ROOKIE, YOU NEED TO MUSTER UP THE WILL TO PULL YOURSELF TOGETHER BEFORE YOU...
--HRRRK--
...LOSE CONTROL OF THE RING.
I REALIZE YOU'RE NEW AT THIS. BUT I'M NOT. HAVE SOME FAITH. THE PLANET IS HERE. YOU JUST NEED TO KNOW THE MAGIC WORDS.
NOK NOK
SPACE SECTOR 2814.

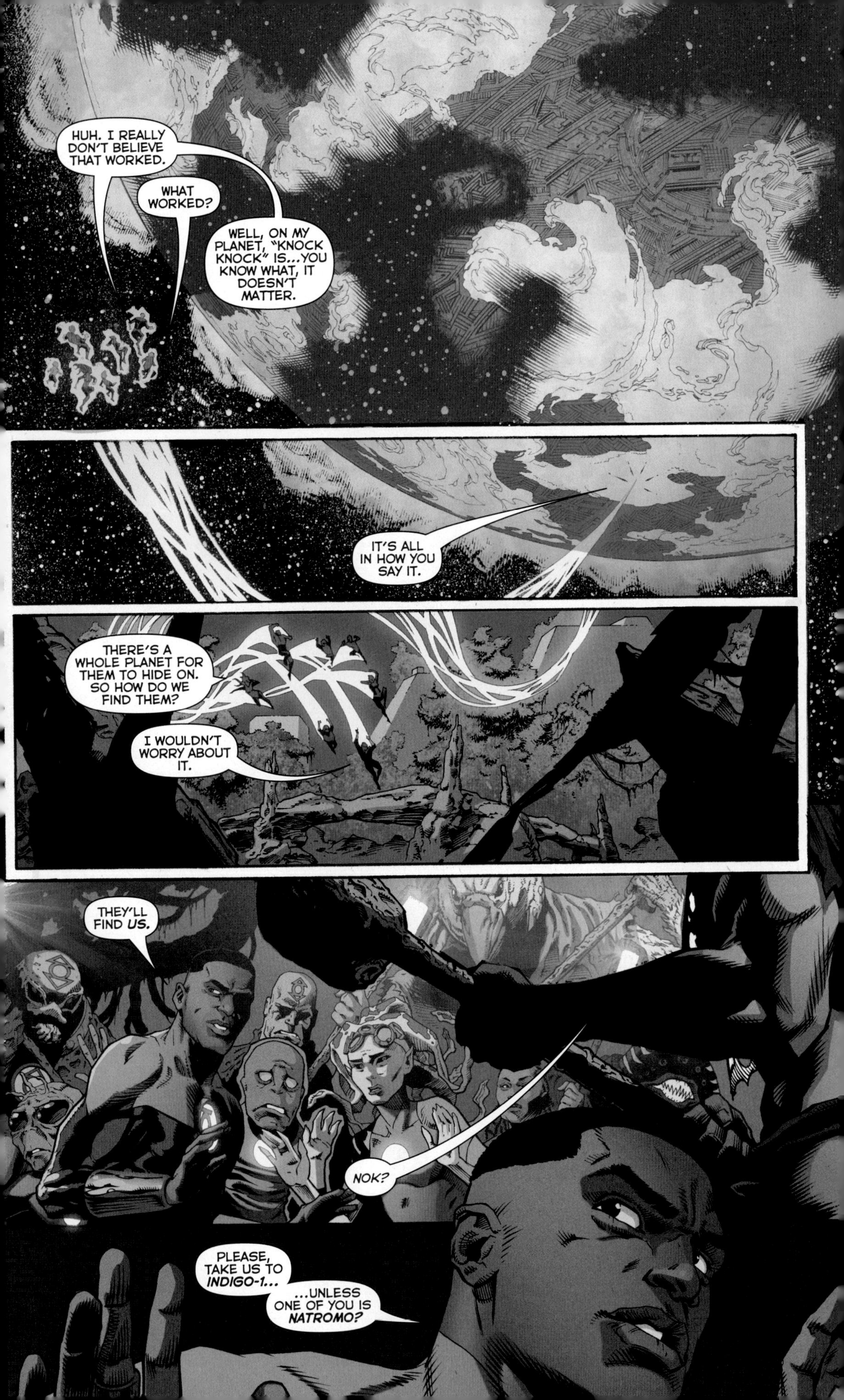
HUH. I REALLY DON'T BELIEVE THAT WORKED.
WHAT WORKED?
WELL, ON MY PLANET, "KNOCK KNOCK" IS...YOU KNOW WHAT, IT DOESN'T MATTER.
IT'S ALL IN HOW YOU SAY IT.
THERE'S A WHOLE PLANET FOR THEM TO HIDE ON. SO HOW DO WE FIND THEM?
I WOULDN'T WORRY ABOUT IT.
THEY'LL FIND US.
NOK?
PLEASE, TAKE US TO INDIGO-1...
...UNLESS ONE OF YOU IS NATROMO?

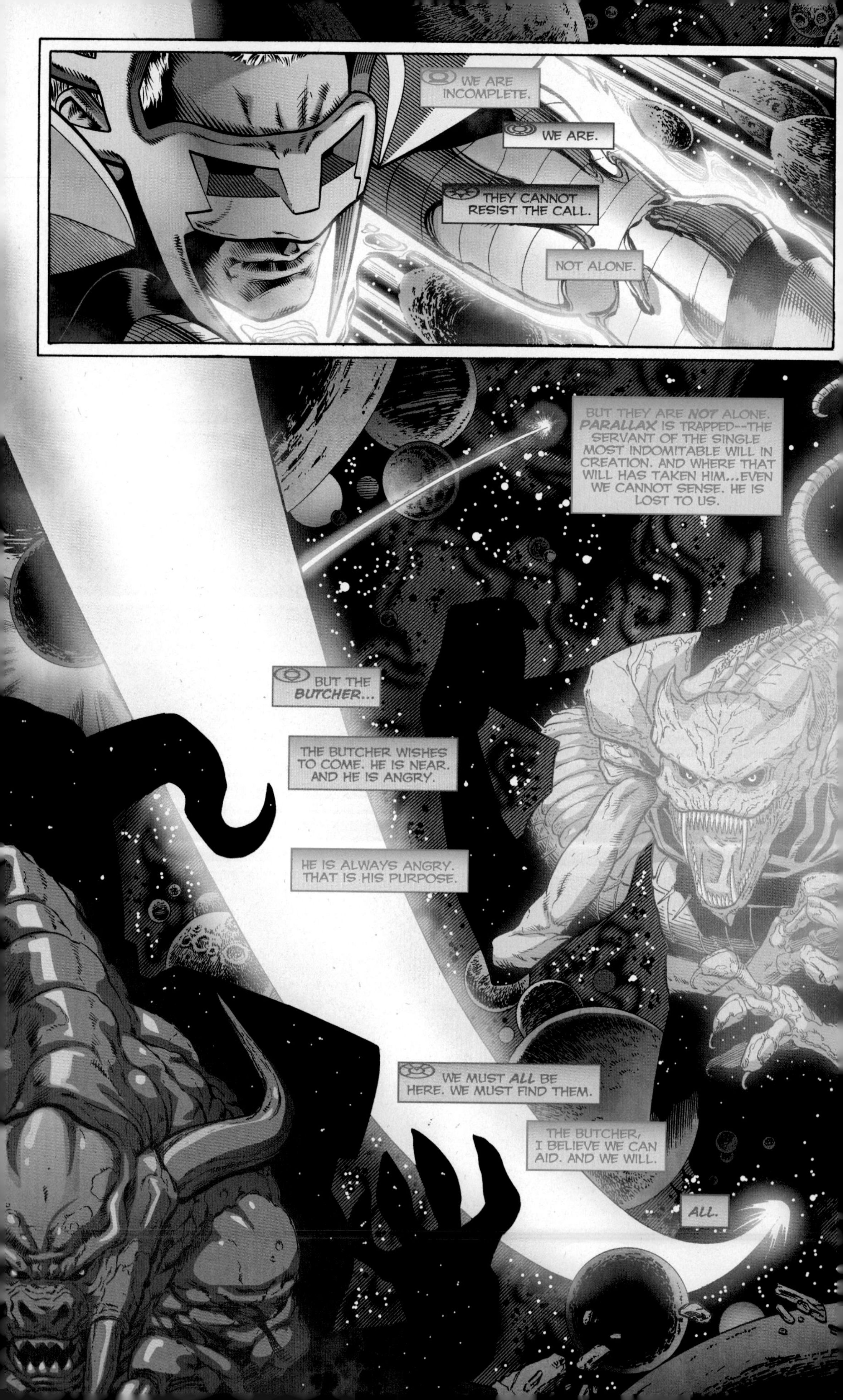
WE ARE INCOMPLETE.
WE ARE.
THEY CANNOT RESIST THE CALL.
NOT ALONE.
BUT THEY ARE NOT ALONE. PARALLAX IS TRAPPED--THE SERVANT OF THE SINGLE MOST INDOMITABLE WILL IN CREATION. AND WHERE THAT WILL HAS TAKEN HIM...EVEN WE CANNOT SENSE. HE IS LOST TO US.
BUT THE BUTCHER...
THE BUTCHER WISHES TO COME. HE IS NEAR. AND HE IS ANGRY.
HE IS ALWAYS ANGRY. THAT IS HIS PURPOSE.
WE MUST ALL BE HERE. WE MUST FIND THEM.
THE BUTCHER, I BELIEVE WE CAN AID. AND WE WILL.
ALL.

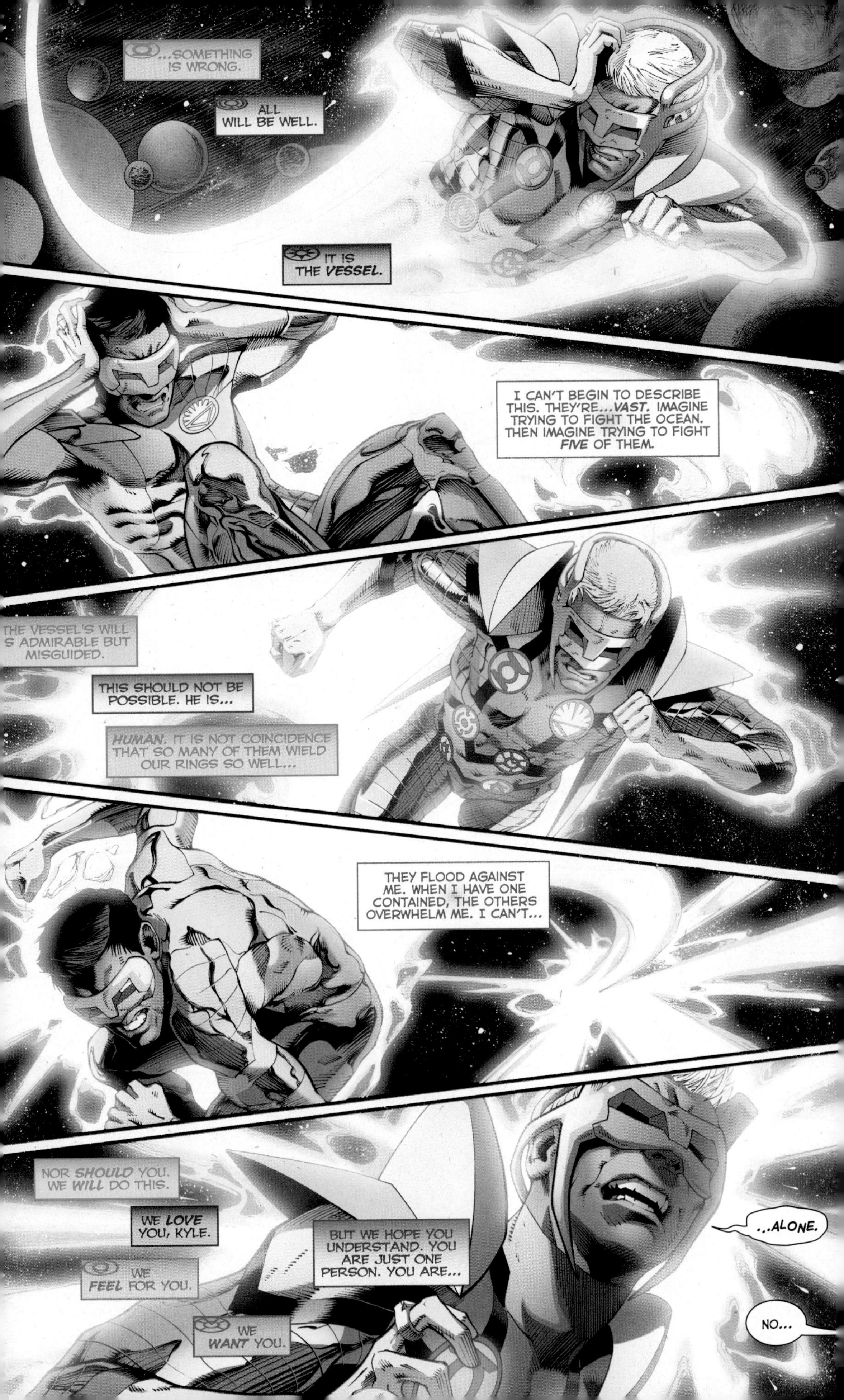
...SOMETHING IS WRONG.
ALL WILL BE WELL.
IT IS THE VESSEL.
I CAN'T BEGIN TO DESCRIBE THIS. THEY'RE...VAST. IMAGINE TRYING TO FIGHT THE OCEAN. THEN IMAGINE TRYING TO FIGHT FIVE OF THEM.
THE VESSEL'S WILL S ADMIRABLE BUT MISGUIDED.
THIS SHOULD NOT BE POSSIBLE. HE IS...
HUMAN. IT IS NOT COINCIDENCE THAT SO MANY OF THEM WIELD OUR RINGS SO WELL...
THEY FLOOD AGAINST ME. WHEN I HAVE ONE CONTAINED, THE OTHERS OVERWHELM ME. I CAN'T...
NOR SHOULD YOU. WE WILL DO THIS.
WE LOVE YOU, KYLE.
WE FEEL FOR YOU.
WE WANT YOU.
BUT WE HOPE YOU UNDERSTAND. YOU ARE JUST ONE PERSON. YOU ARE...
...ALONE.
NO...

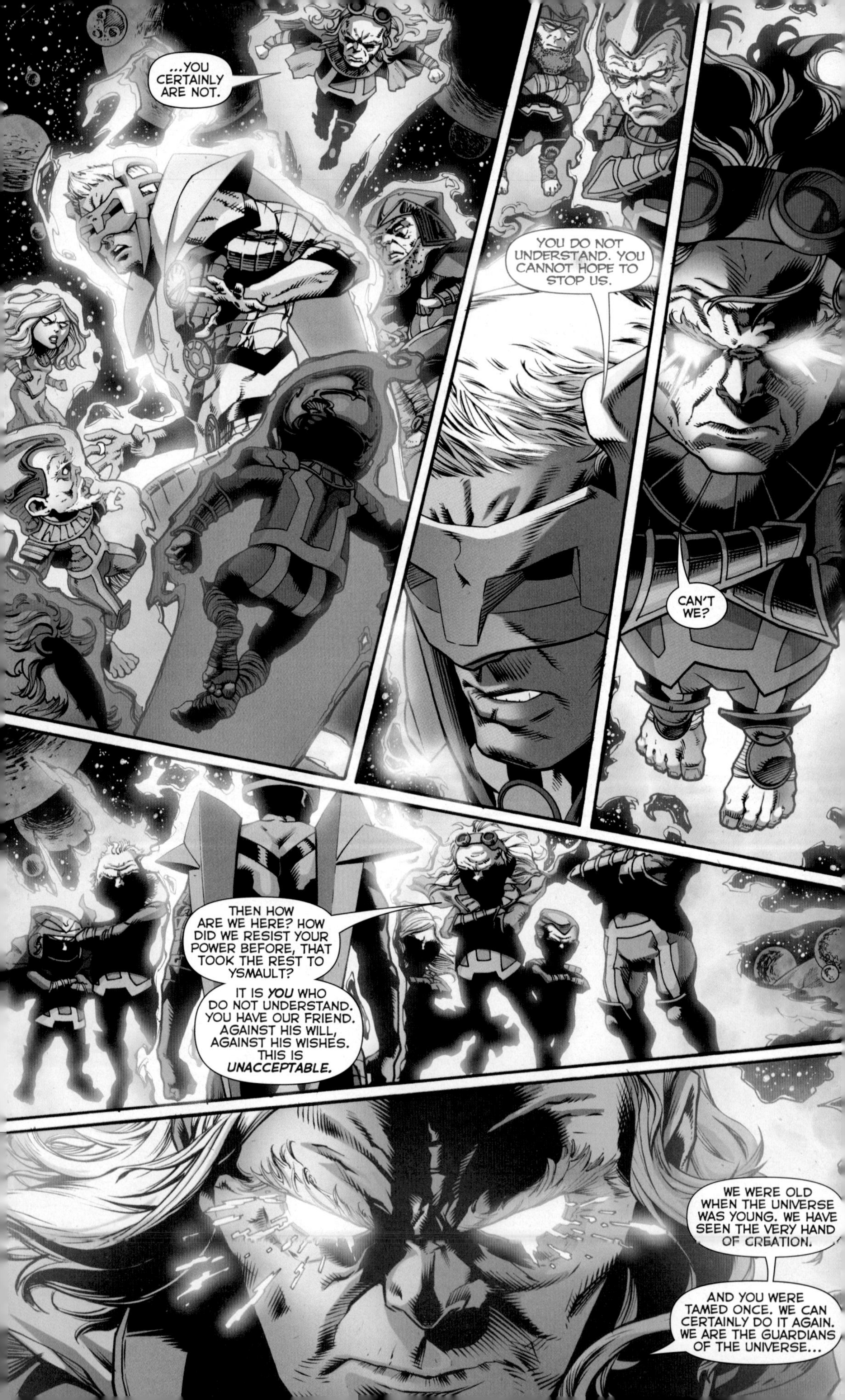
...YOU CERTAINLY ARE NOT.
YOU DO NOT UNDERSTAND. YOU CANNOT HOPE TO STOP US.
CAN'T WE?
THEN HOW ARE WE HERE? HOW DID WE RESIST YOUR POWER BEFORE, THAT TOOK THE REST TO YSMAULT?
IT IS *YOU* WHO DO NOT UNDERSTAND. YOU HAVE OUR FRIEND. AGAINST HIS WILL, AGAINST HIS WISHES. THIS IS ***UNACCEPTABLE.***
WE WERE OLD WHEN THE UNIVERSE WAS YOUNG. WE HAVE SEEN THE VERY HAND OF CREATION.
AND YOU WERE TAMED ONCE. WE CAN CERTAINLY DO IT AGAIN. WE ARE THE GUARDIANS OF THE UNIVERSE...

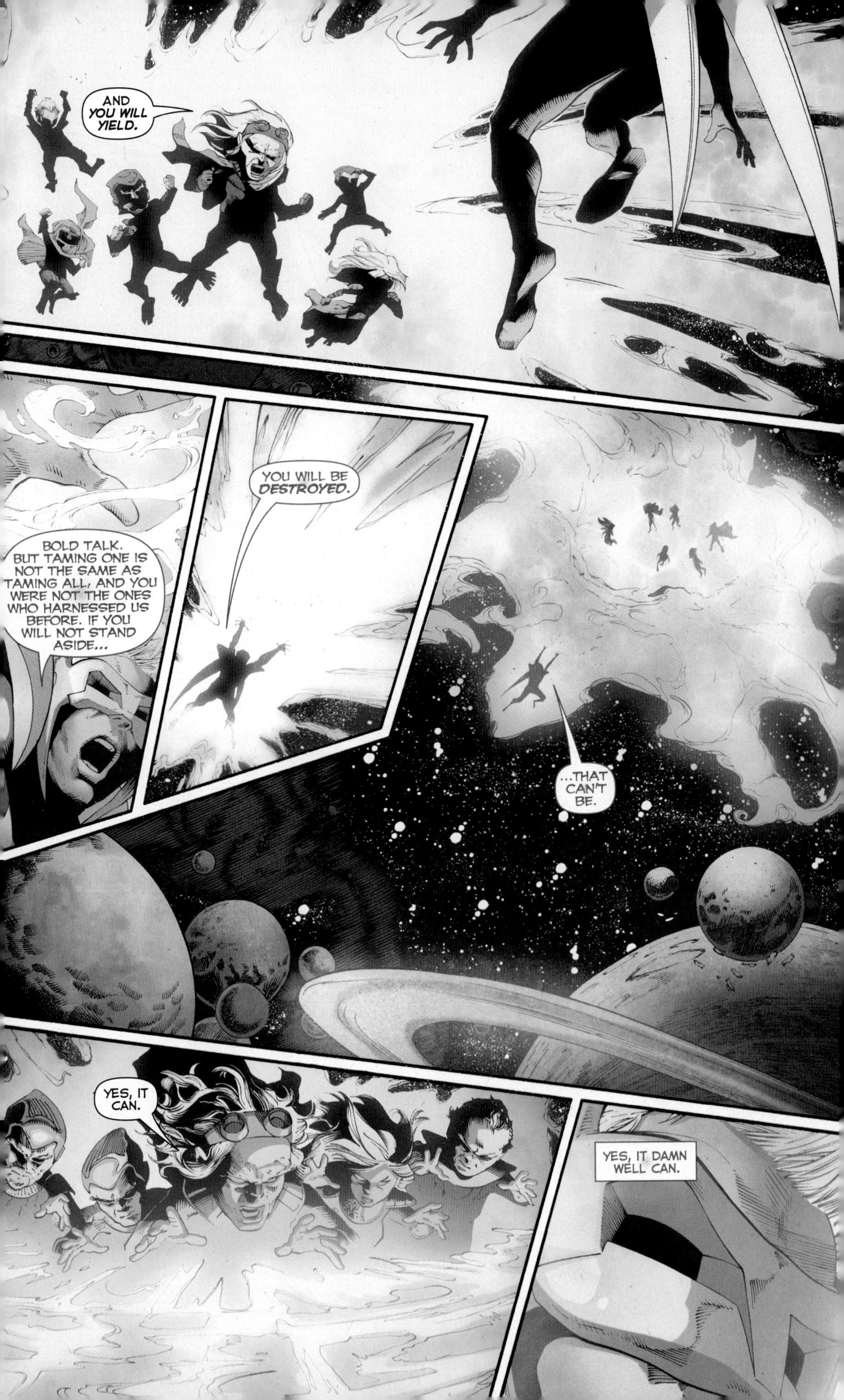
AND YOU WILL YIELD.
YOU WILL BE DESTROYED.
BOLD TALK. BUT TAMING ONE IS NOT THE SAME AS TAMING ALL, AND YOU WERE NOT THE ONES WHO HARNESSED US BEFORE. IF YOU WILL NOT STAND ASIDE...
...THAT CAN'T BE.
YES, IT CAN.
YES, IT DAMN WELL CAN.

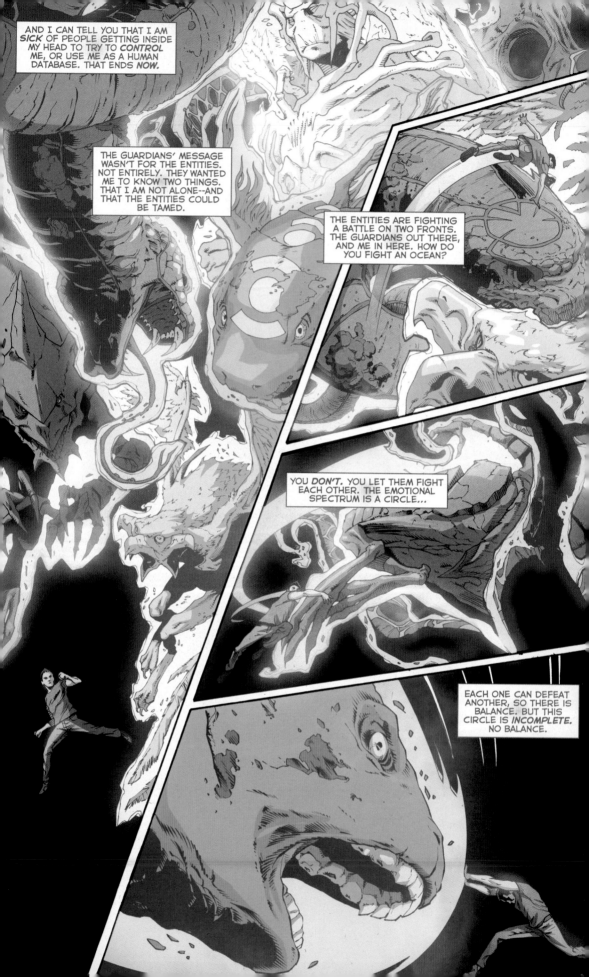

AND I CAN TELL YOU THAT I AM *SICK* OF PEOPLE GETTING INSIDE MY HEAD TO TRY TO *CONTROL* ME, OR USE ME AS A HUMAN DATABASE. THAT ENDS *NOW*.

THE GUARDIANS' MESSAGE WASN'T FOR THE ENTITIES. NOT ENTIRELY. THEY WANTED ME TO KNOW TWO THINGS. THAT I AM NOT ALONE--AND THAT THE ENTITIES COULD BE TAMED.

THE ENTITIES ARE FIGHTING A BATTLE ON TWO FRONTS. THE GUARDIANS OUT THERE, AND ME IN HERE. HOW DO YOU FIGHT AN OCEAN?

YOU *DON'T*. YOU LET THEM FIGHT EACH OTHER. THE EMOTIONAL SPECTRUM IS A CIRCLE...

EACH ONE CAN DEFEAT ANOTHER, SO THERE IS BALANCE. BUT THIS CIRCLE IS *INCOMPLETE*. NO BALANCE.

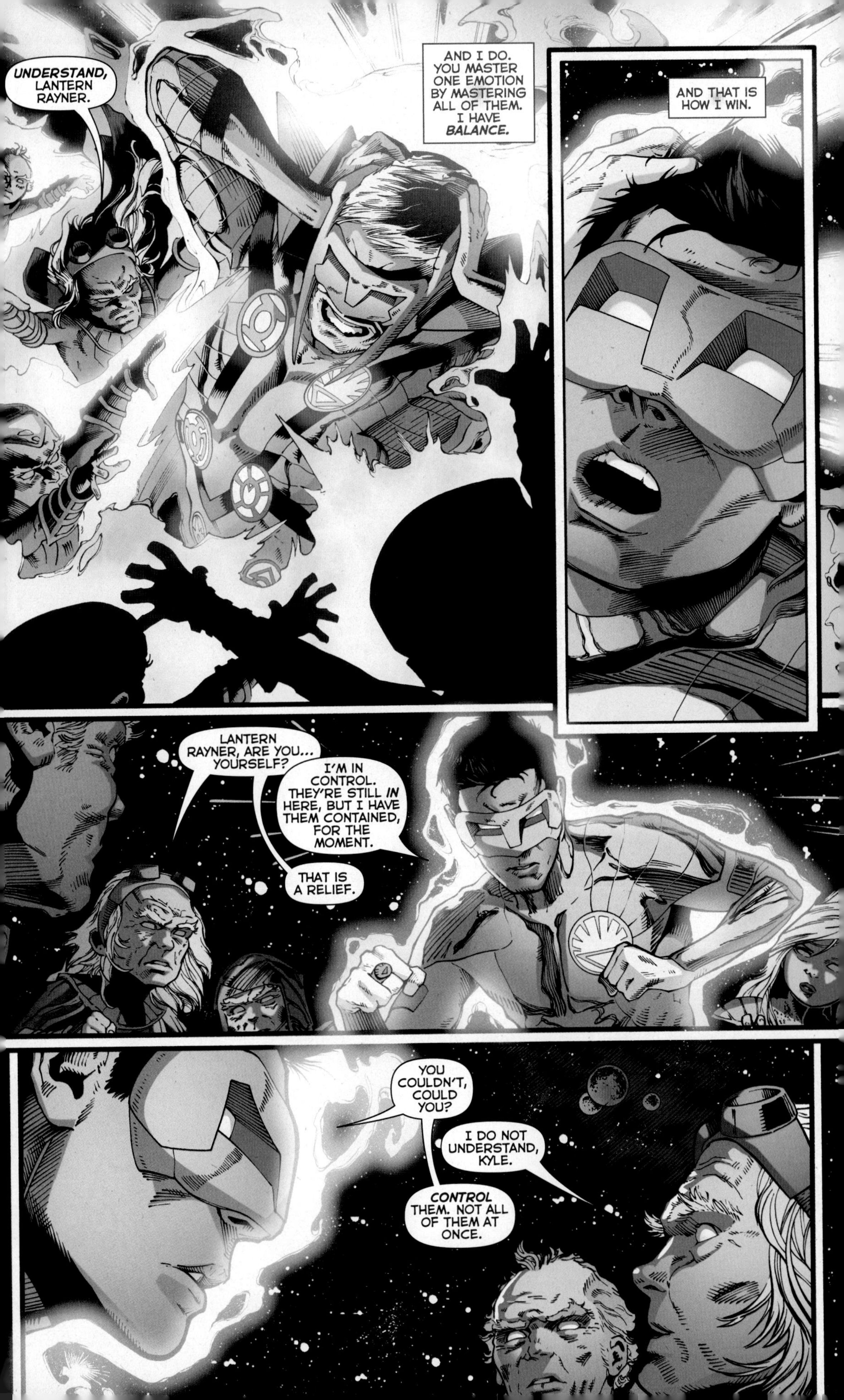
UNDERSTAND, LANTERN RAYNER.
AND I DO. YOU MASTER ONE EMOTION BY MASTERING ALL OF THEM. I HAVE BALANCE.
AND THAT IS HOW I WIN.
LANTERN RAYNER, ARE YOU... YOURSELF?
I'M IN CONTROL. THEY'RE STILL IN HERE, BUT I HAVE THEM CONTAINED, FOR THE MOMENT.
THAT IS A RELIEF.
YOU COULDN'T, COULD YOU?
I DO NOT UNDERSTAND, KYLE.
CONTROL THEM. NOT ALL OF THEM AT ONCE.

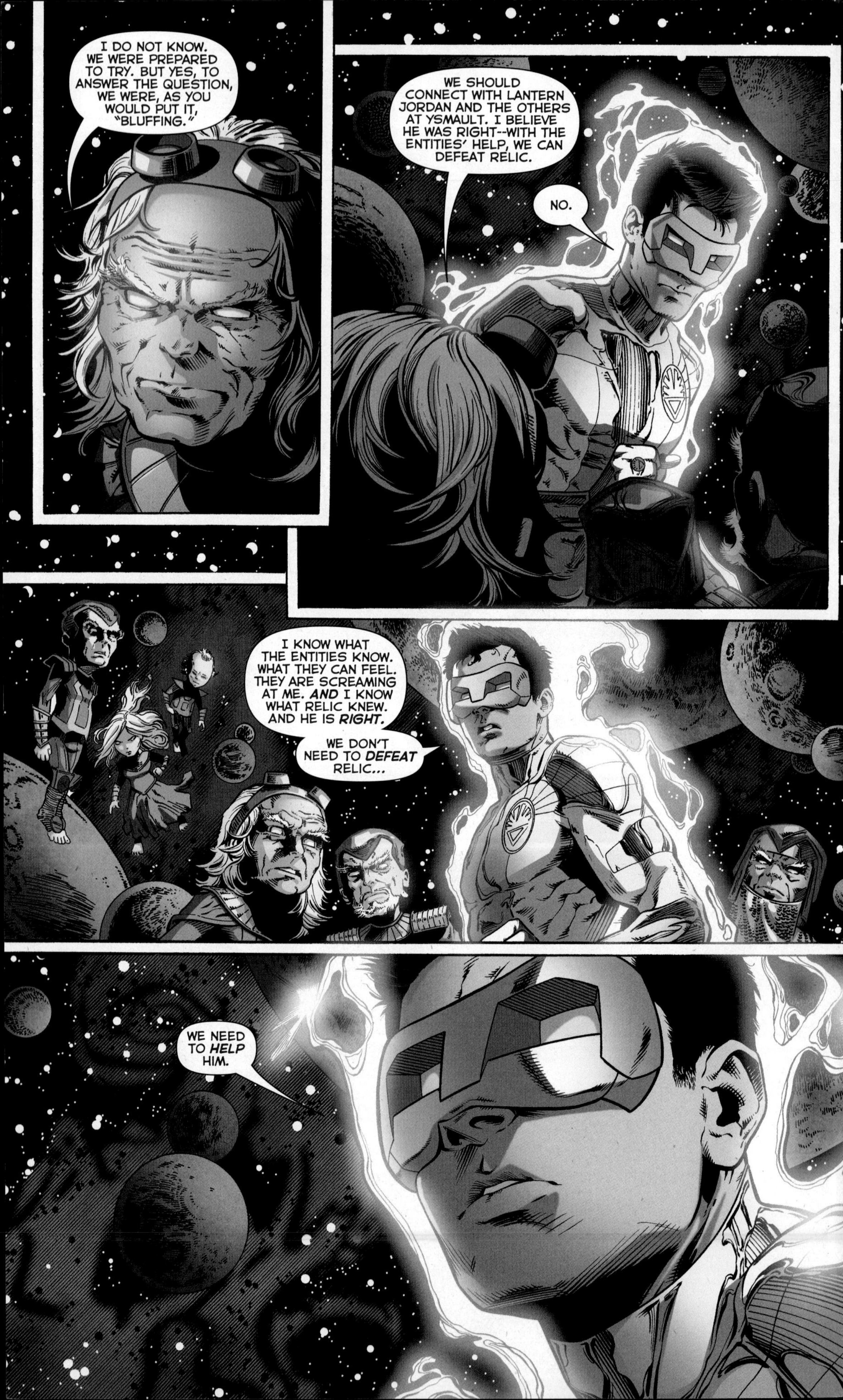
I DO NOT KNOW. WE WERE PREPARED TO TRY. BUT YES, TO ANSWER THE QUESTION, WE WERE, AS YOU WOULD PUT IT, "BLUFFING."
WE SHOULD CONNECT WITH LANTERN JORDAN AND THE OTHERS AT YSMAULT. I BELIEVE HE WAS RIGHT--WITH THE ENTITIES' HELP, WE CAN DEFEAT RELIC.
NO.
I KNOW WHAT THE ENTITIES KNOW. WHAT THEY CAN FEEL. THEY ARE SCREAMING AT ME. AND I KNOW WHAT RELIC KNEW. AND HE IS RIGHT.
WE DON'T NEED TO DEFEAT RELIC...
WE NEED TO HELP HIM.

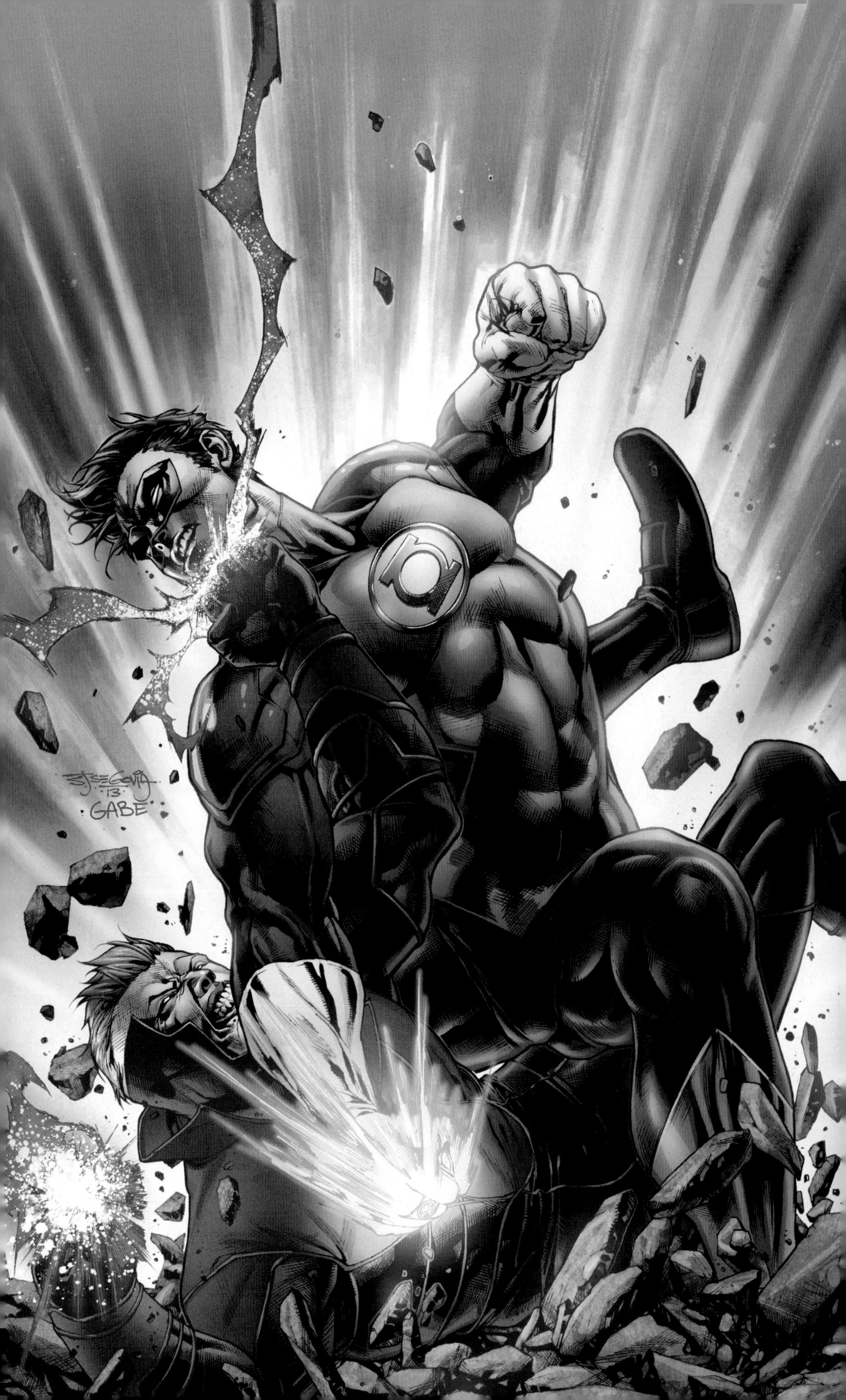
GABE

LIGHTS OUT part four: BLOOD BROTHERS

CHARLES SOULE writer ALESSANDRO VITTI artist GABE ELTAEB colorist STEPHEN SEGOVIA with GABE ELTAEB cover artists

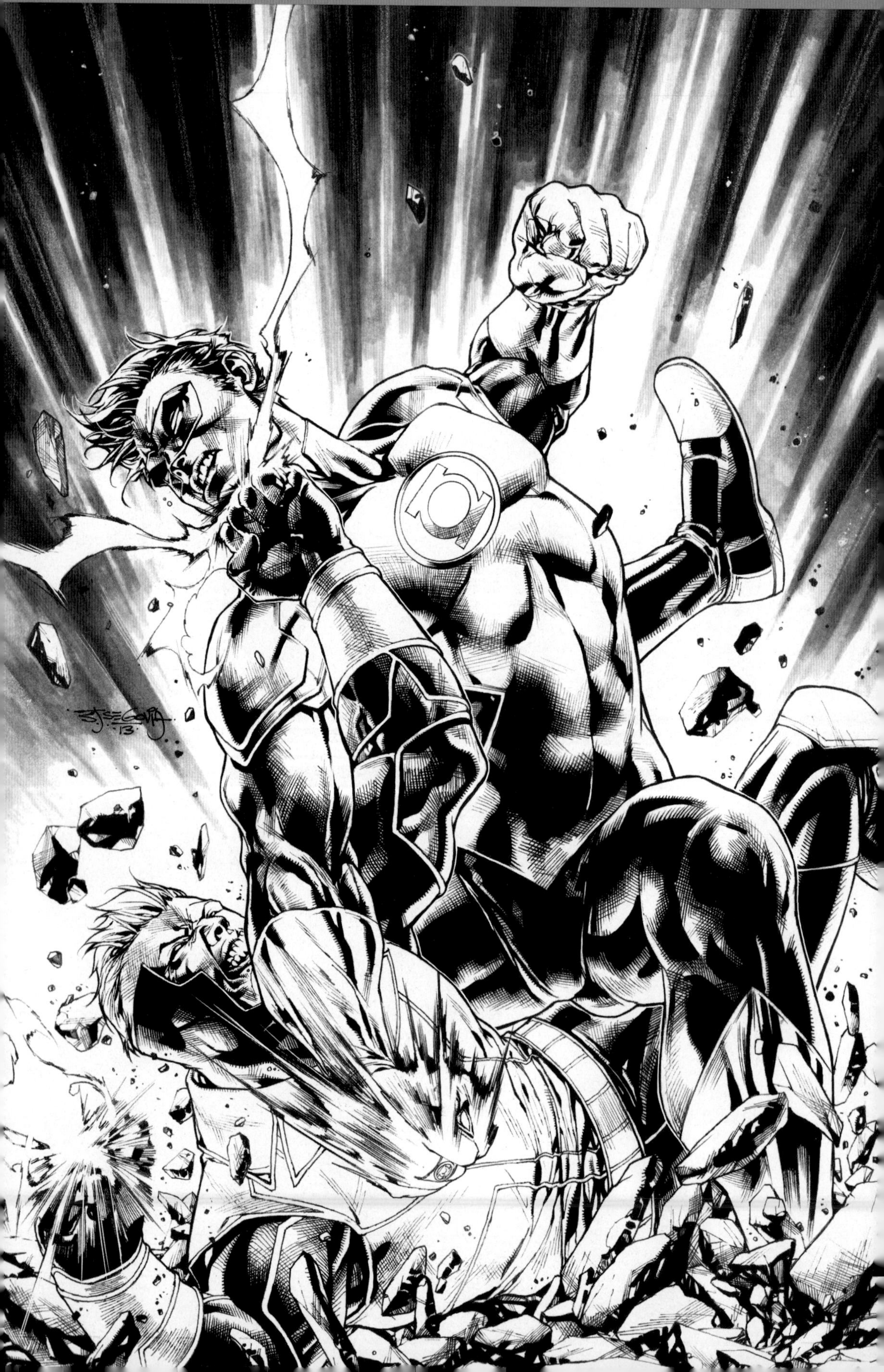

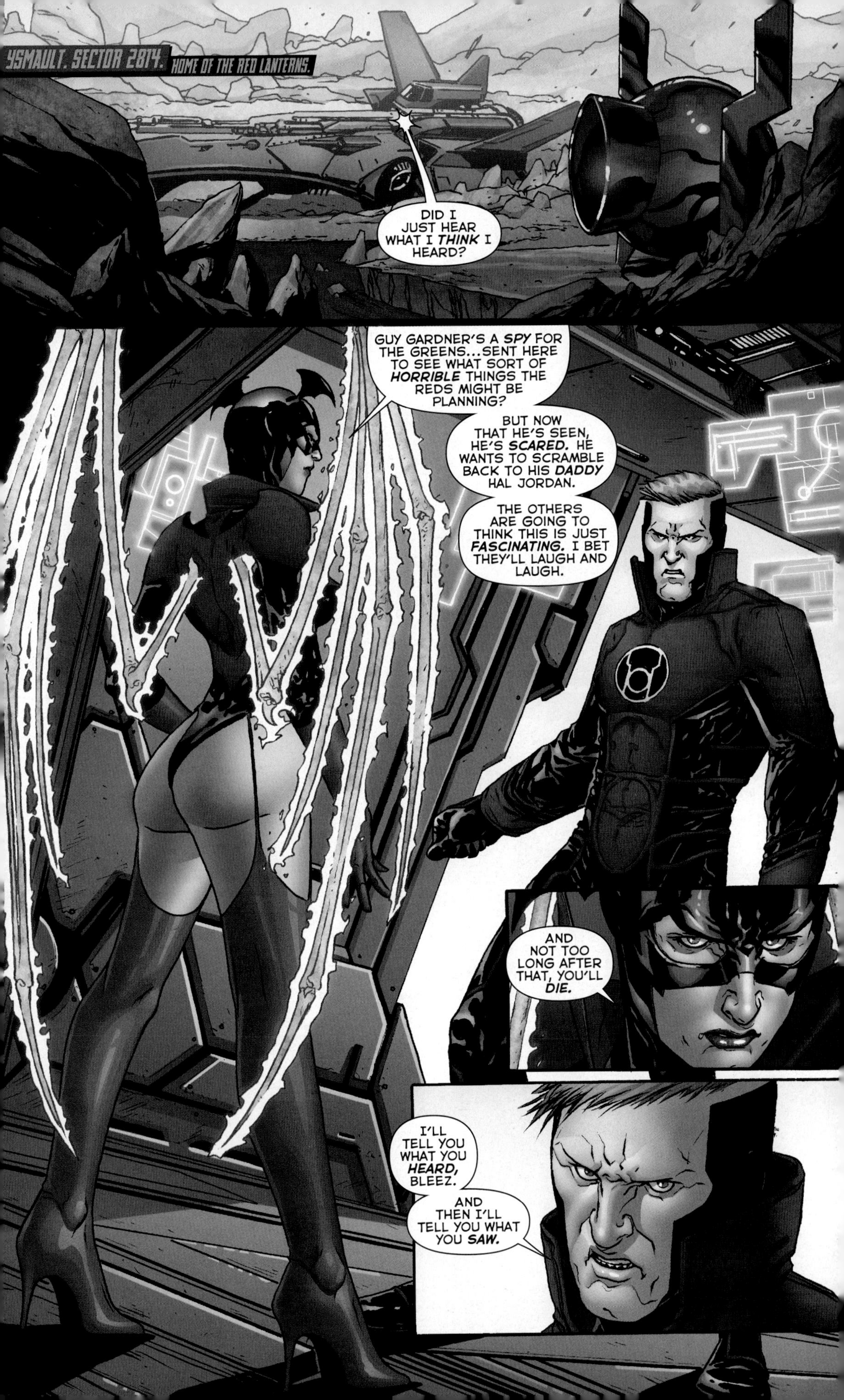
YSMAULT. SECTOR 2814.
HOME OF THE RED LANTERNS.
DID I JUST HEAR WHAT I THINK I HEARD?
GUY GARDNER'S A SPY FOR THE GREENS...SENT HERE TO SEE WHAT SORT OF HORRIBLE THINGS THE REDS MIGHT BE PLANNING?
BUT NOW THAT HE'S SEEN, HE'S SCARED. HE WANTS TO SCRAMBLE BACK TO HIS DADDY HAL JORDAN.
THE OTHERS ARE GOING TO THINK THIS IS JUST FASCINATING. I BET THEY'LL LAUGH AND LAUGH.
AND NOT TOO LONG AFTER THAT, YOU'LL DIE.
I'LL TELL YOU WHAT YOU HEARD, BLEEZ.
AND THEN I'LL TELL YOU WHAT YOU SAW.

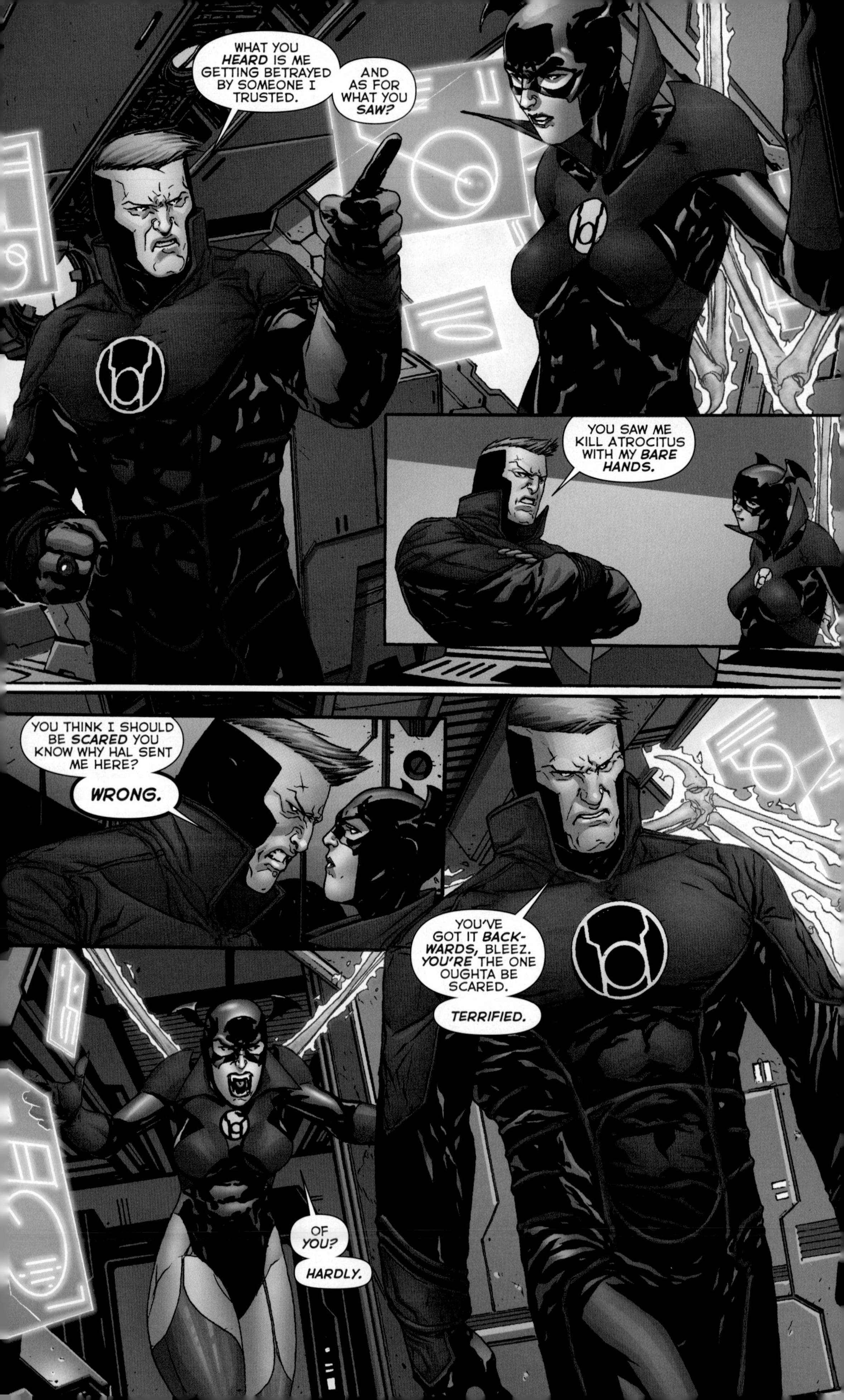
WHAT YOU HEARD IS ME GETTING BETRAYED BY SOMEONE I TRUSTED.
AND AS FOR WHAT YOU SAW?
YOU SAW ME KILL ATROCITUS WITH MY BARE HANDS.
YOU THINK I SHOULD BE SCARED YOU KNOW WHY HAL SENT ME HERE?
WRONG.
YOU'VE GOT IT BACK-WARDS, BLEEZ. YOU'RE THE ONE OUGHTA BE SCARED.
TERRIFIED.
OF YOU?
HARDLY.

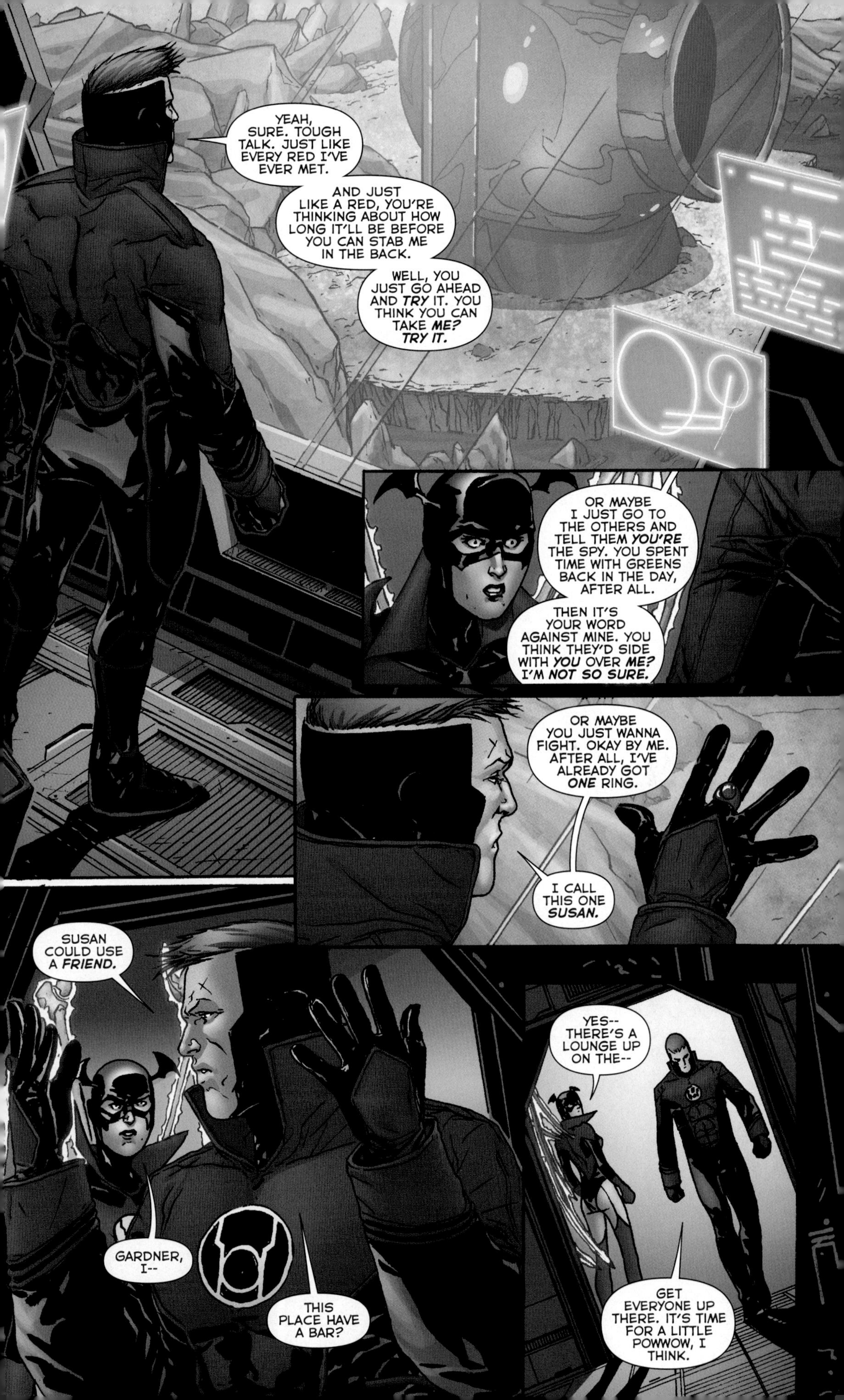
YEAH, SURE. TOUGH TALK. JUST LIKE EVERY RED I'VE EVER MET.
AND JUST LIKE A RED, YOU'RE THINKING ABOUT HOW LONG IT'LL BE BEFORE YOU CAN STAB ME IN THE BACK.
WELL, YOU JUST GO AHEAD AND TRY IT. YOU THINK YOU CAN TAKE ME? TRY IT.
OR MAYBE I JUST GO TO THE OTHERS AND TELL THEM YOU'RE THE SPY. YOU SPENT TIME WITH GREENS BACK IN THE DAY, AFTER ALL.
THEN IT'S YOUR WORD AGAINST MINE. YOU THINK THEY'D SIDE WITH YOU OVER ME? I'M NOT SO SURE.
OR MAYBE YOU JUST WANNA FIGHT. OKAY BY ME. AFTER ALL, I'VE ALREADY GOT ONE RING.
I CALL THIS ONE SUSAN.
SUSAN COULD USE A FRIEND.
GARDNER, I--
THIS PLACE HAVE A BAR?
YES-- THERE'S A LOUNGE UP ON THE--
GET EVERYONE UP THERE. IT'S TIME FOR A LITTLE POWWOW, I THINK.

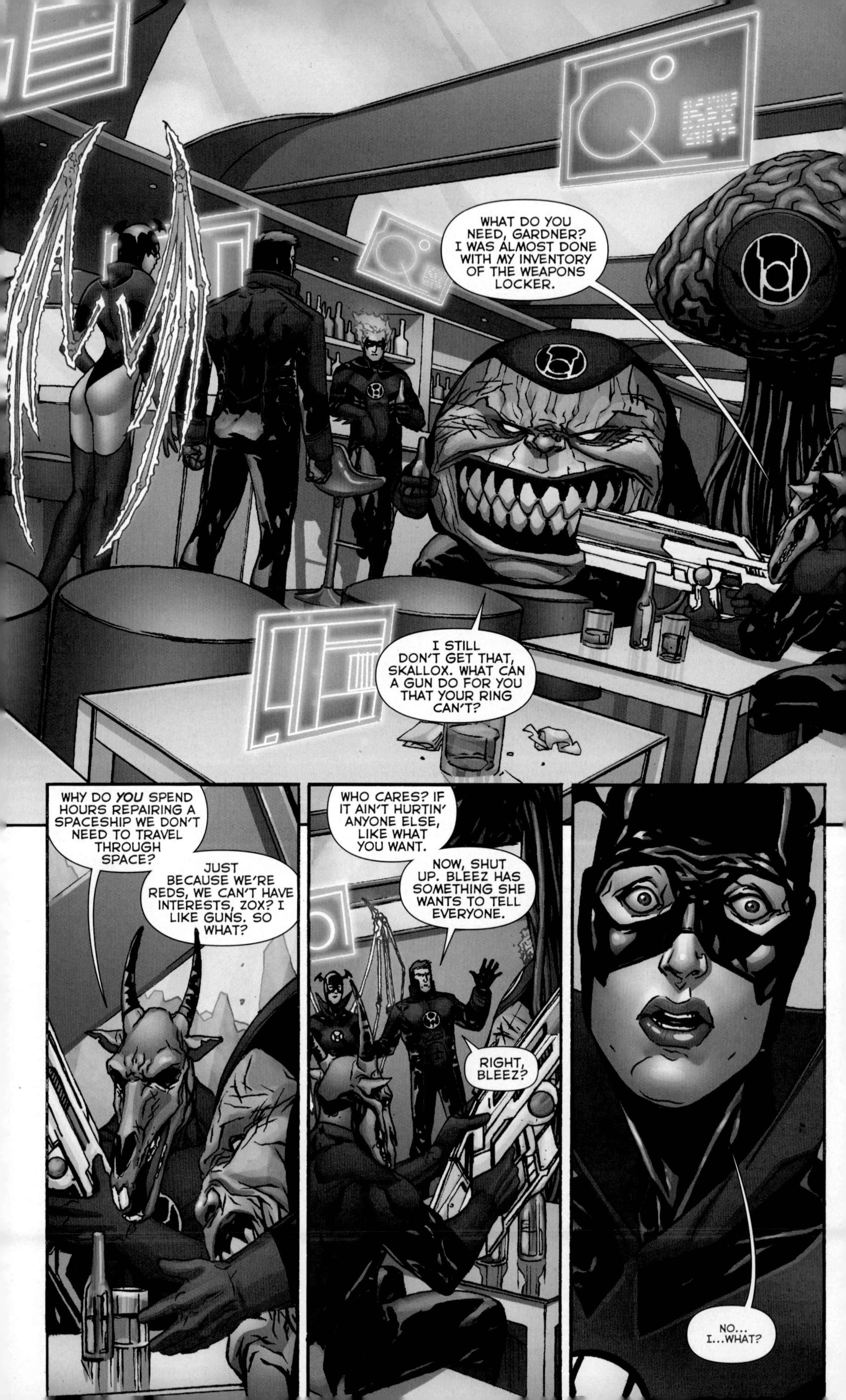
WHAT DO YOU NEED, GARDNER? I WAS ALMOST DONE WITH MY INVENTORY OF THE WEAPONS LOCKER.
I STILL DON'T GET THAT, SKALLOX. WHAT CAN A GUN DO FOR YOU THAT YOUR RING CAN'T?
WHY DO *YOU* SPEND HOURS REPAIRING A SPACESHIP WE DON'T NEED TO TRAVEL THROUGH SPACE?
JUST BECAUSE WE'RE REDS, WE CAN'T HAVE INTERESTS, ZOX? I LIKE GUNS. SO WHAT?
WHO CARES? IF IT AIN'T HURTIN' ANYONE ELSE, LIKE WHAT YOU WANT.
NOW, SHUT UP. BLEEZ HAS SOMETHING SHE WANTS TO TELL EVERYONE.
RIGHT, BLEEZ?
NO... I...WHAT?

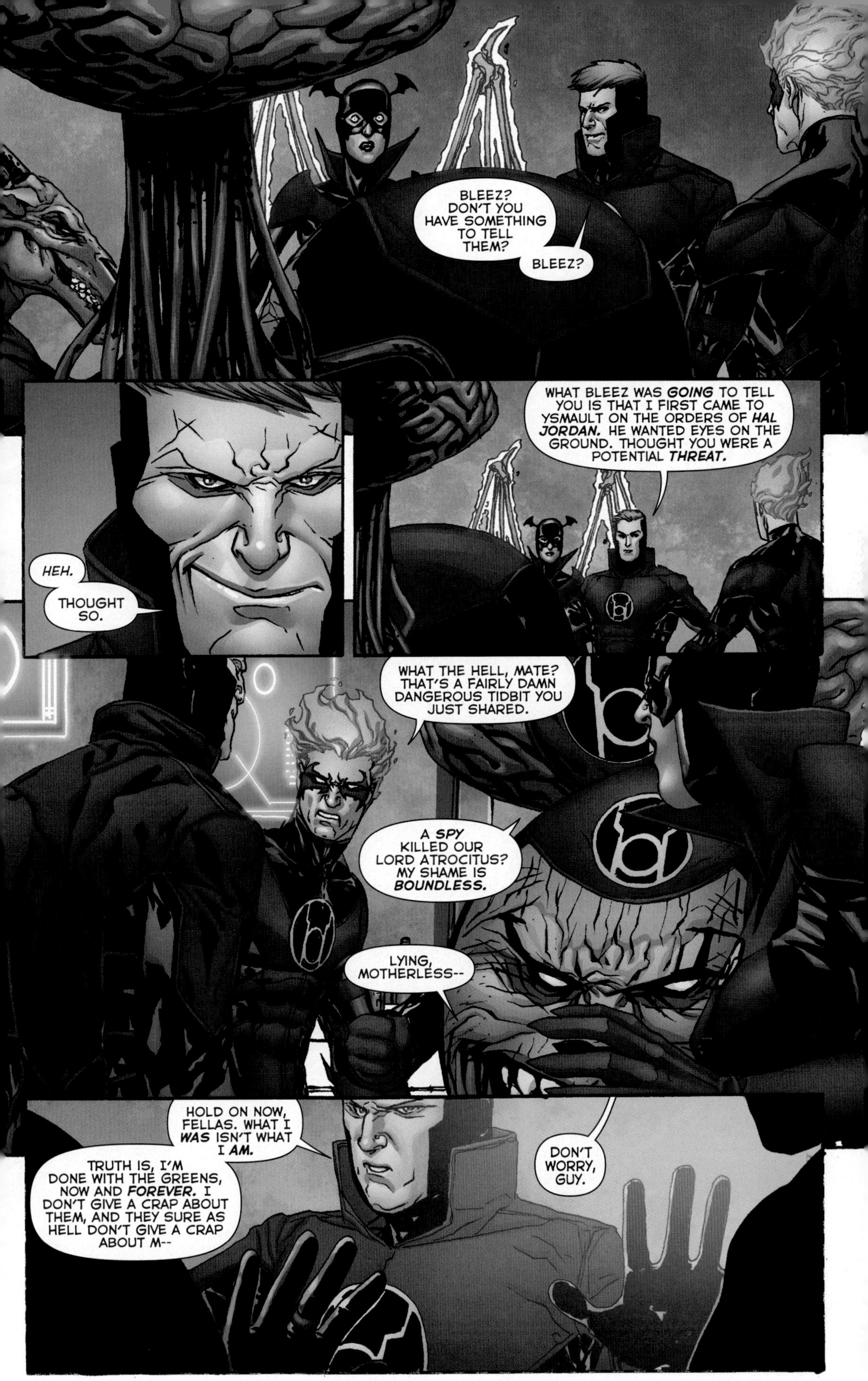
BLEEZ? DON'T YOU HAVE SOMETHING TO TELL THEM?
BLEEZ?
HEH.
THOUGHT SO.
WHAT BLEEZ WAS GOING TO TELL YOU IS THAT I FIRST CAME TO YSMAULT ON THE ORDERS OF HAL JORDAN. HE WANTED EYES ON THE GROUND. THOUGHT YOU WERE A POTENTIAL THREAT.
WHAT THE HELL, MATE? THAT'S A FAIRLY DAMN DANGEROUS TIDBIT YOU JUST SHARED.
A SPY KILLED OUR LORD ATROCITUS? MY SHAME IS BOUNDLESS.
LYING, MOTHERLESS--
HOLD ON NOW, FELLAS. WHAT I WAS ISN'T WHAT I AM.
TRUTH IS, I'M DONE WITH THE GREENS, NOW AND FOREVER. I DON'T GIVE A CRAP ABOUT THEM, AND THEY SURE AS HELL DON'T GIVE A CRAP ABOUT M--
DON'T WORRY, GUY.

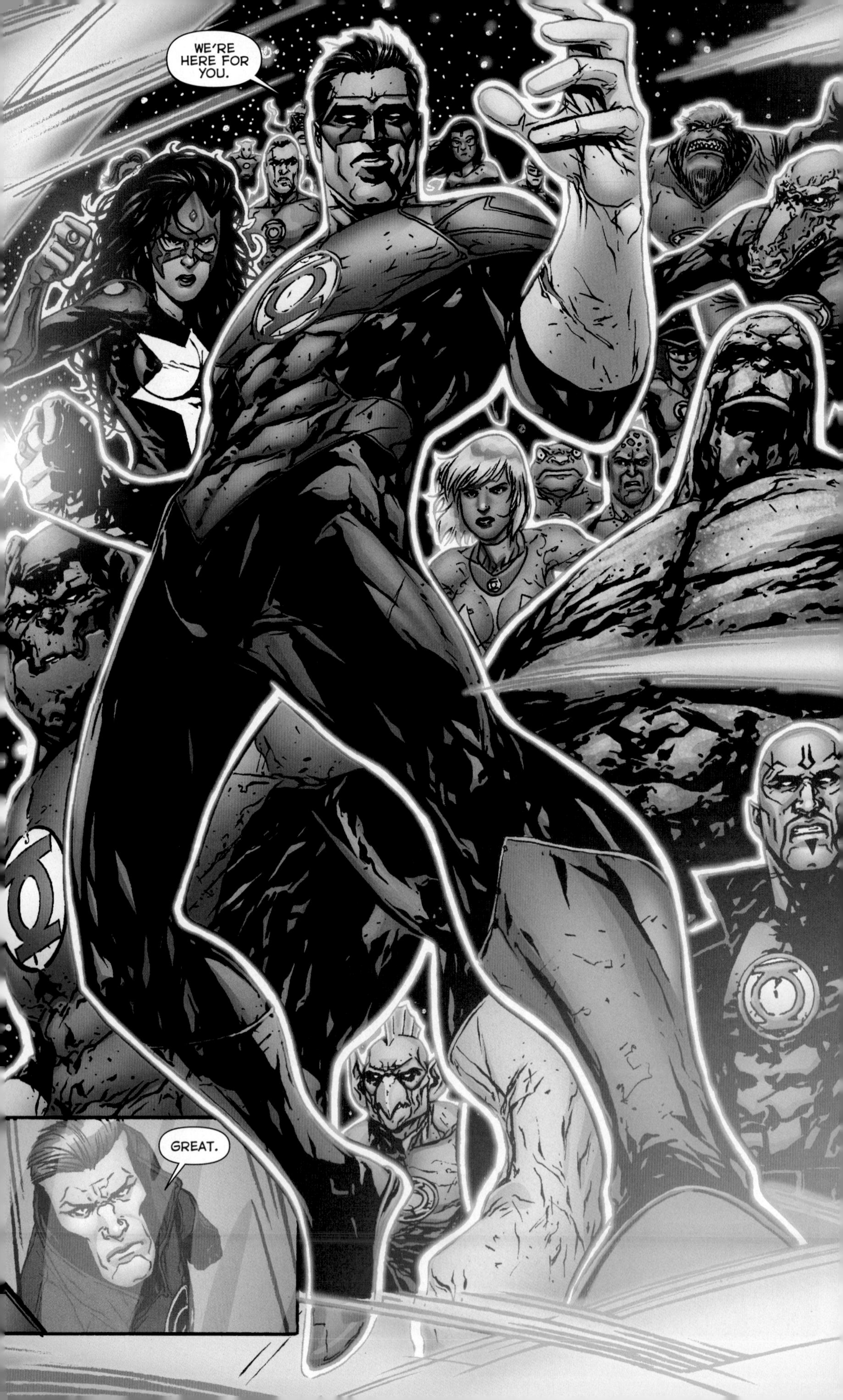
WE'RE HERE FOR YOU.
GREAT.

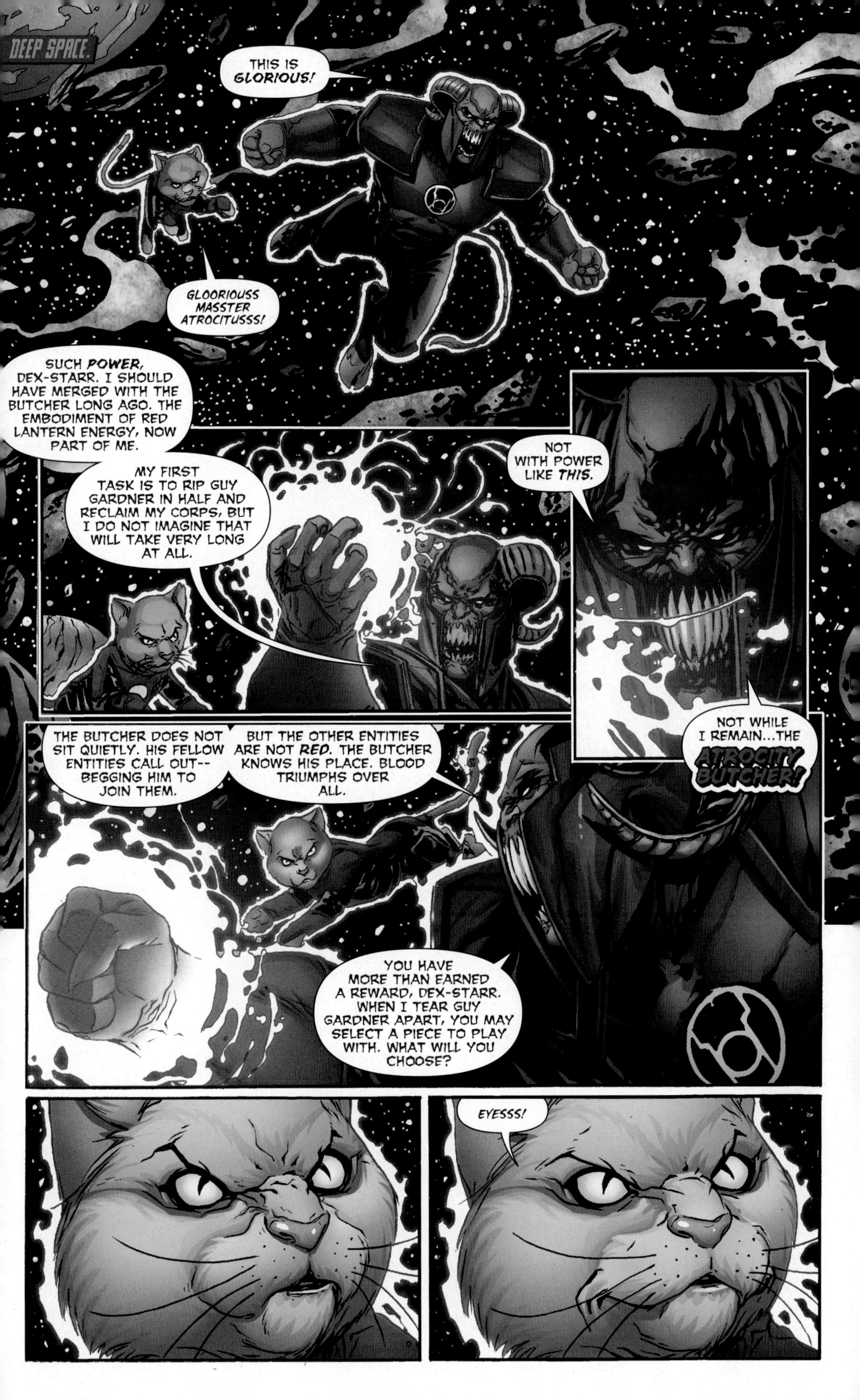
DEEP SPACE.
THIS IS GLORIOUS!
GLOORIOUSS MASSTER ATROCITUSSS!
SUCH POWER, DEX-STARR. I SHOULD HAVE MERGED WITH THE BUTCHER LONG AGO. THE EMBODIMENT OF RED LANTERN ENERGY, NOW PART OF ME.
MY FIRST TASK IS TO RIP GUY GARDNER IN HALF AND RECLAIM MY CORPS, BUT I DO NOT IMAGINE THAT WILL TAKE VERY LONG AT ALL.
NOT WITH POWER LIKE THIS.
NOT WHILE I REMAIN...THE
ATROCITY BUTCHER!
THE BUTCHER DOES NOT SIT QUIETLY. HIS FELLOW ENTITIES CALL OUT-- BEGGING HIM TO JOIN THEM.
BUT THE OTHER ENTITIES ARE NOT RED. THE BUTCHER KNOWS HIS PLACE. BLOOD TRIUMPHS OVER ALL.
YOU HAVE MORE THAN EARNED A REWARD, DEX-STARR. WHEN I TEAR GUY GARDNER APART, YOU MAY SELECT A PIECE TO PLAY WITH. WHAT WILL YOU CHOOSE?
EYESSS!

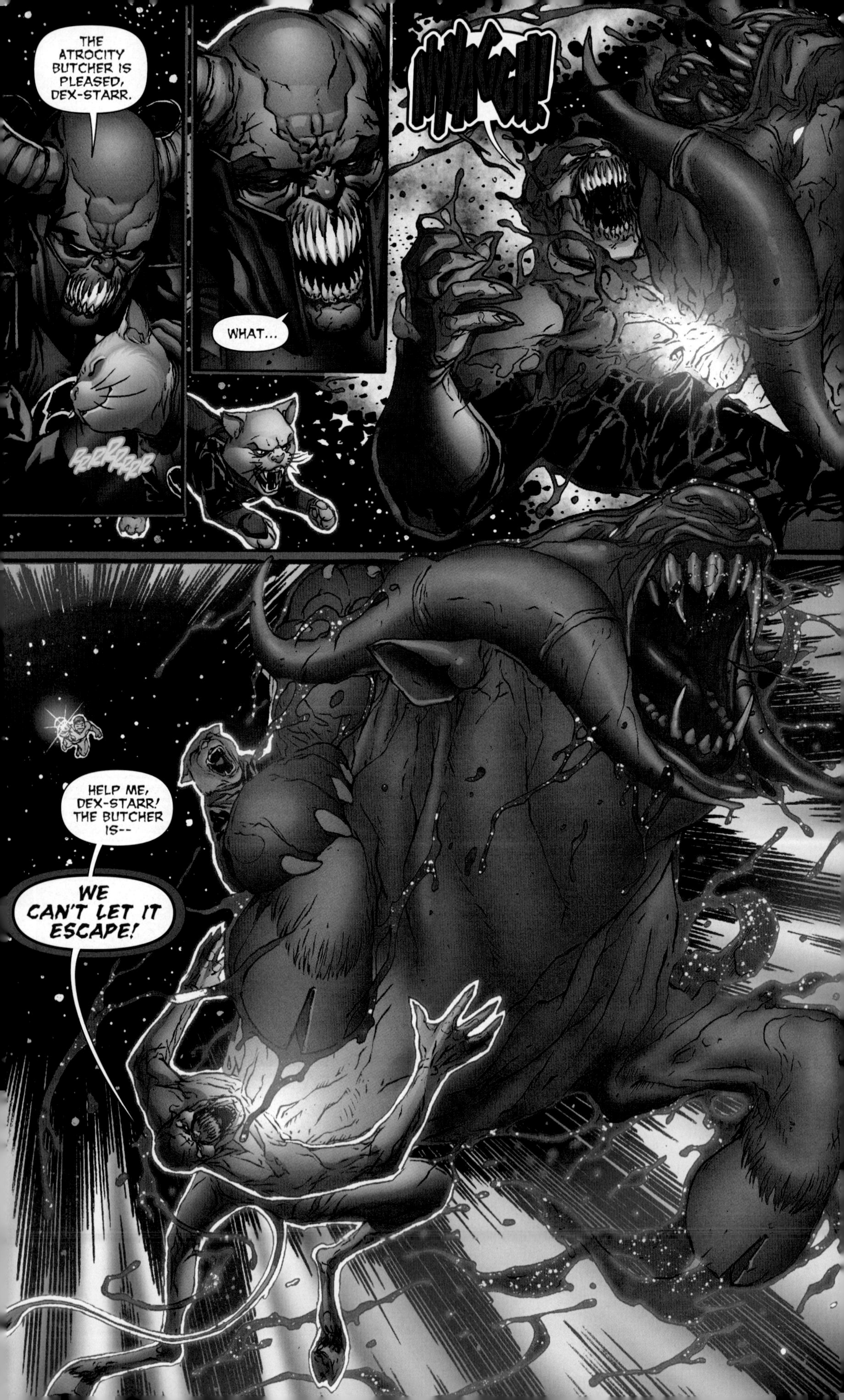
THE ATROCITY BUTCHER IS PLEASED, DEX-STARR.
WHAT...
HELP ME, DEX-STARR! THE BUTCHER IS--
WE CAN'T LET IT ESCAPE!

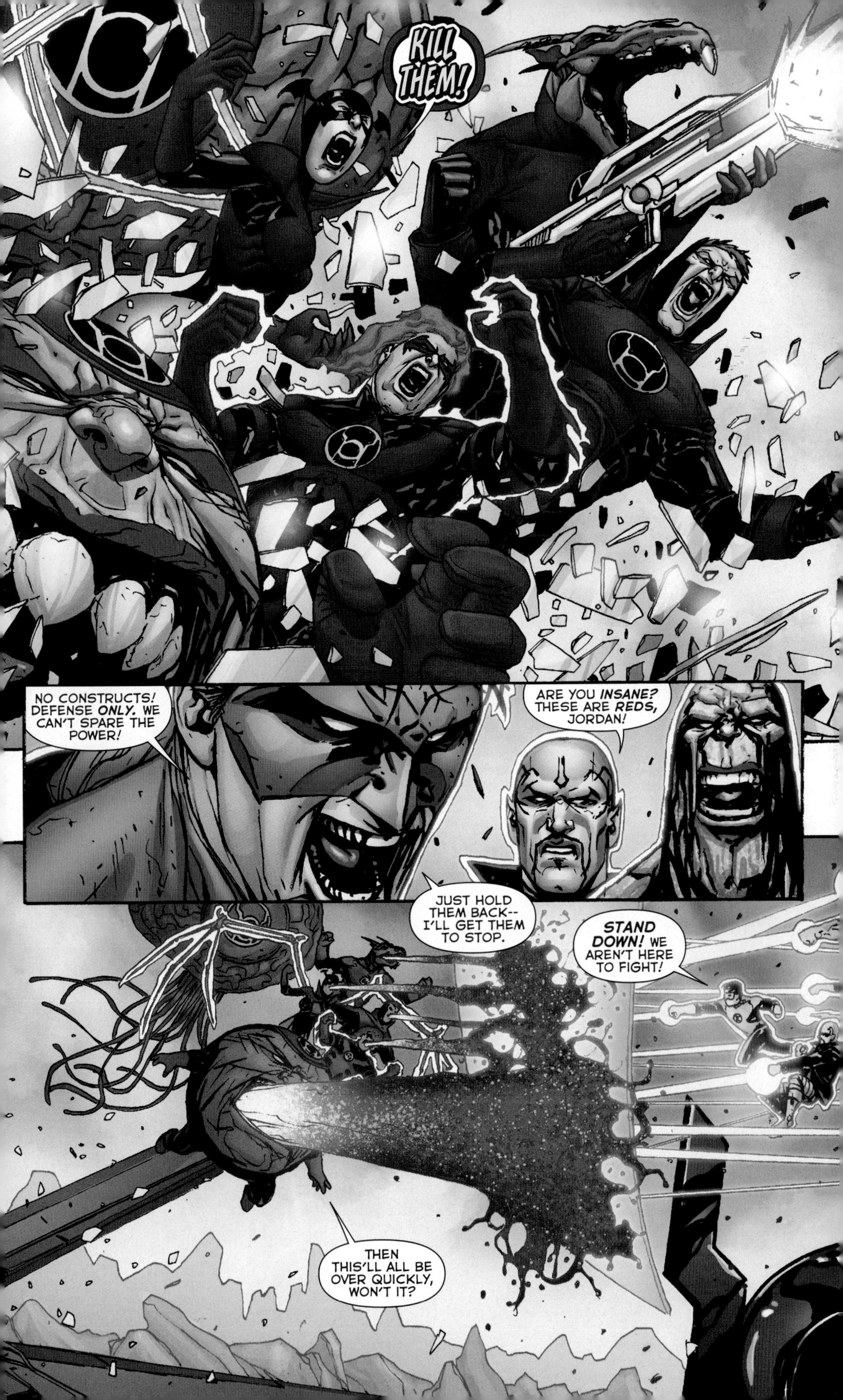
KILL THEM!
NO CONSTRUCTS! DEFENSE ONLY. WE CAN'T SPARE THE POWER!
ARE YOU INSANE? THESE ARE REDS, JORDAN!
JUST HOLD THEM BACK-- I'LL GET THEM TO STOP.
STAND DOWN! WE AREN'T HERE TO FIGHT!
THEN THIS'LL ALL BE OVER QUICKLY, WON'T IT?

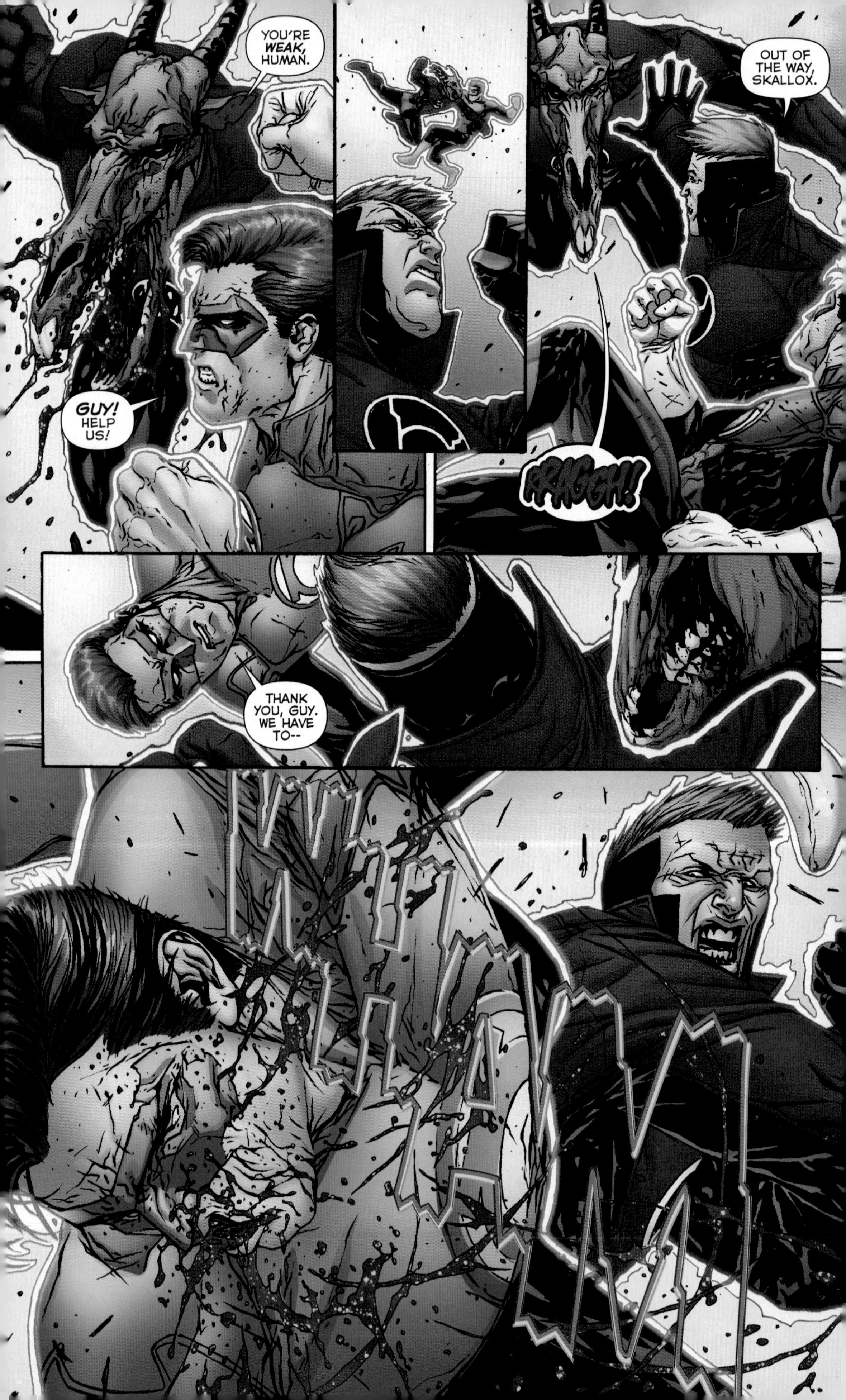

YOU'RE WEAK, HUMAN.
GUY! HELP US!
OUT OF THE WAY, SKALLOX.
KRAGGH!
THANK YOU, GUY. WE HAVE TO--
WHAKAM!

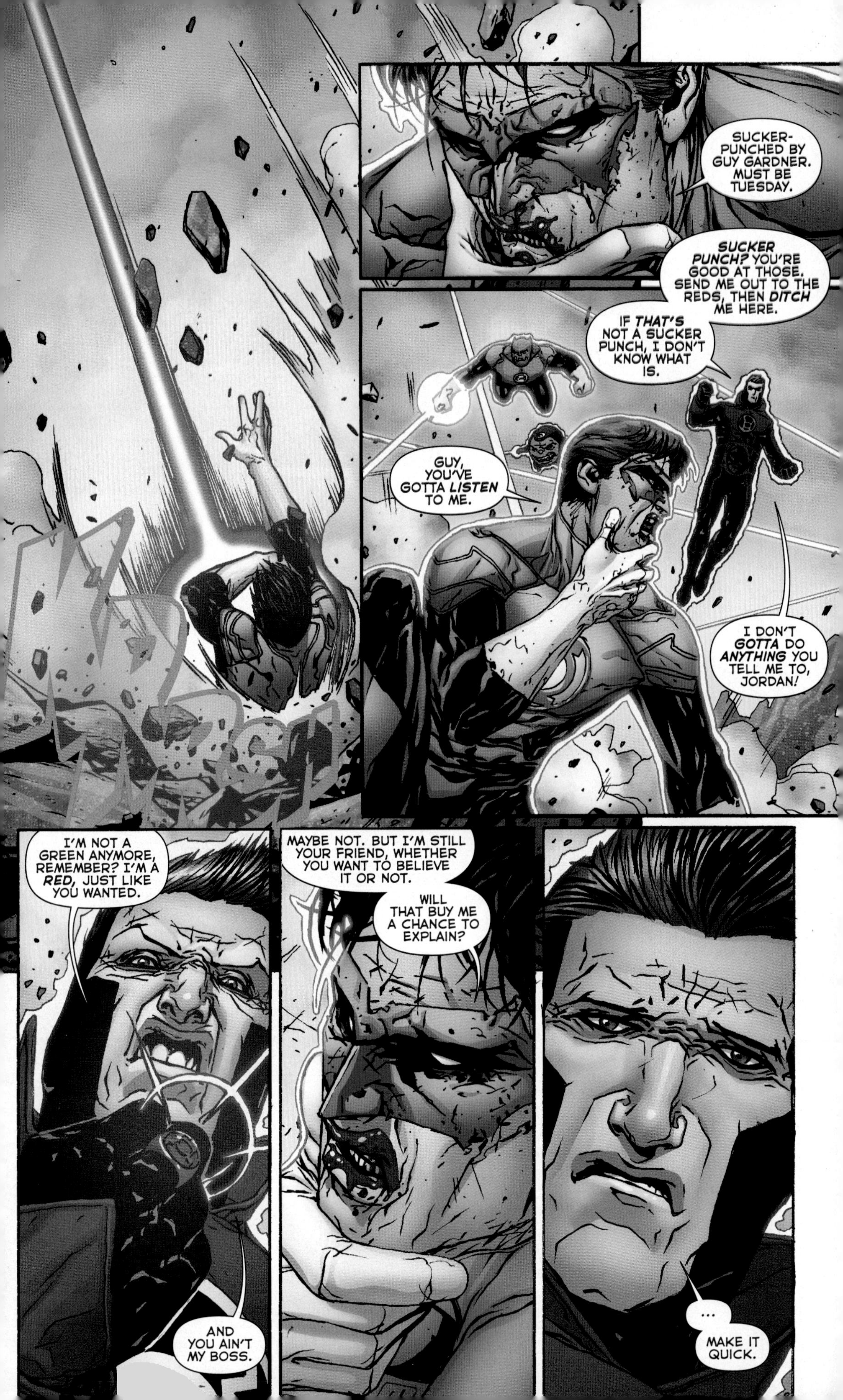
SUCKER-PUNCHED BY GUY GARDNER. MUST BE TUESDAY.
SUCKER PUNCH? YOU'RE GOOD AT THOSE. SEND ME OUT TO THE REDS, THEN DITCH ME HERE.
IF THAT'S NOT A SUCKER PUNCH, I DON'T KNOW WHAT IS.
GUY, YOU'VE GOTTA LISTEN TO ME.
I DON'T GOTTA DO ANYTHING YOU TELL ME TO, JORDAN!
I'M NOT A GREEN ANYMORE, REMEMBER? I'M A RED, JUST LIKE YOU WANTED.
AND YOU AIN'T MY BOSS.
MAYBE NOT. BUT I'M STILL YOUR FRIEND, WHETHER YOU WANT TO BELIEVE IT OR NOT.
WILL THAT BUY ME A CHANCE TO EXPLAIN?
...
MAKE IT QUICK.

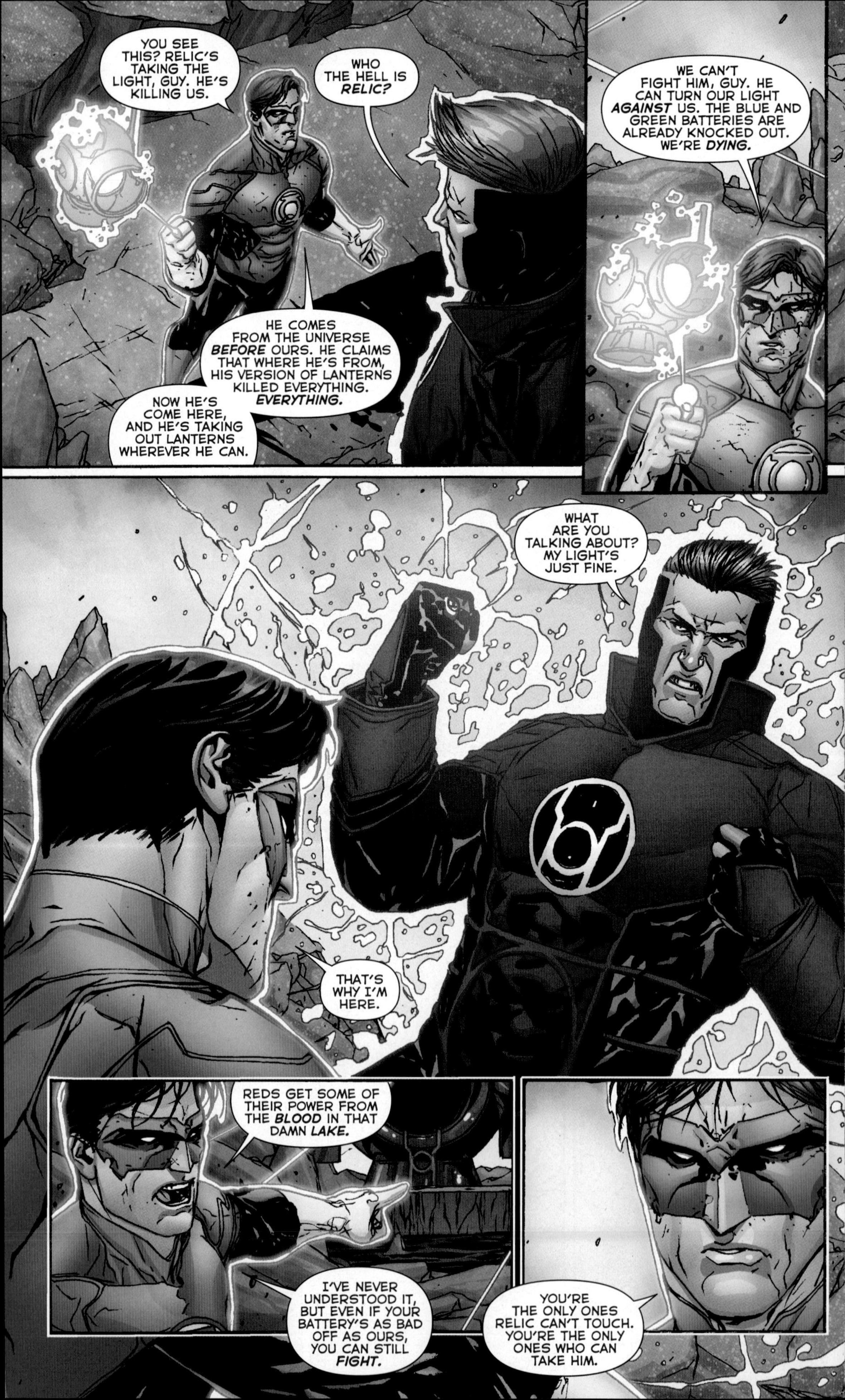

YOU SEE THIS? RELIC'S TAKING THE LIGHT, GUY. HE'S KILLING US.
WHO THE HELL IS *RELIC?*
HE COMES FROM THE UNIVERSE *BEFORE* OURS. HE CLAIMS THAT WHERE HE'S FROM, HIS VERSION OF LANTERNS KILLED EVERYTHING. *EVERYTHING.*
NOW HE'S COME HERE, AND HE'S TAKING OUT LANTERNS WHEREVER HE CAN.
WE CAN'T FIGHT HIM, GUY. HE CAN TURN OUR LIGHT *AGAINST* US. THE BLUE AND GREEN BATTERIES ARE ALREADY KNOCKED OUT. WE'RE *DYING.*
WHAT ARE YOU TALKING ABOUT? MY LIGHT'S JUST FINE.
THAT'S WHY I'M HERE.
REDS GET SOME OF THEIR POWER FROM THE *BLOOD* IN THAT DAMN *LAKE.*
I'VE NEVER UNDERSTOOD IT, BUT EVEN IF YOUR BATTERY'S AS BAD OFF AS OURS, YOU CAN STILL *FIGHT.*
YOU'RE THE ONLY ONES RELIC CAN'T TOUCH. YOU'RE THE ONLY ONES WHO CAN TAKE HIM.

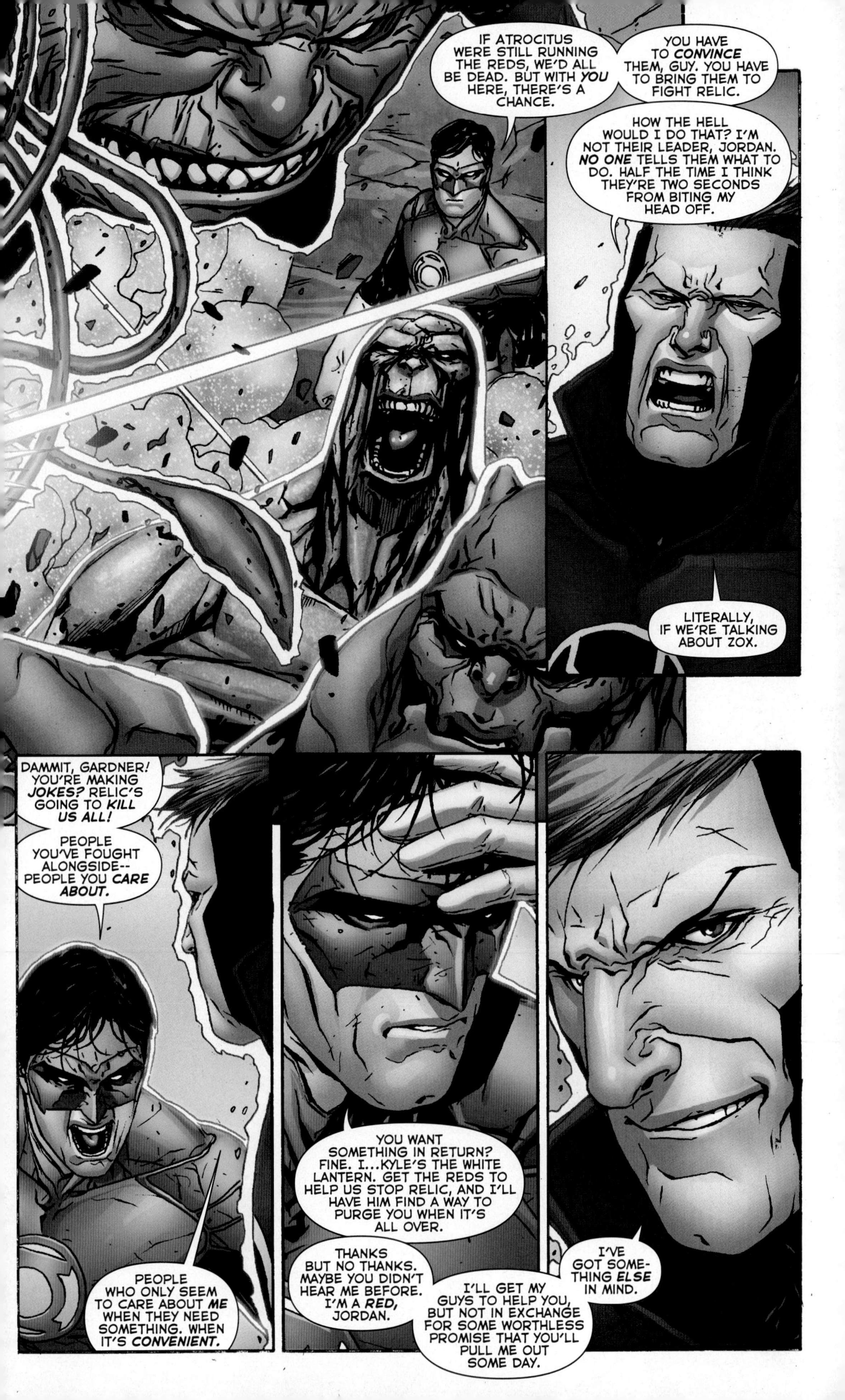
IF ATROCITUS WERE STILL RUNNING THE REDS, WE'D ALL BE DEAD. BUT WITH *YOU* HERE, THERE'S A CHANCE.
YOU HAVE TO *CONVINCE* THEM, GUY. YOU HAVE TO BRING THEM TO FIGHT RELIC.
HOW THE HELL WOULD I DO THAT? I'M NOT THEIR LEADER, JORDAN. *NO ONE* TELLS THEM WHAT TO DO. HALF THE TIME I THINK THEY'RE TWO SECONDS FROM BITING MY HEAD OFF.
LITERALLY, IF WE'RE TALKING ABOUT ZOX.
DAMMIT, GARDNER! YOU'RE MAKING *JOKES?* RELIC'S GOING TO *KILL US ALL!*
PEOPLE YOU'VE FOUGHT ALONGSIDE-- PEOPLE YOU *CARE ABOUT.*
PEOPLE WHO ONLY SEEM TO CARE ABOUT *ME* WHEN THEY NEED SOMETHING. WHEN IT'S *CONVENIENT.*
YOU WANT SOMETHING IN RETURN? FINE. I...KYLE'S THE WHITE LANTERN. GET THE REDS TO HELP US STOP RELIC, AND I'LL HAVE HIM FIND A WAY TO PURGE YOU WHEN IT'S ALL OVER.
THANKS BUT NO THANKS. MAYBE YOU DIDN'T HEAR ME BEFORE. I'M A *RED,* JORDAN.
I'LL GET MY GUYS TO HELP YOU, BUT NOT IN EXCHANGE FOR SOME WORTHLESS PROMISE THAT YOU'LL PULL ME OUT SOME DAY.
I'VE GOT SOME-THING *ELSE* IN MIND.

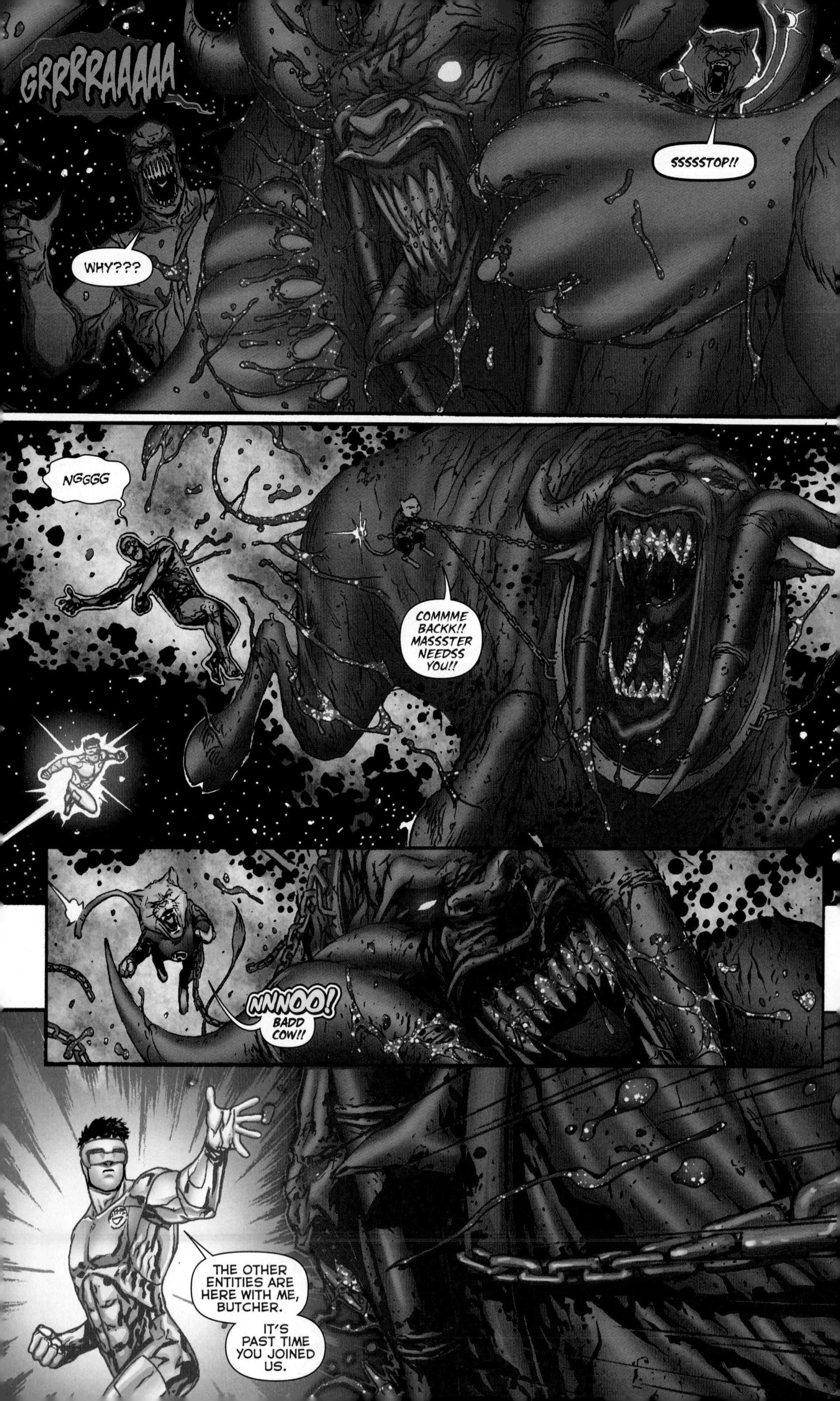
GRRRRAAAAAA
SSSSSTOP!!
WHY???
NGGGG
COMMME BACKK!! MASSSTER NEEDSS YOU!!
NNNOO! BADD COW!!
THE OTHER ENTITIES ARE HERE WITH ME, BUTCHER.
IT'S PAST TIME YOU JOINED US.

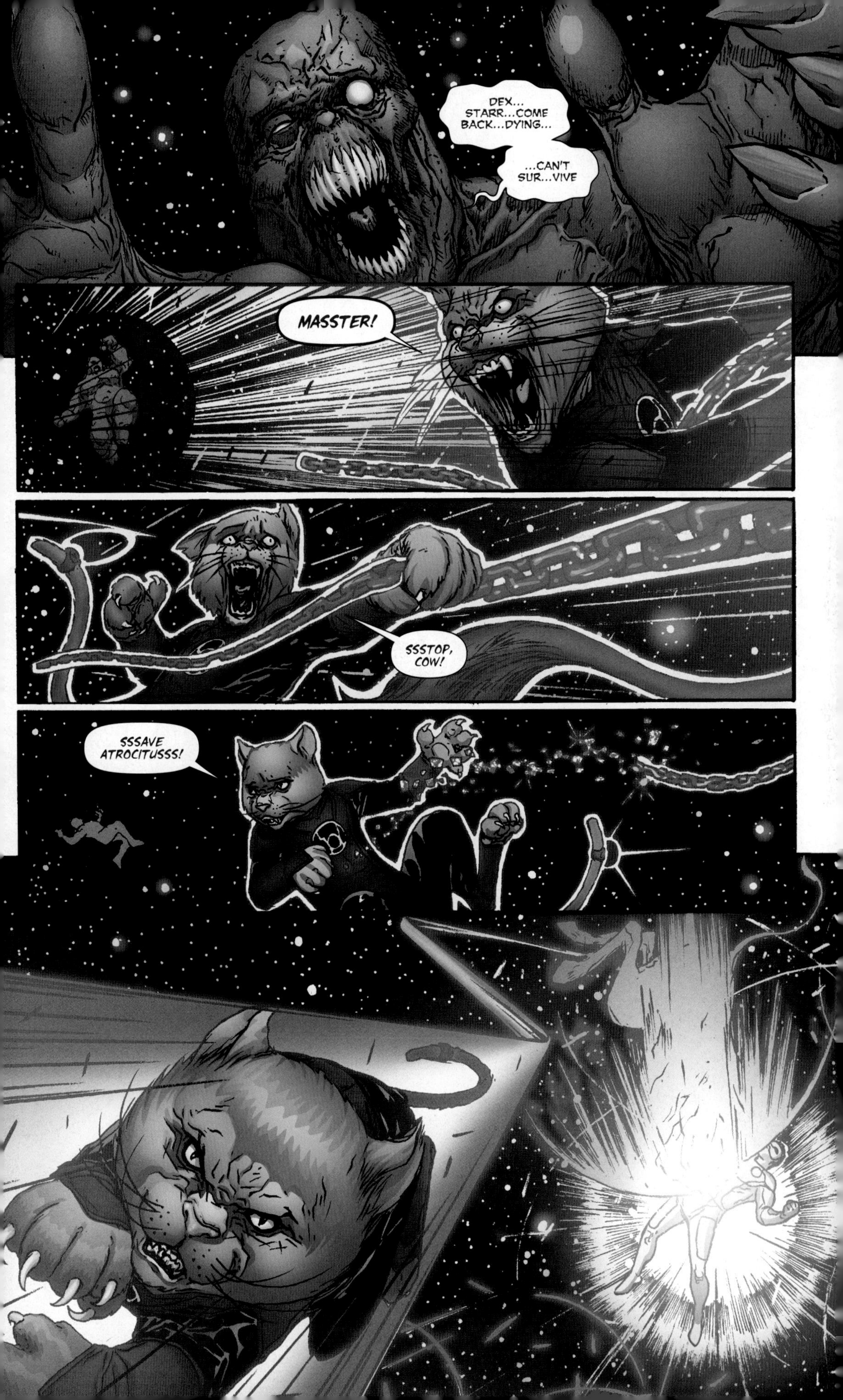

DEX... STARR...COME BACK...DYING...
...CAN'T SUR...VIVE
MASSTER!
SSSTOP, COW!
SSSAVE ATROCITUSSS!

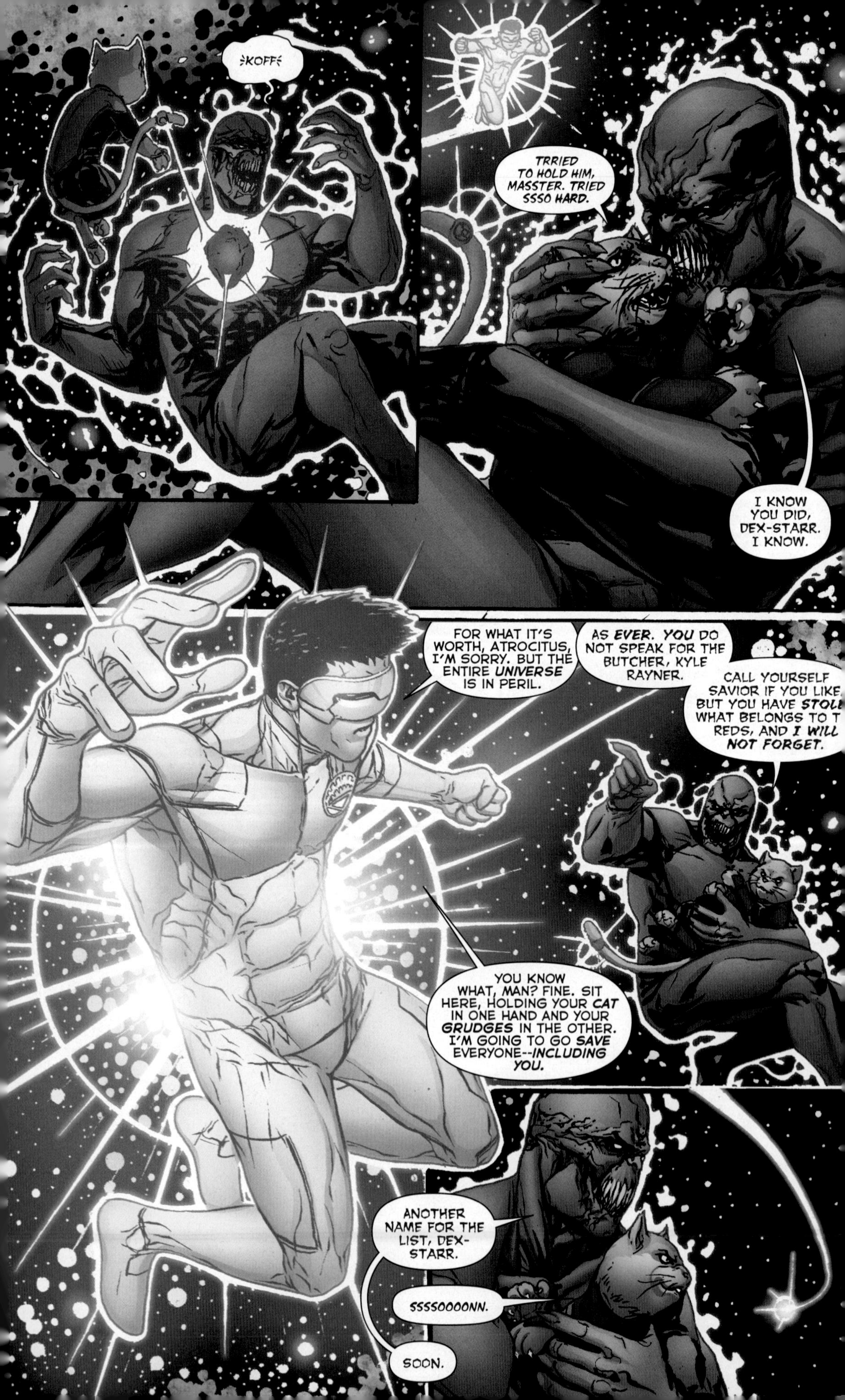

KOFF
TRRIED TO HOLD HIM, MASSTER. TRIED SSSO HARD.
I KNOW YOU DID, DEX-STARR. I KNOW.
FOR WHAT IT'S WORTH, ATROCITUS, I'M SORRY. BUT THE ENTIRE UNIVERSE IS IN PERIL.
AS EVER. YOU DO NOT SPEAK FOR THE BUTCHER, KYLE RAYNER.
CALL YOURSELF SAVIOR IF YOU LIKE, BUT YOU HAVE STOL WHAT BELONGS TO T REDS, AND I WILL NOT FORGET.
YOU KNOW WHAT, MAN? FINE. SIT HERE, HOLDING YOUR CAT IN ONE HAND AND YOUR GRUDGES IN THE OTHER. I'M GOING TO GO SAVE EVERYONE--INCLUDING YOU.
ANOTHER NAME FOR THE LIST, DEX-STARR.
SSSSOOOONN.
SOON.

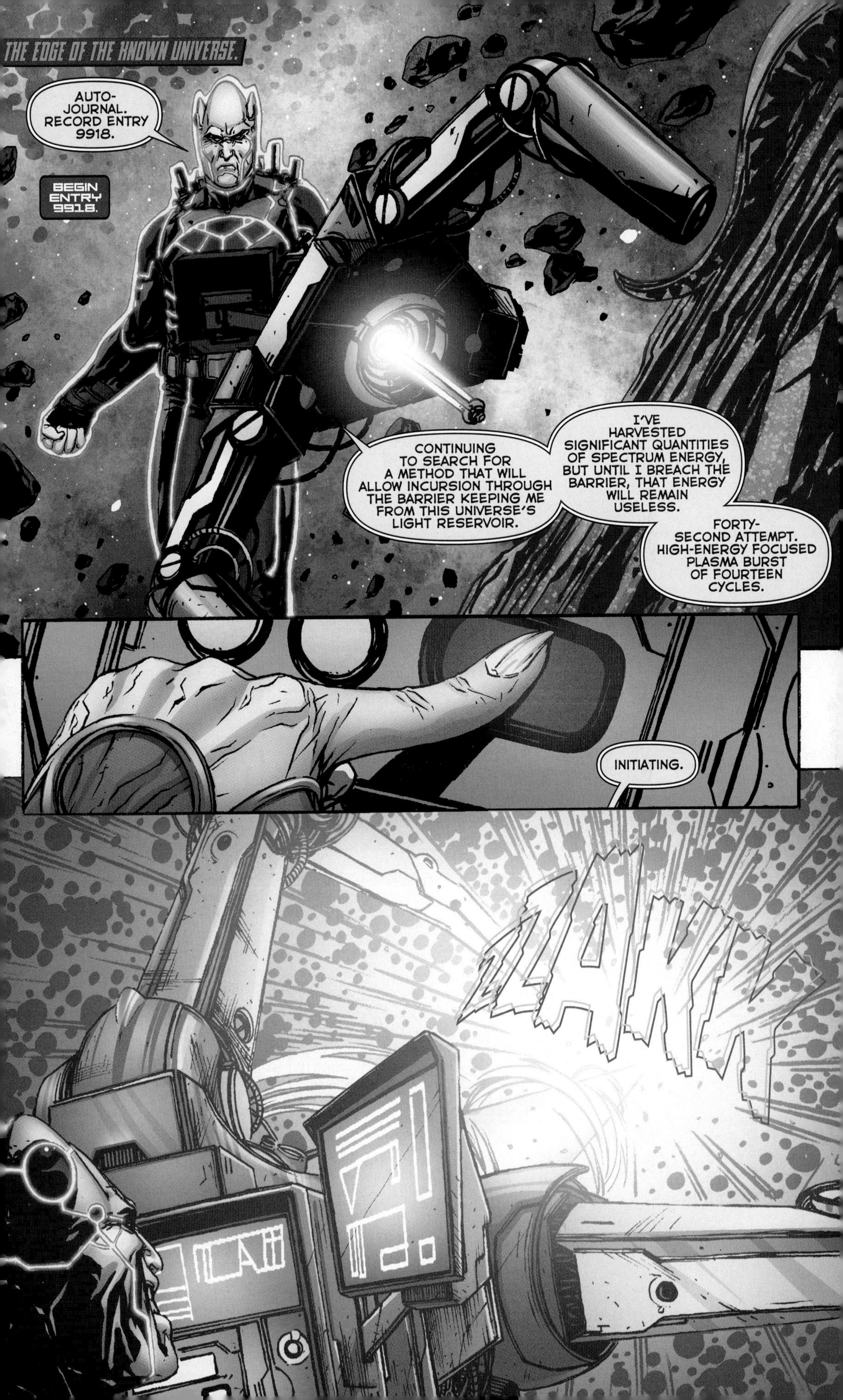
THE EDGE OF THE KNOWN UNIVERSE.
AUTO-JOURNAL. RECORD ENTRY 9918.
BEGIN ENTRY 9918.
CONTINUING TO SEARCH FOR A METHOD THAT WILL ALLOW INCURSION THROUGH THE BARRIER KEEPING ME FROM THIS UNIVERSE'S LIGHT RESERVOIR.
I'VE HARVESTED SIGNIFICANT QUANTITIES OF SPECTRUM ENERGY, BUT UNTIL I BREACH THE BARRIER, THAT ENERGY WILL REMAIN USELESS.
FORTY-SECOND ATTEMPT. HIGH-ENERGY FOCUSED PLASMA BURST OF FOURTEEN CYCLES.
INITIATING.
ZAKK

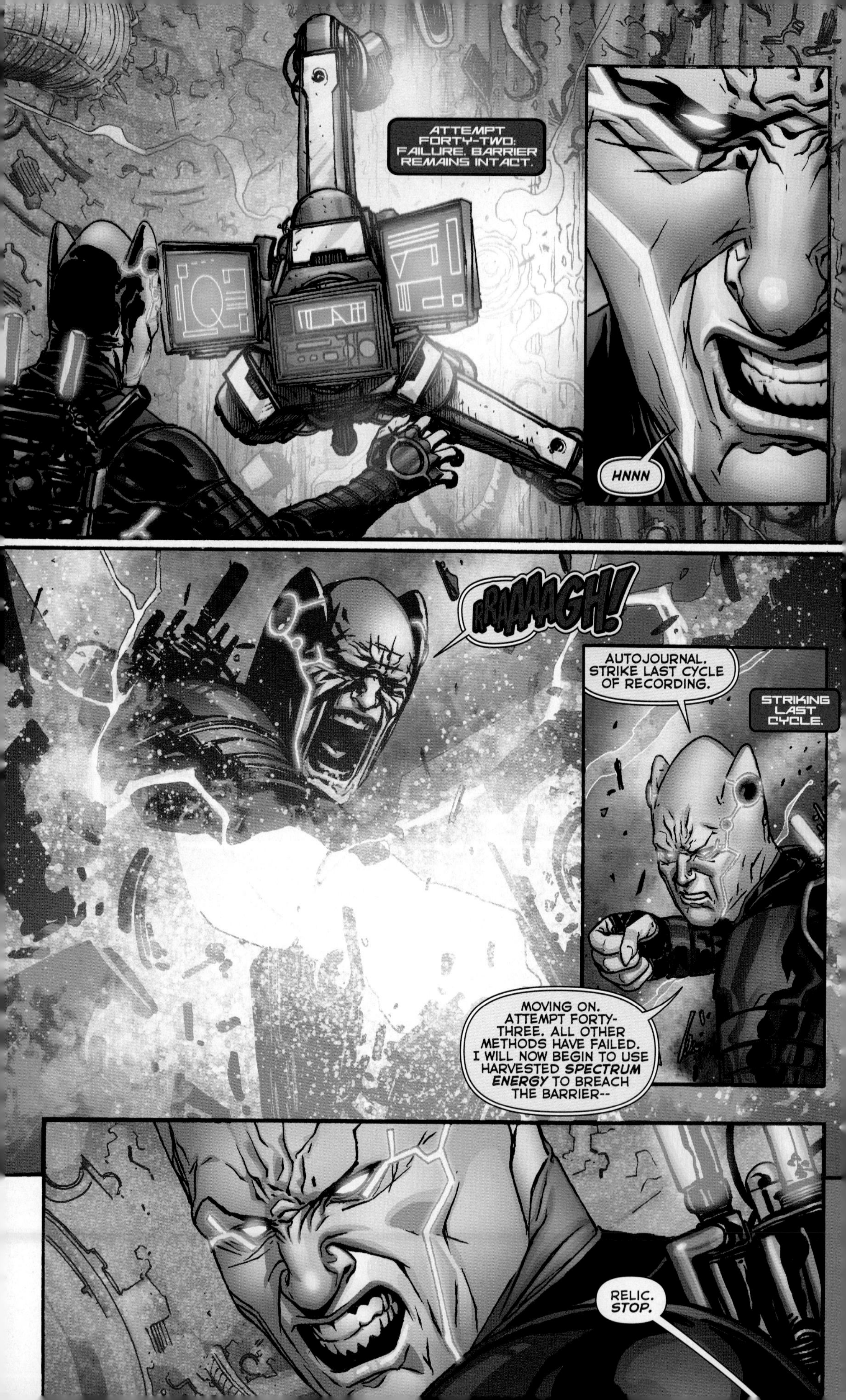
ATTEMPT FORTY-TWO: FAILURE. BARRIER REMAINS INTACT.
HNNN
RRAAAAAGH!
AUTOJOURNAL. STRIKE LAST CYCLE OF RECORDING.
STRIKING LAST CYCLE.
MOVING ON. ATTEMPT FORTY-THREE. ALL OTHER METHODS HAVE FAILED. I WILL NOW BEGIN TO USE HARVESTED *SPECTRUM ENERGY* TO BREACH THE BARRIER--
RELIC. STOP.

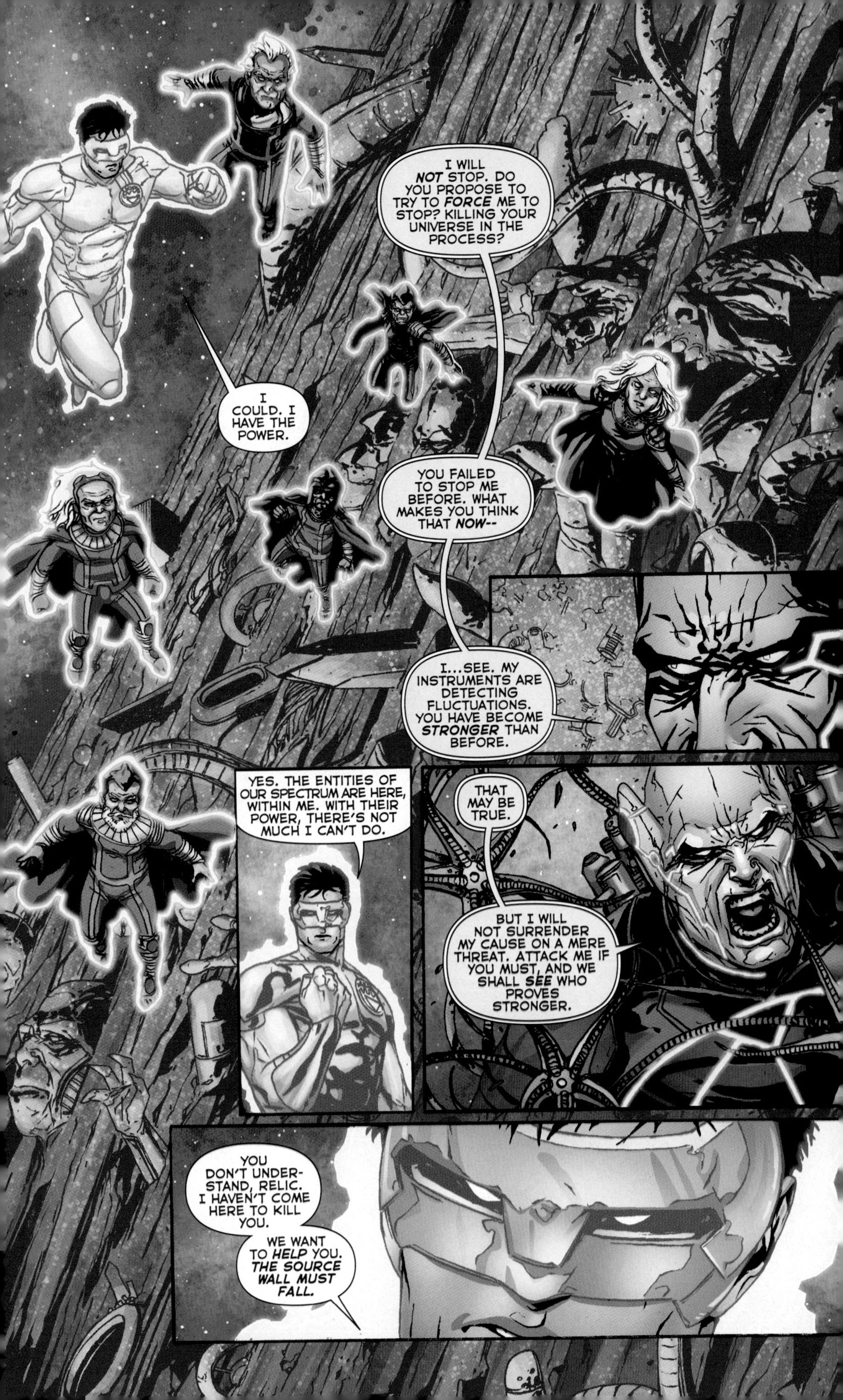
I WILL NOT STOP. DO YOU PROPOSE TO TRY TO FORCE ME TO STOP? KILLING YOUR UNIVERSE IN THE PROCESS?
I COULD. I HAVE THE POWER.
YOU FAILED TO STOP ME BEFORE. WHAT MAKES YOU THINK THAT NOW--
I...SEE. MY INSTRUMENTS ARE DETECTING FLUCTUATIONS. YOU HAVE BECOME STRONGER THAN BEFORE.
YES. THE ENTITIES OF OUR SPECTRUM ARE HERE, WITHIN ME. WITH THEIR POWER, THERE'S NOT MUCH I CAN'T DO.
THAT MAY BE TRUE.
BUT I WILL NOT SURRENDER MY CAUSE ON A MERE THREAT. ATTACK ME IF YOU MUST, AND WE SHALL SEE WHO PROVES STRONGER.
YOU DON'T UNDER-STAND, RELIC. I HAVEN'T COME HERE TO KILL YOU.
WE WANT TO HELP YOU. THE SOURCE WALL MUST FALL.

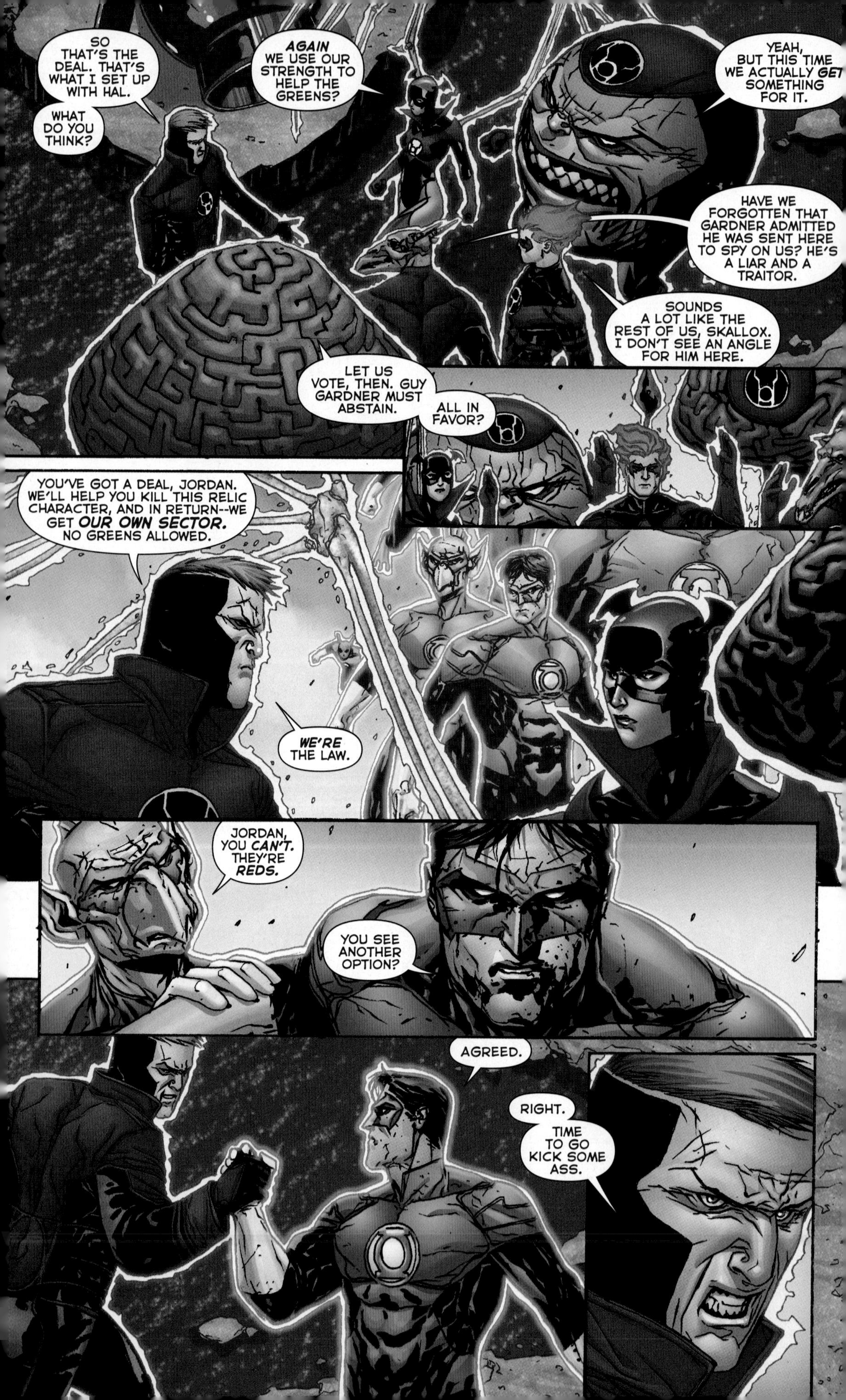

SO THAT'S THE DEAL. THAT'S WHAT I SET UP WITH HAL.
WHAT DO YOU THINK?
AGAIN WE USE OUR STRENGTH TO HELP THE GREENS?
YEAH, BUT THIS TIME WE ACTUALLY GET SOMETHING FOR IT.
HAVE WE FORGOTTEN THAT GARDNER ADMITTED HE WAS SENT HERE TO SPY ON US? HE'S A LIAR AND A TRAITOR.
SOUNDS A LOT LIKE THE REST OF US, SKALLOX. I DON'T SEE AN ANGLE FOR HIM HERE.
LET US VOTE, THEN. GUY GARDNER MUST ABSTAIN.
ALL IN FAVOR?
YOU'VE GOT A DEAL, JORDAN. WE'LL HELP YOU KILL THIS RELIC CHARACTER, AND IN RETURN--WE GET OUR OWN SECTOR. NO GREENS ALLOWED.
WE'RE THE LAW.
JORDAN, YOU CAN'T. THEY'RE REDS.
YOU SEE ANOTHER OPTION?
AGREED.
RIGHT.
TIME TO GO KICK SOME ASS.

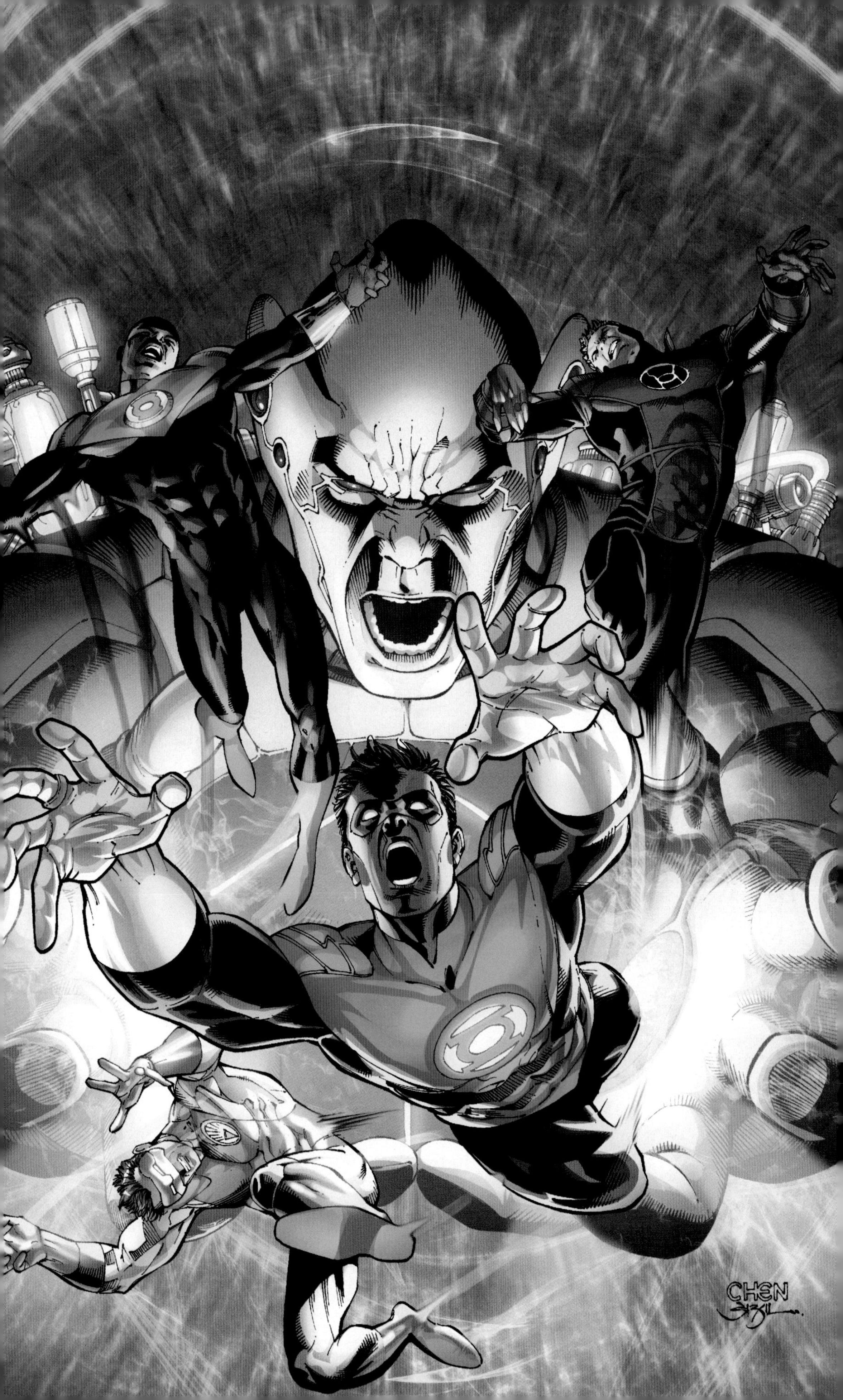
CHEN

LIGHTS OUT part five: THE SOURCE

ROBERT VENDITTI writer SEAN CHEN penciller JON SIBAL with WALDEN WONG inkers
ANDREW DALHOUSE with WIL QUINTANA colorists SEAN CHEN with JON SIBAL and ALEX SINCLAIR cover artists

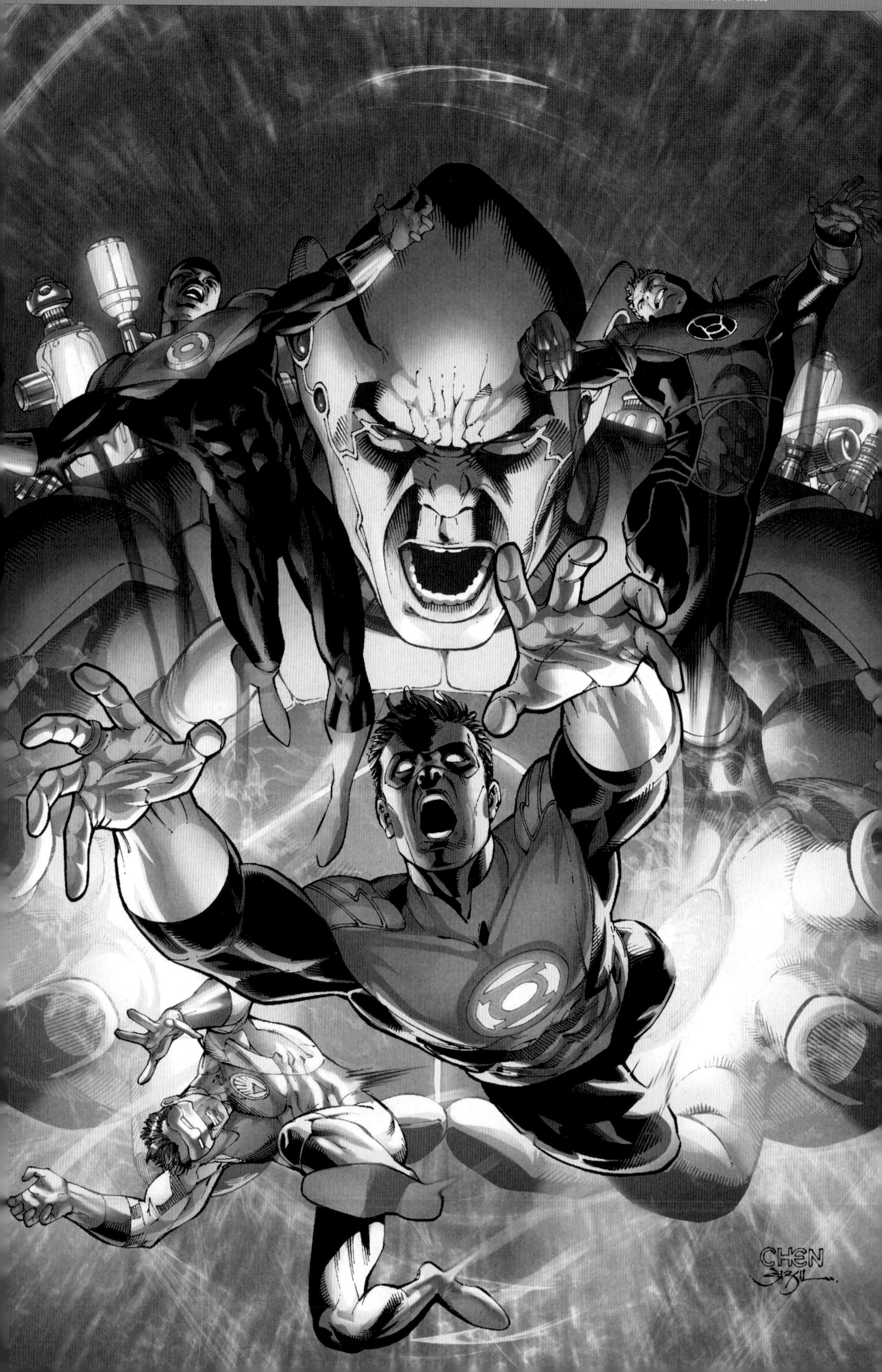
CHEN
SIBAL

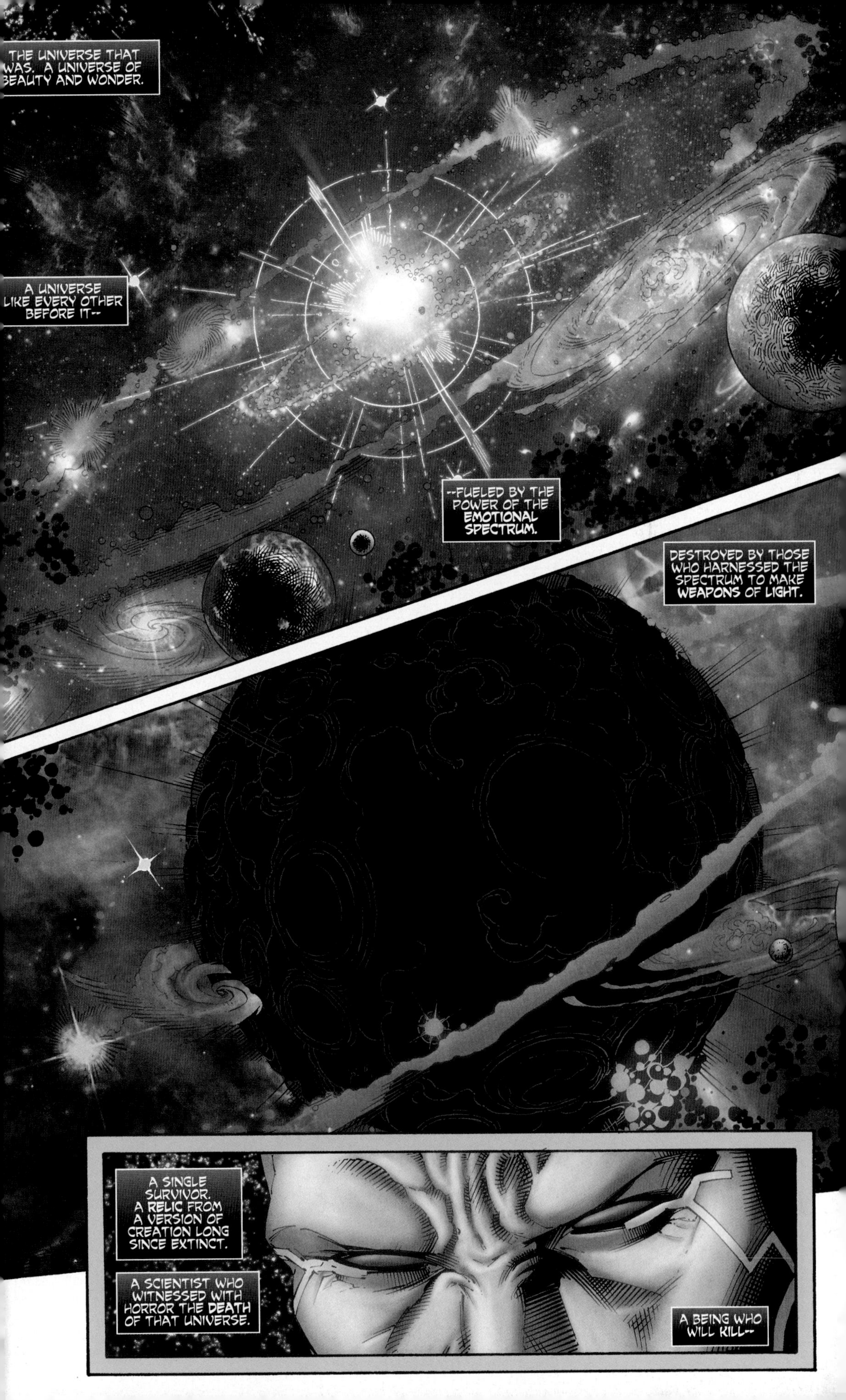
THE UNIVERSE THAT WAS. A UNIVERSE OF BEAUTY AND WONDER.
A UNIVERSE LIKE EVERY OTHER BEFORE IT--
--FUELED BY THE POWER OF THE EMOTIONAL SPECTRUM.
DESTROYED BY THOSE WHO HARNESSED THE SPECTRUM TO MAKE WEAPONS OF LIGHT.
A SINGLE SURVIVOR. A RELIC FROM A VERSION OF CREATION LONG SINCE EXTINCT.
A SCIENTIST WHO WITNESSED WITH HORROR THE DEATH OF THAT UNIVERSE.
A BEING WHO WILL KILL--

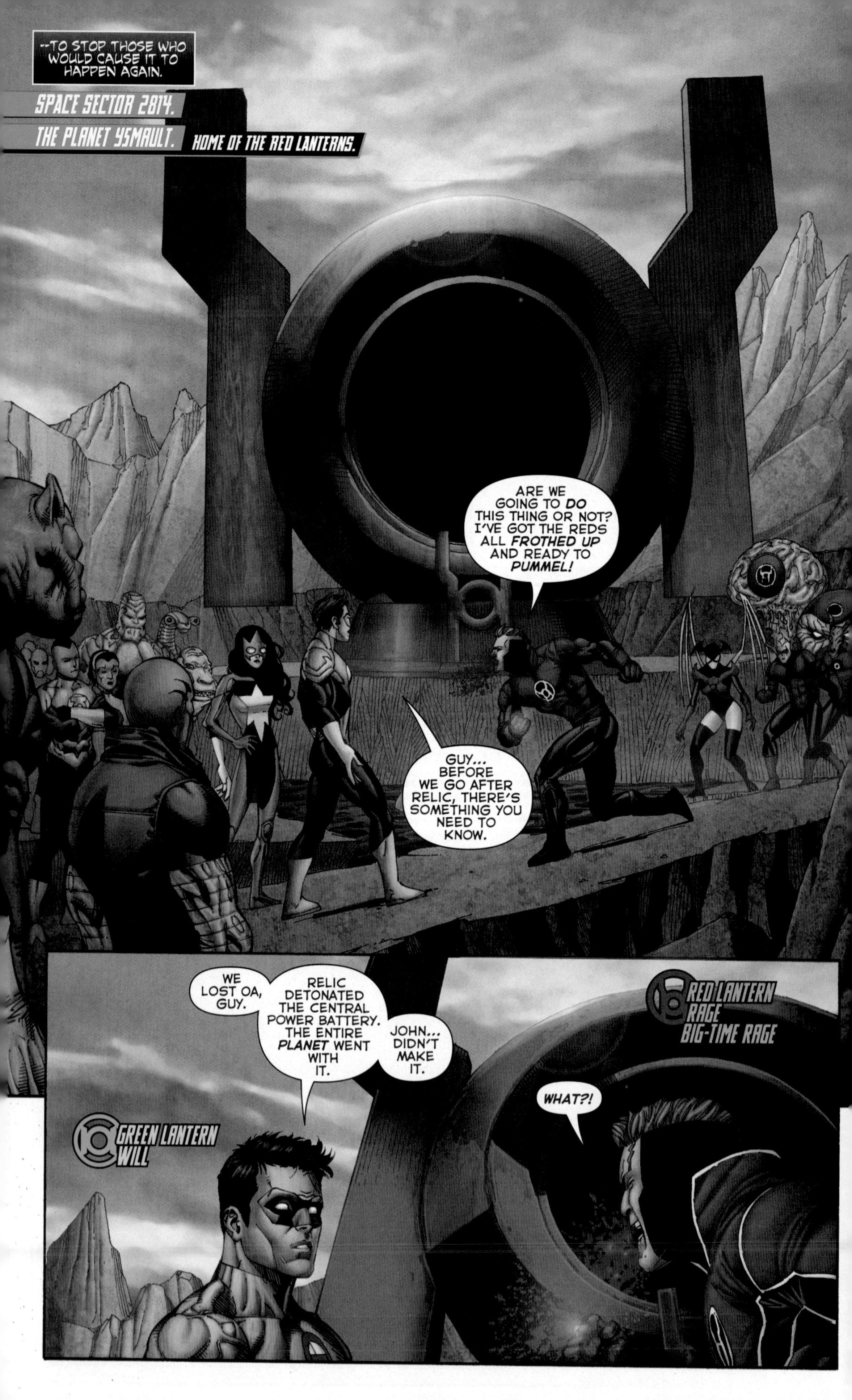
--TO STOP THOSE WHO WOULD CAUSE IT TO HAPPEN AGAIN.
SPACE SECTOR 2814.
THE PLANET YSMAULT.
HOME OF THE RED LANTERNS.
ARE WE GOING TO DO THIS THING OR NOT? I'VE GOT THE REDS ALL FROTHED UP AND READY TO PUMMEL!
GUY... BEFORE WE GO AFTER RELIC, THERE'S SOMETHING YOU NEED TO KNOW.
WE LOST OA, GUY.
RELIC DETONATED THE CENTRAL POWER BATTERY. THE ENTIRE PLANET WENT WITH IT.
JOHN... DIDN'T MAKE IT.
RED LANTERN RAGE BIG-TIME RAGE
WHAT?!
GREEN LANTERN WILL

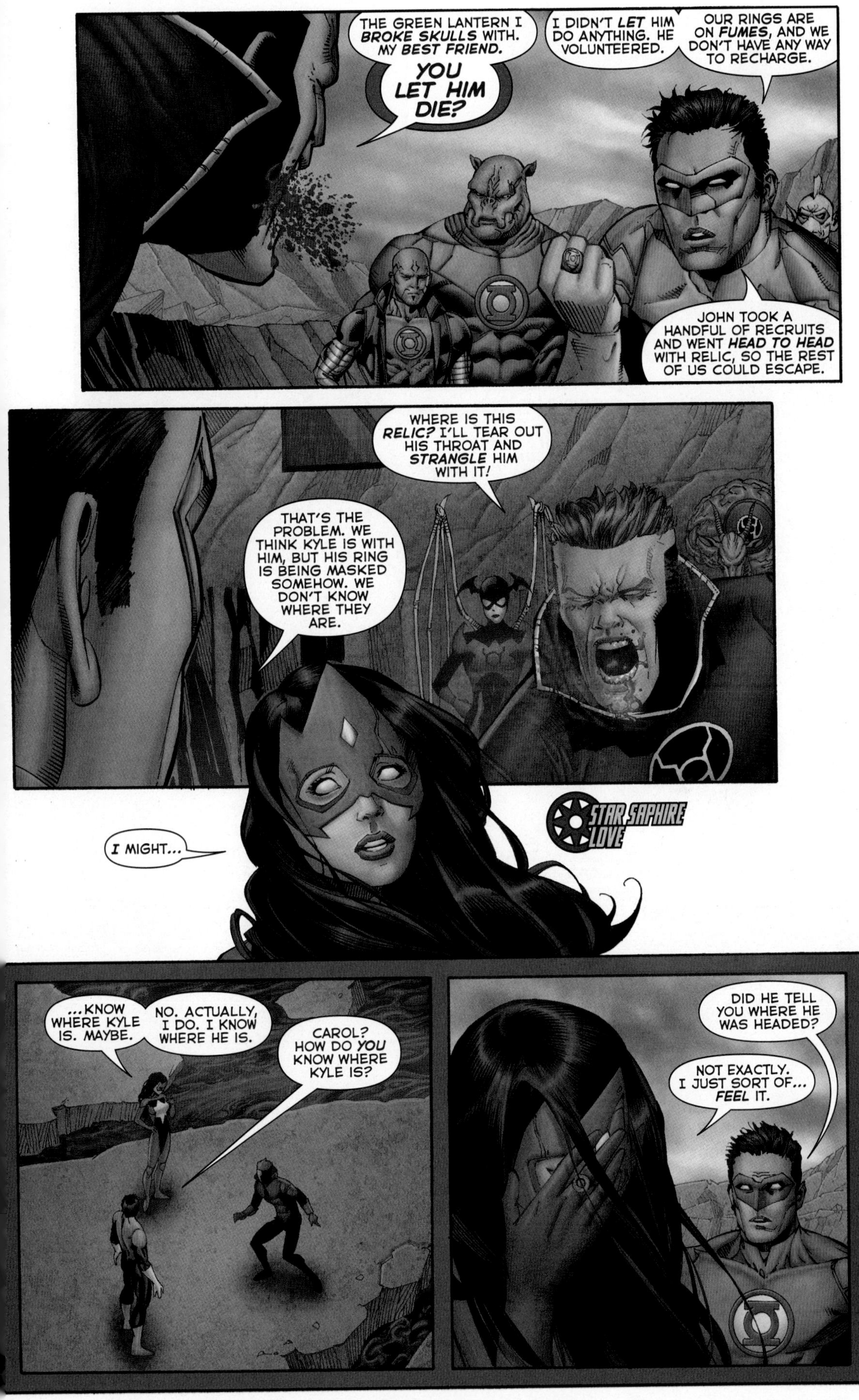
THE GREEN LANTERN I BROKE SKULLS WITH. MY BEST FRIEND.
YOU LET HIM DIE?
I DIDN'T LET HIM DO ANYTHING. HE VOLUNTEERED.
OUR RINGS ARE ON FUMES, AND WE DON'T HAVE ANY WAY TO RECHARGE.
JOHN TOOK A HANDFUL OF RECRUITS AND WENT HEAD TO HEAD WITH RELIC, SO THE REST OF US COULD ESCAPE.
WHERE IS THIS RELIC? I'LL TEAR OUT HIS THROAT AND STRANGLE HIM WITH IT!
THAT'S THE PROBLEM. WE THINK KYLE IS WITH HIM, BUT HIS RING IS BEING MASKED SOMEHOW. WE DON'T KNOW WHERE THEY ARE.
STAR SAPHIRE LOVE
I MIGHT...
...KNOW WHERE KYLE IS. MAYBE.
NO. ACTUALLY, I DO. I KNOW WHERE HE IS.
CAROL? HOW DO YOU KNOW WHERE KYLE IS?
DID HE TELL YOU WHERE HE WAS HEADED?
NOT EXACTLY. I JUST SORT OF... FEEL IT.

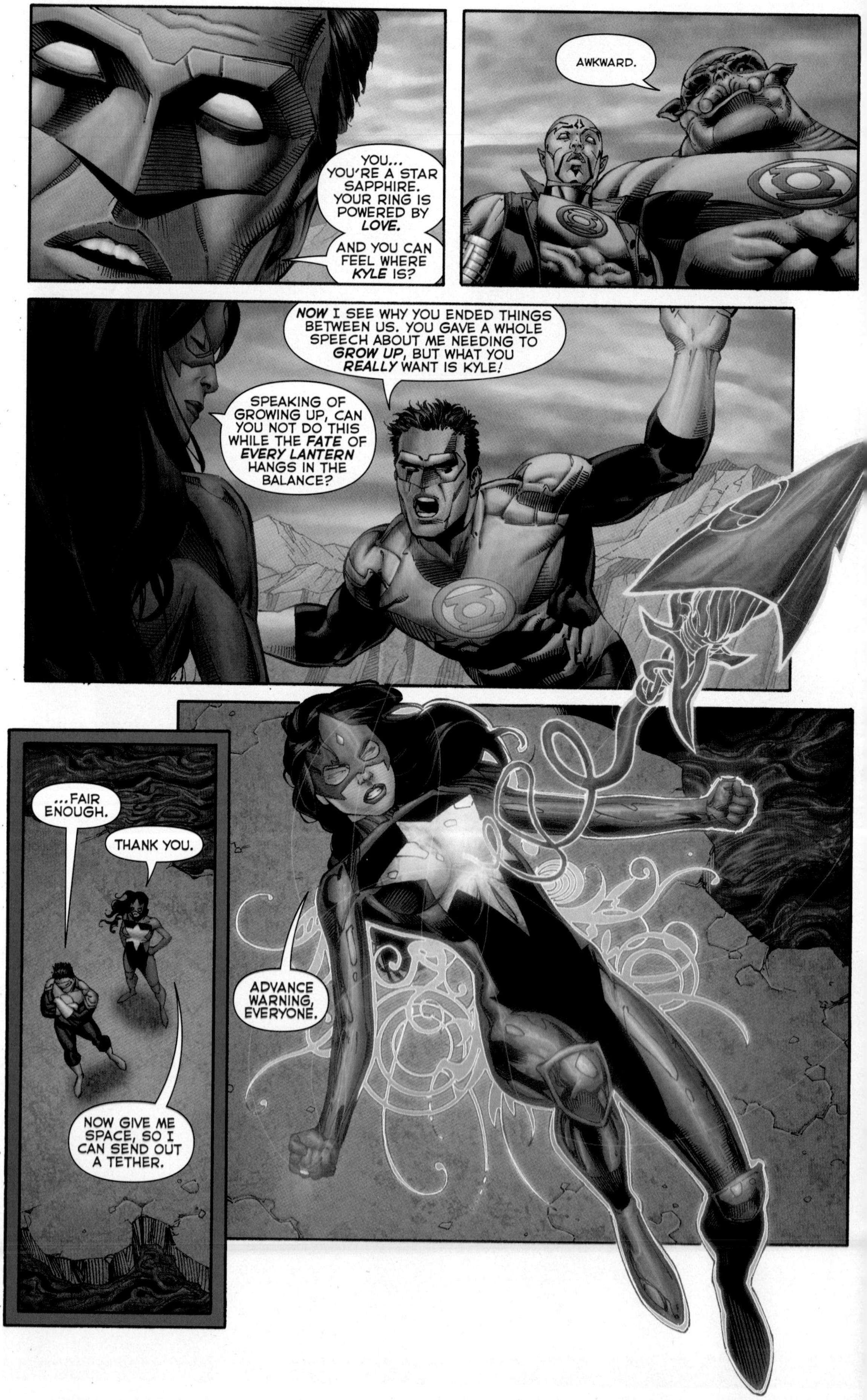
YOU... YOU'RE A STAR SAPPHIRE. YOUR RING IS POWERED BY LOVE.
AND YOU CAN FEEL WHERE KYLE IS?
AWKWARD.
NOW I SEE WHY YOU ENDED THINGS BETWEEN US. YOU GAVE A WHOLE SPEECH ABOUT ME NEEDING TO GROW UP, BUT WHAT YOU REALLY WANT IS KYLE!
SPEAKING OF GROWING UP, CAN YOU NOT DO THIS WHILE THE FATE OF EVERY LANTERN HANGS IN THE BALANCE?
...FAIR ENOUGH.
THANK YOU.
NOW GIVE ME SPACE, SO I CAN SEND OUT A TETHER.
ADVANCE WARNING, EVERYONE.

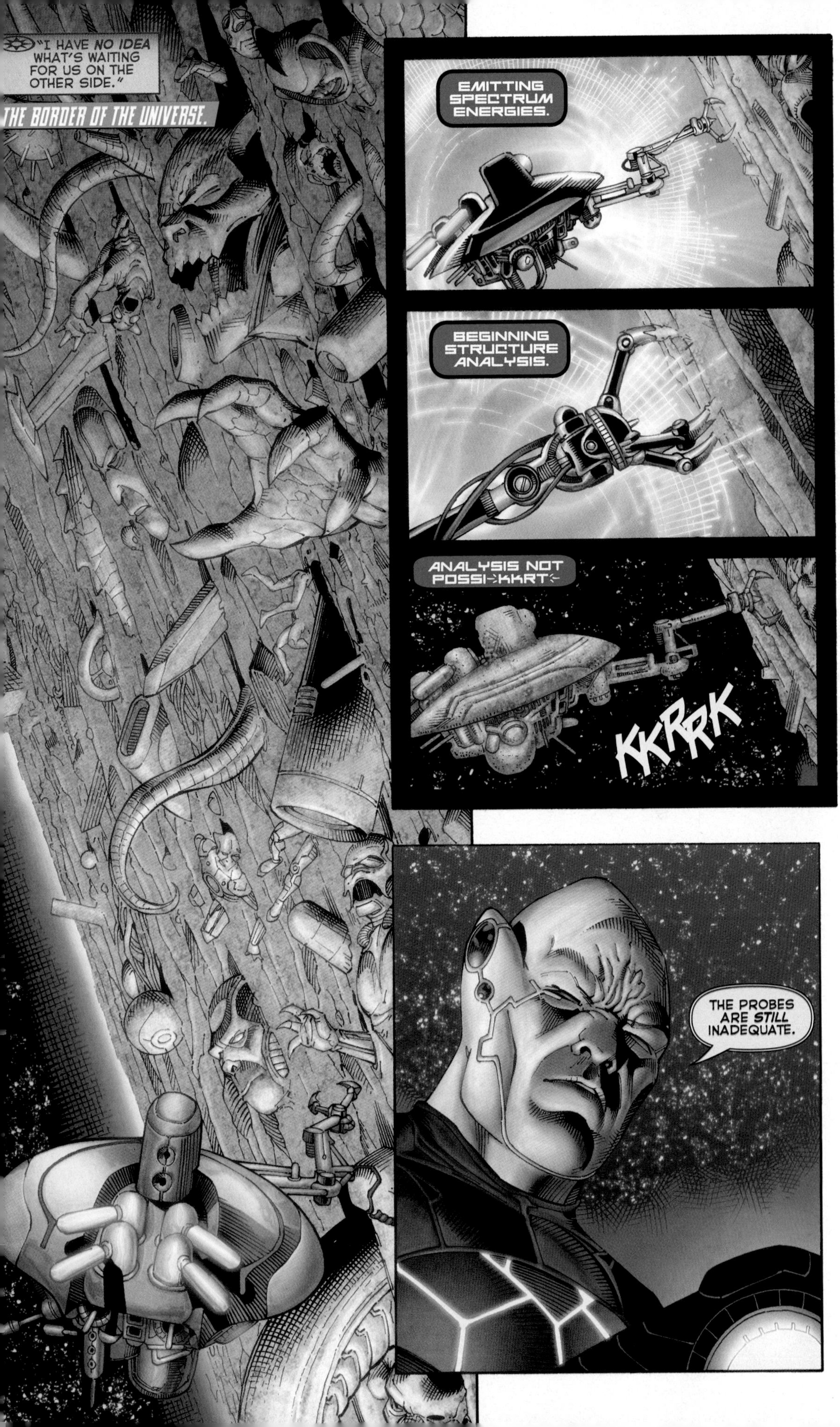
"I HAVE NO IDEA WHAT'S WAITING FOR US ON THE OTHER SIDE."
THE BORDER OF THE UNIVERSE.
EMITTING SPECTRUM ENERGIES.
BEGINNING STRUCTURE ANALYSIS.
ANALYSIS NOT POSSI-KKRT-
KKRRK
THE PROBES ARE STILL INADEQUATE.

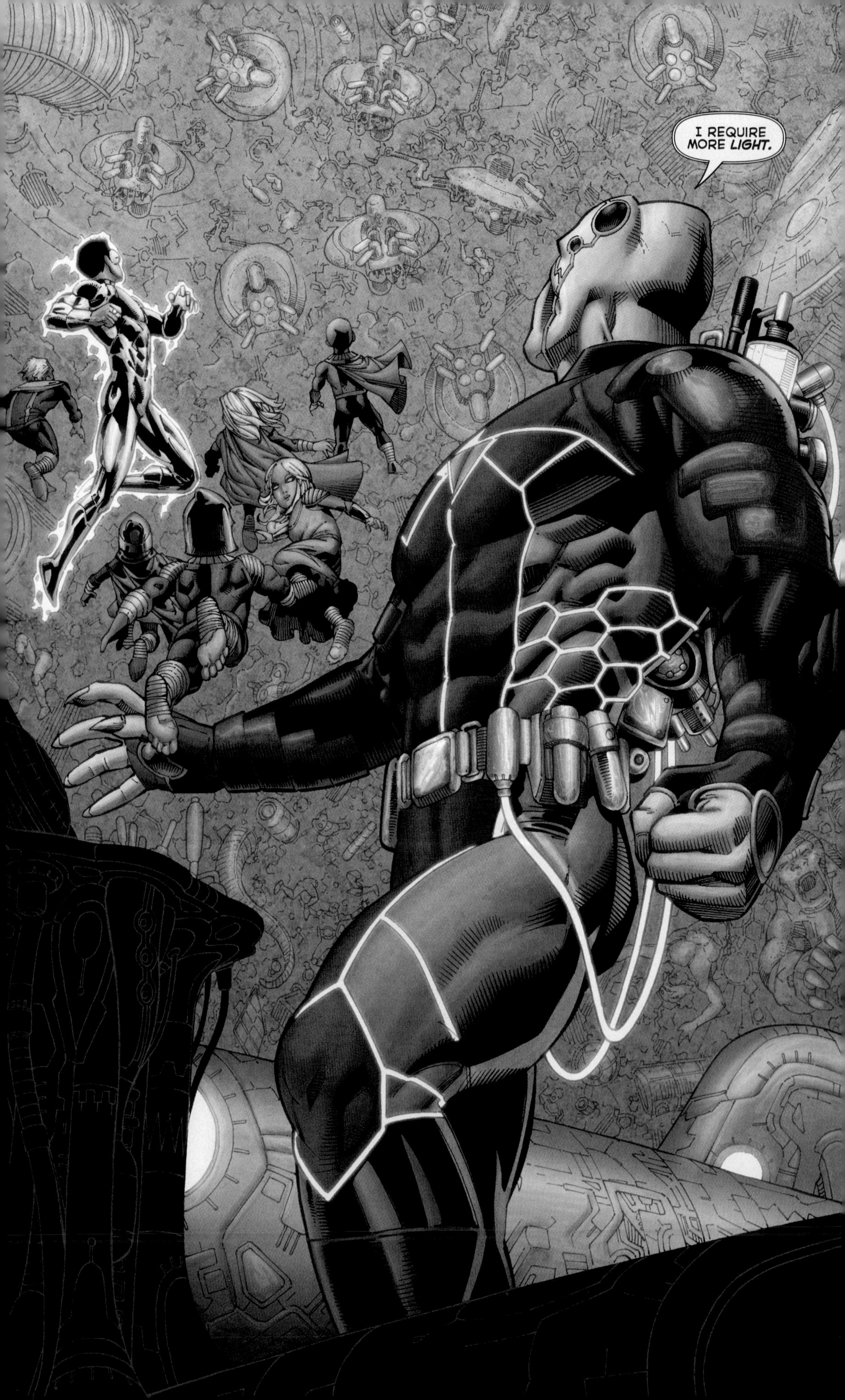
I REQUIRE MORE *LIGHT*.

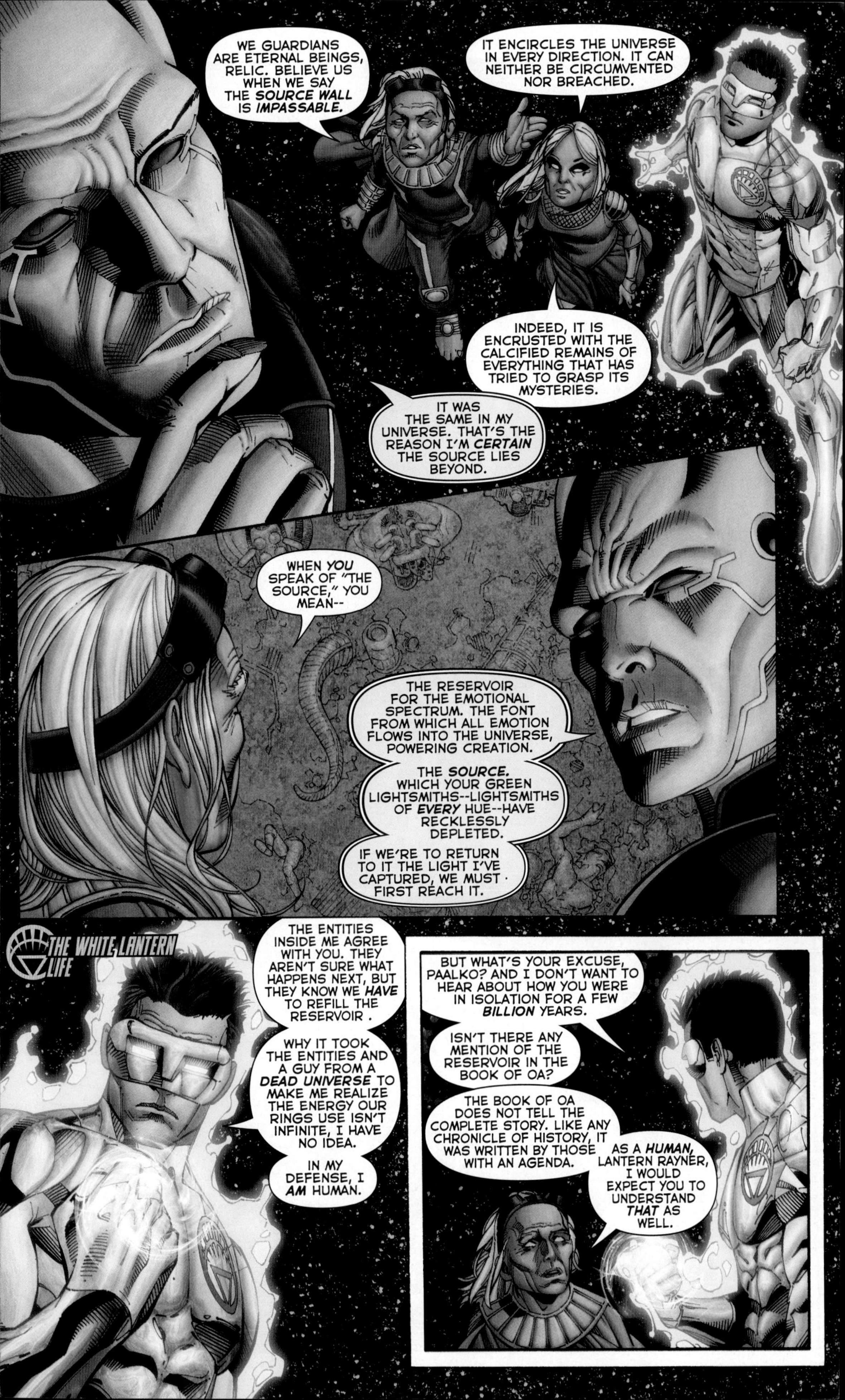
WE GUARDIANS ARE ETERNAL BEINGS, RELIC. BELIEVE US WHEN WE SAY THE SOURCE WALL IS IMPASSABLE.
IT ENCIRCLES THE UNIVERSE IN EVERY DIRECTION. IT CAN NEITHER BE CIRCUMVENTED NOR BREACHED.
INDEED, IT IS ENCRUSTED WITH THE CALCIFIED REMAINS OF EVERYTHING THAT HAS TRIED TO GRASP ITS MYSTERIES.
IT WAS THE SAME IN MY UNIVERSE. THAT'S THE REASON I'M CERTAIN THE SOURCE LIES BEYOND.
WHEN YOU SPEAK OF "THE SOURCE," YOU MEAN--
THE RESERVOIR FOR THE EMOTIONAL SPECTRUM. THE FONT FROM WHICH ALL EMOTION FLOWS INTO THE UNIVERSE, POWERING CREATION.
THE SOURCE. WHICH YOUR GREEN LIGHTSMITHS--LIGHTSMITHS OF EVERY HUE--HAVE RECKLESSLY DEPLETED.
IF WE'RE TO RETURN TO IT THE LIGHT I'VE CAPTURED, WE MUST FIRST REACH IT.
THE WHITE LANTERN LIFE
THE ENTITIES INSIDE ME AGREE WITH YOU. THEY AREN'T SURE WHAT HAPPENS NEXT, BUT THEY KNOW WE HAVE TO REFILL THE RESERVOIR .
WHY IT TOOK THE ENTITIES AND A GUY FROM A DEAD UNIVERSE TO MAKE ME REALIZE THE ENERGY OUR RINGS USE ISN'T INFINITE, I HAVE NO IDEA.
IN MY DEFENSE, I AM HUMAN.
BUT WHAT'S YOUR EXCUSE, PAALKO? AND I DON'T WANT TO HEAR ABOUT HOW YOU WERE IN ISOLATION FOR A FEW BILLION YEARS.
ISN'T THERE ANY MENTION OF THE RESERVOIR IN THE BOOK OF OA?
THE BOOK OF OA DOES NOT TELL THE COMPLETE STORY. LIKE ANY CHRONICLE OF HISTORY, IT WAS WRITTEN BY THOSE WITH AN AGENDA.
AS A HUMAN, LANTERN RAYNER, I WOULD EXPECT YOU TO UNDERSTAND THAT AS WELL.

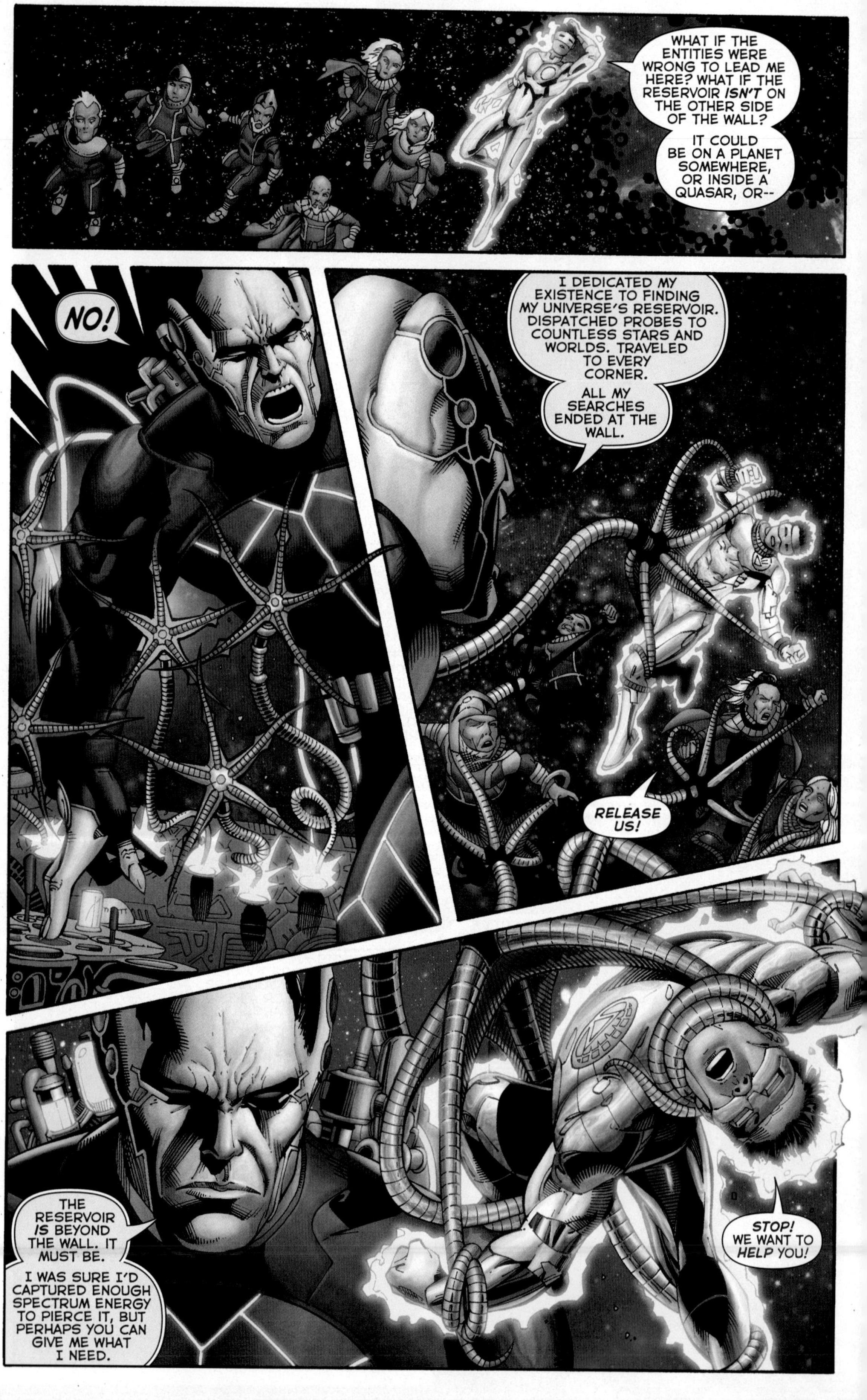
WHAT IF THE ENTITIES WERE WRONG TO LEAD ME HERE? WHAT IF THE RESERVOIR ISN'T ON THE OTHER SIDE OF THE WALL?
IT COULD BE ON A PLANET SOMEWHERE, OR INSIDE A QUASAR, OR--
NO!
I DEDICATED MY EXISTENCE TO FINDING MY UNIVERSE'S RESERVOIR. DISPATCHED PROBES TO COUNTLESS STARS AND WORLDS. TRAVELED TO EVERY CORNER.
ALL MY SEARCHES ENDED AT THE WALL.
RELEASE US!
THE RESERVOIR IS BEYOND THE WALL. IT MUST BE.
I WAS SURE I'D CAPTURED ENOUGH SPECTRUM ENERGY TO PIERCE IT, BUT PERHAPS YOU CAN GIVE ME WHAT I NEED.
STOP! WE WANT TO HELP YOU!

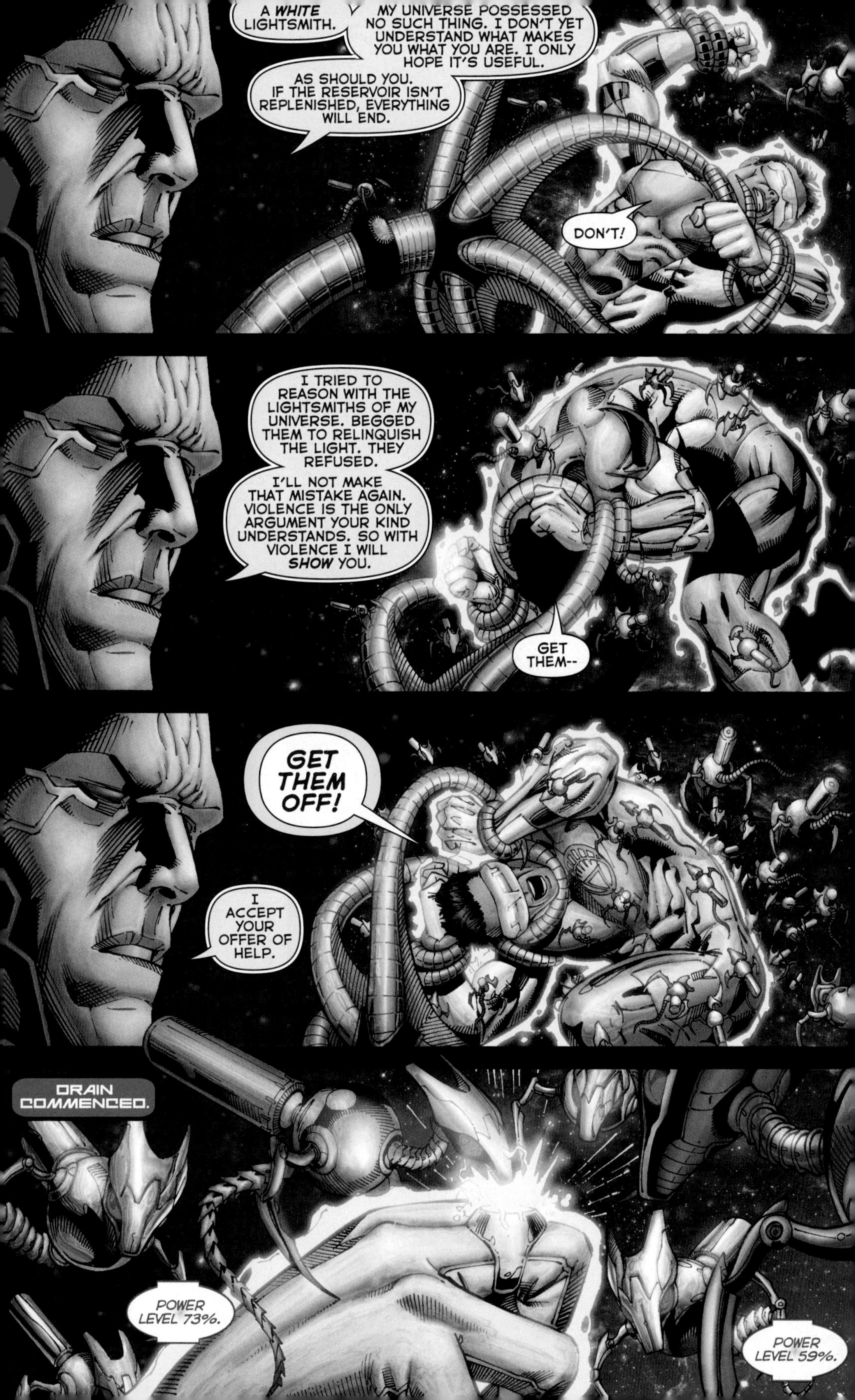

A WHITE LIGHTSMITH.
MY UNIVERSE POSSESSED NO SUCH THING. I DON'T YET UNDERSTAND WHAT MAKES YOU WHAT YOU ARE. I ONLY HOPE IT'S USEFUL.
AS SHOULD YOU. IF THE RESERVOIR ISN'T REPLENISHED, EVERYTHING WILL END.
DON'T!
I TRIED TO REASON WITH THE LIGHTSMITHS OF MY UNIVERSE. BEGGED THEM TO RELINQUISH THE LIGHT. THEY REFUSED.
I'LL NOT MAKE THAT MISTAKE AGAIN. VIOLENCE IS THE ONLY ARGUMENT YOUR KIND UNDERSTANDS. SO WITH VIOLENCE I WILL SHOW YOU.
GET THEM--
GET THEM OFF!
I ACCEPT YOUR OFFER OF HELP.
DRAIN COMMENCED.
POWER LEVEL 73%.
POWER LEVEL 59%.

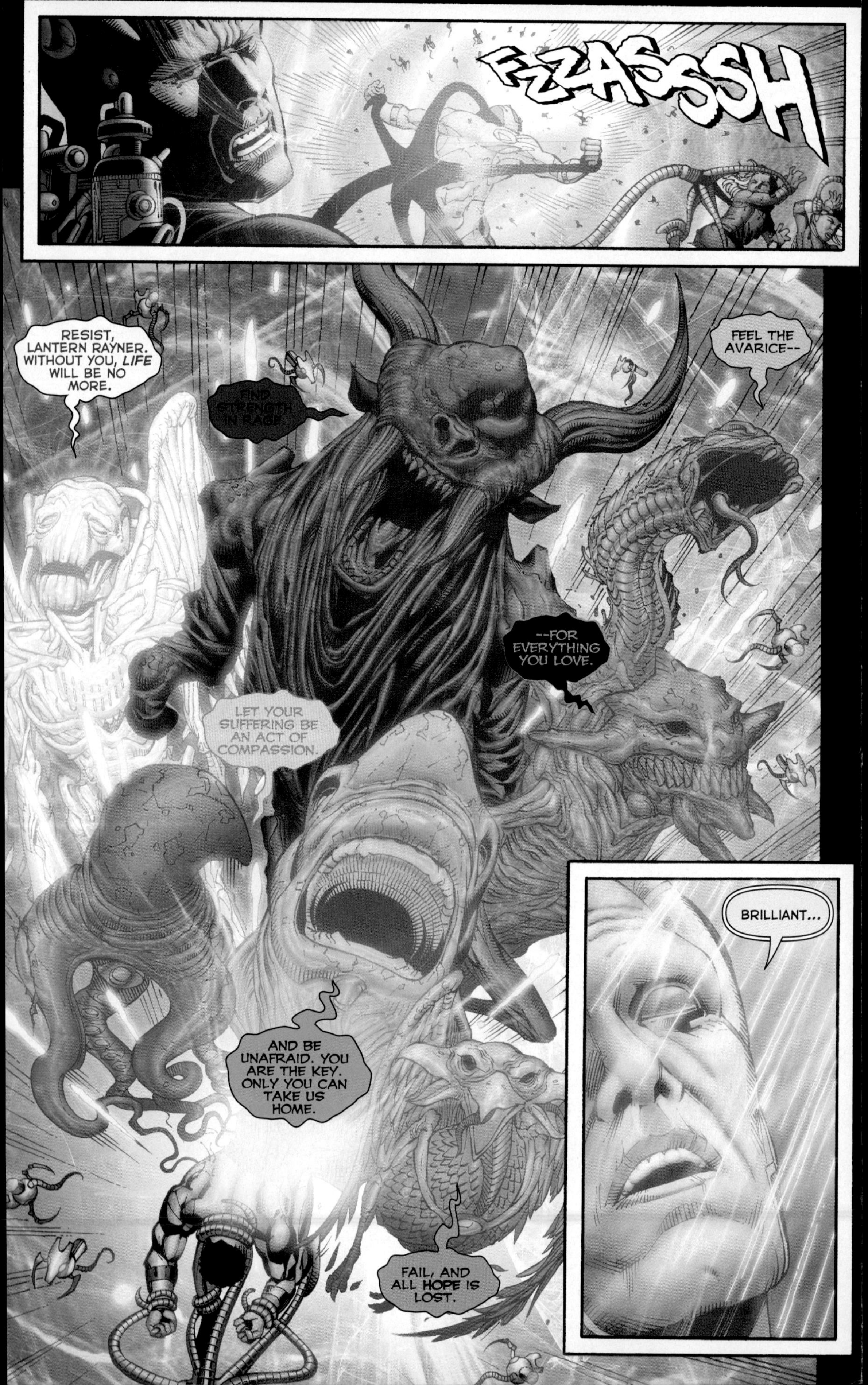
FZZASSSH
RESIST, LANTERN RAYNER. WITHOUT YOU, *LIFE* WILL BE NO MORE.
FIND STRENGTH IN RAGE.
FEEL THE AVARICE--
--FOR EVERYTHING YOU LOVE.
LET YOUR SUFFERING BE AN ACT OF COMPASSION.
AND BE UNAFRAID. YOU ARE THE KEY. ONLY YOU CAN TAKE US HOME.
FAIL, AND ALL **HOPE** IS LOST.
BRILLIANT...

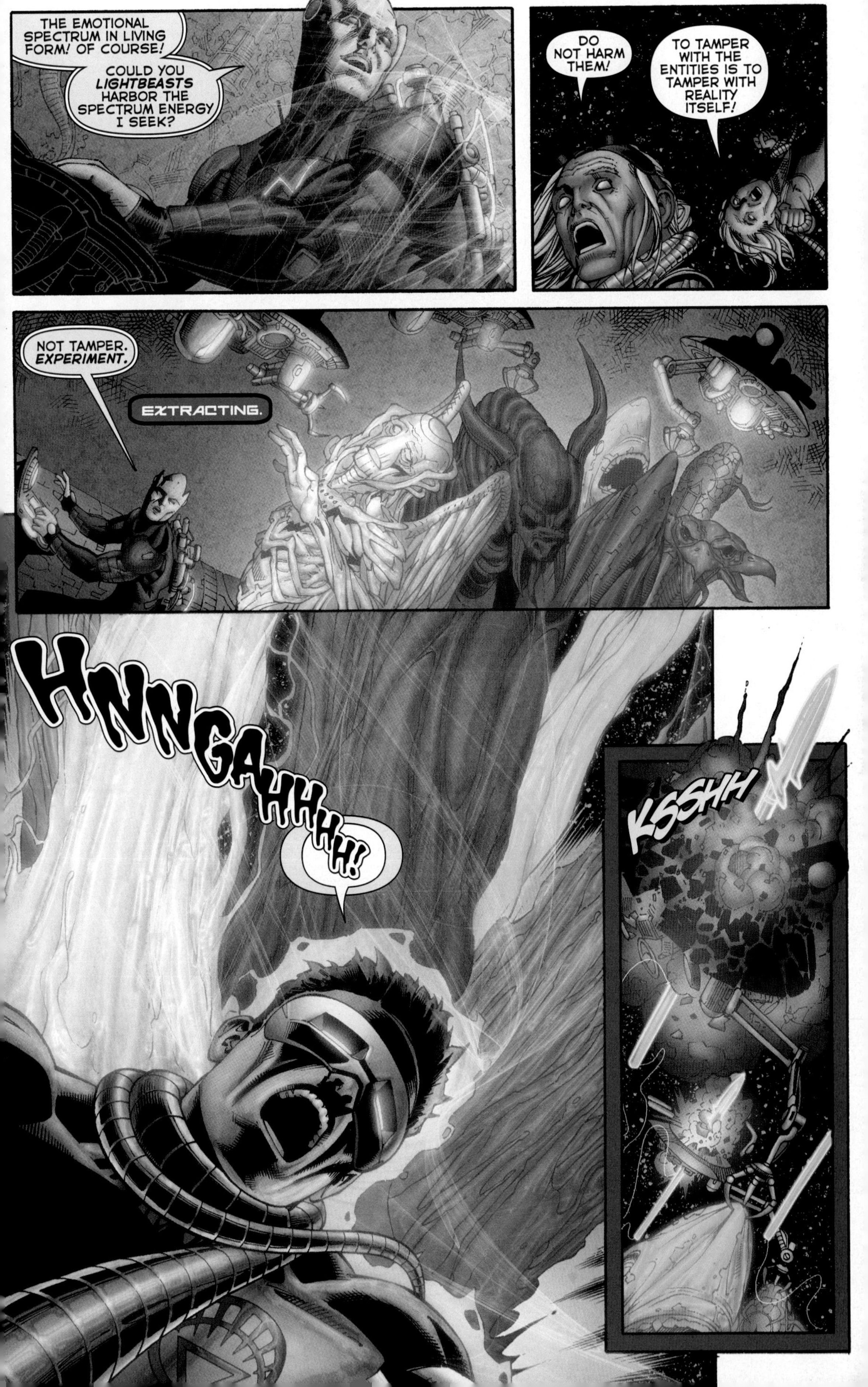

THE EMOTIONAL SPECTRUM IN LIVING FORM! OF COURSE!
COULD YOU LIGHTBEASTS HARBOR THE SPECTRUM ENERGY I SEEK?
DO NOT HARM THEM!
TO TAMPER WITH THE ENTITIES IS TO TAMPER WITH REALITY ITSELF!
NOT TAMPER. EXPERIMENT.
EXTRACTING.
HNNGAHHHHH!
KSSHH

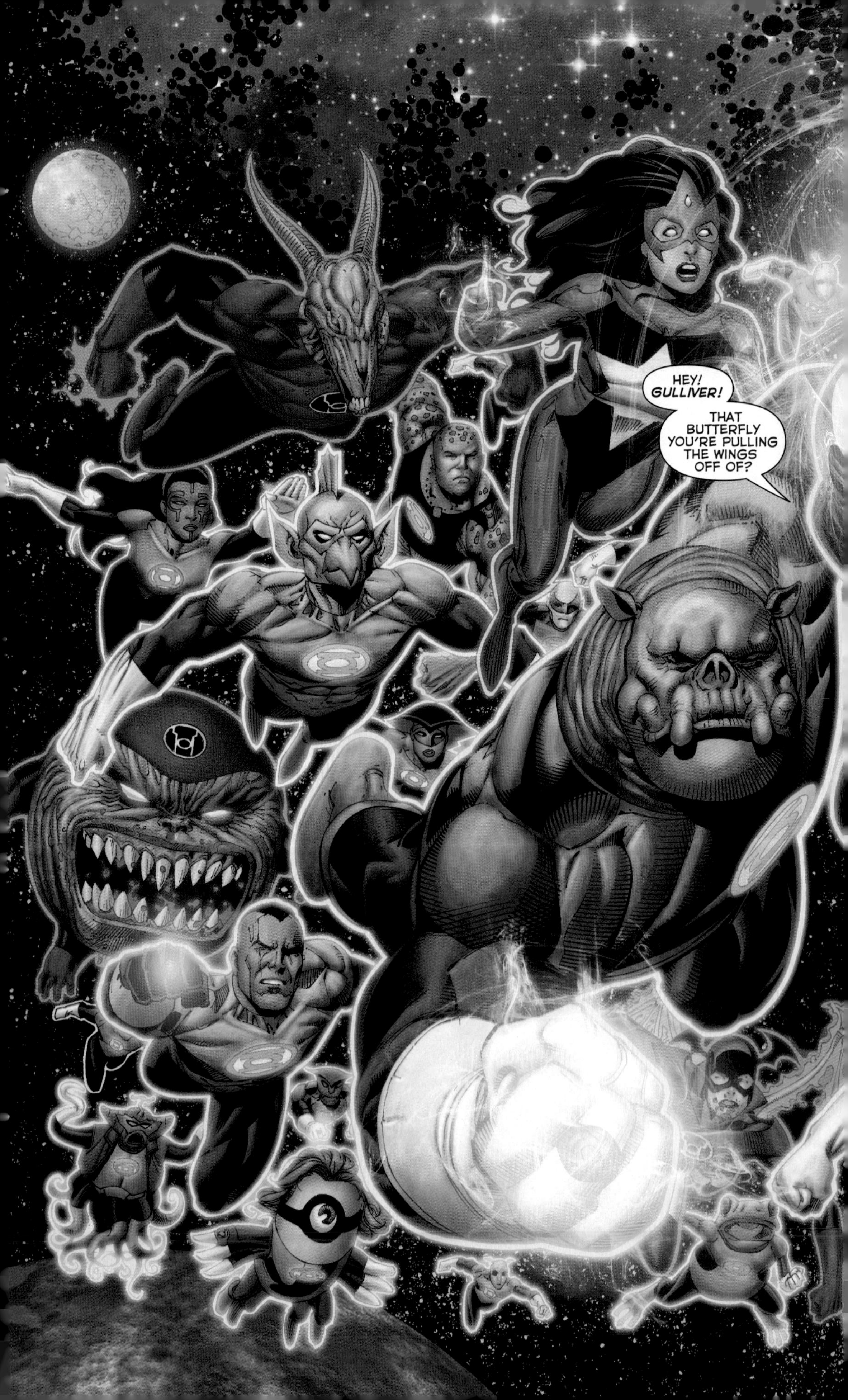
HEY! GULLIVER!
THAT BUTTERFLY YOU'RE PULLING THE WINGS OFF OF?

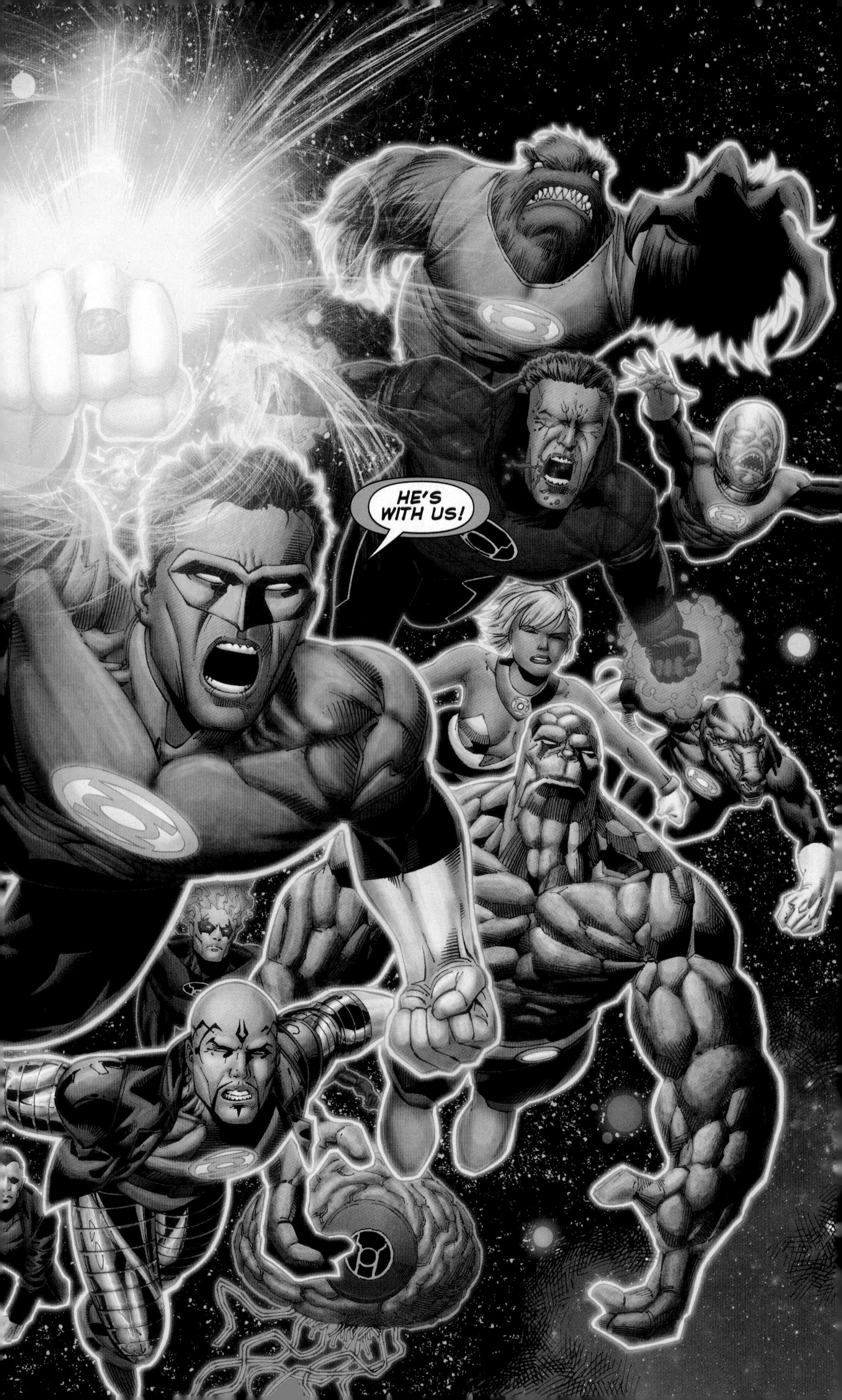
HE'S WITH US!

THEN YOU CAN *EXPIRE* WITH HIM!

AUTOMATED DEFENSES ACTIVATED.

SSKKRROOM

SSKKRROON

SSKKRROON

LANTERNS, IF THERE WAS EVER A TIME TO *SHINE*--

--IT'S *NOW!*

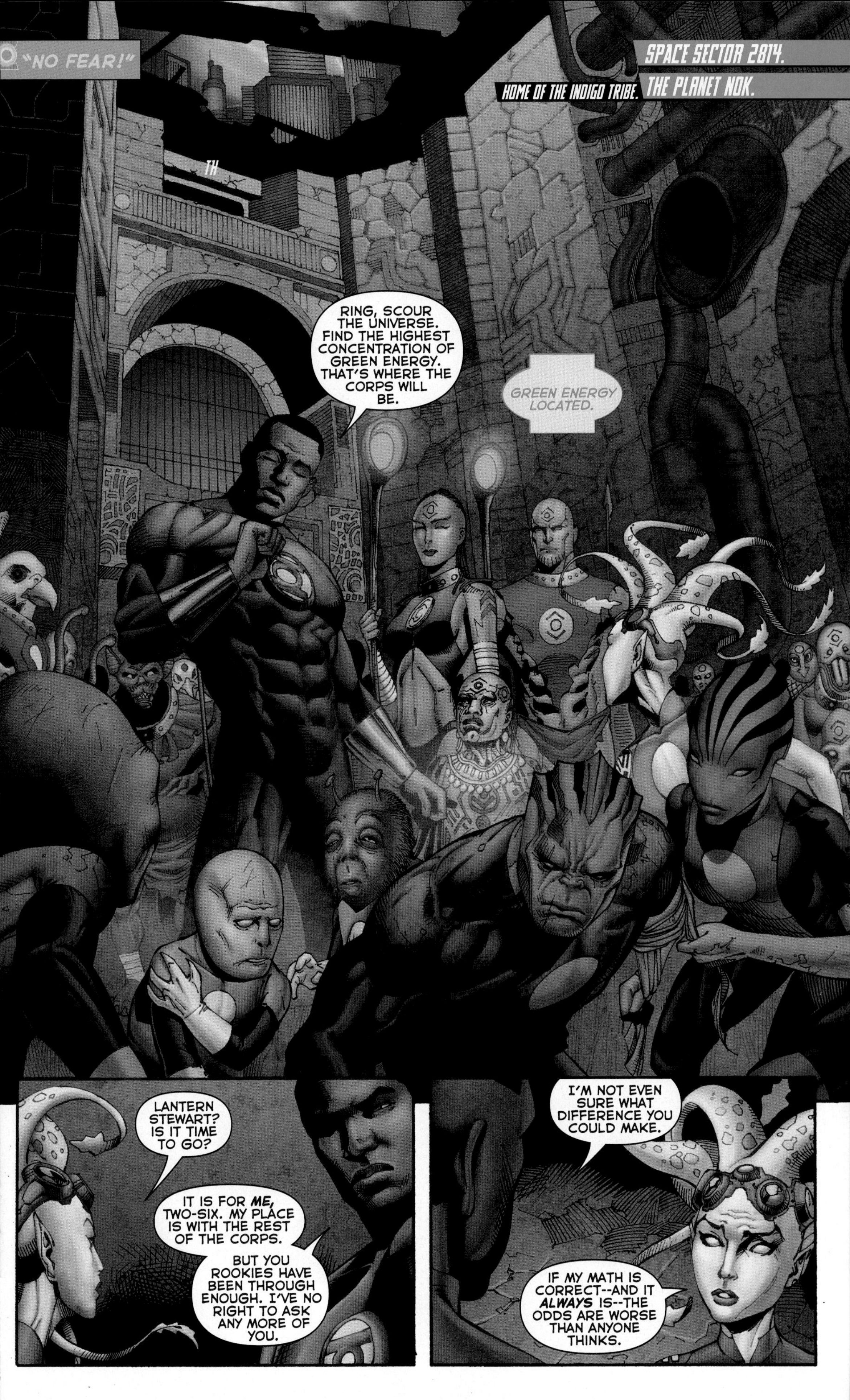

"NO FEAR!"
SPACE SECTOR 2814.
THE PLANET NOK.
HOME OF THE INDIGO TRIBE.
RING, SCOUR THE UNIVERSE. FIND THE HIGHEST CONCENTRATION OF GREEN ENERGY. THAT'S WHERE THE CORPS WILL BE.
GREEN ENERGY LOCATED.
LANTERN STEWART? IS IT TIME TO GO?
IT IS FOR ME, TWO-SIX. MY PLACE IS WITH THE REST OF THE CORPS.
BUT YOU ROOKIES HAVE BEEN THROUGH ENOUGH. I'VE NO RIGHT TO ASK ANY MORE OF YOU.
I'M NOT EVEN SURE WHAT DIFFERENCE YOU COULD MAKE.
IF MY MATH IS CORRECT--AND IT ALWAYS IS--THE ODDS ARE WORSE THAN ANYONE THINKS.

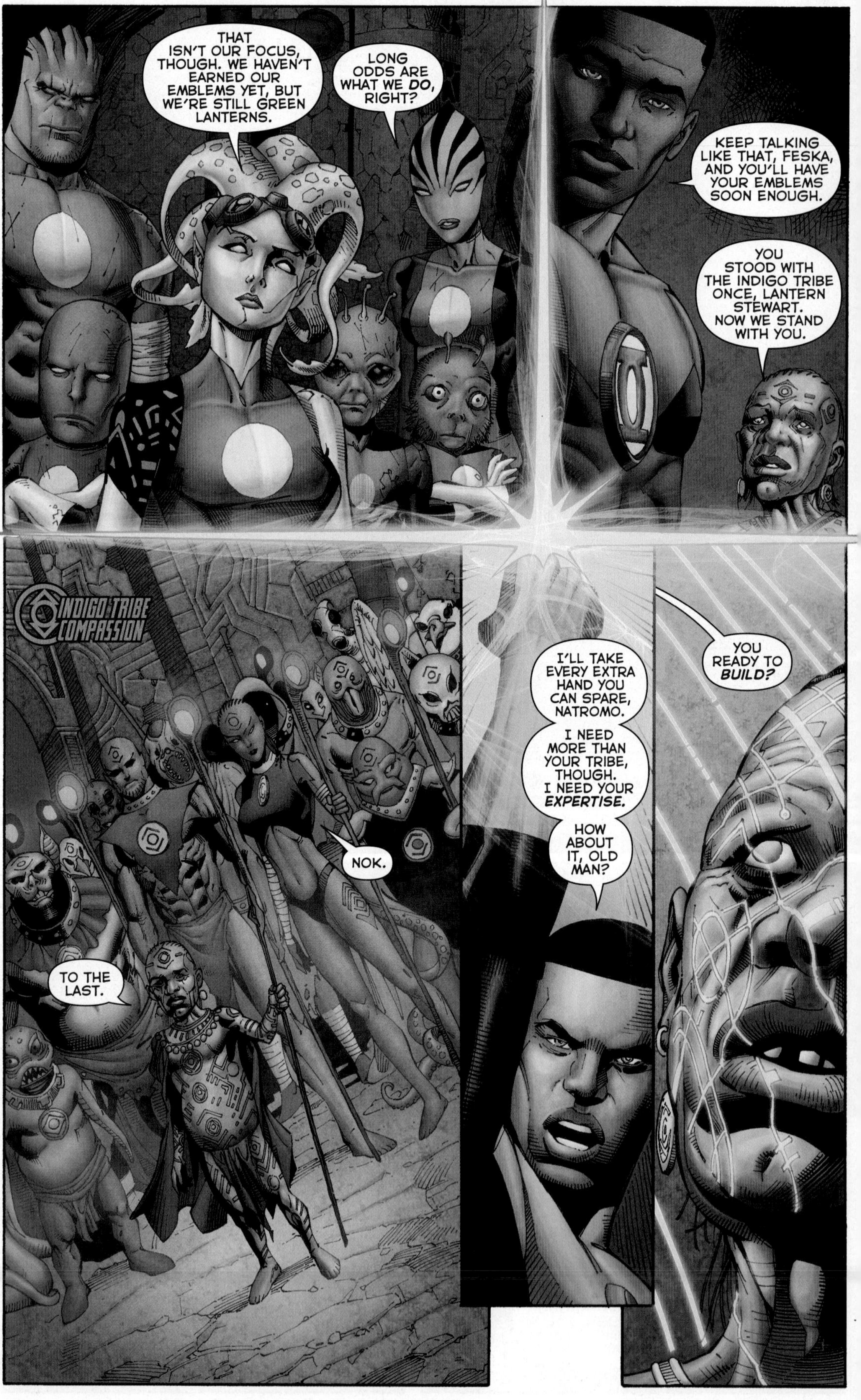
THAT ISN'T OUR FOCUS, THOUGH. WE HAVEN'T EARNED OUR EMBLEMS YET, BUT WE'RE STILL GREEN LANTERNS.
LONG ODDS ARE WHAT WE *DO*, RIGHT?
KEEP TALKING LIKE THAT, FESKA, AND YOU'LL HAVE YOUR EMBLEMS SOON ENOUGH.
YOU STOOD WITH THE INDIGO TRIBE ONCE, LANTERN STEWART. NOW WE STAND WITH YOU.
INDIGO TRIBE COMPASSION
NOK.
TO THE LAST.
I'LL TAKE EVERY EXTRA HAND YOU CAN SPARE, NATROMO.
I NEED MORE THAN YOUR TRIBE, THOUGH. I NEED YOUR *EXPERTISE.*
HOW ABOUT IT, OLD MAN?
YOU READY TO *BUILD?*

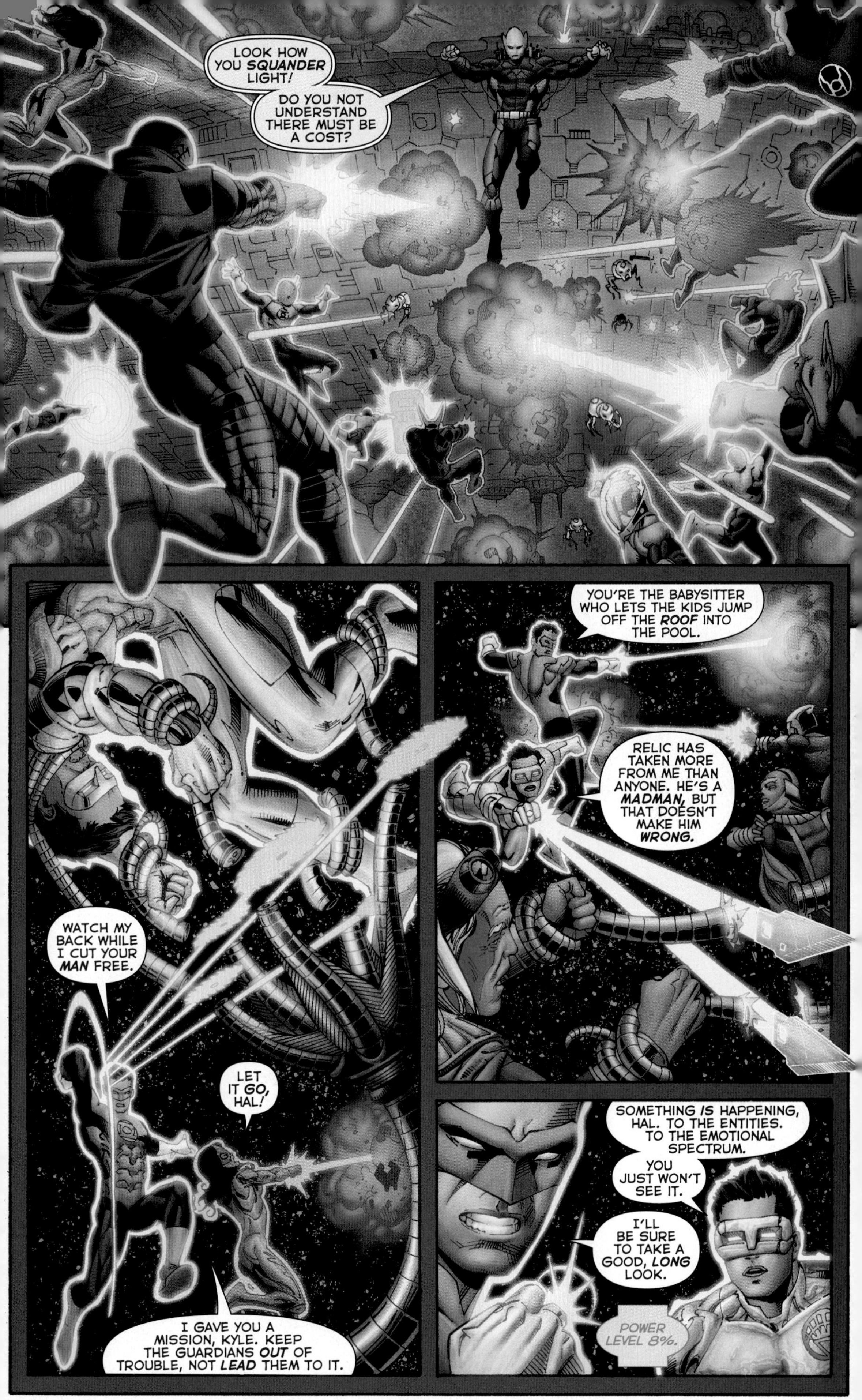

LOOK HOW YOU SQUANDER LIGHT!
DO YOU NOT UNDERSTAND THERE MUST BE A COST?
WATCH MY BACK WHILE I CUT YOUR MAN FREE.
LET IT GO, HAL!
I GAVE YOU A MISSION, KYLE. KEEP THE GUARDIANS OUT OF TROUBLE, NOT LEAD THEM TO IT.
YOU'RE THE BABYSITTER WHO LETS THE KIDS JUMP OFF THE ROOF INTO THE POOL.
RELIC HAS TAKEN MORE FROM ME THAN ANYONE. HE'S A MADMAN, BUT THAT DOESN'T MAKE HIM WRONG.
SOMETHING IS HAPPENING, HAL. TO THE ENTITIES. TO THE EMOTIONAL SPECTRUM.
YOU JUST WON'T SEE IT.
I'LL BE SURE TO TAKE A GOOD, LONG LOOK.
POWER LEVEL 8%.

AFTER I MAKE SURE NO MORE LANTERNS GET KILLED.

HEY, TALL, PALE, AND UGLY! EVER TANGLED WITH THE CHARM CITY P.D.?

CAPTURING SPECTRUM ENERGY.

FOOLISH LIGHTSMITH.

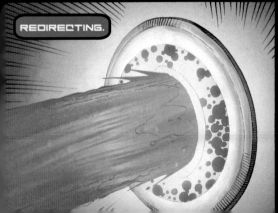

REDIRECTING.

OOPS.

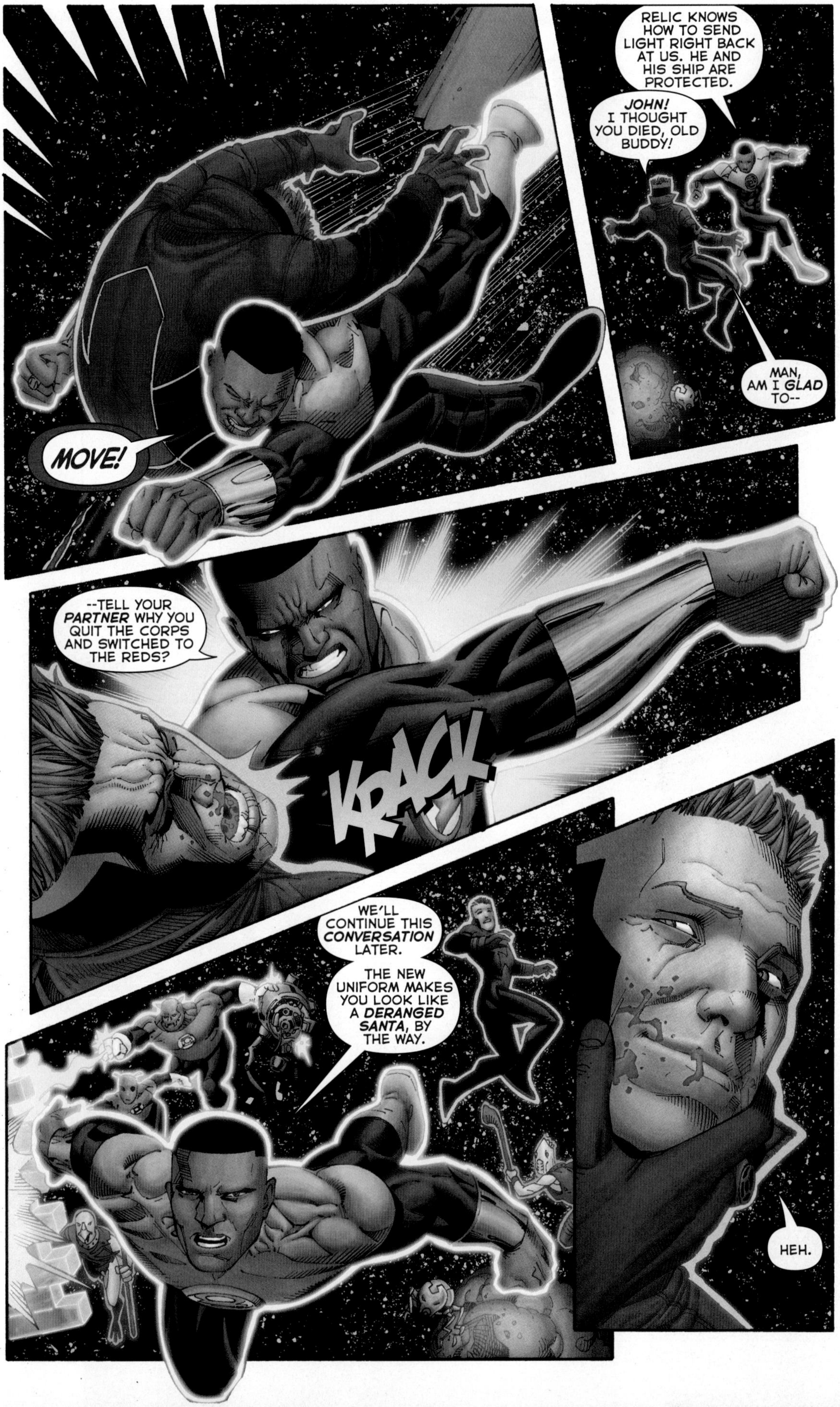

MOVE!
RELIC KNOWS HOW TO SEND LIGHT RIGHT BACK AT US. HE AND HIS SHIP ARE PROTECTED.
JOHN! I THOUGHT YOU DIED, OLD BUDDY!
MAN, AM I GLAD TO--
--TELL YOUR PARTNER WHY YOU QUIT THE CORPS AND SWITCHED TO THE REDS?
KRACK
WE'LL CONTINUE THIS CONVERSATION LATER.
THE NEW UNIFORM MAKES YOU LOOK LIKE A DERANGED SANTA, BY THE WAY.
HEH.

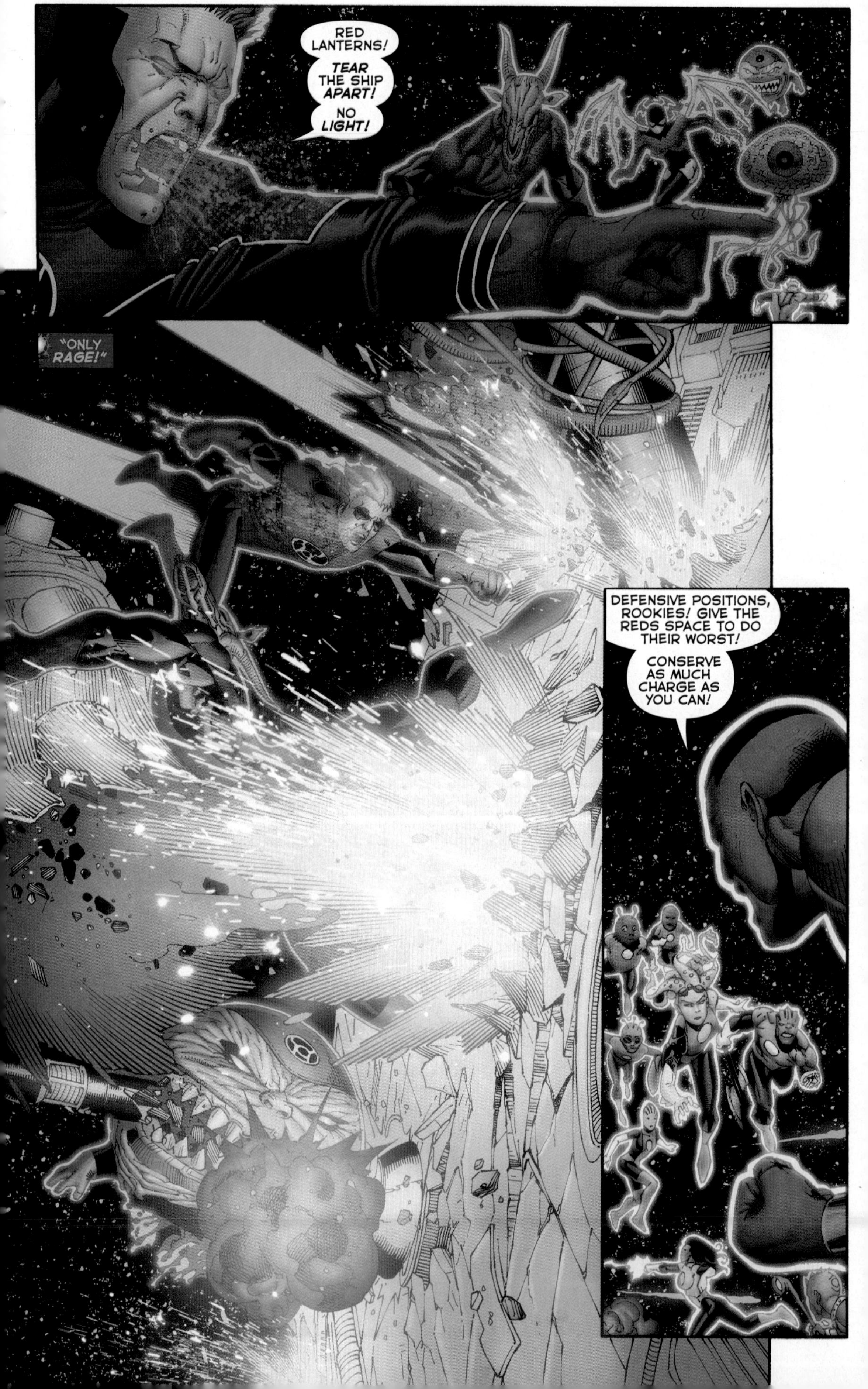
RED LANTERNS!
TEAR THE SHIP *APART!*
NO *LIGHT!*
"ONLY *RAGE!*"
DEFENSIVE POSITIONS, ROOKIES! GIVE THE REDS SPACE TO DO THEIR WORST!
CONSERVE AS MUCH CHARGE AS YOU CAN!

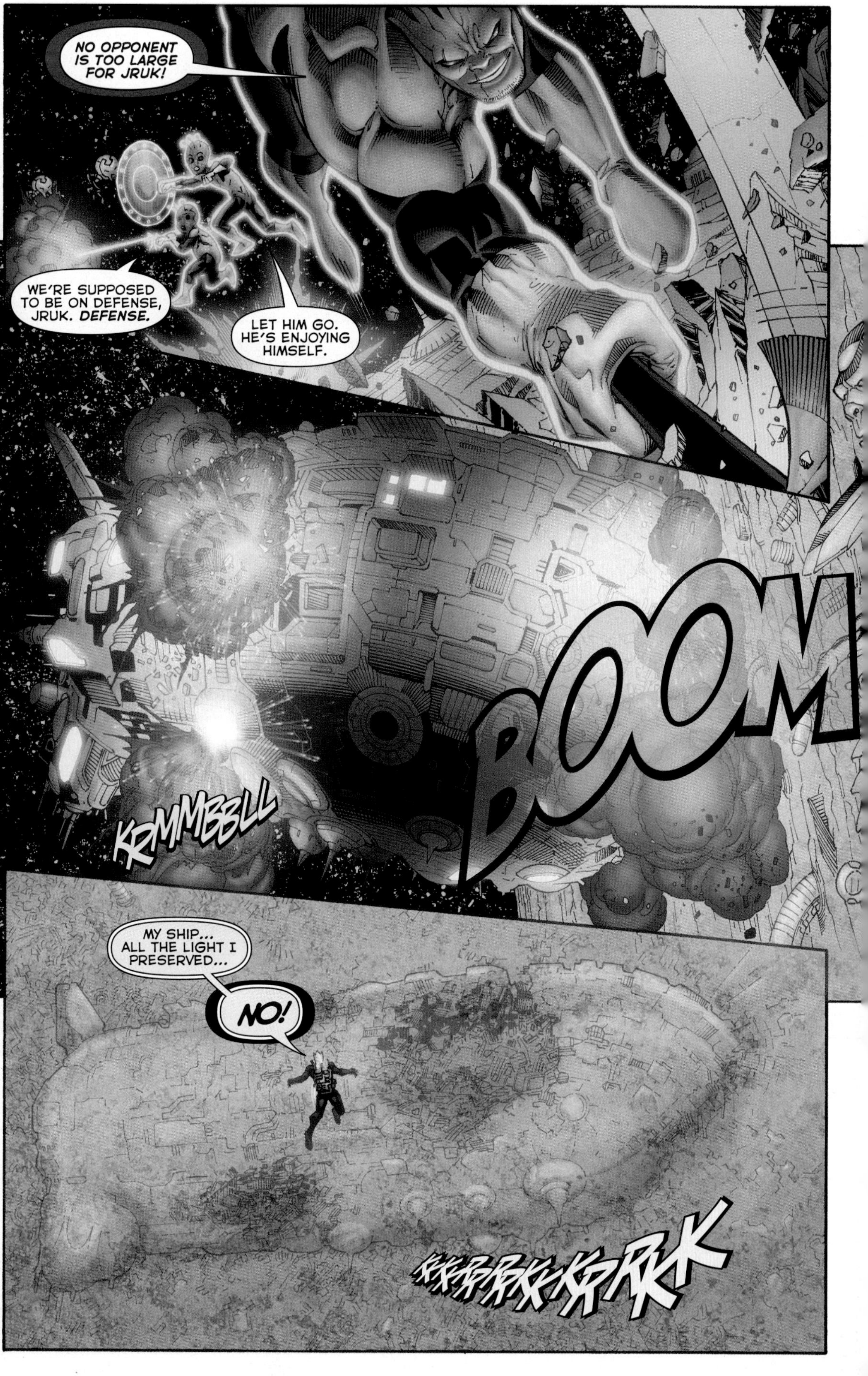
NO OPPONENT IS TOO LARGE FOR JRUK!
WE'RE SUPPOSED TO BE ON DEFENSE, JRUK. *DEFENSE.*
LET HIM GO. HE'S ENJOYING HIMSELF.
BOOM
KRMMBBLL
MY SHIP... ALL THE LIGHT I PRESERVED...
NO!
KKKRRKKKRRKK

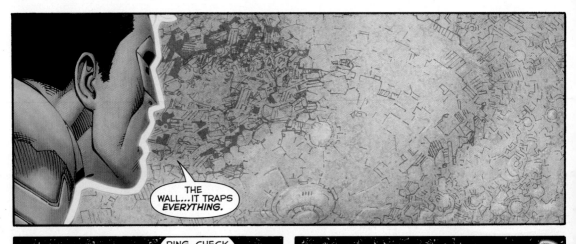

THE WALL...IT TRAPS *EVERYTHING.*

RING, CHECK EVERYONE'S CHARGES. AND KEEP US UPDATED.

POWER LEVEL 5%.

POWER LEVEL 28%.

POWER LEVEL 12%.

POWER LEVEL 6%.

HEY, RAYNER. GET IN THE FIGHT, WHY DON'T YOU?

KYLE ASIDE, WE'VE GOT ENOUGH POWER FOR *ONE MORE* RUN. BUT WE CAN'T WASTE OUR CHARGES ON BLASTS OR CONSTRUCTS.

SO, YOU GUYS READY FOR A GAME OF GOOD OLD-FASHIONED *CHICKEN?*

INDIGO-1, CAN YOU TELEPORT US BETWEEN RELIC AND HIS REFLECTORS-- AND *KEEP* US THERE?

NOK.

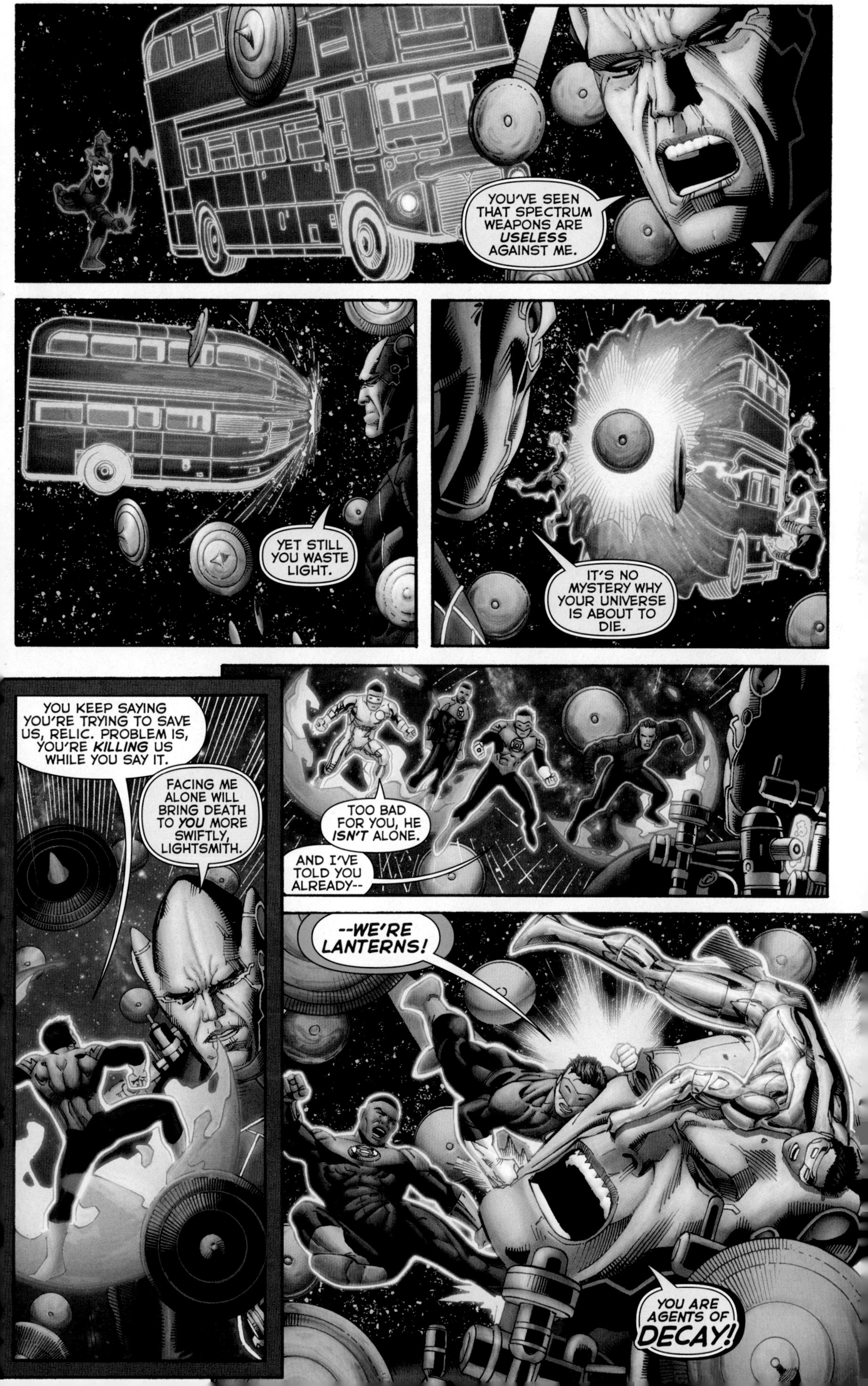

YOU'VE SEEN THAT SPECTRUM WEAPONS ARE USELESS AGAINST ME.
YET STILL YOU WASTE LIGHT.
IT'S NO MYSTERY WHY YOUR UNIVERSE IS ABOUT TO DIE.
YOU KEEP SAYING YOU'RE TRYING TO SAVE US, RELIC. PROBLEM IS, YOU'RE KILLING US WHILE YOU SAY IT.
FACING ME ALONE WILL BRING DEATH TO YOU MORE SWIFTLY, LIGHTSMITH.
TOO BAD FOR YOU, HE ISN'T ALONE.
AND I'VE TOLD YOU ALREADY--
--WE'RE LANTERNS!
YOU ARE AGENTS OF DECAY!

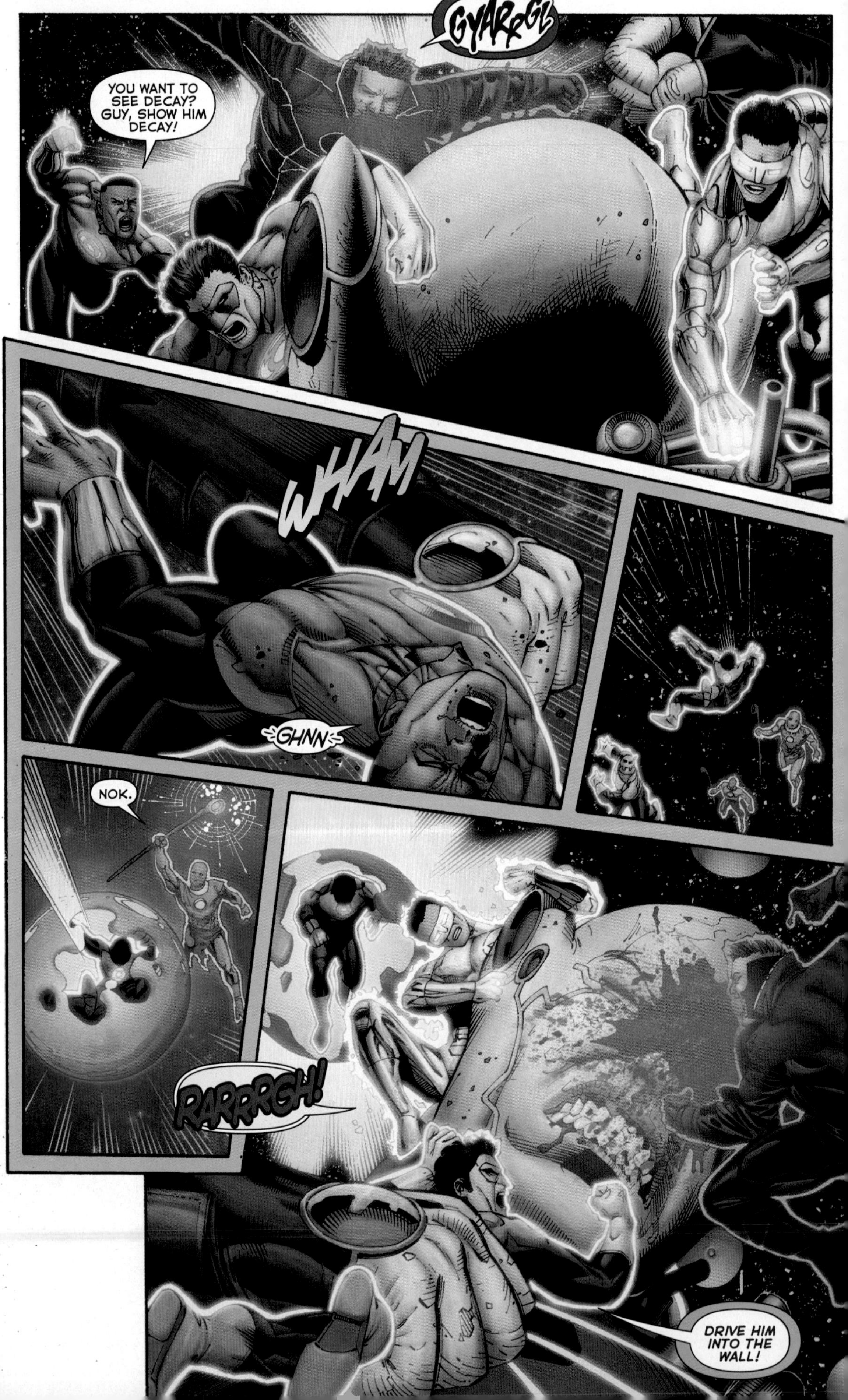
GYARRGL
YOU WANT TO SEE DECAY? GUY, SHOW HIM DECAY!
WHAM
GHNN
NOK.
RARRRGH!
DRIVE HIM INTO THE WALL!

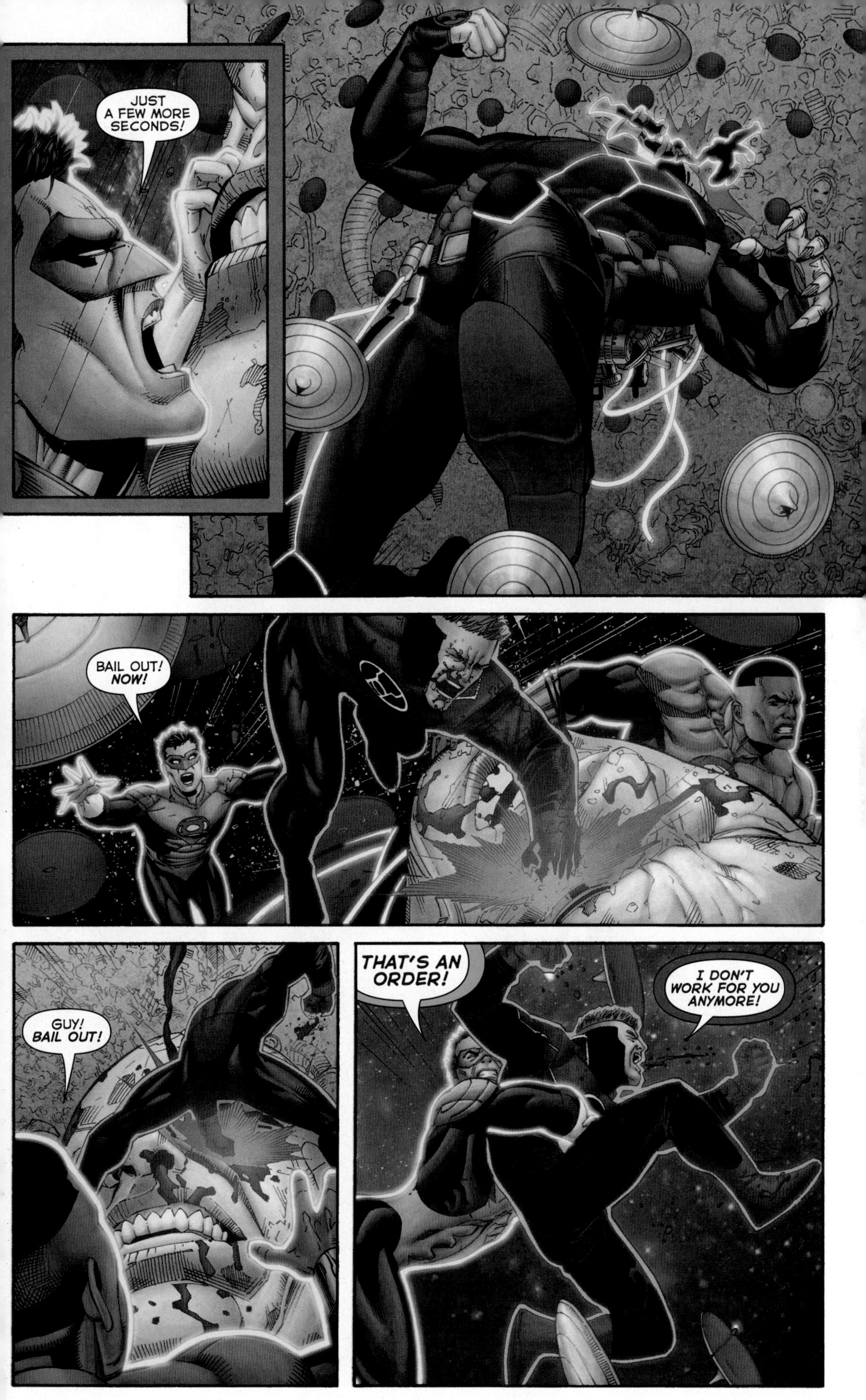
JUST A FEW MORE SECONDS!
BAIL OUT! NOW!
GUY! BAIL OUT!
THAT'S AN ORDER!
I DON'T WORK FOR YOU ANYMORE!

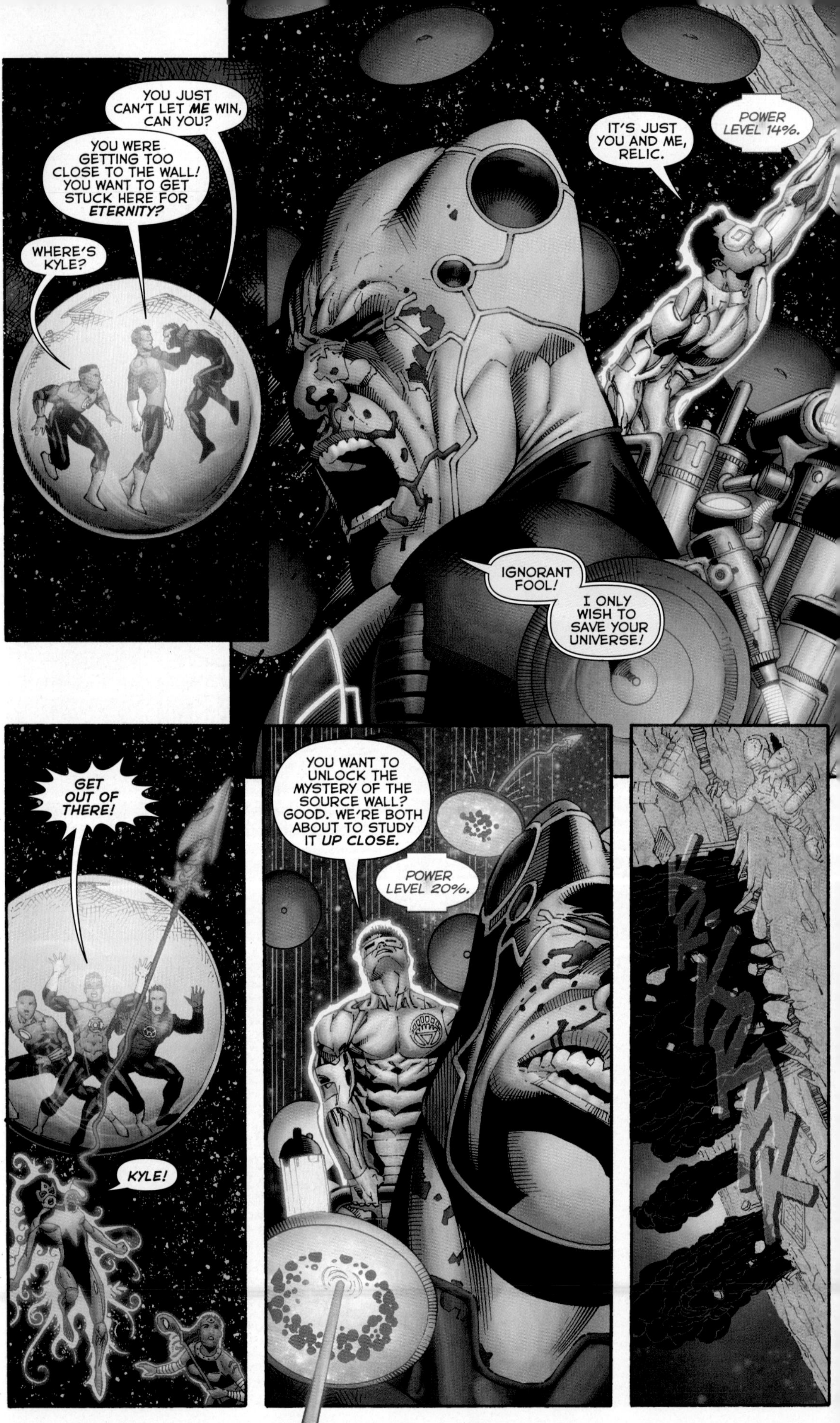
YOU JUST CAN'T LET *ME* WIN, CAN YOU?
YOU WERE GETTING TOO CLOSE TO THE WALL! YOU WANT TO GET STUCK HERE FOR *ETERNITY?*
WHERE'S KYLE?
IT'S JUST YOU AND ME, RELIC.
POWER LEVEL 14%.
IGNORANT FOOL!
I ONLY WISH TO SAVE YOUR UNIVERSE!
GET OUT OF THERE!
KYLE!
YOU WANT TO UNLOCK THE MYSTERY OF THE SOURCE WALL? GOOD. WE'RE BOTH ABOUT TO STUDY IT *UP CLOSE.*
POWER LEVEL 20%.

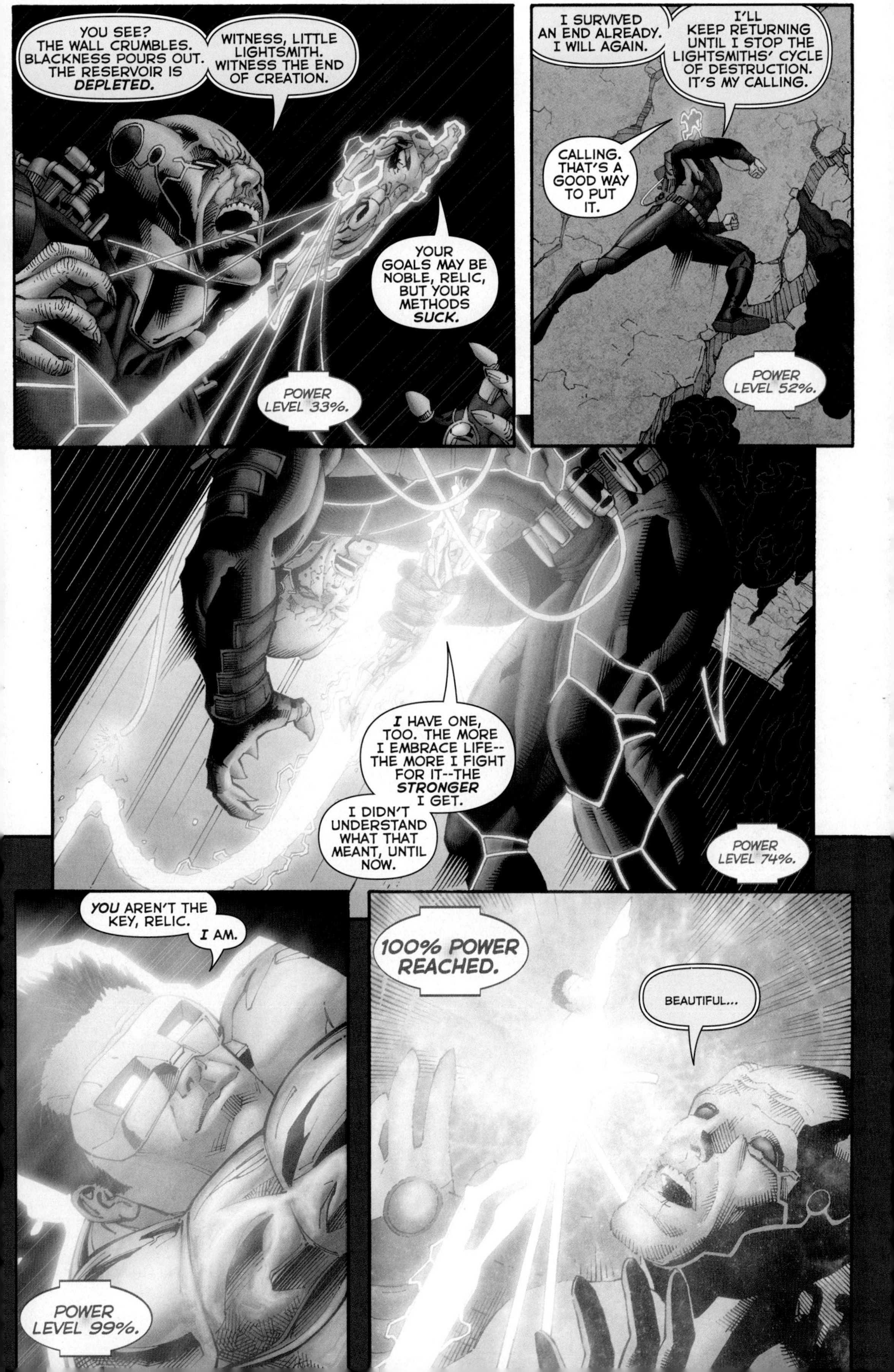
YOU SEE? THE WALL CRUMBLES. BLACKNESS POURS OUT. THE RESERVOIR IS *DEPLETED.*
WITNESS, LITTLE LIGHTSMITH. WITNESS THE END OF CREATION.
YOUR GOALS MAY BE NOBLE, RELIC, BUT YOUR METHODS *SUCK.*
POWER LEVEL 33%.
I SURVIVED AN END ALREADY. I WILL AGAIN.
I'LL KEEP RETURNING UNTIL I STOP THE LIGHTSMITHS' CYCLE OF DESTRUCTION. IT'S MY CALLING.
CALLING. THAT'S A GOOD WAY TO PUT IT.
POWER LEVEL 52%.
I HAVE ONE, TOO. THE MORE I EMBRACE LIFE-- THE MORE I FIGHT FOR IT--THE *STRONGER* I GET.
I DIDN'T UNDERSTAND WHAT THAT MEANT, UNTIL NOW.
POWER LEVEL 74%.
YOU AREN'T THE KEY, RELIC.
I AM.
POWER LEVEL 99%.
100% POWER REACHED.
BEAUTIFUL...

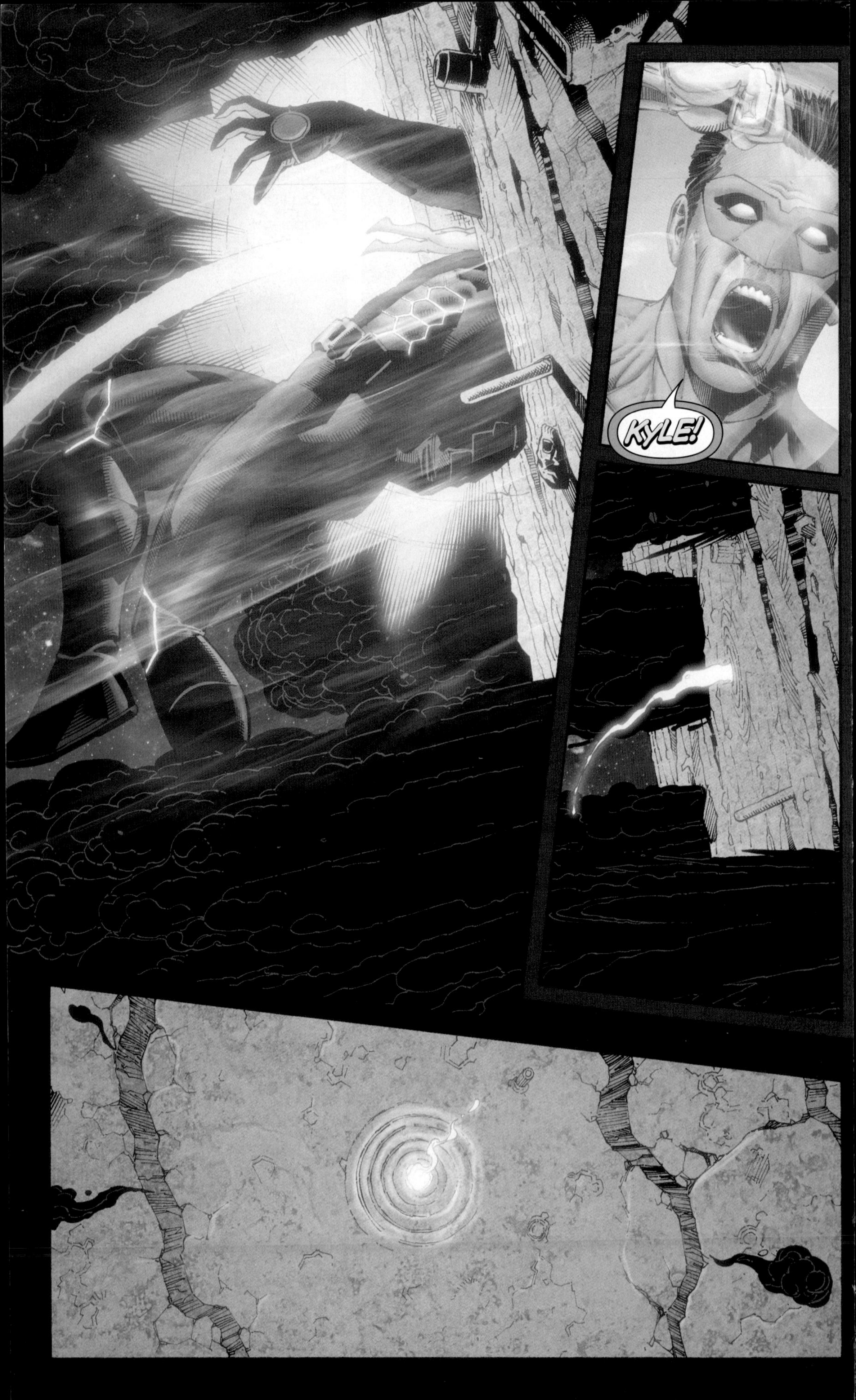
KYLE!

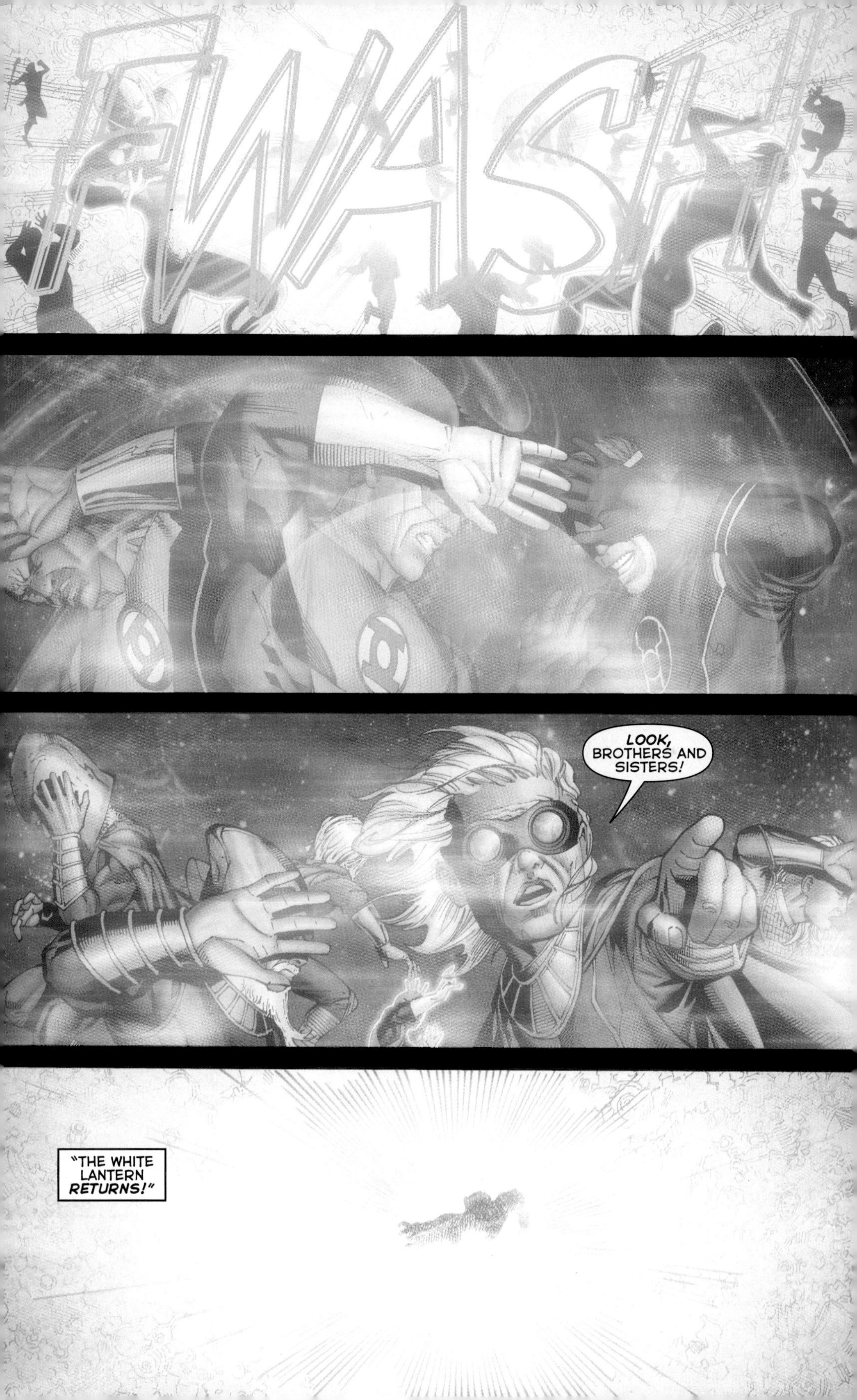
FWASH!
LOOK, BROTHERS AND SISTERS!
"THE WHITE LANTERN RETURNS!"

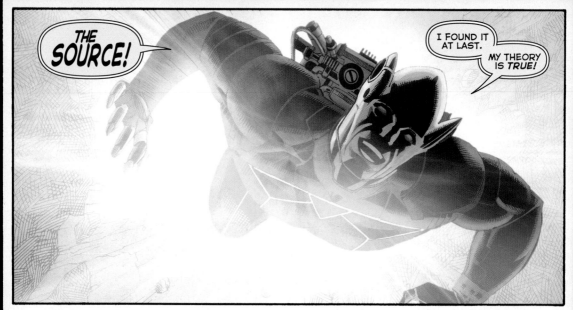

THE SOURCE!

I FOUND IT AT LAST. MY THEORY IS TRUE!

THE RESERVOIR HAS BEEN REPLENISHED.

THE WHITE LIGHTSMITH WAS THE SOLUTION!

RESPECT THE OPPORTUNITY YOU'VE BEEN GIVEN.

MY WORK... IS FINISHED.

KRRKK KRRKK KRRKK

DMFLLN NNNG

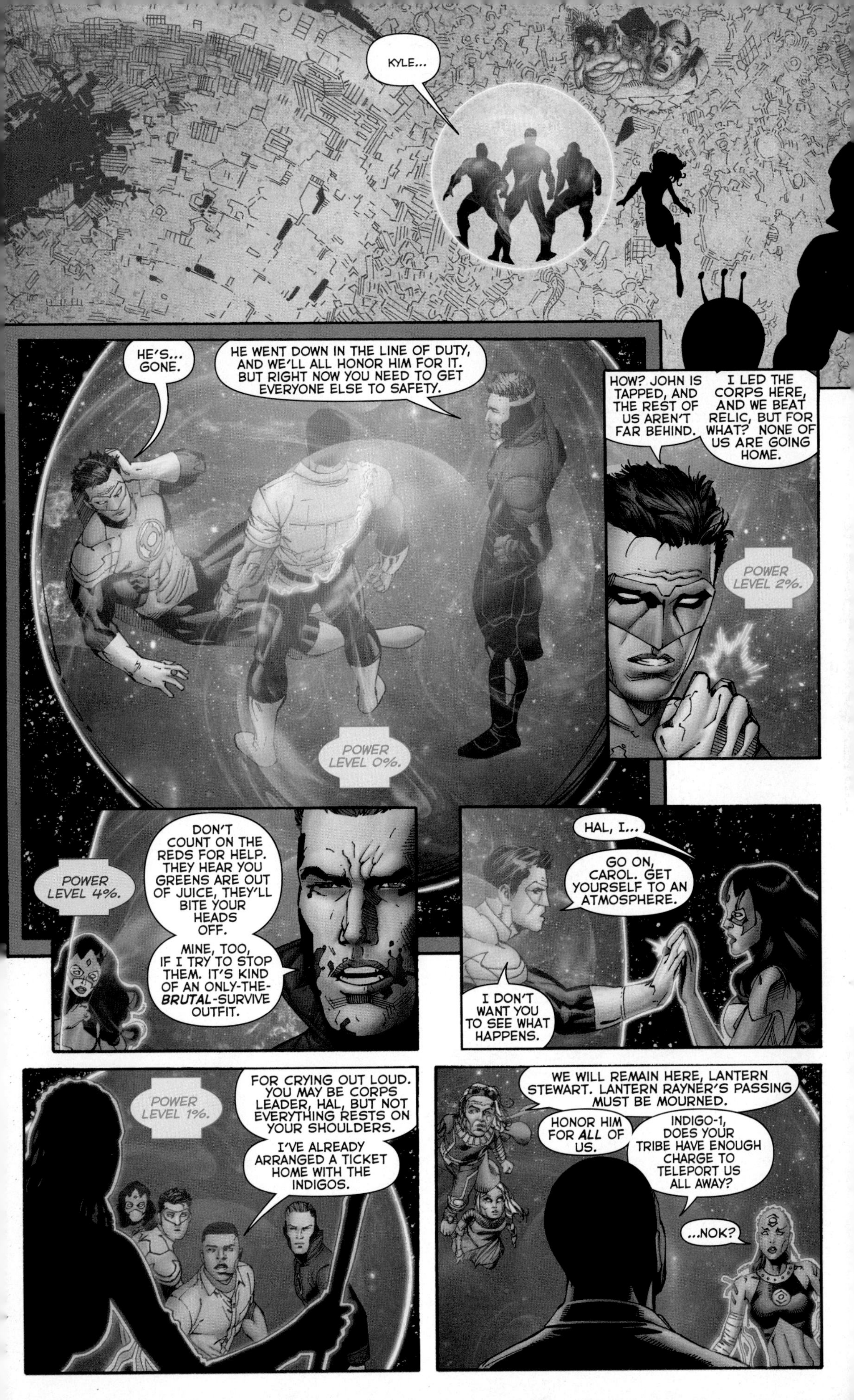
KYLE...
HE'S... GONE.
HE WENT DOWN IN THE LINE OF DUTY, AND WE'LL ALL HONOR HIM FOR IT. BUT RIGHT NOW YOU NEED TO GET EVERYONE ELSE TO SAFETY.
POWER LEVEL 0%.
HOW? JOHN IS TAPPED, AND THE REST OF US AREN'T FAR BEHIND.
I LED THE CORPS HERE, AND WE BEAT RELIC, BUT FOR WHAT? NONE OF US ARE GOING HOME.
POWER LEVEL 2%.
POWER LEVEL 4%.
DON'T COUNT ON THE REDS FOR HELP. THEY HEAR YOU GREENS ARE OUT OF JUICE, THEY'LL BITE YOUR HEADS OFF.
MINE, TOO, IF I TRY TO STOP THEM. IT'S KIND OF AN ONLY-THE-*BRUTAL*-SURVIVE OUTFIT.
HAL, I...
GO ON, CAROL. GET YOURSELF TO AN ATMOSPHERE.
I DON'T WANT YOU TO SEE WHAT HAPPENS.
POWER LEVEL 1%.
FOR CRYING OUT LOUD. YOU MAY BE CORPS LEADER, HAL, BUT NOT EVERYTHING RESTS ON YOUR SHOULDERS.
I'VE ALREADY ARRANGED A TICKET HOME WITH THE INDIGOS.
WE WILL REMAIN HERE, LANTERN STEWART. LANTERN RAYNER'S PASSING MUST BE MOURNED.
HONOR HIM FOR *ALL* OF US.
INDIGO-1, DOES YOUR TRIBE HAVE ENOUGH CHARGE TO TELEPORT US ALL AWAY?
...NOK?

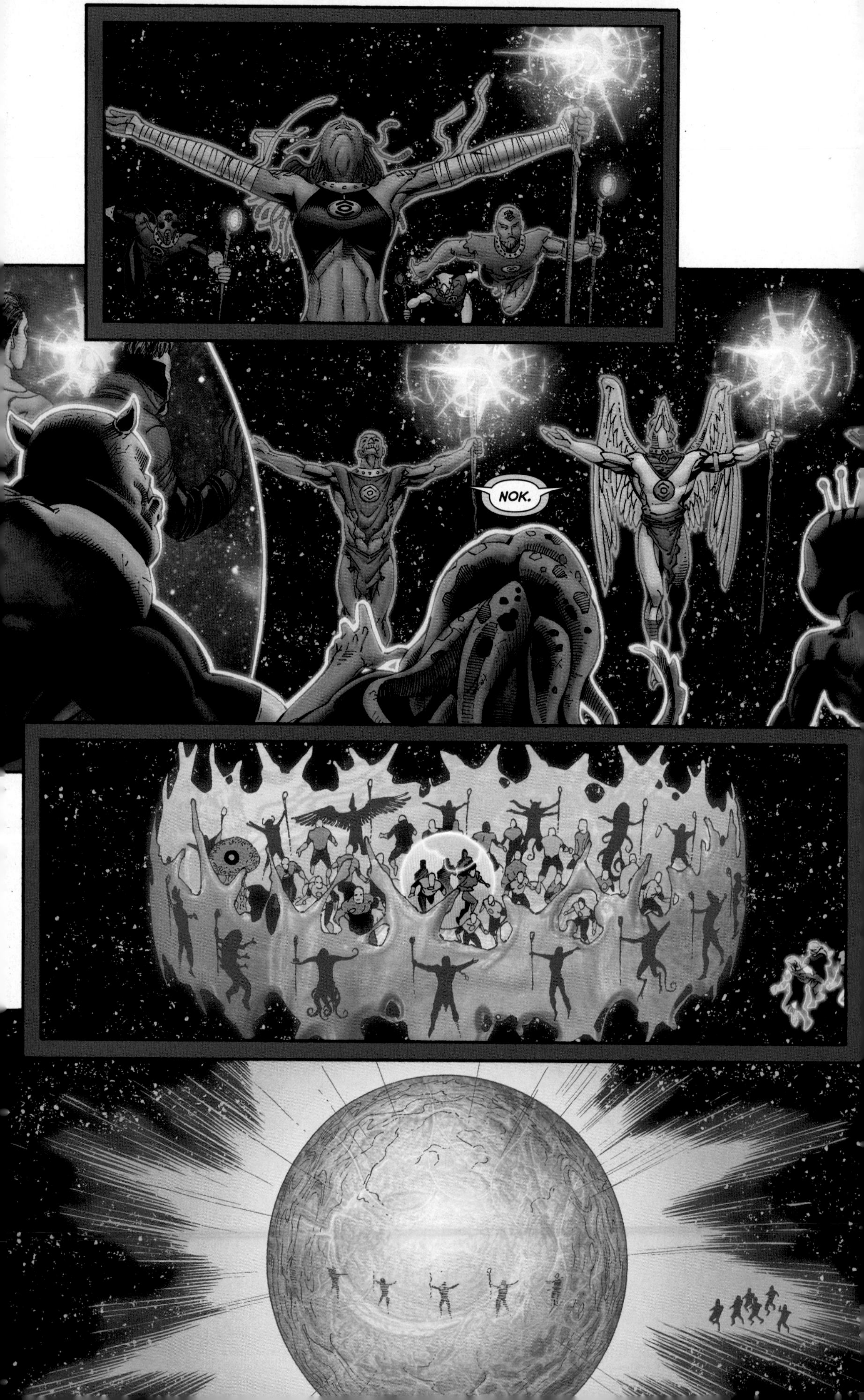
NOK.

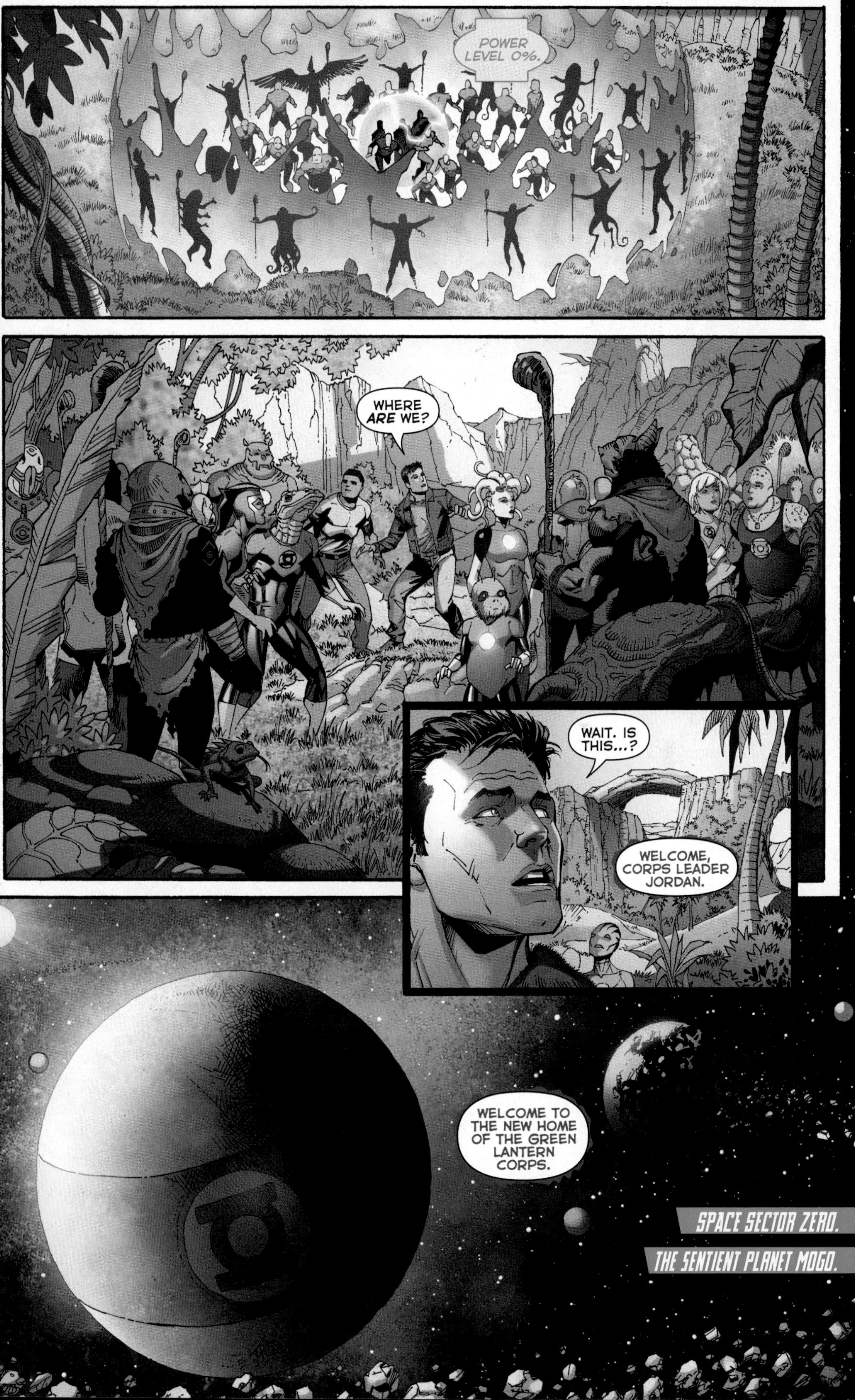
POWER LEVEL 0%.
WHERE ARE WE?
WAIT. IS THIS...?
WELCOME, CORPS LEADER JORDAN.
WELCOME TO THE NEW HOME OF THE GREEN LANTERN CORPS.
SPACE SECTOR ZERO.
THE SENTIENT PLANET MOGO.

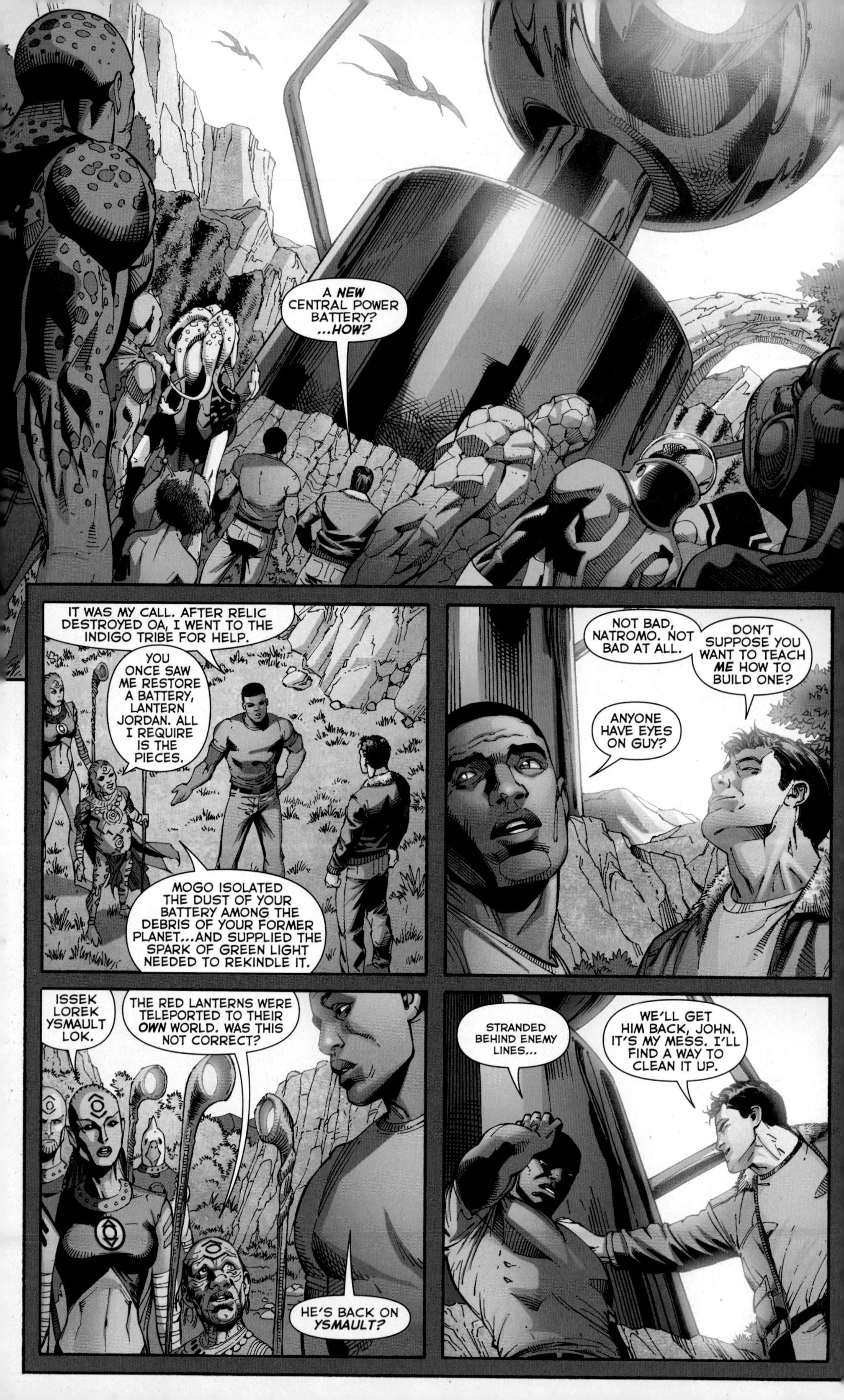
A NEW CENTRAL POWER BATTERY? ...HOW?
IT WAS MY CALL. AFTER RELIC DESTROYED OA, I WENT TO THE INDIGO TRIBE FOR HELP.
YOU ONCE SAW ME RESTORE A BATTERY, LANTERN JORDAN. ALL I REQUIRE IS THE PIECES.
MOGO ISOLATED THE DUST OF YOUR BATTERY AMONG THE DEBRIS OF YOUR FORMER PLANET...AND SUPPLIED THE SPARK OF GREEN LIGHT NEEDED TO REKINDLE IT.
NOT BAD, NATROMO. NOT BAD AT ALL.
DON'T SUPPOSE YOU WANT TO TEACH ME HOW TO BUILD ONE?
ANYONE HAVE EYES ON GUY?
ISSEK LOREK YSMAULT LOK.
THE RED LANTERNS WERE TELEPORTED TO THEIR OWN WORLD. WAS THIS NOT CORRECT?
HE'S BACK ON YSMAULT?
STRANDED BEHIND ENEMY LINES...
WE'LL GET HIM BACK, JOHN. IT'S MY MESS. I'LL FIND A WAY TO CLEAN IT UP.

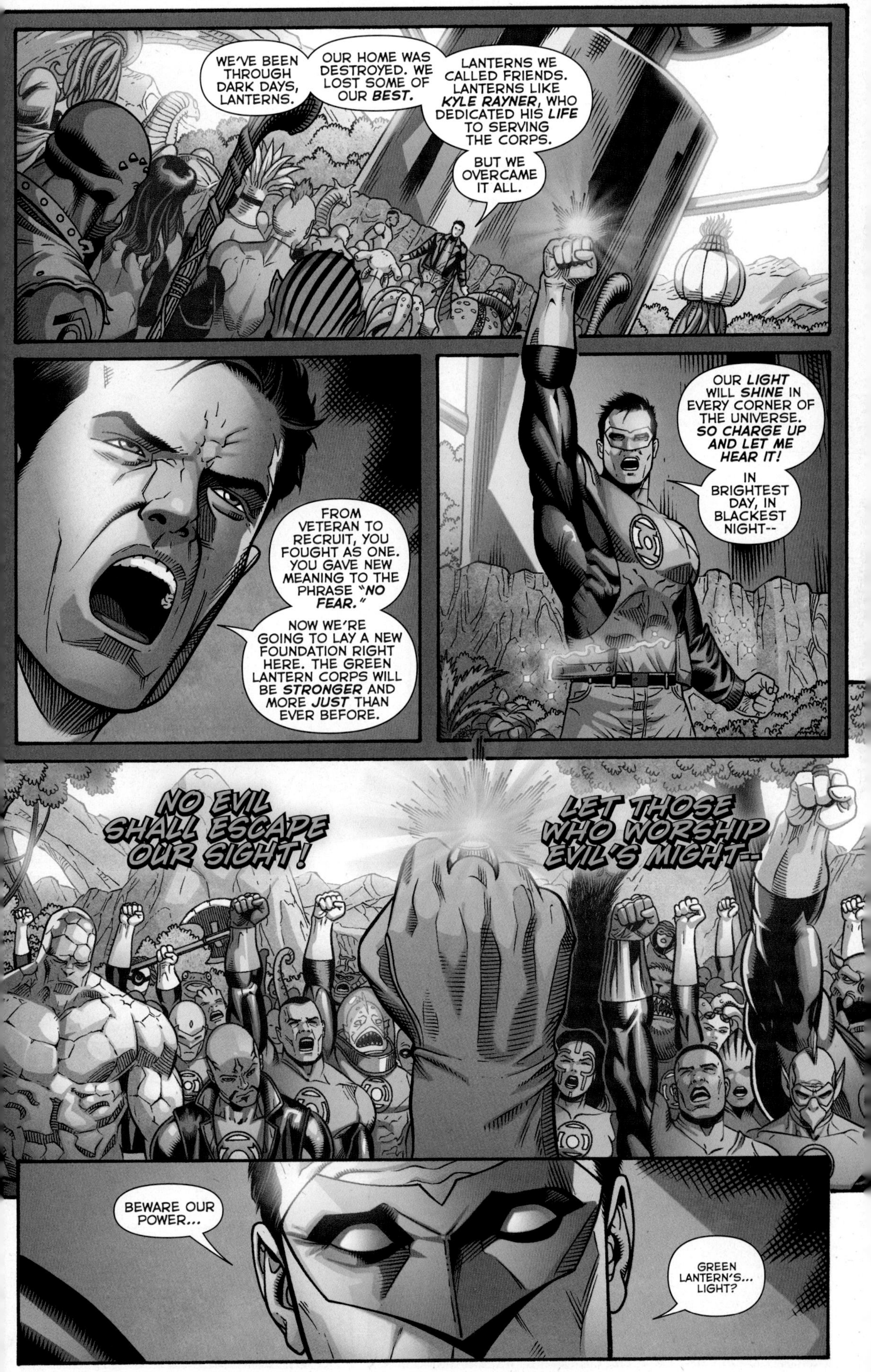
WE'VE BEEN THROUGH DARK DAYS, LANTERNS.
OUR HOME WAS DESTROYED. WE LOST SOME OF OUR BEST.
LANTERNS WE CALLED FRIENDS. LANTERNS LIKE KYLE RAYNER, WHO DEDICATED HIS LIFE TO SERVING THE CORPS.
BUT WE OVERCAME IT ALL.
FROM VETERAN TO RECRUIT, YOU FOUGHT AS ONE. YOU GAVE NEW MEANING TO THE PHRASE "NO FEAR."
NOW WE'RE GOING TO LAY A NEW FOUNDATION RIGHT HERE. THE GREEN LANTERN CORPS WILL BE STRONGER AND MORE JUST THAN EVER BEFORE.
OUR LIGHT WILL SHINE IN EVERY CORNER OF THE UNIVERSE. SO CHARGE UP AND LET ME HEAR IT!
IN BRIGHTEST DAY, IN BLACKEST NIGHT--
NO EVIL SHALL ESCAPE OUR SIGHT!
LET THOSE WHO WORSHIP EVIL'S MIGHT--
BEWARE OUR POWER...
GREEN LANTERN'S... LIGHT?

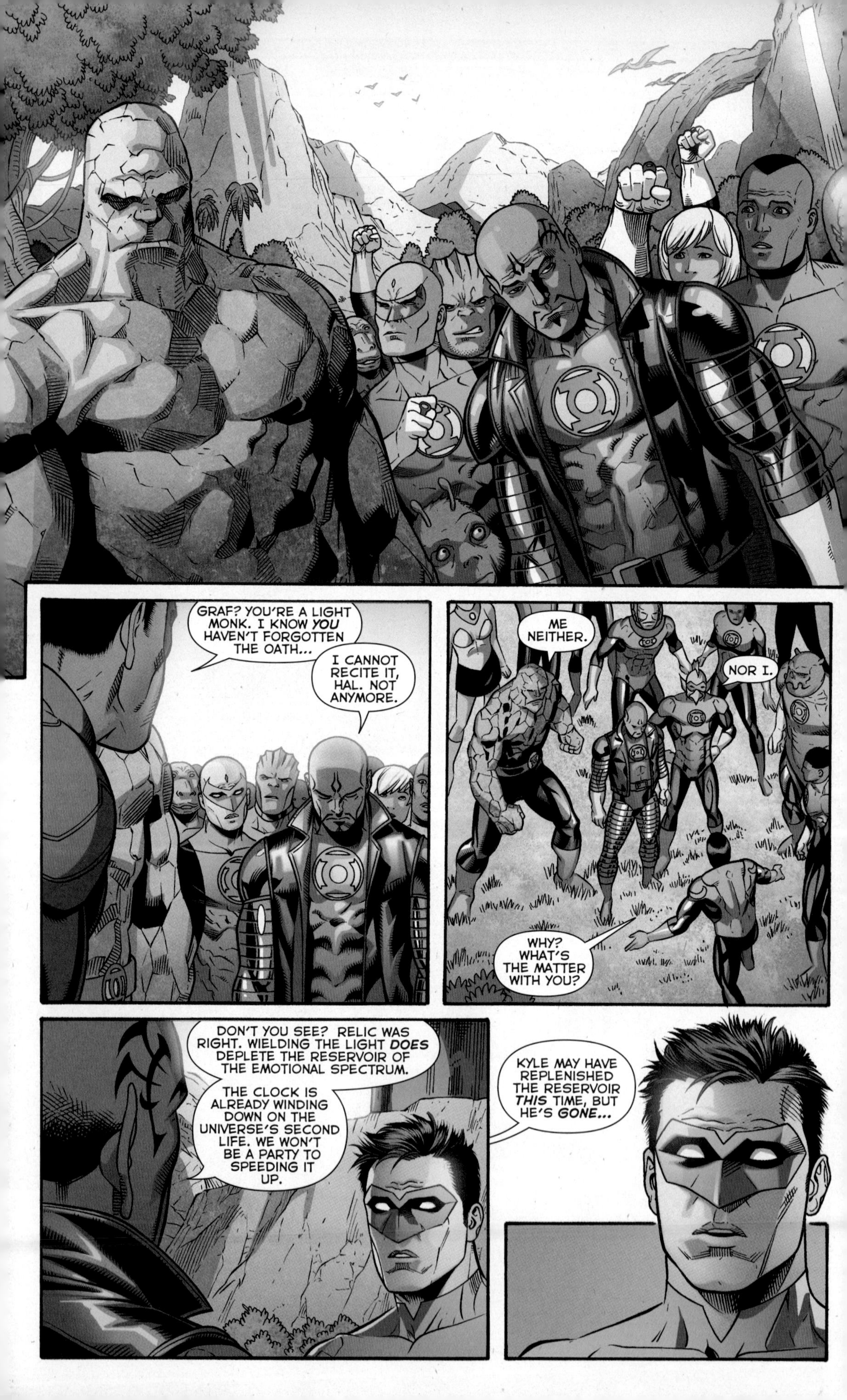

GRAF? YOU'RE A LIGHT MONK. I KNOW YOU HAVEN'T FORGOTTEN THE OATH...
I CANNOT RECITE IT, HAL. NOT ANYMORE.
ME NEITHER.
NOR I.
WHY? WHAT'S THE MATTER WITH YOU?
DON'T YOU SEE? RELIC WAS RIGHT. WIELDING THE LIGHT DOES DEPLETE THE RESERVOIR OF THE EMOTIONAL SPECTRUM.
THE CLOCK IS ALREADY WINDING DOWN ON THE UNIVERSE'S SECOND LIFE. WE WON'T BE A PARTY TO SPEEDING IT UP.
KYLE MAY HAVE REPLENISHED THE RESERVOIR THIS TIME, BUT HE'S GONE...

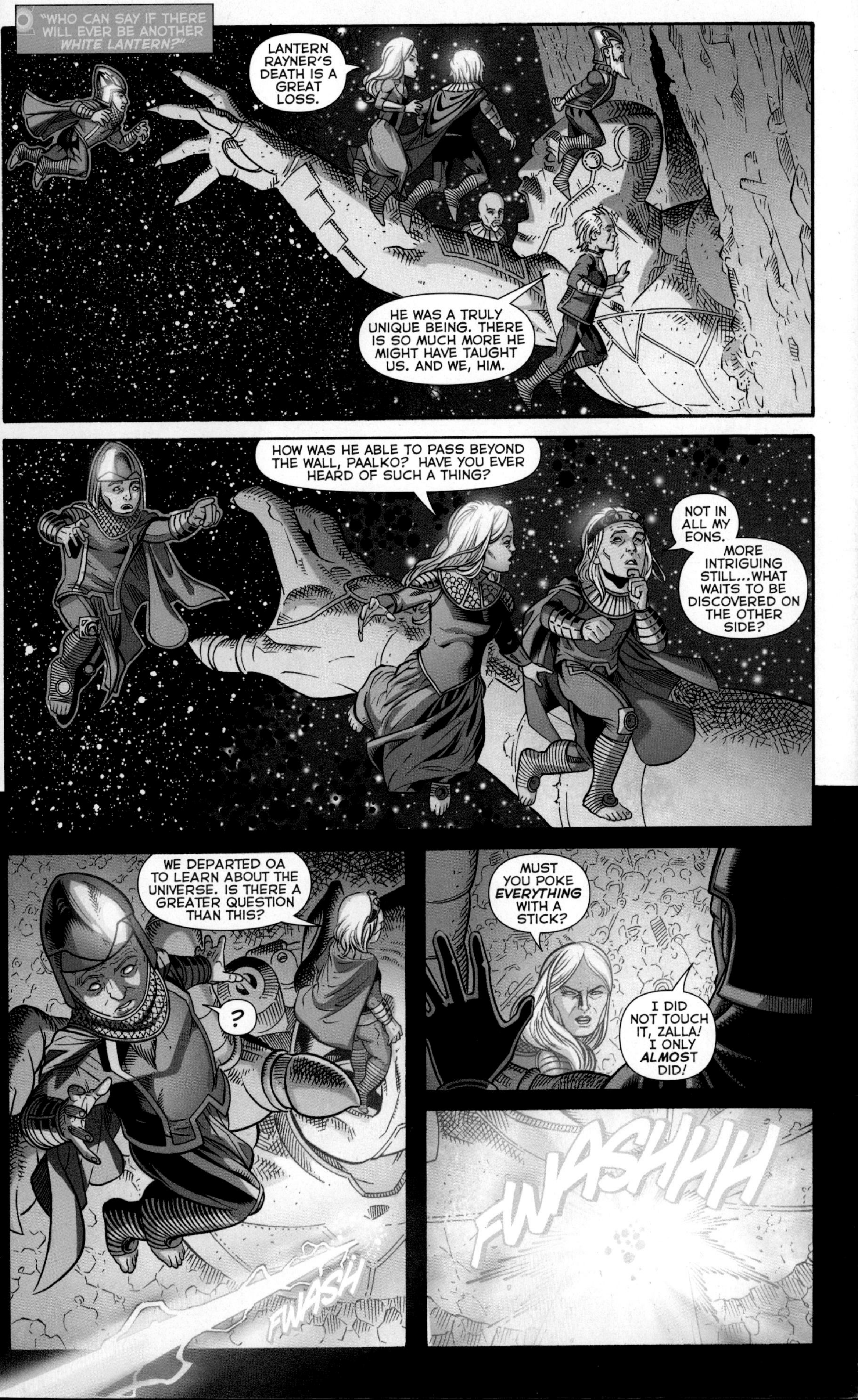
"WHO CAN SAY IF THERE WILL EVER BE ANOTHER *WHITE LANTERN?*"
LANTERN RAYNER'S DEATH IS A GREAT LOSS.
HE WAS A TRULY UNIQUE BEING. THERE IS SO MUCH MORE HE MIGHT HAVE TAUGHT US. AND WE, HIM.
HOW WAS HE ABLE TO PASS BEYOND THE WALL, PAALKO? HAVE YOU EVER HEARD OF SUCH A THING?
NOT IN ALL MY EONS.
MORE INTRIGUING STILL...WHAT WAITS TO BE DISCOVERED ON THE OTHER SIDE?
WE DEPARTED OA TO LEARN ABOUT THE UNIVERSE. IS THERE A GREATER QUESTION THAN THIS?
?
FWASH
MUST YOU POKE **EVERYTHING** WITH A STICK?
I DID NOT TOUCH IT, ZALLA! I ONLY **ALMOST** DID!
FWASHHH

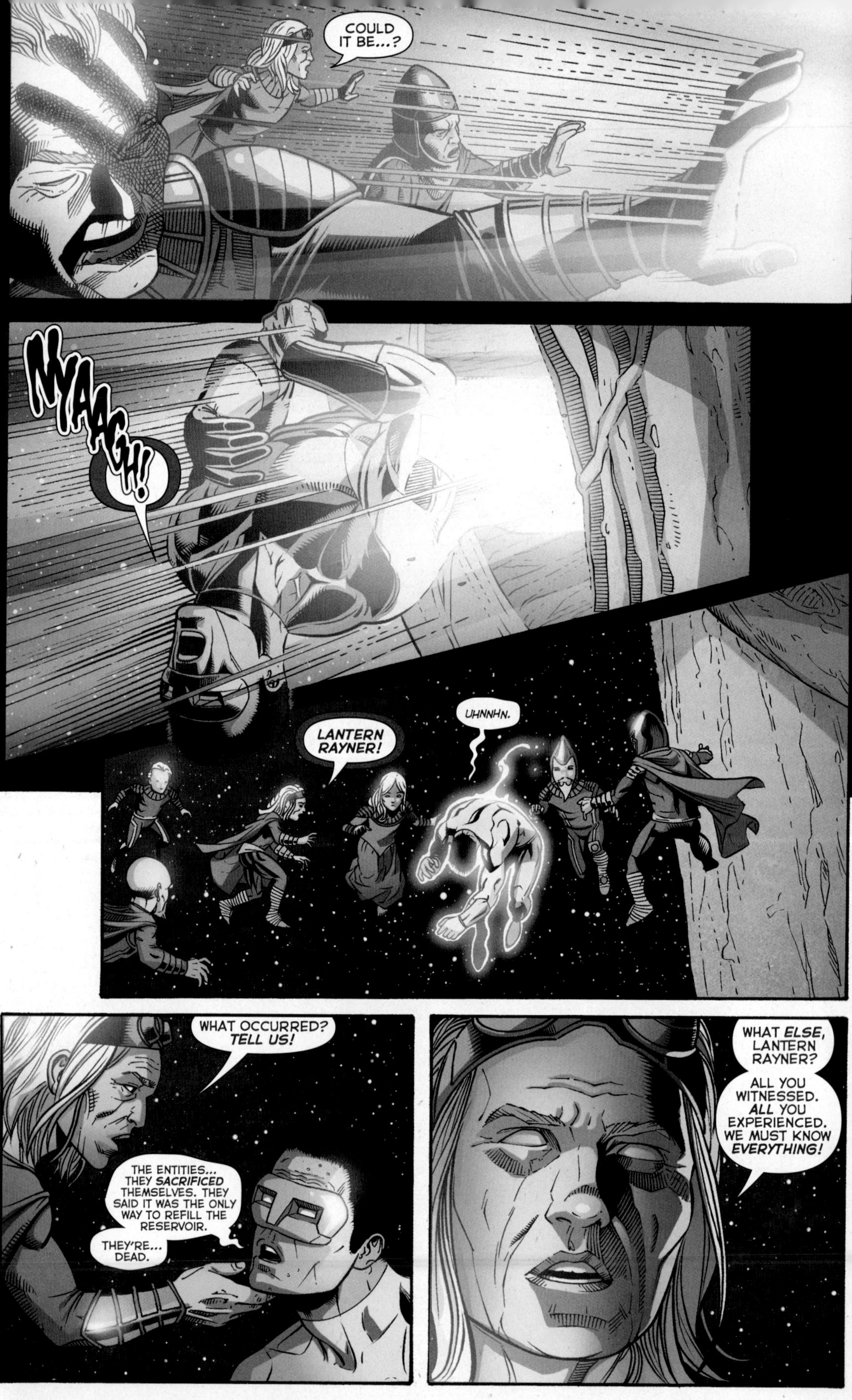

COULD IT BE...?
NYAAAGH!
LANTERN RAYNER!
UHNNHN.
WHAT OCCURRED? TELL US!
THE ENTITIES... THEY SACRIFICED THEMSELVES. THEY SAID IT WAS THE ONLY WAY TO REFILL THE RESERVOIR.
THEY'RE... DEAD.
WHAT ELSE, LANTERN RAYNER?
ALL YOU WITNESSED. ALL YOU EXPERIENCED. WE MUST KNOW EVERYTHING!

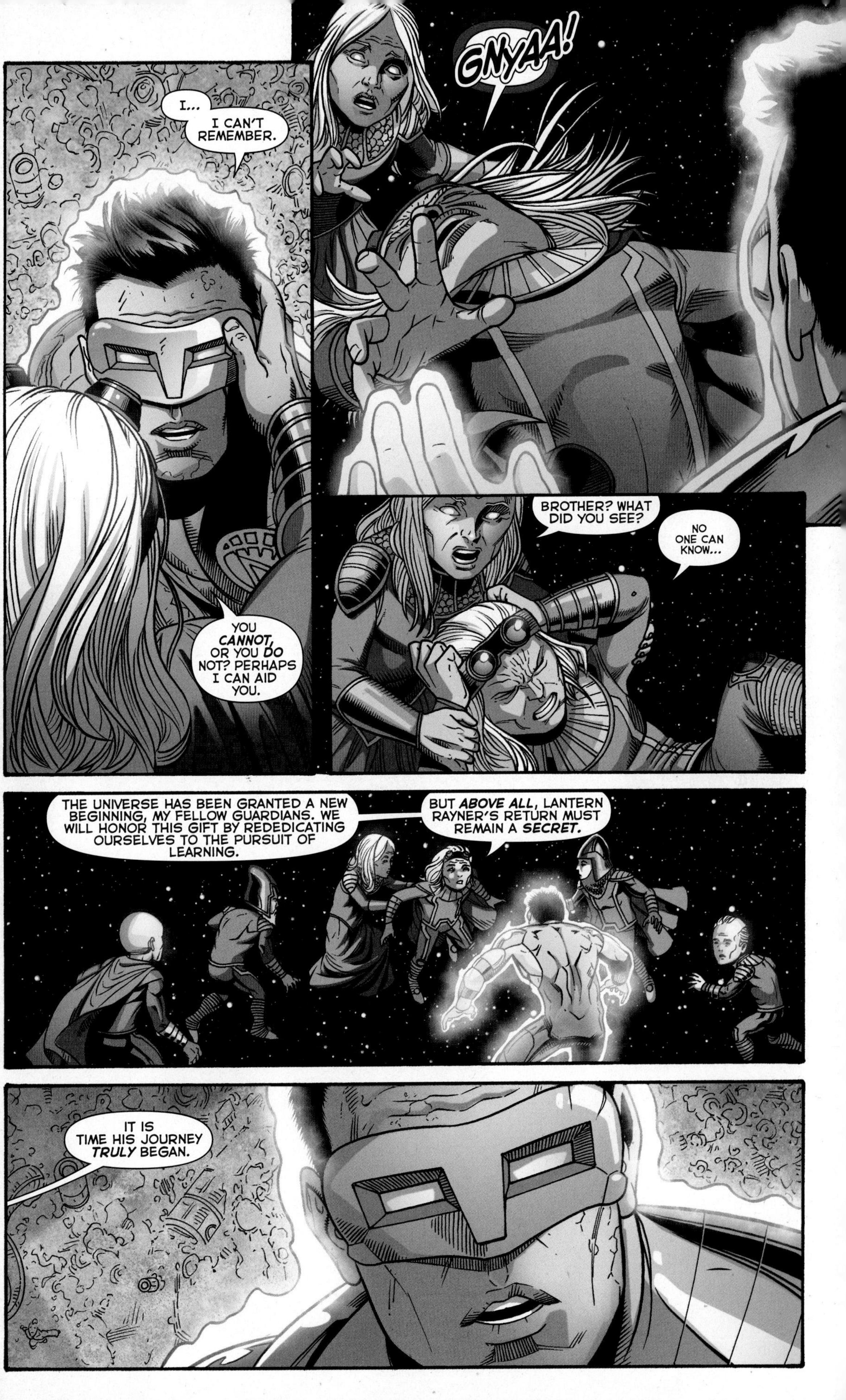
I... I CAN'T REMEMBER.
GNYAA!
YOU CANNOT, OR YOU DO NOT? PERHAPS I CAN AID YOU.
BROTHER? WHAT DID YOU SEE?
NO ONE CAN KNOW...
THE UNIVERSE HAS BEEN GRANTED A NEW BEGINNING, MY FELLOW GUARDIANS. WE WILL HONOR THIS GIFT BY REDEDICATING OURSELVES TO THE PURSUIT OF LEARNING.
BUT ABOVE ALL, LANTERN RAYNER'S RETURN MUST REMAIN A SECRET.
IT IS TIME HIS JOURNEY TRULY BEGAN.

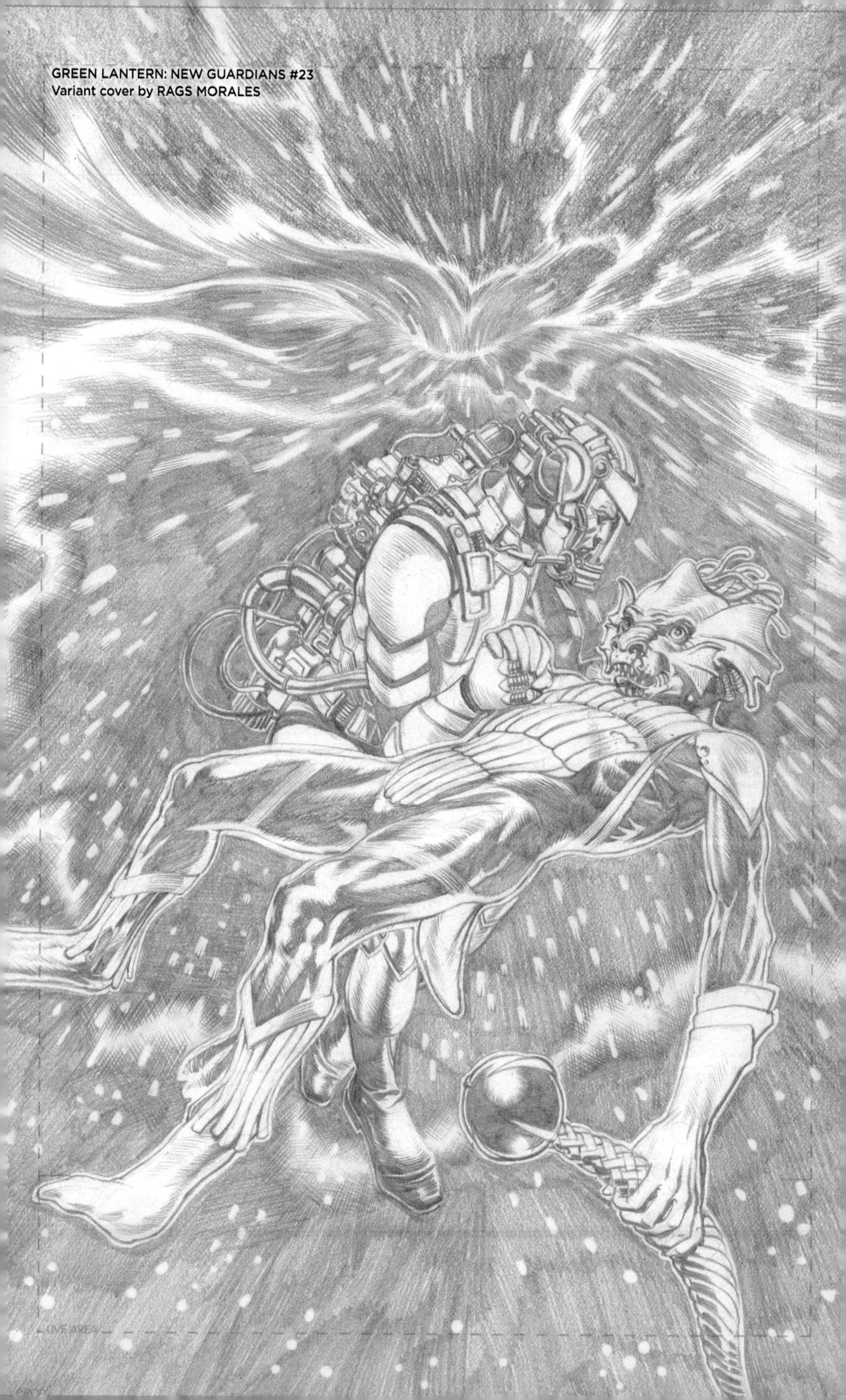
LIVE AREA
GREEN LANTERN: NEW GUARDIANS #23
Variant cover by RAGS MORALES

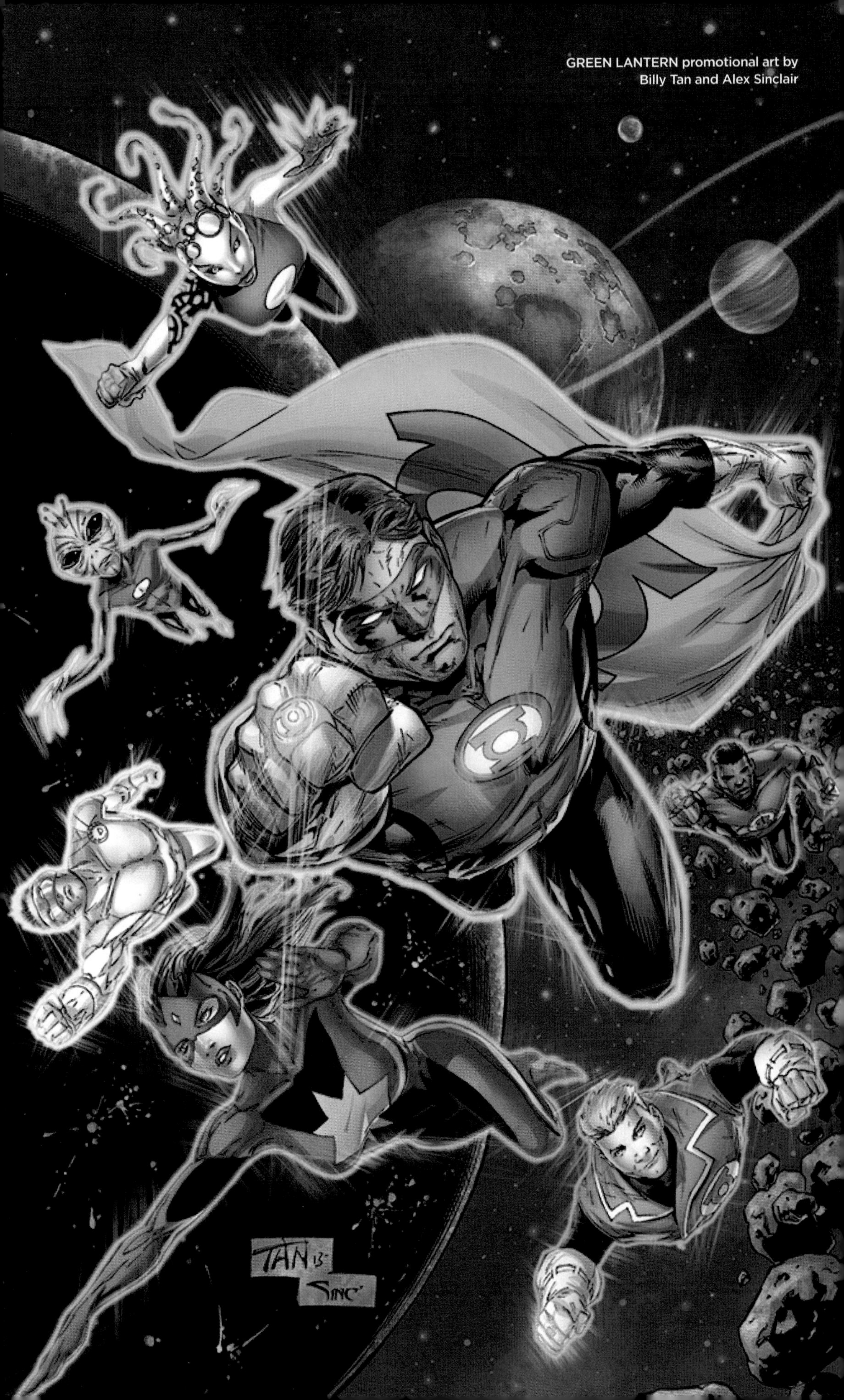

GREEN LANTERN promotional art by
Billy Tan and Alex Sinclair

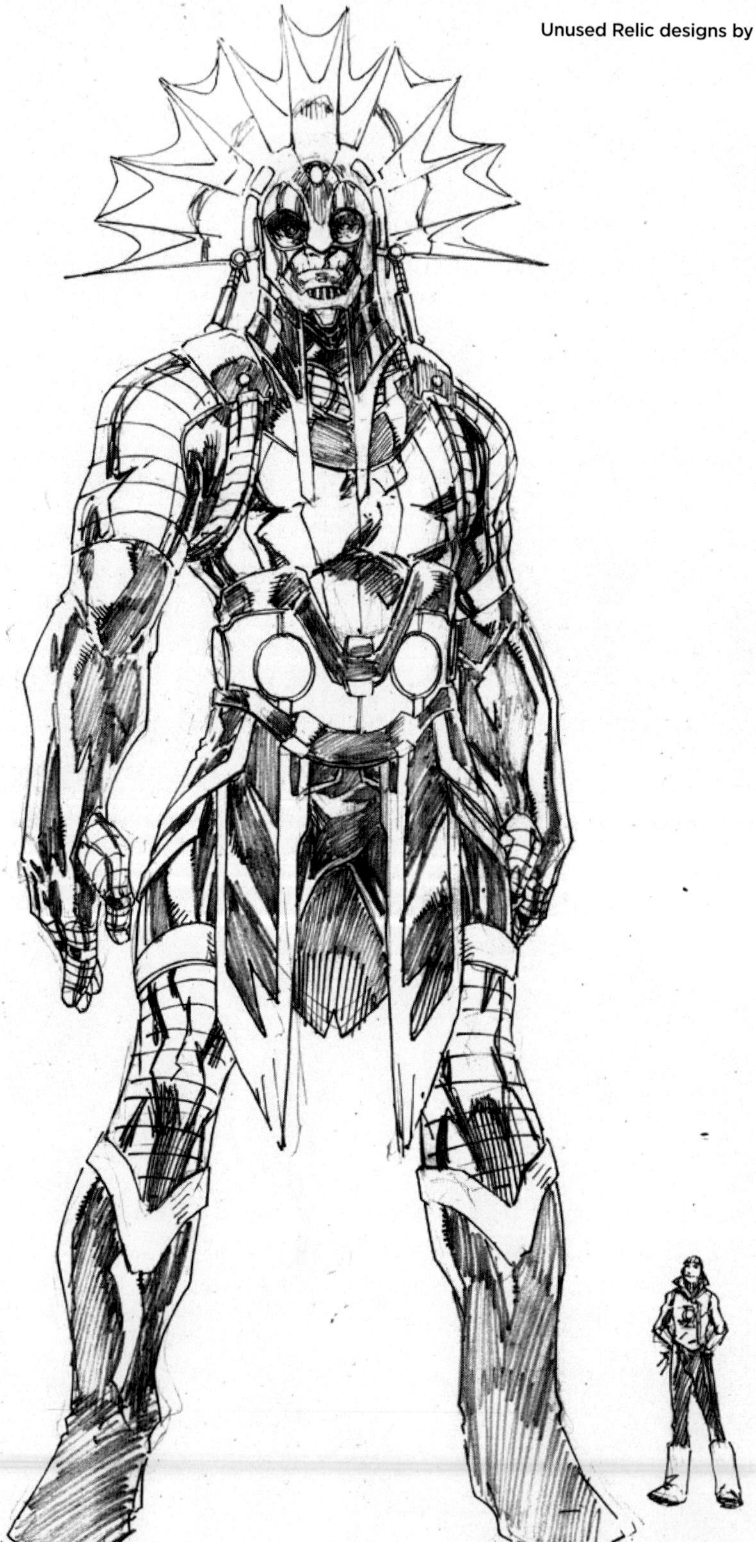

Unused Relic designs by Brett Booth

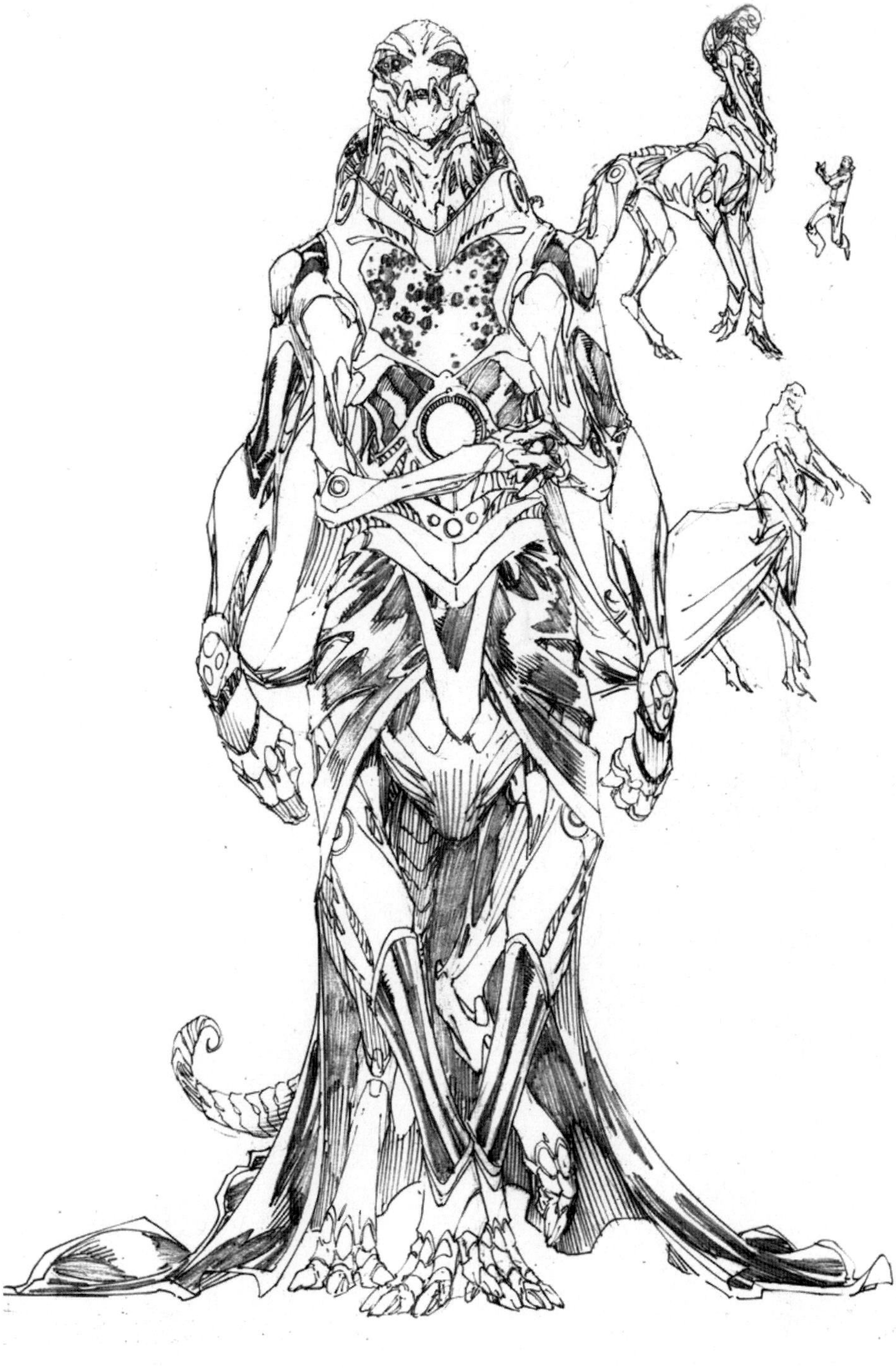

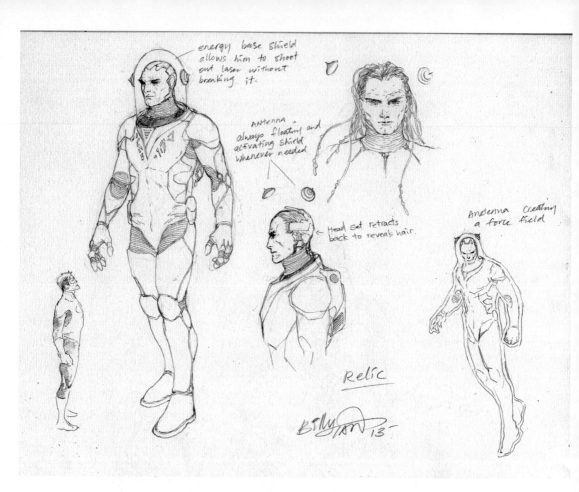

energy base shield
allows him to shoot
out laser without
breaking it.

ANTenna
always floating and
activating shield
whenever needed

Head set retracts
back to reveals hair.

Antenna creating
a force field

Relic

Billy Tan 13

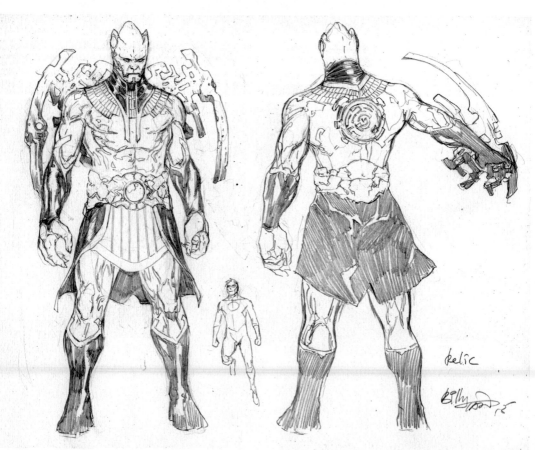

Relic

Billy Tan 15

Relic designs by Billy Tan

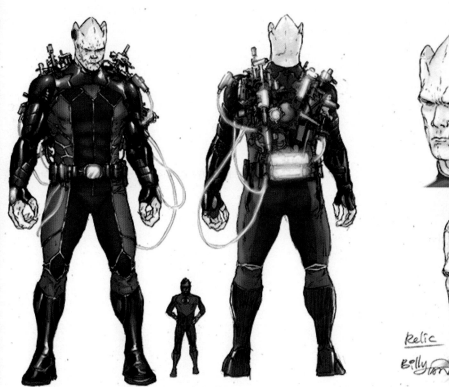

Relic

Billy Tan 2013

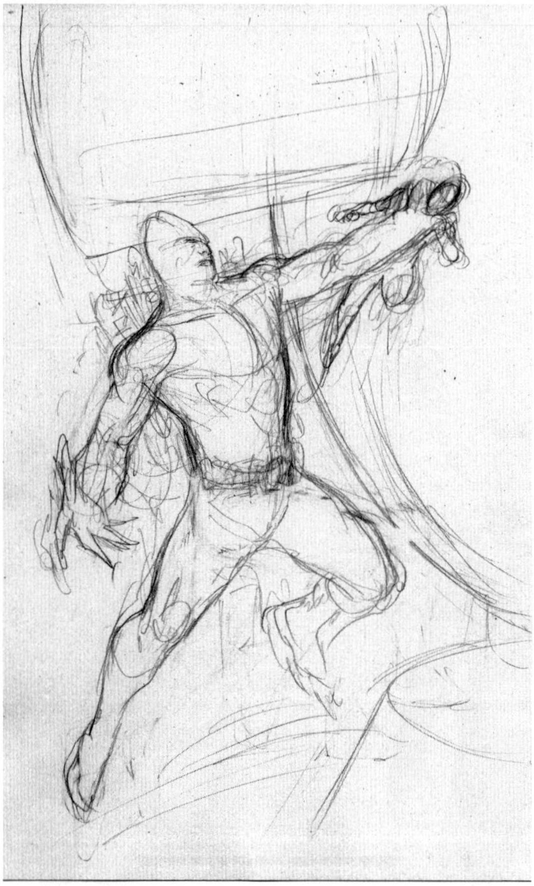

GREEN LANTERN #24 cover sketches by Billy Tan

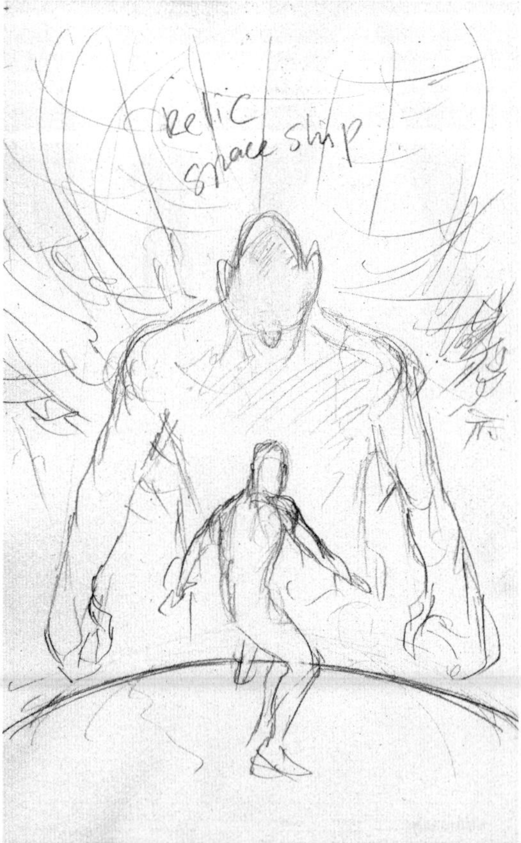
relic
space ship

GREEN LANTERN CORPS #24 cover sketches by J.G. Jones

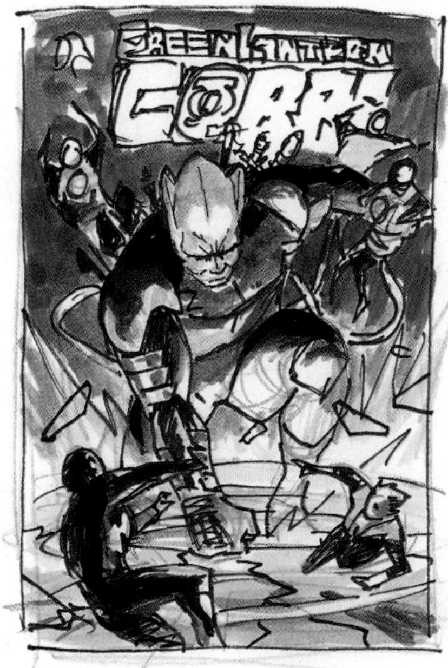

HAL

Relic
smashes
GL symbol

Soranik

Jon

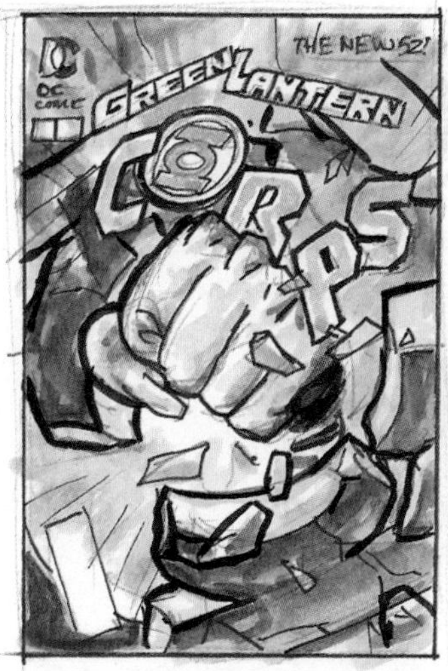
THE NEW 52!
GREEN LANTERN

RELIC'S
FIST
SMASHING
GL BATTERY

CAN WE HAVE
IT SMASH UP
THE LOGO &
TRADE DRESS, TOO?

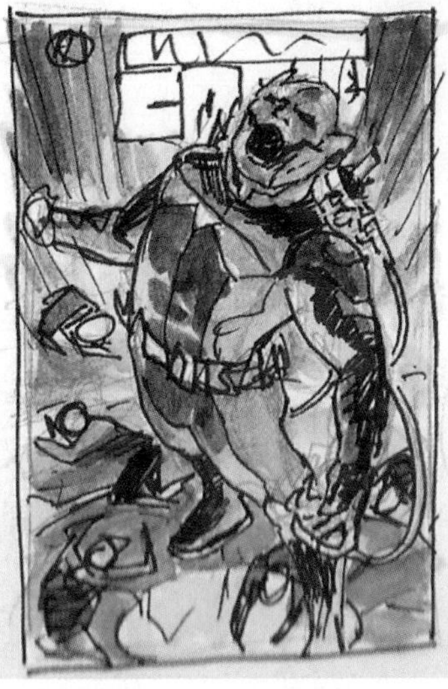

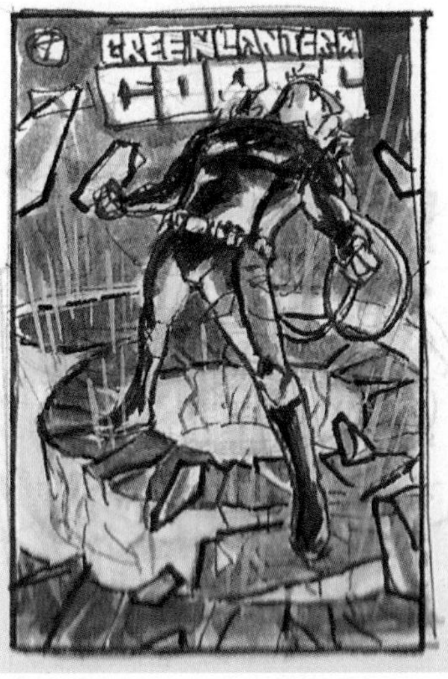

RELIC
STANDS
ON
CRACKED
AND
SHATTERED
LANTERN
LOGO

HEAD
BACK

GREEN LANTERN: NEW GUARDIANS #24 cover sketches by Rafael Albuquerque

NEW G

LIGHT

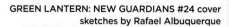